Through gripping narrative … vivid character portraits and deft anecdotes, Winn offers the reader an intimate, indelible portrait of a major world region in the throes of serious social change.
— Alfred W. McCoy, author of *The Politics of Heroin: CIA Complicity in the Global Drug Trade*

Drawing on a decade of on-the-ground reporting in Southeast Asia … *Hello, Shadowlands* is a sweeping work of investigative journalism that reads like a thriller you can't put down. Winn demonstrates how the breakneck economic growth that has lifted so many fortunes in Southeast Asia has also set the stage for a new golden age of drug trafficking – aided by corruption, despotism and the absence of law … a quintessential read for anyone who wants to understand the dark side of Southeast Asia's economic gains.
— Megha Rajagopalan, China bureau chief, *Buzzfeed News*

Brilliantly crafted and thrilling to read … a page-turner with soul.
— Tom Vitale, director of *Anthony Bourdain: Parts Unknown*

Patrick Winn writes in a vibrant, readable style, uses years of hardcore field reporting and adds thought-provoking analysis to expose a side of global crime that we all need to better understand. His vivid descriptions take you deep into surreal and at times heartbreaking worlds but he also steps away to give wider meaning to these tales and their place in the economic and political systems. Anyone who wants to make sense [of] modern global capitalism needs to read it.
— Ioan Grillo, author of *El Narco* and *Gangster Warlords*

Not inappropriately billed as *Fear and Loathing* meets *McMafia*, this is a compelling expose of Southeast Asia's criminal underworld, and the dark underbelly of some popular holiday destinations by an award-winning US journalist resident in Thailand … the chapters on Myanmar [are] particularly illuminating.
— *The Bookseller*

HELLO, SHADOWLANDS

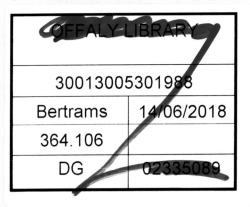

HELLO, SHADOWLANDS

INSIDE THE METH FIEFDOMS, REBEL HIDEOUTS
AND BOMB-SCARRED PARTY TOWNS OF SOUTHEAST ASIA

PATRICK WINN

ICON

Published in the UK in 2018
by Icon Books Ltd, Omnibus Business Centre,
39–41 North Road, London N7 9DP
email: info@iconbooks.com
www.iconbooks.com

Sold in the UK, Europe and Asia
by Faber & Faber Ltd, Bloomsbury House,
74–77 Great Russell Street,
London WC1B 3DA or their agents

Distributed in the UK, Europe and Asia
by Grantham Book Services,
Trent Road, Grantham NG31 7XQ

Distributed in the USA
by Publishers Group West,
1700 Fourth Street, Berkeley, CA 94710

Distributed in Australia and New Zealand
by Allen & Unwin Pty Ltd,
PO Box 8500, 83 Alexander Street,
Crows Nest, NSW 2065

Distributed in South Africa
by Jonathan Ball, Office B4, The District,
41 Sir Lowry Road, Woodstock 7925

Distributed in India by Penguin Books India,
7th Floor, Infinity Tower – C, DLF Cyber City,
Gurgaon 122002, Haryana

Distributed in Canada by Publishers Group Canada,
76 Stafford Street, Unit 300
Toronto, Ontario M6J 2S1

ISBN: 978-178578-347-0

Typeset in Albertina by Marie Doherty

Printed and bound in the UK by Clays Ltd, St Ives plc

Contents

人

Dedicated to Pailin

Prologue

In 2008, I moved to Bangkok with my girlfriend, now wife, who is also a journalist. Both of us were refugees from a collapsing newspaper industry. We sought to escape American newsrooms that were being gutted by layoffs and permeated by gloom – a dreary landscape against which to spend the final years of our twenties.

So we embarked on new lives as freelance correspondents based in Thailand's capital. We began in a leaky shophouse, our meager earnings sustaining a glitchy internet connection and a diet of cheap noodles.

I was drawn towards the intensity of 21st-century Southeast Asia, a region seemingly destined to grow more prosperous despite its war-wracked history. My wife Pailin Wedel – a photojournalist originally from Bangkok – was keen to properly document a region that is so often depicted through crude stereotypes.

For her, this was a homecoming. But for me, it was an odyssey into a world utterly unlike my own. I loved it instantly and threw myself into learning the Thai language. My first years were spent badgering street vendors with tortured grammar, practicing my lilting tones in the shower and watching karaoke DVDs of Thai country singers to absorb bits of rural dialect.

Ten years on, what was unfamiliar has become mundane. Eating a grilled catfish with my bare hands used to be thrilling. Now that's my go-to breakfast. But I've yet to grow bored. That hunger to better understand my adopted home still gnaws at me.

Southeast Asia is heaven for the compulsively curious. This is a world in vibrant flux. Old codes are clashing with modern appetites. The laboring classes are scrambling for cash and status like never before. Meanwhile, the ruling elites grow steadily more cozy in their authoritarianism – and less in thrall to old allies (and former colonial tormenters) in the Western hemisphere.

There is endless drama to document and, for every scintilla of effort I've put into understanding the region, I've been repaid twice over with astonishing stories. I continue to meet people – farmers and aristocrats alike – whose lives demand a thorough telling.

My job, as I see it, is tracking down compelling characters and trying to crystallize their experiences into words. The goal is to capture a twinkle of their humanity – or even just a small episode in their life's journey – and make it available to the world at large. A bit melodramatic, I know. But on my less cynical days, I like to think this work allows readers to take in the splendor and struggles of people they'd never know otherwise.

Over the last decade I've covered coups, street cuisine, ethnic cleansing, pop culture fads and more protests than I can recall. But I've always gravitated back to one subject: organized crime.

This is not a fixation on deranged personalities. Nor is it a true crime-style attraction to the gritty details of shocking murders. Quite the opposite, actually. I'm interested in well-meaning, logic-driven people who choose to live outside the law.

Prologue

I want to understand all of the forces that pushed them towards those often wrenching decisions to go underground – those little moments that progressively turned them into heroin dealers or rebels or bomb-makers. I'm fixated on the economic, cultural and historical currents that have washed trouble into their lives.

I've found that lawlessness itself is often what pushes people over the edge. How do you react when your village or hometown is repeatedly besieged by criminal syndicates – and the police ignore your pleas for help?

Worse yet: what if your government, the appointed arbiter of justice, is actually in collusion with your tormentors?

Do you flee?

Plot vigilante resistance?

Join an armed rebellion?

Or do you seek your own foothold within the underworld so that you might become predator instead of prey?

In the absence of law, people can be driven to make radical decisions. But once closely examined, the choices of those enmeshed in Southeast Asia's underworld – meth barons, dodgy cops, the traffickers and the trafficked – start to make perfect sense.

This pursuit has drawn me into all sorts of jungle hamlets, urban pockets and remote border towns. These are Southeast Asia's shadowlands: zones where the authorities allow organized crime to thrive. They are seldom illuminated to the outside world and the lives of their inhabitants are chronically ignored.

This book doesn't attempt to catalogue every single crime ring in Southeast Asia. Nor have I prioritized only the largest and most fearsome groups. I've instead opted to profile a number of syndicates – in Myanmar, Thailand, Malaysia, Vietnam and the Philippines – that, upon examination, tell us something indispensable about their surroundings.

Many of these syndicates actually operate with the unofficial blessing of the authoritarian states in which they are found. They flourish in spots where officials choose not to enforce order – or at least not as they should. Instead, local police will often function as a protection racket for select criminal operations. In the most forsaken quarters – Myanmar's northern hills, for example – the state actually allows drug barons to rule over its citizens like feudal lords.

Documenting these shadowlands isn't as grim an exercise as it might seem. I've found that humor flourishes in troubled places. So does heroism. I hope to convey the warmth I've felt among guerrillas, brothel workers and vigilantes. Some are among the most impressive people I've ever known. They are men and women who've learned to evade danger with brilliant ingenuity.

Through their stories, I've attempted to sketch a broader portrait of Southeast Asia in the 21st century – a vision filtered through the lens of crime and state power.

X

Let's back up. What exactly is *Southeast Asia* anyways?

The short answer: every nation from Myanmar's frigid peaks running eastward to the balmy Philippine islands. Politically speaking, it's the bloc of ten countries within the Association of Southeast Asian Nations, or ASEAN.

At a glance, this region appears to be defined by proximity and not much else. On the mainland, militaristic Buddhist kingdoms abut a pseudo-communist regime that is, in fact, ravenously capitalistic. All this is half-encircled by a largely Islamic archipelago – one that terminates in islands that are beholden to the Vatican.

This corner of the earth is home to 650 million people, more than in North America or South America or the European Union. But they are not – as in the Middle East – bound by an overarching faith. Nor by a common currency as in Europe. Nor by a common tongue as in Latin America. They are riven by mountains and seas, as well as by language and culture.

Yet in the 21st century, these scattered peoples are increasingly held in common by another force: capitalism – an ideology that America and its allies attempted to pound into this region with millions of bombs.

Those Cold War battles ended in American retreat. But capitalism won out in the end. Markets are roaring in Southeast Asia. Among the world's major economies, only China and India are growing faster than ASEAN.[1]

This economic boom is widely regarded as a success story. But it has also cast the region into an era of social upheaval.

For millennia, families grew what they ate and seldom left their little patch of land. Today, in practically every Southeast Asian nation, traditionally agrarian peoples have abandoned the fields in droves. Millions keep hurling themselves into a cash economy – a fast and plasticky world where basic nourishment comes not from the soil but from 7-Eleven.

Those raised in comfort are often tempted to lament the withering away of idyllic villages. But I've found that anyone who grows up yanking rice stalks from the mud seldom turns down a chance to do something else. A farmer's life is afflicted by nature's cruel whims: drought one year, pestilence the next.

In recent decades, people from Southeast Asia's farming hinterlands have deluged the cities. In these boom towns – Manila, Ho Chi Minh City, Bangkok – the shopping malls are often lavish and the streets are set to a soundtrack of bleeping smartphones.

But when newcomers arrive from the paddies, they're usually swept into an underclass of taxi drivers or sex workers, builders of condos or stitchers of Nikes. They endure this toil in pursuit of the Southeast Asian dream.

What is that dream, exactly? It's a modest set of hopes compared to its fading American counterpart.

It typically includes a new Honda motorbike parked by the front steps. Kids in fresh uniforms, headed to school instead of work. Hopes that those children will someday find jobs in air-conditioned offices and send money home. It's one weekly day of leisure, often spent at the mall, slurping mango ice cream and dithering on Chinese-made mobile phones.

There are daunting barriers in the way of the Southeast Asian dream. They include merciless labor laws, broken education systems, post-colonial class discrimination, loan sharks and police shakedowns.

Still, people persist by the millions. This mass scramble for cash is more than a trend. It is the story of almost every Southeast Asian nation today.

This meta-narrative is also the backdrop to many smaller phenomena in the region – including the expansion of Southeast Asia's criminal underground.

A voracious breed of capitalism is binding together once-fractured Southeast Asian nations like never before. Previously torn apart by land wars, they are now united in trade, digital communication and a mass narrative of upward mobility.

But as the region's overall economy soars, its black markets keep swelling too.

In fact, they've never been bigger.

This is largely down to the fact that there are more cashed-up consumers out there for every good or service you can think of: toothpaste, prostitution, airline tickets, crystal meth and so on.

The more-illicit wares are traded in a subterranean realm – one inhabited by syndicates large and small. It's home to scrappy players such as part-time gun-runners or pet-thief gangs. But it also encompasses the planet's largest methamphetamine empire – a billion-dollar complex churning out more speed pills each year than McDonald's serves Big Macs worldwide.

The United Nations values Southeast Asian organized crime at $100 billion and growing. That's equal to the entire economy of Washington DC. Or every single transaction made in Las Vegas for an entire year – and this is cited as a lowball estimate.[2]

To be clear: this book is a narrative plunge into the Southeast Asian criminal underworld. It's not an academic treatise. But in my years of reporting, I've developed a hypothesis of sorts: Southeast Asia is veering into a golden age of organized crime.

Before diving into these shadowlands, I'd like to briefly sketch out a few trends that support this conclusion. Some explain why transnational criminal operations are in a position to flourish. Others indicate that, if nothing else, the near future is unlikely to bring any major threats to Southeast Asia's melange of smugglers, pushers and traffickers.

Authoritarianism is here to stay

The West once had great political hopes for Southeast Asia. America in particular has long envisioned a string of just and orderly pro-US democracies triumphantly prospering in China's backyard.

Today, that vision looks more like a hallucination. Southeast Asia has become the domain of unelected authoritarians – or worse yet, elected leaders who behave like despots.

Let's briefly scan the region. Vietnam and Laos are run by entrenched, Chinese-style communist parties. Cambodia has been controlled for three decades by Hun Sen, Asia's longest-running strongman. Thailand is ruled by a prickly military junta. Myanmar, now superficially democratic, is actually in the grip of its ruthless army.

Turning southward, both Malaysia and Singapore are effectively one-party states. The West may claim Indonesia as a bright spot – the world's third-largest democracy! – yet its scattered islands and institutional rot make it difficult to govern. Moving eastward, the Philippines is run by an elected leader with the bloodlust and dangerous unpredictability of a dictator.

This is the present and future of Southeast Asia: hyper-capitalistic but deeply illiberal. This autocratic sweep doesn't just benefit the entrenched political dynasties that run these nations.

It's also a blessing for organized crime.

Southeast Asia doesn't breed the sort of authoritarianism that offers squeaky-clean streets and criminals cowering in fear. (Tiny Singapore, with less than 1 per cent of ASEAN's population, is an exception.) To varying degrees, police throughout the region instill just enough order to keep the economy humming along.

Their prime duties include squashing dissidents while protecting the upper classes and their property. The cops are far less keen on breaking up crime rings – particularly the ones that pay on time.

Despite incessant claims to the contrary, most politicians in Southeast Asia fully expect their police forces to indulge in corruption. I don't mean a little dabbling here and there. From Mandalay to Manila, bribery is an essential source of funding for law enforcement.

Without this flow of illicit cash, many police departments would risk collapse. They simply wouldn't be able to pay officers enough to come to work. On paper, the region's cops are offered miserable wages: roughly $100 to $700 per month*, depending on the country.

But these official salaries are comparable to the $3-per-hour wages paid to American waiting staff. The real money comes from tips.

Cops generate off-the-books money through a dazzling variety of methods. They can shore up petty cash by shaking down motorists or small-time vendors. But the much bigger

---

* These police wages would be paid in local currency – Thai baht, Philippine pesos, Vietnamese dong, etc. – but figures throughout the book are generally presented in US dollars.

payments come from brothels, underground gambling halls or smugglers of people, wildlife and drugs.

For a monthly fee, these illegal operations will pay for a tantalizing benefit: immunity from prosecution or, at the very least, a warning if crackdowns are imminent.

As Southeast Asian governments grow increasingly authoritarian and opaque, their security forces grow more untouchable. This allows police and military officers to run their departments like entrepreneurial businesses. Give them a big umbrella of impunity and they will permit criminals – for the right price – to take shelter underneath.

There is a financial logic to this model. Governments willing to overlook police bribery can pay their security forces dismal salaries and then foist these labor costs onto the black market.

I'm painting in broad strokes here. Police corruption in Southeast Asia is an incredibly complex ecosystem – a theme that will become clear over the course of this book.

In each country of the region, you can find workaday cops who may feel genuinely fed up with vice in their ranks. They may be heartened by sporadic anti-corruption drives, orchestrated by politicians, that take down a handful of low- and mid-tier officers. Or they may place faith in some phony drug war that never actually imprisons any of the top kingpins.

These campaigns are designed not to upturn the status quo but to deflate public anger or to shore up some leader's tough-on-crime bona fides. Often the state is selective in its targets. They may order police units to go hard on sellers of endangered wildlife, perhaps, while tolerating collusion with speed traffickers.

But no matter what, the overall model remains intact.

This is a system that perversely incentivizes cops to focus on the wellbeing of criminal figures – their paying customers – above the civilians they've sworn to defend.

New arteries for the criminal underground

You may regard infrastructure as boring. Smugglers tend to disagree.

In the 21st century, Southeast Asia is increasingly interlinked by roads, bridges, docks, runways and railway lines. This has proven utterly transformative – and the boom has just begun.

Over the next two decades, large parts of Asia will be interlaced by new infrastructure worth trillions of dollars. Much of this will be underwritten by Beijing, which is now building its Silk Road redux – a matrix of highways and ports that link the Chinese motherland to its backyard and beyond.[3]

Southeast Asia's punishing landscape of tall mountains and deep inlets is finally being tamed by concrete and steel. These new land and sea lanes aren't being created for malevolent purposes. They're simply meant to increase the flow of stuff and people: oil barrels and motherboards, traders and tour groups.

But they are also a boon to crime syndicates, which need to move forbidden goods and substances (as well as undocumented migrants) from points A to B.

Gone are the days of rebels in Myanmar strapping heroin to mules that clomp through malarial jungles. Old paths that were once used to trade opium and tiger bones across the Golden Triangle are being paved over and rebranded as 'economic corridors'. Drug runners can now truck their wares along these new highways, hiding their illicit bundles under sacks of grain or pallets of toys.

Police don't stand a chance of keeping up. They are so overwhelmed by the new rush of transnational trade that, according to UN experts, they catch only about 5 to 10 per cent of the narcotics flowing across Southeast Asia's mainland borders.[4]

Now factor in new powers of communication that would have astounded the poppy kingpins of the 1960s. Mobile phone towers are sprouting up everywhere – even in remote valleys that still lack regular electricity.

This is a blessing for long-isolated peoples, many of them mesmerized by the glowing screens of their $100 Huawei smartphones. But this mobile phone revolution is even more wondrous for criminals seeking to expand their cross-border trade.

Smugglers benefit from constant communication. They need tipoffs from police to steer clear of surprise checkpoints. They require a clean flow of information across a long chain of suppliers, truckers and armed guards. With the proliferation of cell towers, there's never been a better time to move speed, people, wildlife and weapons around Southeast Asia.

The moralizing Western order is wilting

Western diplomacy towards Southeast Asian nations has often assumed the tone of a disappointed dad. America is particularly fond of reacting to any serious abuse of power – from coups to protest crackdowns – with 'deep concern'.

To leaders around the region, the US can come off like a nag, forever harping on about 'human rights' and 'the rule of law'. These are more than just ideals. They are measuring sticks, used to size up Southeast Asian nations and gauge their virtue.

Aspire to be more like us, America tells both its allies and foes. Promise to do better by signing memoranda and conventions on slavery, narcotics, land mines and human trafficking. Go after your corrupt police and officialdom at the highest levels and make a big show of locking them up.

When Southeast Asian nations fail to live up to these expectations – as they frequently do – the US Foreign Service will attempt to prod and shame their governments into better behavior.

But it's always been a bit bizarre to watch America hover over Southeast Asia as a self-appointed guiding moral light. After all, no other foreign power has brought so much mechanized death to this region.

During the US–Vietnam War, American planes disgorged more bombs over Vietnam, Cambodia and Laos than were dropped from all Allied planes during the Second World War.[5] In the late 1960s, the White House was, by its own admission, overseeing the killing or maiming of 'more than 1,000 non-combatants a week' in the war against communism.[6] Even today, children are still getting killed by US explosives that remain buried in the mud.

Of course, none of the officials who masterminded these crimes are in prison. Henry Kissinger is not only free but fêted in Washington DC. It is difficult to understate the extent to which war planners of his ilk have shaped modern Southeast Asia through violence: annihilating entire cities, altering maps and propping up powerful cliques at the expense of others.

This hypocrisy is not lost on Southeast Asian leaders.

But the flipside to American aggression has been bountiful aid: a torrent of cash that many nations – such as Thailand, Cambodia and the Philippines – have relied upon.

This has given America and its allies enough clout to browbeat leaders into launching occasional police campaigns (some superficial, some legit) against certain breeds of criminality such as sex trafficking, child soldiering or people smuggling. The US Foreign Service's stated rationale is that human rights will not just 'combat crime' but 'strengthen democracies' – a notion harkening back to the Cold War.

Governments that refuse to cooperate with these demands risk losing aid or, worse yet, incurring economy-shattering sanctions. But some good does occasionally comes from this pressure exerted from afar.

One of the better modern-day examples is an offensive against seafaring slave traders operating from Thailand to Indonesia. In the past decade, these traders have duped thousands of poor villagers, mostly from Myanmar, onto deep-sea trawlers. The men are then forced to fish without pay.

This trade was going strongest around 2012, right about the time that then-President Barack Obama promised to champion 'one of the great human rights causes of our time' – a global fight against the 'injustice, the outrage, of human trafficking, which must be called by its true name: modern slavery.'[7] It is a scourge, he said, that 'fuels violence and organized crime'.

My own encounters with slave-driving boatmen bear this out. In Samut Sakhon, a port city in Thailand, I once met a deputy boat captain named Jord. His face was dominated by a scar running in a pink groove from his scalp to his nose bridge.

He and his crew mates shared tales that recalled the horrors of the Middle Passage: Burmese men purchased for $600 a head, their bodies brutally exploited out on the anarchy of the sea.[8] They spoke of slaves traded from boat to boat, never coming ashore for five years or more. The maimed or diseased, they said, are often bludgeoned and dumped overboard.

A few years later, when it grew painfully obvious that slave-caught fish were being sold in Western supermarkets, the US, EU and UK pushed Thailand to kick off a region-wide crackdown. Raids against boat captains and people smugglers followed and Thai officials began surveilling boat crews more closely. The region's fishing industry remains murky but the worst abuses – such as murdering migrant workers at sea – were diminished.

This was presented as a victory for the American-led global order of rules and rights, which is always in need of a public relations win. Obama's soaring rhetoric was a thin veneer over US misadventures in Iraq, Afghanistan and Libya – not to mention its long history of supporting dictatorships from Southeast Asia to Latin America.

But pushing back against Southeast Asian slavery may have been one of this system's last hurrahs. Just a few years on, the idea of a US-led international order looks more wobbly and morally confused than before – so much so that it's hard to imagine another campaign on this scale.

Under the presidency of Donald Trump, the White House doesn't even pretend that it cares more about individual suffering than about corporate interests. This is an administration that believes fretting over 'human dignity' is an 'obstacle' to advancing America's business interests.[9]

Wondering aloud about abuses in Asia, Trump's national security adviser asks: 'How much does it help to yell about these problems?'[10] The US is turning inward: gutting its diplomatic corps and eviscerating foreign aid. American evangelizing about the 'rule of law' was dubious before. Now it looks absurd.

In 2016, the volatile and self-avowedly murderous president of the Philippines, Rodrigo Duterte, rolled out a crowd-pleasing 'war on drugs' to purge his nation of 'junkies'. This crusade is mostly wiping out poor meth smokers, not well-connected traffickers. The upshot is that meth sales continue while Philippine cops, more than ever, have been gifted an unrestricted license to kill.

So far, this massacre has ended the lives of more than 10,000 people.[11] That's a death toll which exceeds that of the Srebrenica massacre, the worst mass killing in Europe since the Second World War. And it's actually receiving kudos from the White House.

Trump never expresses (as his predecessors surely would have) 'deep concern' about this killing spree. Instead, he's called the Philippine president to 'congratulate you because I am hearing of the unbelievable job on the drug problem'. As a US senator later lamented: 'We are watching in real time as the American human rights bully pulpit disintegrates into ash.'[12]

Oh, well. The era of pious American patronage is probably doomed no matter who leads the US. The future of Asia belongs to China, soon to become the world's dominant economy.

China is Southeast Asia's top trading partner. Many nations here have already adopted its philosophy of government: authoritarian capitalism. As American largesse becomes more fickle and weak, these nations increasingly turn to Beijing for aid, weapons, rail lines and counsel.

That China offers its backing without resorting to belittling harangues is quite refreshing to leaders in Southeast Asia. These are men (and a few powerful women) who crave respect as much as fortune and power.

China's political dream is to dominate Asia and share global power with the US as an equal. This world is taking shape faster than many predicted.

Even after Trump is gone, America will find itself jockeying for influence in Southeast Asia from a weakened position – one too weak, perhaps, to sporadically cajole governments into the embarrassing work of uprooting traffickers and dodgy police.

X

In finishing, I'd like to ask for a favor.

This is a book filled with tales of predation and survival. But it mustn't be read as a portrait of a region succumbing to wholesale disorder or haphazard violence. That simply isn't accurate. In fact, many of the places profiled here are statistically less dangerous than parts of the US.

On the whole, Southeast Asia is not a dreary place. In surveys taken in almost every country in the region, people report feeling quite optimistic about their future. This can't be said about Americans or Western Europeans, whose feelings tend to portend decline.[13]

Nothing I describe here should convince you to cancel your holiday to Southeast Asia. You won't encounter jihadis or stick-wielding vigilantes on your street food crawl in Bangkok or your Bagan temple tour. The mainstream tourist trail is quite safe.

Much of the criminality described in this book is quarantined to specific areas where travelers seldom venture. Moreover, organized crime need not correlate with an increase in pickpockets, muggers or other predators who target strangers at random. I've actually encountered very little petty crime in Southeast Asia – even in places that are largely abandoned by police.

I've written this book in part to exorcise frustrations over the way parts of Southeast Asia are portrayed by Western media. The denizens of these places are too often depicted as unicellular organisms, easily victimized or casually roused to violence.

Seldom do we hear about rational, complex actors in brothels or drug dens or rebel battlefields. If you spend enough time with people in these environments – as I've been fortunate enough to do – you'll find a multiplicity of motives, some nakedly selfish and others quite noble.

I am deeply grateful to the lawbreakers who've expanded my understanding of the human condition. I've met very few genuine sadists out there. I've more often found people who demonstrate a deep capacity for sacrifice – especially when their family members are under threat.

I hope this book will help you think about the agonizing decisions any of us might make if our police and courts left us to fend for ourselves. Those who would prefer a tabloid-style account of black-hearted villains will find this book exasperating – and perhaps guilty of moral relativism.

So be it.

Author's Note

Journalism is a tribe with a deeply held set of convictions and mores. My membership in this tribe is central to my identity. So I want to be totally transparent about the ways in which I plan to deviate from its norms.

My biggest transgression concerns chronology. Every event in this book happened. Most happened in the order in which they're presented. But in select cases, I've opted to depict events out of sequence. For example, if I've interviewed an individual two or three times, I'll condense those talks into a single conversation.

Also, I've occasionally stumbled into a revelatory experience or piece of intel very early into an investigation – and the significance can't be appreciated without a proper lead up. For clarity's sake, I've shifted some of these occurrences forward in time. These alterations, applied very judiciously, have allowed for a narrative that remains honest if not chronologically pure.

Investigative journalism doesn't unfold like a Scooby Doo episode with cascading clues building to a neat conclusion. Some of the narratives in this book were compiled over multiple years. Long lapses were taken when time or expenses ran short. Were this book written exactly as events occurred, it would be twice as long and thrice as confusing.

This is a book about the underworld so, naturally, I've changed quite a few names. Anyone whose appearance here might lead to legal harassment or, worse yet, getting dragged from their home at 1am – either by police or outlaws – has been given a pseudonym. In very isolated cases, I've slightly altered the description of a source's appearance to protect their identity.

Note that this anonymity has not been extended to high-ranking officials, warlords or insurgent chieftains who enjoy positions of great power. For the record: none of them asked.

Some conversations in this book were reconstructed from my handwritten notes. This is an imperfect process, subject to my fallible memory, but I've made every effort to preserve accuracy.

Also, in select cases, I've had to excise field producers from the storyline. Among reporters, these people are called 'fixers'. But that term doesn't adequately value their work and, frankly, implies a value beneath the lofty title of 'foreign correspondent'.

Nothing could be further from the truth. A good field producer can arrange tricky interviews, negotiate access to hidden places and distract authorities who intend to sabotage your reporting. I'd be useless without them.

On top of that, these field producers have to translate. I only speak English and Thai. So any conversation in this book held in Vietnamese, Tagalog, Burmese, Kachin (a language spoken in northern Myanmar) or Korean was filtered through an interpreter.

You'll meet many of these field producers in this book. Those who may face repercussions, however, have been removed from the story. This is terribly unfair – and it reflects my privileged status as an American, often immune to the worst penalties doled out by authoritarian states.

Author's Note

Police are reluctant to risk the diplomatic grief that comes with locking up journalists with US passports. They reserve the cruelest treatment for their own citizens. But without the wit and persistence of my field-producer colleagues, this book would not exist.

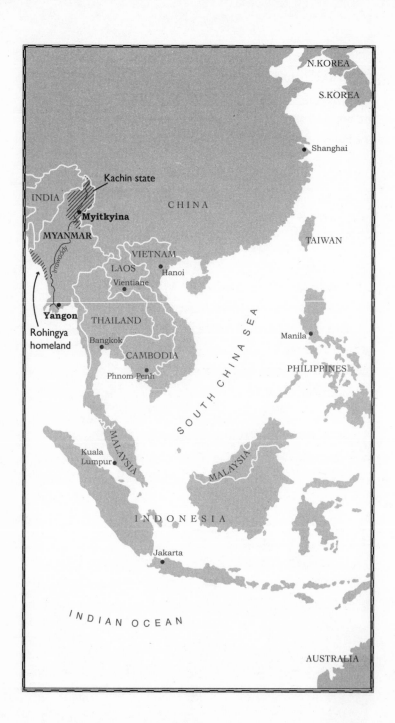

CHAPTER I

Hot Pink Speed

Location: Myitkyina, Myanmar

Where drug barons churn out candy-colored meth

The town of Myitkyina is the last outpost before Myanmar disintegrates into its chaotic frontier. When the British Empire laid railroad tracks throughout this territory – which was then called Burma – its sinews of steel reached these foothills but went no further.

This town now functions as the government's northernmost terminal station. Beyond it lie hilltops ruled by guerrillas and armed clans.

Just a few miles from the town's decrepit railway station, inside the attic of a wooden home, a ritual is set to commence. The windows have been shuttered, nosy kids ordered to scram. Sunday morning sunshine seeps through cracks in the blinds, casting blades of warm light on the floor planks. The room is otherwise dim.

Leading this ritual is Zau Ring, sitting in the lotus position. He is 40 or so, a tad gaunt, clad in a beige sarong and an unbuttoned plaid shirt. I'm crouching nearby, watching him work.

Zau Ring slides a hand into his sarong and fishes a foreign object out of his underwear. It looks like a lumpy wad of electrical tape, roughly the size of his palm. But when Zau

Ring peels away the layers of tape, he reveals a ziplock baggie concealed within.

He squeezes open the baggie's plastic mouth. Out pour two dozen methamphetamine tablets, which rattle across the floorboards. Each pill is as pink as Barbie's Corvette.

All hard drugs evoke a certain counterculture. Opium conjures old-world mystique. Cocaine screams fast-money excess. Meth, in the West at least, is seen as a gutter drug – a tooth-rotting, low-life disgrace. But what I am about to witness will play out more like a sacrament than some dirty fix.

Zau Ring has an array of paraphernalia at his feet: strips of aluminum foil, colorful bendy straws, one roll of electrical tape, a half-empty bottle of water. From these household items, he begins to assemble a funny-looking hookah.

With a lit cigarette, he burns a circular hole into the side of the water bottle. Into this orifice he inserts a foot-long length of piping. It's made from interlocked plastic drinking straws. This is the hookah's hose. He applies some tape to seal up leaks, gives it a test suck and the contraption bubbles into life.

Strangely, a strong aroma permeates the room before the hookah has been lit. This is the signature scent of Myanmar speed tablets – a chemical sweetness that smells exactly like vanilla cake frosting. The pills reek even before they are put to flame.

The smell is derived from some mysterious additive favored by meth chemists – the legions of drug lab mixologists, operating in those lawless hills beyond the tracks.

Perhaps this is a fluke of their recipe. Maybe it's a marketing strategy to render meth pills more candy-like. Regardless, it's so aromatic that addicts such as Zau Ring won't carry meth pills in public without triple-wrapping their baggies in tape. That scent is a dead giveaway. You can smell this stuff across a large room – especially an airless attic.

Outside the attic's entrance, Zau Ring and I hear loud creaking – the sound of a wooden staircase bending under the weight of grown men. Our heads jerk towards the doorway as three figures approach.

But it's just Gideon, the home's owner, followed by two anemic-looking younger guys.

'You startled me, Gideon,' I say. 'I keep worrying your wife and kids will barge in.'

'Relax,' he says. 'They're at church already. Can't you hear?'

Indeed, for the past ten minutes, Zau Ring's prep work has been set to a soothing soundtrack: harmonious choir singing. The attic overlooks the courtyard of a Baptist church next door. The voices, high-pitched and adolescent, carry easily through the attic's thin walls.

These are Myitkyina's churchgoing hours – an ideal time to sneak away and sin in peace.

I'm relieved that Gideon has returned to the room. He's like a brotherly confidant, the only friend I've got in this town. Zau Ring and these other men? To me, they're total strangers.

Gideon is in his late thirties with raven-black hair styled into an Elvis swoosh. Like most guys around here, he almost exclusively wears flip-flops and sarongs. Up top, however, he favors Magnum PI-style flamboyant shirts: lots of button-ups with floral patterns and fleurs-de-lis. They're always partially undone to reveal his hairless chest, which is smooth as a mango.

I prefer to keep Gideon close. Here, in Myanmar's far north, survival hinges on knowing the dos and don'ts. Whom to flatter. What laws you can safely ignore. Which officials to bribe. When to shut up. Where to smoke meth without getting caught.

Gideon, a Myitkyina native, is my guide to this world. He's helping me navigate this thicket of unwritten codes. It's a vital skill. Doubly vital considering our plans for the next few weeks. It will involve consorting with quite a few law-breakers – starting with the men in this attic.

Gideon corralled them here at my request. Actually, I just requested one guy – any user willing to show off his stash and chat about the local drug scene. Gideon, with his heavy appetite for mischief, was more than happy to oblige. He even offered up his own attic, assuring me that the cops would never think of raiding his home.

Only Zau Ring was invited this morning. But soon after he arrived, Gideon's phone started chirping. A few of Zau Ring's pals had caught word of our little drug scrum and they were already loitering outside, desperate to join. Gideon obliged, ducking out of the room so he could unlock his front gate and discreetly guide them up to this hideaway.

Now he's back and we're all here. Both of the newcomers are far more conspicuous than Zau Ring. One is shirtless, his back and arms inked up with crudely-drawn tattoos. The other is wraith-like, tall and painfully slender, a lichen-esque goatee clinging to his chin.

As soon as they mount the stairs, the two newcomers spot the pink meth. Like ants to sugar, they scuttle over and kneel by Zau Ring's feet, inspecting and sniffing at the pills arrayed on the floor. Zau Ring swats them away.

They back off and assume sitting positions on the floor, encircling the meth hookah like it's some sort of altar.

'So,' I ask, 'how do you guys know each other?'

Long pause.

'We're all mechanics,' says the tatted-up guy. Head downcast, he fidgets with his toes. 'I do air-conditioners.'

'I work on generators,' murmurs the goateed man, the youngest of the three.

'Generators?' I say. 'Well, you must get a lot of work.' Myanmar's state-run electrical grid is so glitchy that shops and homes require diesel generators to power through daily blackouts. They're noisy machines, big as refrigerators, and they're always breaking down.

'Yeah, sure,' he says in a pained murmur. 'Very busy.'

This is like chatting up guys in a long bathroom line. Their minds are consumed by the looming promise of physical relief. No one here seems keen on small talk with a foreigner – some weirdo who apparently traveled to the far edge of Myanmar to watch strangers get high.

'Almost done here,' Zau Ring says, tinkering with his hookah, giving it one final quality inspection. 'Let's not waste any more time.'

At last, the ritual begins. Zau Ring picks up a long strip of foil and pinches it into a silvery canoe. He takes one of the pills – about the size of a baby aspirin – and drops it into the foil. Then he lovingly treats the underside of the strip with candle flame.

Heat makes the little pill dance. It shimmies on the bed of aluminum, charring at the edges, liquefying and quickly losing its shape. All the while, white vapor rises from the foil.

Zau Ring holds the foil beneath an air valve carved into the water-bottle hookah. When he sucks on the hookah's hose, the meth smoke is hoovered into the apparatus, where it mixes with burbling water. This softens the acrid notes that would otherwise sting the throat.

Zau Ring holds the smoke inside his lungs for a beat. Then he releases twin torrents from his nostrils. So this thing actually works. A few more rounds and the pill is a blackened squirt on the foil.

One pill leads to another. And another. The other men have their turn. Gideon is standing in the corner, grinning, meth clouds swirling at his legs. I'm stationed closer to the hookah, entranced by the rite, trying to catch whiffs. You'd think these pills would smell like burnt Oreos when cooked. But the smoke is nearly scentless.

The smokers' malaise has lifted. They sit with upright spines. I attempt another question. At the first syllable, their heads swivel towards me in unison like startled owls.

'So tell me,' I say. 'What's so great about meth?'

The answers come quick and loud. They speak all at once, six eyes laser-locked on mine. Gideon gestures for them to keep their voices down but it's no use. I can hardly keep track of who's saying what.

'This stuff gives you incredible alertness. You become so focused you forget to eat and …'

'… yeah, it's like you can achieve anything. You're not sleepy nor drunk nor hungry nor fatigued and you just go and go and go …'

'… so it's like our medicine, right? As we say, use a bit and it's medicine, use a lot and it's poison. But it's really hard to moderate …'

'… true, like, once I scored ten pills and said, "I'll just use one per day for ten days" but then I smoked all ten pills in one morning …'

'… which is how you ruin your body. Smoke too much and you'll stay awake for three days, dim-witted and paranoid, flying into a rage at some small remark …'

'… and that's the real problem with *ya ma*. You always think one more pill will bring perfect bliss. But it never comes. It's always one more pill away …'

'… but it's worth it, just to feel that power. Like no one can stand in your way. Like no one can take you down.'

Ya ma. That's what they call these pills in Myanmar. Translation: horse pills. If swallowed or smoked, the pills bring stallionesque intensity to any task: sex, plowing rice fields, partying, assembling sneakers in a factory, shooting the shit in some dusty attic.

This drug scene is steeped in slang. In neighboring Thailand, a prime consumer of Myanmar's meth, these tablets are known by a more sinister name: *ya ba* – madness pills. That's the term preferred by police across Southeast Asia.

But Zau Ring and his crew are not tilting towards face-chewing insanity – the sort of crazed behavior caricatured in anti-drug propaganda. They seem no more psychotic than a few grad students snorting powder-blue rails of Adderall off a physics textbook.[1] (Still, if Adderall is Bombay Sapphire, this is bathtub gin: noxious, strong stuff riddled with adulterants.)

As the men tell it, meth positively dazzles. Euphoria? That doesn't quite capture it. It's more like sublime confidence. Your ego is electrified. Your enemies seem small. Your day crackles with brilliant potential.

On meth, you are essential. You matter. You are in control.

What better drug to transfix the inhabitants of Myanmar's borderlands? They are remote hill dwellers – neglected by the government, bullied by warlords, forgotten by the world.

Zau Ring grows fidgety and, soon enough, another pill drops onto the foil. Now he's on his knees, crouching over the hookah, sucking so hard that the jade amulet around his neck sways like a pendulum. He has stripped to the waist.

The pill sizzles. Sweat streaks his back, drippy rivulets soaking into the sarong pulled snug around his hips.

While Zau Ring smokes, I find myself tracing a finger along the wooden floor planks. Each swipe sends little plumes of dust spiraling upwards and, when they drift towards sunbeams, their sooty particles twinkle magnificently in the light. How intensely mesmerizing. I notice my other hand tapping out a manic drumroll on the floor.

'Gideon, I have a question,' I say. 'Can I get a contact high just by sitting here?'

'Maybe,' he says from the far corner of the room. 'These pills are 88s. Extra strong. Take a look.'

I lean over to scrutinize the remaining pills – only half remain – and see that each pill is imprinted with the number 88.[2] It's a brand. Like BAYER etched into aspirin.

'You know, 1988?' Gideon says. 'The big democracy protest year.'

Everyone in Myanmar knows the significance of 1988. The digits are burned into the nation's psyche. That was the year roaring masses poured into the streets of every major city (Myitkyina included) to demand that the military junta loosen its kleptocratic death grip on the country.

The uprising failed. Thousands were slaughtered.[3] Yet this flash of defiance is still acid-etched into the souls of millions – just as the Boston Tea Party or the 1963 March on Washington is held sacred by Americans.

These days, it seems the uprising's appeal is also being exploited to brand meth. 'How odd,' I say. 'I would never associate drugs with that protest.'

'Yeah, well, the number just means democracy. So it's cool,' Zau Ring says. 'Eighty-eights are the finest pills on the market.'

We are interrupted by another round of hymns resounding from the church outside. This time the singers are backed by an organ, blaring chords through a cheap amplifier. Its sound waves cause the attic's windowpanes to buzz.

This song's melody is startlingly familiar, stirring my own memories from 1988: the back row of a Baptist church, small-town North Carolina, my mother imploring me to stop sulking and sing along.

There's a reason the hymn outside sounds so recognizable to my American ears. This patch of Myanmar was Christianized more than a century ago by Baptists from the US – and those proselytizers left behind their hymnals.

To this day, come Sunday mornings, Baptists around here belt out the same old-time gospel songs as their American counterparts. The lyrics, however, are translated into the local tongue: Kachin.

We are, after all, in Myanmar's Kachin State. It's a region about the size of Portugal and is inhabited by its namesake: the Kachin people. Their language is spoken by roughly a million people, including the four Kachin men in this attic. But their speech is unintelligible to the Burmese, who make up the dominant ethnicity in Myanmar.

'Hear that?' Gideon says. 'That's the last round of singing. Time to finish up. The service will end soon.' After that, he says, the streets will fill with church folk. Best for the meth smokers to clear out and head home.

Last call for horse pills.

'Now that you're high,' I say, 'will you guys feel a bit anxious walking the streets?'

They nod affirmatively. 'These days, you've got to watch your back,' he says. '*Pat Jasan* is everywhere.'

Ah, *Pat Jasan*. The word on everyone's lips in Kachin State.

Pat Jasan, I'm told, is a newly formed group of Christian anti-drug vigilantes. Their name is a compound word, mashing together the Kachin-language verbs 'block' (*Pat*) and 'cleanse' (*Jasan*). They are hunters of addicts, stalkers of dealers, raiders of drug dens. Though they seemingly coalesced out of nowhere, these grass-roots hardliners are metastasizing with great speed. Their goal is to purify Kachin society of narcotics, one addict at a time.

People say *Pat Jasan* will charge into your bedroom, kick over your bong and drag you screaming into the road. They'll abduct you, stuff you into a cage, make you beg for God's clemency. Run afoul of *Pat Jasan* and you will vanish for days, sometimes months, resurfacing with bloody welts, vowing never to touch meth again.

'*Pat Jasan* is changing everything,' Zau Ring says. 'They have spies on every street. Hell, half of that church over there is probably cooperating with *Pat Jasan*.'

'Wow,' I say, 'so you guys are really that scared of church folk? What about police?'

The baffled smirks curling across their lips indicate that I've asked a stupid question. Around here, everyone knows that copping speed is as easy as buying eggs. Kachin State cops are notoriously lenient on drugs.

There's another reason these guys aren't too worried about cops at the moment. Gideon – the very man who organized this gathering – is himself a low-level police operative. Is this foreigner really that clueless? Has Gideon never told him? Ever the rascal, Gideon lets them wonder, savoring the awkward silence.

Yes, I'm well aware that Gideon works with the police. I've known that ever since we were connected through a network of Kachin friends.

My contacts had suggested that, in Gideon, I might enlist an interlocutor with a deep knowledge of the local black market. Once we met here in Myitkyina, Gideon and I got along easily, building trust over many mugs of beer and cups of milk tea.

Honestly, I couldn't have found a more perfect conspirator than a plainclothes police agent. Gideon operates in the murky space where the state and the underworld overlap. And I've come here to figure out how Myanmar gave rise to the biggest meth trade on the planet – all with suspiciously little government pushback.

Here's what I know so far.

Myanmar's billion-dollar meth syndicates now collectively rake in more profit than many Fortune 500 companies.[4] This cabal of drug barons currently commands the weaponry and political clout of a small nation. Their power and cash is largely owed to their top-selling product: those little pink pills.

Hanging with meth smokers in a musty attic? This is a decent start. But my ultimate goal is to push beyond the customers and uncover the supply chain. To reveal this drug trade's inner workings, I'll need to penetrate that murky purgatory where officialdom seethes with criminality. This is a realm that Gideon knows well.

)(

You probably think of Myanmar as a single, unified country. It sure looks like one on the map – a misshapen diamond with a spit of land jutting south like a kite's tail.

These are Myanmar's official borders, drawn by (who else?) the British. For millennia, this area was an amalgam of small kingdoms and loosely-run territories inhabited by a dizzying variety of ethnic groups. In the 19th century, however, the British Empire glued them into one big blob and called it Burma.

Never mind that many of these groups had been clashing for centuries. Under British rule, they now belonged to one common territory. But when the Empire ended its more than 120-year occupation of Myanmar after the Second World War, the country was left with a puzzle.

How to preserve this weak fiction of nationhood?

Enter a brilliant Burmese rebel named Aung San, beloved for orchestrating the British Empire's ouster. In the waning day of British Burma, Aung San emerged as the leading voice for a population eager to construct its own state. Aung San vouched for a plan that would prevent minority groups from breaking away. Why not let the so-called 'hill peoples' run their own semi-autonomous states in the frontier?[5]

They could swear allegiance to a national union, which would look after defense and foreign affairs. Day to day, however, the minorities would manage their own turf – just as they'd done for ages. This recalled the United States' post-colonial era, when George Washington tried to cobble together a nation out of many squabbling states.

This plan, however, was annulled with bloodshed. A Burmese clique in collusion with British officers mowed Aung San and his crew down with Tommy guns, inside a government building. The exact motives behind this assassination remain murky. But the reigning theory is that they feared Aung San would veer Burma towards communism.[6] Regardless, the upshot of his murder would be prolonged national disunity.

The following decade was marked by uprisings and political chaos. Then, in 1962, Myanmar's army seized absolute control. They proposed a darker solution to the country's externally-imposed diversity puzzle. Deploy brute power. Force the minorities to their knees. Propagate a myth of racial supremacy.

(In a jab to the British, they later gave the nation a post-colonial title: Myanmar. The meaning is virtually identical. Myanmar is just a slightly more poetic word for the Burmese race.)

The nation of Myanmar remains a melange of 100-plus ethnicities. But there are seven major minority groups: Shan, Karen, Chin, Rakhine, Mon, Kachin and Karenni. If you grow up in Myanmar, you learn these racial categories at around the same time you learn to count.

Lording it over all minorities, however, are the Burmese. They are the heirs to a grand civilization spanning two millennia. They are the builders of glimmering temples, the pious disciples of Buddha, the conquerors of savages. Without

∧

Burmese might, the borderland barbarians would run amok and Myanmar would come unglued.

So goes the narrative proffered by the Burmese army propagandists.

Those at the nation's fringe have a different view. In their eyes, the Burmese-dominated army – which effectively embodies the state – is not some valiant protector of nationhood. It's more like a voracious squid-beast, tentacles flared in all directions.

The beast's head rests in the central plains. This is Myanmar's low country, a fat ribbon of fertile land. It begins in a sun-baked plateau, runs southward into soggy river delta and finally melts into the Bay of Bengal. This land is the nation's soft and populous center, lush with rice fields, scattered with the ruins of ancient kingdoms. This is native soil for the nation's ethnic-religious majority: Burmese Buddhists.

Perhaps your aunt, college roommate or neighbor went on holiday in Myanmar and came back gushing about golden spires and barefoot monks? This is where they went. It's the Myanmar of coffee table books and travel sites that tout the world's top ten hottest new destinations.

This is also the army's home turf – and it is indeed safe for tourists. But the central region is not without problems. The first among them is punishing poverty.

Belonging to the top ethnicity does not confer prosperity to the Burmese. The military beast hoards the national wealth all for itself, enriching a coterie of generals and cronies. The masses – of whatever ethnicity – are left to feed off the few crumbs that dribble from its jaws.

The army devours much of the national budget, leaving between 1 and 3 per cent of GDP for health care and education.[7] Such stinginess makes the governments of Liberia or Sudan look charitable.

As a result, many of Myanmar's hospitals are eaten by black mold. So are the schools, where teachers are sometimes paid so poorly that the students sustain them with donated sacks of rice.

Many kids never make it to class at all. Instead, they report each morning to the dockyards or the quarry. According to the United Nations, one in five of Myanmar's kids (aged ten to seventeen) holds down a job.[8] They are often pulled out of school by sick parents who've been made invalid by treatable illnesses, casualties of the broken health care system.

In Yangon, Myanmar's principal city, state neglect is actually a tourist attraction. Foreign visitors are inevitably charmed by the city's grandiose Victorian-era British architecture. But they are often surprised to learn that bureaucrats still have to work inside some of these crumbling structures. The buildings – spectacular in their decay – have become exotic backdrops for selfie-snapping tourists.

This is the bleak status quo in Myanmar's center. And yet, compared to those in the hills, the people who live in this low country are comparatively fortunate.

Follow the beast's tentacles out of native Burmese terrain in any northerly direction. You will begin winding uphill into the mountains that encircle the plains. Keep going and you will reach the 'black zones' – army parlance for the jungles that are teeming with 'terrorist' minorities. Here, in lieu of clinics or classrooms, the army has invested in death. Its troops have sown some of the densest mine fields in Asia.

These black zones – large swaths of Karen, Kachin, Shan and other states – officially belong to Myanmar. In reality,

MYANMAR'S BLACK ZONES : MOUNTAINOUS AREAS CONTESTED
BY REBELS OR CONTROLLED BY ARMY-ALIGNED MILITIAS

Hpakant
jade mines

Area contested
by Kachin
Independence
Army (KIA)

Area controlled
by the warlord
Ting Ying

Myitkyina

INDIA

Mandalay

CHINA

BANGLADESH

MYANMAR

Rohingya
Homeland

Irrawaddy River

LAOS

Yangon

THAILAND

areas contested by
rebel groups

areas controlled by
militias aligned to the
army

they are disputed battlefields, chewed by the beast but not quite swallowed up.

For the minorities who live here, life is a struggle to keep those tentacles from wrapping around their throats. As with mountain cultures the world over, from the Ozarks to Tibet, the high altitude seems to breed rebellion. These hills are filled with men and women whose distrust of low-land authoritarians is felt down in their marrow.

Much of Myanmar – nearly half, by some estimates – is contested by various armed groups.[9] But they are not galvanized behind a single resistance force. Instead there is a messy jumble of territories, divided up by language and clan. In more extreme terrain, each new valley seems to contain a different ethnicity with its own dialect and band of fighters. There are now so many guerrilla factions in Myanmar – many dozens of them, large and small – that even experts struggle to recall all of them from memory.

Though united in suspicion of the beast, these armed groups are driven by diverse motives. Within a 50-mile radius, you may find Jesus-loving freedom fighters, ex-communists and river pirates. Some groups control proto-states, defended by anti-aircraft cannons and thousands of uniformed grunts. Other factions amount to just a few guys in flip-flops with mud-splattered carbines.

A range of colorful rebel leaders have emerged from these black zones. Among them is Olive Yang, a female warlord who, in the 1950s, once commanded 1,000 fighting men.[10] Also, in the early 2000s, there were the Htoo twins: cute twelve year olds with shoulder-length brown locks. Despite resembling an armed wing of the boy band Hanson, these pre-teens attracted adult guerrillas to their side by claiming wizard-like powers.

Myanmar's armed minorities aren't just defending land and honor. They're also protecting the natural bounty beneath their feet. Gems and timber are key sources of rebel income. But the beast also hungers for all those jade stones, rubies and gold – anything of value that can be yanked from the earth and raked into its maw.

The rebels' job is to fend off the soldiers. But the military often triumphs.

The proceeds from all this army plunder adds up to billions. Much of it disappears into the generals' pockets. But profits are also plowed back into the killing machine: bullets and fighter jets, RPGs and even surveillance drones. This perpetual warfare has killed approximately 150,000 people since the colonials chugged back to Britain.[11]

⋊⋉

Hold up. Isn't Myanmar on the mend?

Didn't former US President Barack Obama fly to Yangon in 2012 to announce that a 'dictatorship of five decades has loosened its grip'? Didn't he stand before crowds of Myanmar citizens and tell them 'you can taste freedom'?[12]

Myanmar has indeed loosened up – especially in the government-dominated low country. Back in 2011, the army removed many of its North Korea-style shackles on society. Mobile phones, once available only to the super-rich, are now enjoyed by the masses. Reporters and rock bands alike no longer have to filter their words through stodgy censors. The army even freed thousands of political prisoners. Some had been wasting away for nothing more than handing out pro-democracy pamphlets.

This was no minor transformation. In big cities such as Yangon and Mandalay, the Orwellian vibe has genuinely dissipated. These reforms have helped generals negotiate for the end of American and European sanctions. At last, multinational conglomerates – Unilever, KFC, Ford – are selling their soap, chicken and trucks inside this long-secluded nation.

Most celebrated of all, of course, is the rise of State Counsellor Aung San Suu Kyi to the throne of government.

After decades of direct totalitarian rule, the army generals finally permitted a free general election in 2015. Aung San Suu Kyi – the child of the slain independence hero Aung San – won in a landslide along with her party. This was a dramatic reversal for a woman who'd spent much of the 1990s and 2000s under military-imposed house arrest – an attempt to dim her dreams of one day governing the nation.

Her victory was no great shock. Aung San Suu Kyi is the most famous human being from Myanmar, living or dead. To the Burmese, she is akin to George Washington's daughter. On the evening of her big win, I watched block parties break out across Yangon. Old and young alike sobbed and sang in the streets. The city thrummed with mass catharsis.

Western diplomats were giddy too. They had long hailed Aung San Suu Kyi as a champion of the meek. She is prim and poised, and can offer mellifluous odes to democracy in her crisp Oxford-educated English. Through embargoes and condemnation, they've spent decades pressuring the army to allow her release and ascent to power.

At last, the diplomats had actualized their dream. They still tell themselves they've midwifed Asia's newest democracy – a triumph of freedom lovers over tyrants. According to

US statements, Myanmar has 'overcome decades of military rule to achieve a democratic state'.[13]

But, sadly, this is a fairy tale.

Before it handed over sections of the government, the army filled one quarter of Myanmar's parliament with unelected officers. They can veto any law that might sap the military's power.

The beast also retains its most powerful tentacles. Generals still control the battalions that torment the hills as well as a nearly untouchable police force. Aung San Suu Kyi has no real authority over the nation's paddy wagons or howitzers.

Moreover, the most lucrative government revenue streams – namely those tied to resource extraction – are still dominated by the army officers, their kin and their cronies. They derive billions from secretive army-run corporations that own banks, jade mines and shipping fleets. They even run breweries.[14] Each evening, when backpackers and Burmese alike crack open bottles of Myanmar Beer (the nation's top-selling brew), some awful old men get a little bit richer.

As for Aung San Suu Kyi and her party? They are the new stewards of a public sector that rotted under military rule. Collapsing bridges? Hospitals lacking penicillin? Don't protest against the army. Take your complaints to 'Aunty Suu'.

The military beast has at last been liberated from its most-hated chore: tending to its citizens' welfare. You might now expect the generals to lapse into leisure, spending languid days enjoying foot rubs and Scotch inside their gaudy estates.

If only. They have instead channeled their superfluous energy into accelerating the siege of the hinterlands. Their long-running wars along the Thai and Chinese borders are now as intense as they've been in decades. The generals are gambling that Myanmar's democracy project will help to distract attention from their ethnic cleansing campaigns – and, to a degree, they've been proven right.

Not long after Aung San Suu Kyi's coronation, the army expanded its northern battlefront – surging into a tea-growing region near China and bombarding the Kachin hilltops with attack choppers. At the opposite end of the country, along the marshy coast, troops have redoubled efforts to purge the Rohingya, a Muslim group that has been described by state-run newspapers as 'human fleas'.[15]

The army's strategy in this ongoing campaign has been to march into Rohingya settlements, rape women in plain view, kill the men who try to stop them and, finally, reduce the village to smoldering ash. This tactic has proven scarily effective. In 2016–17, more than half a million Muslims were sent fleeing into neighboring Bangladesh.[16]

In the West, this ethnic-cleansing spree – Asia's worst in recent memory – has knocked Aung San Suu Kyi off her gilded pedestal. Those who imagined the Nobel Peace Prize laureate as a saint have been horrified to watch her deny the atrocities are even taking place.

Worse yet, her offices have mocked well-documented Rohingya claims of sexual torture as 'fake rape' and insisted that Muslims torched their own homes for media sympathy.[17] They've even used the Trumpian phrase 'fake news' when lashing out at critical reporting.

This is the state of Myanmar following its much-hyped reboot. Sure, the monks are on Facebook, its golden temples are swarmed by foreign tour groups and teenage boys can court their girlfriends over a KFC value meal. But both ends of the nation are on fire.

Up in the hinterlands, no one is tasting the freedom. Old dreams of democracy are reduced to a sick joke – '88' – stamped onto a speed pill. In the black zones, minorities still answer to their local warlord or rebel chieftain, not the central state.

More than ever, Myanmar's mountainous fringe belongs to no nation. It is a patchwork of semi-anarchic enclaves cut off from the world. For those marooned there, life can be a rough slog.

But what a superb place to run a meth lab.

※

Between 2 to 6 billion meth pills. According to UN narcotics officials, that's how much *ya ba* gets churned out of Myanmar's black zones each year.[18]

Let's throw this into perspective.

Two billion speed pills? That is, at a bare minimum, triple the number of coffees served each year by Starbucks worldwide.[19] Go with the higher estimate, 6 billion, and you've got Myanmar drug lords serving up more meth tablets each year than McDonald's serves Big Macs. By a factor of ten.[20]

Myanmar is the beating heart of mainland Southeast Asia's meth industry, the largest illicit speed market in the world. The UN values this trade at $15 billion – higher than the net income of Walmart, double that of Pfizer.[21]

The government of Myanmar would like you to believe that this is the work of a few rebel gangs slinking around the jungle. But this is a drug empire, run from powerful narco-fiefdoms. They rival Mexican cartels, if not in violence, then in scale and even myth-making. As in Sinaloa, Medellin or Sicily, this trade has given rise to flamboyant killers and folk heroes alike.

But Myanmar's kingpins don't get dramatized by Hollywood. They're rarely brought up by Western diplomats. Foreign Service emissaries have spent years crowing about Myanmar's dawning democracy. They're less keen to talk about the vast numbers of people living under drug lords – petty tyrants who are about as democratic as 9th-century Viking kings.

Meth is far and away the biggest narcotic exported from Myanmar. In fact, it's one of the country's biggest exports, period – far more valuable than on-the-books exports such as natural gas or vegetables.

Its number two narcotic export is heroin. Myanmar is the second-largest poppy grower in the world, following Afghanistan. It produces twice as much poppy as Mexico, the prime source of heroin sold in the US.[22]

In Myanmar, opium and heroin belong to a far older tradition than synthetic speed pills. But these days, among drug syndicates, tending poppy fields is increasingly seen as a terrible headache. To understand this shift from heroin to meth, you've got to think like a drug baron.

Your poppy fields are outdoors, exposed to crop-ruining cold spells – not to mention satellite cameras hovering in the sky. Specialists with the United Nations or the US Drug Enforcement Agency (DEA) can snoop on your crops from space. Occasionally, these foreign troublemakers manage to shame the army into half-heartedly hacking down some of your poppies with weed whackers. It's a real drag.

Manufacturing meth, meanwhile, is a far more appealing venture. You start by smuggling over chemical 'precursors' (namely drums of pseudoephedrine) from unscrupulous factories in India or China.[23] No need to fear the police: they've got rusty pistols, you've got RPGs – and besides, they're all bought off.

As for those meddling UN narcs? They're no real threat. From their satellite cameras, your meth lab looks like any old warehouse or school.

Next step: hire someone with college-level chemistry skills to synthesize your pseudoephedrine into a narcotic slurry. They'll combine that with binding agents, caffeine powder (which pads out the mix), pink dye and other additives. Once it's all blended and dried, the meth is pressed into Tylenol-sized tablets.

This is *ya ma* (or *ya ba*) and its popularity is hard to underestimate. Forget pot. Across Asia, pink speed is now the go-to drug.

In Thailand, meth now accounts for more than 90 per cent of drug arrests.[24] Over in China, *ya ba* along with *bingdu* (crystal meth) has overtaken heroin as the nation's most popular narcotic. Roughly five out of every 1,000 Chinese citizens are believed to use meth – double the percentage found in the US.[25] Even in Muslim-majority Bangladesh, to the west of Myanmar, millions are getting high on black-zone speed.

Authoritarian governments across Southeast Asia have responded to this meth wave with a mix of ineptitude and obscene violence. Thailand was the first to launch a drug war in 2003. The kingdom's police kill-squads wiped out thousands of people – many of them labeled as suspected addicts or dealers and executed without trial.[26] When the campaign ended, however, meth sales rebounded. They're now stronger than ever.

The region's most recent meth-related panic kicked off in the Philippines during the summer of 2016. The death toll from the island nation's drug war, also perpetrated by police death squads, hovers around 10,000 people – among the bloodiest massacres in recent Southeast Asian history.

Yet in Myanmar's northern hinterlands, where meth is produced, officials don't expend much energy chasing down drug users. For the most part, they just sit back and allow narcotics to course through minority territories. It's not like this down in the Burmese low country. There, a pocket full of pills can bring many years in some disease-ridden prison. But up in border towns like Myitkyina, buying speed or heroin is as simple as ordering a pizza.

Each morning, meth dealers zip around on motorbikes, making their deliveries. In tea shops, heroin-addled school-boys nod off in plain sight, track marks dotting their spindly arms like spider bites. At one internet cafe, I've seen signage requesting that patrons refrain from shooting up while checking their email.

Worse yet, at the region's bastion of higher learning, Myitkyina University, the bathrooms are outfitted with metal biohazard boxes. They're syringe depositories for students who want to dose on the toilet before class.

Drug use in the countryside is even more flagrant. This is a source of immense grief for the Kachin, who view the pastoral backcountry as their heartland. Each Sunday, pastors mount the pulpit to lament grim scenes: village after village where scrappy farmers are reduced to skeletal men, selling their family's last chicken for another hit.

Like cocaine in Peru, or heroin in Afghanistan, meth in Myanmar's upcountry is pervasive and dirt-cheap, often selling for a mere $1–$3 per pill. At those prices, even poor villagers can afford a twitchy, eight-hour high – especially if they're willing to forego a few meals.

If drug war massacres lie at one extreme, this is what lies at the other: suffering wrought by extreme negligence.

The best place to witness this human toll is in the quasi-underground rehabs that pop up in and around Myitkyina. These places are part-gulag, part-Bible camp, where rapturous singing mingles with agonized groans.

)(

Morning dawns over Myitkyina. I've got about one hour before Gideon and I will drive out to a jungle rehab camp. Half awake, I slink into a tea shop outside my hotel. I've been in town long enough for the child waiter – he must be eleven, tops – to scream out my usual order to the kitchen as soon I enter the shop.

'*Laphet yee boma dti kwe!*'

I squeeze in and find an empty seat, a dollhouse-sized plastic stool no taller than my calves. By the time I've delicately lowered myself into a sitting position, the tea arrives: a little ceramic cup, gushing steam, clattering down on the bamboo table.

This stuff is brown, viscous magic. It's Burmese-style tea, the life force of Myanmar. A few gulps and your consciousness positively crackles. Best of all is the globule of sweetened condensed milk coagulating at the bottom of the teacup. They're little pearl-colored dollops of nirvana.

The last slurp of tea brings the day's first dilemma. Noodles or samosas?

Kachin State is shaped like an arrowhead, jutting northward. To the east of this jagged triangle is China. To the west, India. And come breakfast time, you can smell this geographical confluence out on Myitkyina's streets.

Each morning by the roadside, ladies plop samosas into bubbling woks. Minutes later, they spoon out little morsels of pillowy mashed potatoes encased in crisp pastry. These Indian snacks, a tea shop staple, cost mere pennies.

But in eateries down the block, an even heartier meal awaits. Near the central market, grandmas tend to cauldrons of Chinese-style pork broth. Poured over rice noodles, flecked with herbs, this savory brew is served with chopsticks and a spoon. One bowl will stave off hunger for many hours.

This morning, I'm opting for the noodles. We've got a long drive ahead of us. I might not encounter another hot meal until after dark.

For all its troubles, Myitkyina is easy to love. It's a town where children sit in tree branches, munching wild fruit. Almost all of the women smear their faces with tree-bark paste. And some men even carry swords, fastening them to their hips, and passing them down to their sons once they grow old.

Myitkyina is a government-run town, an outpost of the Burmese state. But most of the inhabitants are Kachin. They are beholden to a parallel society emanating from the distant hills. It operates on a distinctly non-Burmese set of codes: tribe over nation, Jesus over Buddha.

The town is nestled in an oxbow of Myanmar's largest river, the Irrawaddy. The current is mostly ice melt from Himalayan glaciers. In the day's first hours, the water shimmers silvery blue. The river runs alongside Myitkyina's downtown, a jumble of wooden and cement structures. Most are topped with A-frame tin roofs, splotched with orange rust. It feels more like an overgrown country trading post than a regional capital.

On my walk to the noodle joint, I pass wrinkled men selling onions from a pushcart. On another block, a salesgirl at a mobile phone shop – filled with out-of-date Samsungs – gives her display case a good squeegee.

Closer to the market, vendors sitting on blankets display the bounty of the heartland: baskets of rice, sugarcane stalks, oranges arranged in a neat pyramid. I kneel down, pick out a few oranges and pass some cash to the vendor. Might be good to have some fruit handy for the road.

Today, Gideon and I are headed out into that Kachin heartland – over the river, past the military checkpoints, into places where police seldom venture. That's where the rehab camp is located. It's run by a cleric named Master Ahja. He's reputed to possess Christ-like healing powers.

Mindful of the time, I quicken my pace to the noodle shop. Best to fill my belly quickly and head back to the hotel before Gideon arrives to pick me up.

※

Down in the low country, it's not unusual for Burmese drivers to display a photo of Aung San Suu Kyi inside their cars – almost like a Virgin Mary-style good luck charm.

But on Gideon's dashboard, he's taped up a picture of someone else. It's some whiskery gentleman in a flannel shirt. Everywhere we drive, this guy is smiling at us.

'I've been meaning to ask you something,' I say. 'Who is that guy? And why is he so happy?'

'That's Yup Zau Hkawng. He's the richest Kachin man in the world.'

'What's so great about him?'

'I just told you. He's rich.'

'That's it?'

'That's it, brother,' Gideon says. 'Do you know how hard it is for a Kachin to get rich? It's damn near impossible. For that alone, you have to respect him.'

Gideon calls me 'brother' because that's the custom in Myanmar. But our rapport is more akin to a patient uncle and an overly inquisitive nephew. I've got more than an hour to badger him with questions before we reach the rehab camp.

'How did Yup Zau Hkawng get so rich?'

Gideon pops open his glove compartment, retrieves a stone and drops it into my lap. It's about the size of a goose egg. Parts of the stone are chipped, revealing an inner vein of greenness similar in color to creamed spinach.

'Jade.'

Once Kachin men reach adulthood, Gideon says, they're generally forced to choose from three livelihoods: farmer, rebel or miner. Yup Zau Hkawng opted for the latter. He supposedly started off as a gem-scrounging prospector.

Many who enter the Kachin State mines crawl out years later with broken dreams, not to mention limbs. But Yup Zau Hkawng? He emerged as a tycoon.

This was no minor feat, Gideon says. Myanmar's jade business is dominated by army generals who impose a racial hierarchy on its supply chain. Kachin men are supposed to toil in the pits while Burmese generals (and their Chinese financiers) hover above, sucking up the profits.

The Kachin aren't meant to ascend into the jade-mining elite. But Yup Zau Hkawng was able to jockey for power and slowly amass his millions.

His defiance of the odds engenders a Jay-Z-esque adulation among the Kachin. They're thrilled to see one of their own beat the system. 'That big mansion downtown? With the high walls and security cameras?' Gideon says. 'That's his house. One of them, anyways.'

In the photo on Gideon's dash, however, Yup Zau Hkawng looks like the antithesis of a coiffed, bejeweled Burmese aristocrat. He's wearing an L.L. Bean-style plaid shirt and, on his cheeks, three days of scruff.

'How come he doesn't dress like a rich guy?' I ask.

'He wants to come off as a man of the people,' Gideon says. This lumberjack chic is meant to offset an uncomfortable truth. No jade dealer gets that rich without consorting with the Burmese generals – men viewed by Kachin society as villains. Yup Zau Hkawng makes penance for this sin, Gideon says, by building public parks and roads in Kachin State.

'He's a good guy,' Gideon says. 'Deep down, he probably doesn't like the military. But what choice does he have? What choice does any Kachin have? The Burmese control everything. You want to make it in life? You have to work under them.'

Among diehard Kachin nationalists, collaborating with the beast is treason. But Gideon isn't a hardliner. He's a colluder too – a paid intermediary between Kachin society and the quasi-imperial police force.

In the hinterlands, most cops are Burmese men imported

from the low country. They see everything about Kachin State – the language, the faith, the local clan hierarchy – as alien, so they employ a cohort of Kachin to serve as their conduits to the local culture.

These intermediaries are often paid off the books. But they're invaluable to the police force. They provide critical intel. They hunt down suspects. They help plan and execute raids on drug houses.

Part of Gideon's job requires rounding up drug users so that the cops can meet their meager arrest quotas. He claims to scoop up only the most shriveled addicts, men and women teetering towards death. He steers the cops away from well-behaved drug users and dealers who don't bring trouble into their neighborhoods.

'I'm only arresting really sad cases. People who can barely feed themselves. People who are better off drying out in jail,' he says. 'The sort of people you're about to see at this rehab camp.'

'How do you get them to cooperate?'

'Some people go down fighting. But my specialty is showing up alone and convincing them to turn themselves in. No guns, no handcuffs.'

Smooth talking addicts into custody? It sounds absurd, but I buy it. Gideon radiates an irresistibly impish charm. He's like a hostage negotiator who strolls into the bank, cracks a few filthy jokes and, minutes later, walks out arm in arm with the robber, his new best friend.

In awkward moments, Gideon can tap his canon of folksy-yet-obscene parables to lighten the mood. Or he'll bust out some silly anecdote, channeling tension into laughs. He also knows when to blend into the background and just listen – soaking up information that may prove useful later.

We've come to an iron bridge spanning the Irrawaddy River. Above, I can see a canopy of ancient-looking iron latticework. Below, gray waters reflect mid-morning sunshine. Squadrons of bored-looking soldiers lurk at both ends of the bridge.

'Don't stare at them,' Gideon says. 'Just look straight ahead.'

We pass through without incident. Not long after we cross the bridge, Gideon veers off onto an unmarked gravel path.

Initially the road is flanked by leafy vegetable crops – a sign of human activity. But this landscape soon devolves into wild shrubbery. Thick vines intrude upon the lane. Before long, the road disintegrates further, giving way to a dirt track pocked by craters. The undercarriage of Gideon's car is noisily pelted by pebbles flung up from below.

For the next twenty minutes, we occasionally pass tiny villages: rattan homes on stilts, moms boiling rice over charcoal fires, trouserless kids playing in the mud. But there is mostly jungle, creating a pleasing sense of nowhereness.

Then our serenity is interrupted by two human silhouettes in the distance.

'That jade in your hand,' Gideon says. 'Put it away.'

Gideon cranks down his window, a warm breeze ruffling his rayon shirt collar. As we approach, the silhouettes become skinny males. They're standing before a painted wooden pole that blocks the road. One has a rifle slung across his back.

'Who are these guys?' I ask.

'*Pyi Thu Sit.*' Translation: People's Militia Forces. Private militia aligned with the military. Highly unpredictable.

'Don't talk to them,' Gideon says.

When he pulls up, the young men crowd the window. Gideon hits them with some friendly Kachin banter and cigarettes. I just smile in silence.

The gawky dude with the gun – a new-model hunting rifle with a wooden stock – is clad in mismatched army-surplus greens. The other is wearing a sweater and Crocs.

Next thing I know, Gideon is palming off cash to the Crocs guy. With his free hand, the guy tugs a string fed into a pulley that raises the wooden pole. Our path is now clear.

The militia boys wave us onward.

※

Try to recall the worst flu you've ever felt: joints throbbing, guts curdling, fluid leaking from every orifice.

Now imagine enduring all that inside a cement cell filled with other nauseated strangers. Everyone has diarrhea. There's no sit-down toilet, just a cavity in the floor. No running water. No air-conditioning. No television. No mobile phones.

You never really sleep. At night, your fever dreams are intruded upon by the other inmates' sickly whimpering. Come morning, your captors crank up loudspeakers positioned just outside the cell. The playlist? Contemporary Christian rock.

Such is the fate that awaits incoming addicts at the 'Youth for Christ' rehab camp.

The prison cell's walls are brick. Its floors are polished concrete. The only way in is through a wrought-iron door, secured with an industrial-strength padlock. The only way out is to renounce all drugs and beg for Christ's mercy.

Release is also contingent upon convincing the jailers that you won't run off in search of more heroin or meth. In years past, when this prison was made of bamboo, addicts would claw through the floor. But the new cell is a fortress that, so far, has proven impervious to escape.

I'm peering through a grille in the cell's iron door. There are four half-naked men sprawled on the concrete. I suppose that's the coolest surface in the chamber.

Their backs are scribbled up with DIY tattoos. On their skin, I can make out inky creatures real and imaginary: dragons and cobras, demons and carp. Most of the tats are as crude as cave paintings.

One of the men – nude except for some loose-fitting black trunks – notices me, rubs his eyes and squints in my direction. He lifts his head from the floor to get a better look. His eyes are shellacked by yellow film.

'Hey, brother,' I say. 'How long you been in here?'

'Two days.'

'How's it going?'

'Horrible. Can't sleep. The Number Four is still working its way out of my system.'

Number Four. That's local slang for heroin – a reference to the number of chemical procedures needed to synthesize opium goo into a grey powder that can be turned into a solution for injection.

This guy is clearly in the savage throes of first-week withdrawal. I don't want to pester him too much. 'Sorry to hear that,' I say. 'I'm off to speak with Master Ahja. Before I go, do you want an orange?'

From my backpack, I produce an orange, small as a snooker ball, and stick my arm through the door's grille. With great effort, he pulls himself off the floor and waddles over to retrieve the fruit from my outstretched hand. Then he melts back into the floor. I expect him to peel the orange but he just lays there, squeezing it in his fist.

This gulag aside, the Youth for Christ rehab camp is actually kind of charming. It's like a tiny village along the Irrawaddy River. The camp amounts to a few structures built mostly from forested materials: logs, rattan, bamboo – all held together with nails and rope. Out back, there's a herb garden. The camp is fronted by a grassy hill that slopes down-ward towards the riverbanks.

The addicts' day begins with a sleepy shuffle 50 paces down to the chilly water. Cold muck sucking at their ankles, the men wade in the river a bit before dragging themselves back up the hill. Up top, in an open-air mess hall, they receive breakfast: fresh eggs, herbal soup, a huge mound of rice.

Take away the dope-sick guys, convert the gulag into a yoga studio, and you could brand this as an organic eco-lodge. Just throw in some tiki torches and backpackers would pay $500 per week.

For Kachin addicts, however, lodging is 100 per cent free.

The chieftain of this camp is Master Ahja. He is a rangy man, in his forties, built of lean muscle. All day long he speed-walks around the grounds, seizing his so-called 'patients' by the shoulders and bombarding them with 90-second ser-mons. His intensity glows all the more brightly against the addicts' gloom.

I walk over towards the camp's largest structure: a two-story clubhouse built of bamboo and logs. In the back, there's a stage set up with second-hand amps, guitars and mics – all powered by a diesel generator.

This is where Ahja, himself a former heroin user, preaches salvation to his captive audience: three dozen addicts in recovery. He is stylishly disheveled – a bit of goatee fuzz, a few holes in his sweater – like some grunge cleric. Here, in this hideaway, the addicts confess their sins together. They weep together. They rock together. No one can hear their lamentations but the frogs in the river and the songbirds in the trees.

I find Ahja in the rapturous final act of a rock 'n' roll sermon. He is backed by a band composed of his more musically talented patients. They jam as he preaches. Cymbals crash, a bass guitar thumps and Ahja paces the stage like an upright cheetah. He's wearing a sarong decorated in a purple and green tartan pattern. As he moves, the fabric swishes violently at his bare feet.

Aside from a few newcomers, swaying lethargically, most of the patients are totally feeling it. Two guys are straight-up catching the Holy Ghost. The pair – one in Buddy Holly glasses, the other with shoulder-length surfer hair – cry out to God with eyes squinted. Their arms jut skywards like radio antennae.

When the sermon ends, I attempt to pull Ahja aside. But I'm too late. He's already dragging some of the more desperate-looking guys into a private prayer huddle.

So I talk to Buddy Holly and surfer-hair guy instead. They introduce themselves as La Htoi, a former jade trafficker in his mid-thirties, and Hawng Dai, early twenties, an ex-militia kid.

'I've only been here a few months,' Hawng Dai says. 'I got kicked out of a militia near the Chinese border and needed a place to get clean.'

'I've been here longer,' La Htoi says. 'I came after my jade business fell apart. Satan was slowly calling me to hell.'

Like most guys here, they've dabbled with both meth and heroin. They say the local consensus is that, between the two, meth can turn you into a bigger nuisance when you're high – especially on the fifth sleepless day, when your shadows become assassins chasing your tail.

But once you're ready to go clean, they say, meth is easier to kick than heroin. Ridding your body of opiates, they tell me, is pure heartache. Even a breeze on your arm hairs can hurt. Your thoughts move at the speed of sludge. Food tastes like cardboard. Whatever you manage to swallow is soon expunged.

Plus, once that warm, blanketing high lifts, you can suddenly feel emotions with agonizing rawness. Seemingly random triggers – a child's voice, a kitten's mewling – bring on pathetic sobs.

'I have a question for you guys,' I say. 'I hope it's not too personal.'

'It's OK, brother,' Hawng Dai says. 'We're strong enough.'

'I've heard plenty about detoxing. I'm more curious about the experience of getting high on heroin. Why do people keep doing it even in the face of death? Is it really that amazing?'

Hawng Dai inhales deeply. 'I can only speak for myself. And my answer is not short,' he says. 'You would have to hear my whole story.'

I spy Ahja in the corner of the room, furiously preaching to his huddle.

'We've got time,' I say. 'Go for it.'

Hawng Dai tells me he was a soldier in a militia called the 'NDA–K' or New Democratic Army – Kachin. This band of former communists is about as 'democratic' as the Democratic People's Republic of North Korea. For this cabal, 'democracy' is a meaningless slogan slapped onto a family crime syndicate.

The militia, which boasts roughly 1,000 soldiers, is run by a Kachin warlord named Ting Ying. He controls crucial smuggling routes into China. Though his minions, he taxes the hell out of all the timber, jade, meth and heroin flowing over the border.

'I sort of joined them as a joke,' Hawng Dai says. 'One of my friends said, "Hey, my dad is a soldier in the militia. They need new recruits. I bet you guys are too cowardly to join."'

'Eight of us joined the next day,' he says. 'The oldest was seventeen. The youngest was twelve.'

'Jesus, man. How old were you?'

'About fourteen. They gave me a .22-caliber rifle, put me in a hut on the roadside and told me to tax every truck that came through.'

'Did they pay you?'

'Yeah,' he says, 'About 30,000 kyat per month.' Roughly $30. 'But I made my real money as an errand boy for Burmese officers.'

'Burmese officers?' I ask. 'Isn't this a Kachin militia?'

'Yes,' he says, 'but it's allied with the central army. So we had a lot of high-ranking Burmese officers from the low country hanging around.'

'The Burmese always wanted to try the local "Number Four". They'd tell me, "Hey, you're a Kachin kid. You know where to get drugs." I took a cut of each purchase. But soon enough,' Hawng Dai says, 'I was using along with them.'

Hawng Dai's body is wiry and boyish, like a figurine made from pipe cleaners. His squeaky voice, the way he flips his Kurt Cobain-esque locks – it's all so childlike.

He must have been even smaller when he joined this militia. I'm trying to imagine a grown man handing him a rifle and ordering him to shake down meth-smuggling truckers. Or instructing a barely teenage Hawng Dai to go fetch packets of heroin.

'How bad was your habit?' I ask.

'At least one *Tite Nar Lone* per day.'

More Myanmar drug slang. A *Tite Nar Lone* is a little cylinder, about the size of an okra pod, stuffed with high-purity heroin. 'I got it straight from the producers. So it was cheap. About 7,000 kyat.' Only seven bucks. 'That habit dragged on for years.'

Hawng Dai has so thoroughly circumnavigated my question about getting high that I suspect he'd rather not answer. Which is fine. Asking a recovering addict to rhapsodize about the wonders of heroin is probably bad form.

But then he arrives at the point of his story: 'Out on the roadside, alone, I just didn't want to be there. Number Four allowed me to travel to new worlds in my mind. If you'd seen me back then, you'd wonder, "Why is he sleepily staring at the grass like a fool?" But I would have been in the most beautiful daydream. It was my only escape.'

La Htoi butts in: 'You see? This is why we must remain in the camp,' he says. 'The temptation to use again is too overpowering.'

La Htoi seems eager to share his own backstory. 'The only

reason I dragged myself here,' he says, 'is because I got sick. I contracted HIV.' The admission rolls out with a surprising casualness.

'You see, my friends and I, we thought you could only get HIV from prostitutes hanging around the jade mines. We had no idea it would enter our bodies through the needle.'

'On your first day here,' I ask, 'did Master Ahja put you in that cell?'

Both nod. 'When I arrived,' La Htoi says, 'I was so weak. A drop of water could have knocked me down. And yet withdrawals made me desperate to escape from this camp and get more drugs.'

'But out there,' he says, gesturing to the jungle beyond, 'I was a breathing corpse. Here, my brothers and I are coming back to life – thanks to almighty Christ.'

)(

The Kachin weren't always so tight with Jesus. Christianizing the tribe was a long effort undertaken by many Western evangelists. Among the first to make serious inroads was William Henry Roberts. He was a veteran of the American Civil War who fought under General Robert E. Lee.

After the confederate defeat, Roberts became a missionary. In the 1870s, the mustachioed ginger apostle sailed to Burma to meet Thibaw, the Burmese kingdom's monarch. Roberts requested permission to travel north into Kachin lands. He was keen to evangelize among the hill tribes.

The king just snickered. If that pleases you, he said, go for it. But you might as well try to teach Bible scriptures to the palace dog.

Or so the (possibly apocryphal) story goes. Soon after this glib dismissal, Thibaw was yanked from the throne by British troops, and foreign missionaries were more freely able to spread the gospel in remote Kachin villages. The first Kachin baptisms came in 1880 and, by the mid-1900s, the faith had become central to the Kachin identity – as it is today.

But for much of the 19th century, Kachin territory was regarded as too forbidding for missionary work. The Kachin were known as 'a war-like people ... and the government prevents Europeans from traveling through these parts lest they should be killed and the expense of a punitive expedition should have to be incurred.'[27]

So wrote the British missionary William C.B. Purser in the early 1900s. Like his peers at the time, he fretted over the souls of Burma's 'illiterate savages' – all while oozing contempt for their culture.

The missionaries were both steadfast anthropologists and crass racists. Their documentation of customs, tribal relations and linguistics is vital to our understanding of Burma in the 1800s. But it's impossible to read their journals without cringing.

They tended to dismiss any local custom as vulgar. This ugly suspicion of the unfamiliar even seeped into Purser's food reviews. A meal in Burma, he wrote, is 'never considered complete unless accompanied by an evil-smelling concoction of putrid fish called *nga pi*'.[28] (Blasphemy! *Nga pi* is heavenly stuff.)

As the British Empire strove to subdue all of Burma's tribes and administer them under a common flag, the missionaries felt they were in a race against time. A unified Burma would bring the so-called 'savages' out of isolation and expose their unpolluted minds to the low-country way of life.

The Bible-thumping Anglos felt they had to reach the tribes first – lest they assimilate into the Buddhist mainstream.

'In Burma, as in many other parts of the world, a great change is coming over these backward tribes who have hitherto inhabited remote mountains and islands – and have remained untouched by modern progress,' Purser wrote in 1911.[29] 'Year by year, they are coming into closer contact with civilization, and if they do not become Christians, they will become Buddhists.'

'If these tribes are to be won for Christ,' he wrote, 'it must be within the next 25 years.'

Enter a wave of Baptists from America. They would answer this call, braving disease and starvation to save souls in the hinterlands.

One of them was a Swedish-American named Ola Hanson, a gifted linguist. He arrived in Burma in around 1890 and lived among Kachin villages for nearly three decades. Kachin Christians still revere him for rendering their spoken language into a written script. He was the first to translate the Holy Bible into Kachin.

But like his contemporaries, Hanson's adventures were stained by unapologetic Euro-Christian chauvinism. His mission was to elevate these 'primitive people' into the realm of the 'more favored and advanced races'.[30]

This was the era of white explorers cataloguing fellow humans by trait – as if they were a newly discovered species of newt. Of the Kachin women, Hanson wrote: 'Most of them are strongly built and able to endure a great deal of hardship.'

Of the men: 'Many are quick tempered … and love above everything to get something for nothing.'

Of both: 'The color of the skin may vary from almost negro black to the sallow tint of the northern Chinaman.'

Even his compliments came out all wrong. In rejoicing over the 'rhythmic proverbs' in Kachin speech, Hanson observed that 'poetry is the natural speech of the savage'. And yet his descriptions of Kachin lands can't help but excite the imagination. It is a 'wild mountain country intersected by narrow valleys and deep gorges … through which flow numerous mountain streams'.

Tigers and leopards are a constant menace. The eagles, he wrote, are sturdy enough to snatch pigs in their talons. Around the village cooking fires, weasels, porcupines and pythons 'present a variety for the curry pot'.

Hanson observed that most Kachin homes rest upon three-foot-high stilts. The space beneath is a livestock pen filled with hogs and fowl. After dinner, any unwanted bones can be pushed through slats in the bamboo floor into a piggy's waiting mouth.

This is a fair description of many rural Kachin dwellings even today. Many other aspects of life also remain constant. The Kachin (like the Burmese) still munch betel nuts, a mild stimulant that offers an espresso-like rush and turns the saliva blood red. Also, just as in Hanson's time, Kachin men are still expected to own a sword with a squarish blade – called the *dha* – that is often hung prominently on the wall.

Despite the missionaries' slander of the Kachin as 'war-like', Hanson observed the opposite. Their society functioned through what he called 'almost ideal socialism'. He noted that 'all the jungle surrounding the village is common property. Anyone can take all the wood and timber he needs.'

If you want dibs on a certain patch of land inside the village, that's not a problem. Put a bamboo fence around it and raise your crops – but expect to share with your neighbors.

You'd think this collectivist spirit might inspire admiration. But Hanson managed to hold it against the Kachin. Their rules on property, he wrote, 'are not nearly as strict as in higher forms of civilization'.[31] Behold the obscenity of colonial logic: the British Empire, which killed tens of thousands to control Burmese lands, were highly civilized. The Kachin, who seldom bothered anyone outside their mountain patch? Savages.

Hanson conceded, however, that Kachin tribes were not genuine warmongers. Unlike the Burmese kingdoms, which actively sought to conquer other cultures, the Kachin would only defend themselves against invaders, such as low-landers trying to establish settlements inside their mountainous sphere.

The Kachin were effective fighters. In Hanson's time, the Burmese 'never really ruled the hills'. In fact, he wrote that no 'Burman village could exist where the hill men were within striking distance … thus the Kachin regarded himself lord of all he surveyed'.

These and other observations are extraordinarily helpful in imagining pre-Christian Kachin life. But this wasn't ethnography for its own sake. All of Hanson's findings were put into the service of his core goal of converting the tribes to Christianity.

He wanted to understand Kachin culture and history so that he could upend it.

Hanson's top concern was ridding the Kachin of animism – that ancient belief, common across Asia, that the world is influenced by a near-innumerable variety of spirits. In Kachin-style animism, cosmic beings rule over vital matters like when it rains or who gets cholera. They also mediate small concerns, such as the success of a hunting trip.

All the world's natural phenomena are attributed to these supernatural creatures. For example, rainbows shoot from the mouths of giant subterranean crabs. As for an eclipse? That's just a space frog trying to gulp down the sun. The Kachin also believed in a great creator: long ago, all of existence was created by a 'mysterious female half-human, half-avian' spirit.

Hanson devoted years to documenting the complexities of Kachin belief. His writing suggests that he was mesmerized by this folklore. And yet he wanted nothing more than to eradicate their spirituality.

Out with the groovy bird goddess. In with the God of Abraham.

✗

How pleased Hanson would be to see the results of Myanmar's latest census. Today, throughout all of Kachin State – population 1.6 million – not even 4,000 people call themselves animist.[32]

Christianity now reigns supreme over Kachin society. Faith is the thread stitching together tribal units. Organized Kachin life largely revolves around two entities. Both are deeply Christian.

One is the Kachin Baptist Convention, a network of

churches that claims nearly half a million members. It is the largest Kachin institution in recorded history and a great arbiter of Kachin spiritual life.

The second is the Kachin Independence Army, or KIA, perhaps the world's largest explicitly Christian rebel group. The KIA is much more than a militia. It is a proto-government, backed by 10,000-plus troops, controlling vast terrain abutting the Chinese border.

The organization funds itself though timber cutting, mid-sized jade mines (frequently besieged by the Burmese military) and borderland taxation.[33] Much of its revenue is used to pay for makeshift school systems, hospitals and courts.

The KIA does not demand an entirely new nation. It merely seeks statehood within the nation of Myanmar. But this must come with a strong degree of autonomy: Kachin-language schools, Kachin integration into the police force, a drawdown of occupying forces and – perhaps most importantly – more control over their natural wealth.

The KIA generals' fundamental job is to protect Kachin society against total Burmese-Buddhist domination. This mission is steeped in Christian philosophy. It's common for these rebel leaders to hold hands and sing Baptist hymns – many of them translated by Hanson – before planning their troop movements.

With the Kachin Baptist Convention and the KIA dominating Kachin society, there is no longer a need for pasty foreigners to trek up here with Bibles. Christianity now pervades all aspects of life. Walk into a Kachin village and you may find parents named Samson and Esther tending to kids named Paul and Mary.

In lieu of proselytizers from Massachusetts or Tennessee, indigenous preachers carry forth God's work. Among them: Master Ahja, a practitioner of American Baptist-style faith healing.

X

Back at the Youth for Christ camp, Ahja has finished praying with his flock. When I pull him away for a chat by the river, I can sense he's still coming down from his sermonizing high.

'This camp is beautiful, Ahja,' I say. 'How did you make this happen?'

Every holy man needs his transformation story. Ahja's begins in the late 1990s. His rock band, Phase II, had a local buzz. After performing, he would party like Slash circa 1989. In Myanmar's frontier, you don't need to be rock-star rich to afford a weekend bacchanal of meth and heroin. About $150 will suffice.

'Every day, I was on both *ya ma* and Number Four,' Ahja tells me. 'The police finally caught up with me and my friends. They burst into our room and found a whole penicillin.' This is more Myanmar drug slang. A 'penicillin' is a unit of heroin, often sold in a small glass bottle that is traditionally used to hold liquid penicillin.

'The cops kicked us around the room,' he says, 'and ground their boots into our thighs. Then they dragged us away.'

'Hold on,' I say. 'I thought police seldom made drug arrests up here.'

'In the countryside, yeah, anything goes. In a city like

Myitkyina, it's also easy to sneak around. But you'll eventually get nabbed if you make a big scene. We were really reckless.'

What followed were nine years in prisons that, as Ahja puts it, were as inhumane as 'Nazi camps'. The food allotment was so scarce, he says, that men 'actually starved to death in there. I've seen guys turn to gay prostitution just to get a meal.'

'How much food can you get for sex?' I ask.

'Two scraps of chicken.'

'You see, it was in prison,' Ahja continues, 'that I learned I had the power to heal people.' I sense that I'm about to hear an origin tale he's delivered hundreds of times before. But I don't mind. Listening to Ahja is electrifying. He has a mystic's habit of staring directly into your eyes, lingering until your surroundings fade away and you feel singularly important.

'There was a man in prison who, from birth, could not walk. I gripped his legs in my hands and he rose to his feet!'

'There was a man who had broken veins in his heart. I held him and, through Christ, his body healed.'

'And today, when these men come to me, after becoming a stain on their community, I lay my healing hands upon them. I hold them, pray with them, and lead them towards the Holy Spirit.'

'Master Ahja,' I say, 'I have to ask about your own prison here at the camp.'

'Well, we don't call it a prison,' he says. 'That's my "special prayer room". Do you think it's wrong?'

'I'm not sure yet,' I say. 'Did they choose to go in there?'

'Some do. Others are dragged out of bed at their community's request.'

'How long do you keep people in there?'

'We put fresh patients in the room for roughly one week. But they're getting constant care. We bathe them, pray with them, massage them. Talk them through their darkest thoughts.'

'Why blast Christian music into their cells all morning?' I ask.

'My intention is for them to hear the word of God constantly. This is a drug ministry. We don't use medication. We don't have doctors. All we have is the word of God.'

'When will you release them?'

'Only when we're convinced they won't run off. It's a long way to town but some still try. Three or four times even. We're good at catching them. I've got some tough guys here to help me out. You know, ex-cons. That gives the runners second thoughts.'

Before arriving here, I'd heard rumors about these Kachin rehab jails. But I hadn't seen one with my own eyes. This form of 'therapy' is condemned within the international aid worker scene. In conversation with officials from the UN Office on Drugs and Crime, I'd even heard the office's senior Myanmar representative – then a Canadian named Jason Eligh – describe these cells as 'deplorable'.

'You're talking about taking someone and locking them in a cage … and expecting that, miraculously, they'll be healed?' he once told me. 'That's just not reality.'

But as Ahja tells it, this is an hour of crisis for the Kachin – and crisis requires extreme counter-measures. The Kachin, he says, are locked in an existential battle against twin threats: narcotics and Myanmar's army.

'The two forces work hand in hand,' he tells me. The military is delighted to see drugs sap the vitality of the Kachin and weaken their ability to resist, Ahja says. Softened up by addiction, the population is easier to subdue and their natural bounty is more vulnerable to plunder.

'This is a drug war, you see,' Ahja says. 'It's a new kind of Opium War. Just like in the history books. Our race is breaking into pieces. We have to do everything in our power.'

Apparently that includes locking sick addicts in cages.

I won't say that Kachin-style prison therapy is morally defensible, but nor can I summon enough outrage to use the word 'deplorable' even after having seen it firsthand.

The Kachin people have long endured outsiders deriding their behavior as barbaric. I don't want to join that chorus. In witnessing the 'special prayer room', I feel like a houseguest stumbling across a filthy closet – an unseemly sight, sure, but not one that demands my judgment.

I also believe in the profound sincerity of Ahja's mission. His faith healing is terribly unscientific. But what else can he muster out here? This isn't some well-financed methadone clinic. It's just a few huts, built with scrounged bamboo, in the militia-run badlands of Myanmar.

Ahja certainly compares favorably to the prominent Baptists of the American South, my birthplace. Take Jerry Falwell, the famed televangelist. He got rich sitting in an air-conditioned studio, proclaiming that gay men are hatching secret plots to spread AIDS.

And here is Ahja, holding bedraggled miners with HIV in his arms, whispering into their ears that God still loves them. He spends his nights inside that vomit-stained prison cell, massaging the shoulders of addicts who want to die.

A few hours later, as Gideon and I prepare to leave, we notice a young man walking unsteadily up the pebbly path leading to the camp. He immediately recognizes Ahja and slinks over, hunchbacked and shamefaced. 'My name is Mala,' he says. 'I just got back from the mines. You have to help me.'

'We're pretty full here right now, little brother,' Ahja says. 'We don't have much food or space to offer. But tell me. What's wrong?'

This guy is scarecrow-thin, his body shriveled by addiction. It takes him a minute to find his words. But Ahja is patient, letting the quiet do its work. Then it all just pours out: 'I found this piece of jade worth a lot of money. But then I spent all the profits on heroin. It just went up into my arms,' Mala says. 'I need your help. I'll try anything. I'm tired of everyone looking at me like I'm garbage.'

'God is here, Master Ahja,' Mala continues. 'I can feel it.'

⋊

Gideon and I decide to spend the rest of the week visiting the other Christian rehab camps scattered around Myitkyina. Most are ramshackle settlements with a Mad-Maxian sense of architecture: structures built of metal scraps, rope, bamboo and lengths of blue PVC piping.

The layout of each camp is fairly consistent. Invariably, they're surrounded by high walls made of tin sheeting. Entrances are manned by tough-looking sentries with wooden staves. These men are akin to prison guards. Inside, there are usually a few dozen inmates – called 'patients' – who are in various states of detoxification.

There is a hierarchy inside the camps. Recovering addicts who've achieved months of sobriety are often anointed as counselors or prayer coaches – a responsibility that they relish. This elevates them over the glassy-eyed newcomers.

Lowest of all are the fresh arrivals, languishing in cells. The rehab cages vary in design. One camp called 'Light of the World' padlocks addicts inside a jumbo-sized chicken coop. At another camp, the cell is as big as a train car with bars made of sanded hardwood.

Aside from the newcomers – groaning and clammy and shouting abuse – everyone seems keen to chat. It seems my visits are a welcome relief from the drudgery of Bible study and self-flagellating confessionals. Within days, I've talked to so many addicts that their woeful backstories blur together.

There is no bigger recovery cliché than the 'rock bottom' tale. But I can't help but ask each patient if there was a singular moment that signaled peak awfulness. For one meth addict, it was defecating blood. For another inmate, it was dredging a used needle from a mud puddle, loading it with heroin and jabbing it into the crook of his arm.

Among the meth users, though, I notice a pattern. Their addiction would often crescendo in some screaming, dish-smashing rampage that provoked the neighbors (or sometimes their own mothers) to alert *Pat Jasan*.

I've yet to meet one of *Pat Jasan*'s vigilantes in person. But I'm already detecting their presence. Their shadowy crusade has left its mark on many of the caged addicts – often literally.

Peering into cages, Gideon and I see purplish contusions striping the flesh of the inmates' calves and backs. The wounds are like ugly ribbons, thick as your thumb, but thrice as long. When I ask about these injuries, the men just mutter '*Pat Jasan*' and wave us off.

'Those are definitely cane marks,' Gideon says. 'These guys were hit with bamboo rods.'

'Gideon,' I ask, 'do you think *Pat Jasan* would talk to me about these beatings?'

'I doubt it. But we can try,' he says. 'They're very secretive, you know. The police hate them.'

And for good reason. What I've seen so far suggests the emergence of a parallel justice system. It seems *Pat Jasan* is doing what the cops won't: hunting down meth smokers and hauling them into the night. The rehab camps serve as a shadow prison network. The pastors who run the camps are, in effect, rogue wardens.

How to justify such radicalism? When I ask the camp overseers, I hear a common refrain. We're at war, they say. Our fighting-age males are succumbing to meth and heroin. If we let this continue, we will be too weak to fend off the Burmese – and the Kachin people will be swallowed by the beast.

At one camp, a crew of counselors insists that I meet one of their newcomers: a child named Li Li. This kid, they tell me, will help you understand their sense of apocalyptic urgency.

They plant me in a little hut and tell me to wait. Five minutes later, in walks a thirteen-year-old boy, rubbing his eyes. The kid has not quite grown into his Dumbo ears. He's wearing pajama pants decorated with cartoon animals. They tell me he's an orphan, now in the care of recovering addicts.

The rehab counselors discovered Li Li living as a ragamuffin, rough and parentless in Myitkyina. The kid says his mother and father are still alive. But they're marooned somewhere in the jungle, sleeping under tarps, living off feral boar his father hunts with a Kachin sword.

'At least that's what they were doing when I left their side.'

'Why,' I ask, 'were you sleeping out in the wild?'

'The army,' Li Li says. 'They torched our village. We were living on the run with about 200 others.'

'My mom and dad were scared that troops would find us living in the jungle,' he says. 'They worried soldiers would take me away and turn me into a porter. So I needed to leave. They pointed me in the direction of Myitkyina and told me to walk.'

Once Li Li reached town, he fell in with a gang of street kids. They survived by running errands for a crew of older meth and heroin addicts. Li Li was properly indoctrinated into the gang when they pulled him into a circle, sprinkled some heroin powder onto a copper plate and held a lighter underneath.

'It starts to bubble and you put your face close to the plate. Then you breathe as hard as you can,' Li Li tells me. 'It's easy.'

He freebased the fumes and then fell back on the grass, swept up into a sweet reverie. Soon enough, his life revolved around that charred plate.

'You know, after my village burned down, my goal was to join the KIA and seek revenge,' Li Li tells me. 'But I forgot about all that once I discovered Number Four. Now? I don't know. I just want to be a good kid again.'

Li Li belongs to what many Kachin call the 'lost generation'. Ask anti-drug crusaders why they resort to midnight abductions and secret jails. You'll hear about all the Li Lis out there, zombified by drugs before puberty, too enfeebled by narcotics to pick up a rifle (or a book) and resist.

Towards the end of my camp tours, I meet Peter Khon

Awng, a clean-cut man in his thirties. He runs a camp called 'Rebirth' in Myitkyina.

Unlike Ahja, Peter has the spiffy bearing of a Sunday school teacher. In lieu of faith healing, he relies on twelve-step literature that he downloads from the internet and translates into Kachin. He too keeps a detention cell out back but, as cages go, it's tidy and spacious – about the size of a small Manhattan studio apartment.

But for all of Peter's poise, his sense of foreboding is no less powerful than that of firebrands like Ahja. 'I know that you've spoken to a lot of people at this point. So I hope you understand our situation. This is a real genocide,' Peter says. 'The government is using drugs to destroy us.'

'Think about it,' he says. 'The army kills the KIA with guns. Then they kill civilians with drugs. Once our race become too weak, they will finally control our land.'

So the theory goes. Among many Kachin, this genocide-through-drugs conspiracy rhetoric is now taken as gospel. Everyone seems convinced that the military is either cranking out meth on its own bases or, at the very least, goading drug lords to pump speed into Kachin villages.

I am reminded of the longstanding allegation that the CIA was complicit in America's 1980s crack wave – a notion derived from the agency's collusion with right-wing Central American coke traffickers.

The charge against Myanmar's army is similarly difficult to pin down. It's not that the military lacks malicious intent. This is an army that grinds down minorities with mortar attacks in the mountains and systematic rape along the coast. Its generals would hardly object to a weaponized meth scheme on moral grounds.

But malice alone does not prove every dark plot. Perhaps there is a simpler explanation: base neglect.

Pastors such as Peter ask why the military allows meth labs to operate so freely in their homeland. But do they really expect the generals to expend energy busting drug rings in minority areas – the same places they're actively trying to conquer? Why would the soldiers who burned down Li Li's hut give a damn if the kid overdoses?

Moreover, anti-drug rhetoric from Kachin Christian networks reeks of hyperbole. They seem all too eager to blame a tangle of complex problems on drugs. Even if Jesus descended from the sky and turned all the meth pills to Skittles, Kachin State would still be mired in land mines, illiteracy and warlordism.

But the vigilantes can't grab illiteracy by the hair and force it to repent. Nor can they toss powerful army generals in their bamboo prisons. However, there is a near-endless supply of addicts for *Pat Jasan* to smack around – all under the banner of cleansing Kachin society.

'People on meth become brain damaged,' Peter says. 'When they finally run out of money, they will steal. If you try to stop them, they won't hesitate to kill.'

'But *Pat Jasan* is violent too,' I say. 'Running into people's houses, beating people up – do you think that's justified?'

Peter, like the other camp leaders, gets squirmy when I bring up *Pat Jasan*. The group's home invasion techniques are an open secret in Myitkyina. But he is careful not to reveal too much to a note-taking foreigner.

'I agree that they have no legal right to beat drug users,' Peter says. 'But they're not just beating people up and then walking away. They bring addicts to places like this to get treatment. And now, some addicts are so scared of *Pat Jasan* that they come running here on their own.'

The Burmese-Buddhist police, I say, are not too fond of minority groups forming their own abduction squads. How much longer can *Pat Jasan* get away with this?

'We're ready for anything,' Peter says. 'Even a showdown with police.'

On that ominous note, I bid goodbye to Peter and signal to Gideon that we're done for the day. We hop in his car and reverse out of the camp, past the gruff men guarding the entrance.

'Look at that,' Gideon says. He's pointing to a crumpled section of the camp's exterior metal fence. The metal sheeting is bent, seemingly folded downwards by some heavy weight that pressed down from above.

'The addicts tell me that's where they jump over and escape,' Gideon says. 'Honestly, this is kind of a bad place to put a rehab. There are loads of places to score nearby.'

⋏

For days on end, Gideon has listened over my shoulder as men like Peter implicate the police in racial-extermination plots. As we rumble down Myitkyina's dirt roads, chassis squeaking over potholes, I ask him straight up: are your police cohorts really plotting genocide against the Kachin people?

'No,' Gideon says. 'All that *Pat Jasan* talk about genocide? It's overblown.'

To hear Gideon tell it, cops in Kachin State are much more concerned with Johnny Walker and kickbacks than ethnic cleansing. They hate leaving their cozy home base in

Myitkyina or other government-controlled areas. They prefer to operate in towns, where the Kachin must bow to their authority.

Out in the rebellious backcountry, the cops feel threatened and outnumbered. Villages go unpoliced. Drug users freely smoke or shoot up. Gideon says this feeds the belief that the state wants drugs to fester among non-Burmese ethnic groups.

Still, that contention that cops in minority areas seldom make drug arrests? It's not an exaggeration. In a typical year, Kachin State police arrest about 1,500 to 2,000 people on drug charges.[34] That's nothing.

Population-wise, Kachin State is on par with Idaho. Yet Idaho's drug arrests are 500 per cent higher. And unlike Myanmar's black zones, the Potato State isn't churning out 2 billion speed pills each year – enough to tweak out every man, woman and child in America for a whole weekend.

Gideon makes the Kachin State police sound more like bumblers than scheming Nazi Schutzstaffel. 'The local police are mostly just going after small-time dealers and sad little addicts,' Gideon says. 'They try not to pick on anyone who can put up a fight.'

'Do suspects ever resist?' I ask.

'It happens. Guys come out swinging Kachin swords. Or waving spears,' Gideon says. 'In that case, I might take out their legs with a slingshot.'

'A slingshot?' I ask. 'Don't you guys have guns?'

'Yeah,' Gideon says. 'The unit I work for has pistols and shotguns and old carbines.'

'So why the slingshot?'

'The Burmese officers hang back with the guns. They send

me in first with the slingshot. I'm Kachin, remember. They won't let me handle a rifle.'

The inept police, Gideon says, are given too much credit by *Pat Jasan*. 'If you want to find a big drug conspiracy, look at the institution that controls the police,' he says. 'Look at the institution that controls the courts, the roads, the whole government.'

'The military,' I say.

'Right,' Gideon says. 'Remember the guys we saw at that checkpoint? *Pyi Thu Sit*. They're a type of militia that works for the army. They control a lot of the meth labs. But our local police are under orders from the army to leave them alone.'

'Suppose they catch some dealer,' he says, 'and squeeze him for information. If he says he's with an army-linked militia? Question time is over.'

'That's it?'

'That's it. Actually, he could just say he's from a *Pyi Thu Sit*-controlled area like Washawng and he'd probably go free.' I recognize the district's name. That's where Li Li's family was driven from their flaming hut.

'What would happen if you tried to raid a meth lab out there?'

'Impossible,' he says. 'The army would never approve.'

'Yeah, but what if?'

'We'd be walking into a gun battle that we wouldn't win. The police have no desire for that, brother. They'd rather go raid some guy's house just to steal his stash.'

We drive for a moment in silence. Gideon is cruising slowly and aimlessly. We're getting overtaken by schoolgirls on motorbikes and smoke-spewing tractors.

'You know,' Gideon says, 'a lot of the cops on the force are actually half-addicted to drugs themselves. They love opium.'

'Opium,' I say. 'Back in the states, we have meth, we have heroin. But to us, opium is very rare. I've never even seen it.'

A naughty smirk curls across Gideon's lips.

'Never even seen it?' he says. 'I know where we're going next.'

)(

Gideon pulls into a gravel driveway outside a featureless cement house. He parks, alights and heads into the back yard. I follow close behind.

He bids a familiar hello to a grandma minding the scene. She's tending a cauldron of chicken soup, frothy and brimming with bones, as it roils over a charcoal fire. Near her legs, a toddler chases a chicken in circles. Gideon makes a goo-goo noise and the kid smiles.

It seems we're not headed inside the cement house. We're walking towards an elevated wooden hut out back. It's a creaky structure perched high above the dirt on hardwood stilts.

We come to a staircase. I slide off my shoes, Gideon kicks off his flip-flops. We ascend. Up top, there's a wooden door. Gideon knocks. There's an affirmative grunt from within.

Inside, we're greeted by a heavyset man in a starched white shirt and sarong. He's sitting cross-legged on the floor. Gideon greets him in Burmese.

The room is tiny and devoid of furniture. Dozens of cigarette packs are stacked in orderly towers against the wall. On the floor, a teapot and tiny glass cups rest on a silvery platter.

'There it is,' says Gideon, motioning to the floor. At the man's feet, I see a few black globs wrapped in cellophane. They look like melted clumps of dark chocolate.

Just what I suspected. Gideon has brought me to an opium den.

More than a century ago, when Hanson was documenting Kachin customs, he stumbled across lots of opium sessions. 'Many Kachins,' he wrote, 'smoke the drug with shredded and dried plantain leaves. The opium is liquefied on a small copper dish and the leaves are saturated with the drug. Then it is smoked in an ordinary pipe – a small pinch at a time.'

With a few exceptions, that description matches the process I'm about to witness.

Gideon sets down a gas-powered hot plate in the center of the floor. He turns its dials and I hear the high-pitched hiss of an open fuel line. With the flick of his lighter, the gas jets are lit and – whoosh – there is a perfect ring of sky-blue flame.

The other guy hands over a wide-mouthed copper ladle. Gideon warms it a bit above the fire. Then he picks up a baggie and shakes loose a sticky black wad. It falls into the ladle with a plop.

'See this stuff?' says Gideon. 'People call this "mouse shit" opium.'

Now he is hovering the ladle about four inches above the flames. Within half a minute, the mouse droppings have liquefied, bubbling like hot motor oil.

'I get the feeling you guys have done this before,' I say. The men smile.

'These are ancient procedures,' says the guy sitting cross-legged on the floor. 'The teenagers today? They don't have the patience for this. They just go straight for the needle. They want to get really high, really fast. Our grandfathers never did anything like that.'

'I'm confused,' I say. 'How do you actually smoke it?'

'With this,' he says, holding up a bamboo bong. It looks utterly unlike Zau Ring's meth hookah, all synthetic and plasticky and held together with tape. This bong is a sturdy wooden pipe, the size of my forearm. It has heft and soul.

'That's a traditional opium pipe,' Gideon says. 'We call it a "ka-boom".'

I am wary of getting too personal in an opium den. But I can't resist asking the stranger what he does for a living.

'I'm an officer in the military,' he says.

I try to squelch my surprise. But my face betrays me.

'Don't worry. I'm not a soldier,' he says. 'I'm just an army doctor.'

Gideon switches off the burner and waits for the opium sludge to cool a bit. Then he produces a chopstick and lightly applies the tip, swirling the liquid blackness in circular patterns, leaving artful trails. The opium thins out on the concave ladle, lacquering its surface.

The doctor passes over a wad of brown plantain leaves, shredded and dried. Gideon places a clump inside the ladle and swishes it all around until the leaves are coated with black opium goop.

The kindling is now saturated. Gideon takes a pinch off the spoon and plugs it into the bong's bowl, which juts from its cylindrical side like a little stem. He passes it over to the doctor, who sticks his face in the ka-boom's wide opening, lights the stem and takes a big gurgly rip. I sure hope this guy is not on call tonight.

'Your turn,' says the doctor.

'Oh,' I say. 'No thanks.'

He squints back at me, eyeing me up and down with that distinct *what-are-you-a-narc?* stare. I sense that I've breached opium-den etiquette. Or worse yet, perhaps I'm arousing suspicion.

A foreigner turns up to the opium spot with Gideon so he can sample the local goods? Weird but plausible. A foreigner shows up, takes a lot of notes, asks too many questions and then refuses to get high? That might be a problem.

'Just a small hit,' says Gideon, pressing the ka-boom into my hands.

⋈

My memories of the ensuing hours are a bit fuddly. Trying to recall precise details is like trying to grasp handfuls of syrup.

I do recall sitting in the back of Gideon's car and gazing up at an electric-peach sky as we drove away from the shack. We skipped dinner that night. He just dropped me at my hotel.

I remember sitting by my window, watching an amber sun descending between two peaks. After that, I was soon ensconced in bed. The 150-thread count sheets felt like orchid petals marinated in lotion. Then everything went dark.

Not long after that evening, Gideon began making inroads with *Pat Jasan*. Setting up a rendezvous required some serious cajoling. But the vigilantes would eventually agree to meet at their operations center – a complex on the grounds of a wooden church, hidden away in the backstreets of Myitkyina.

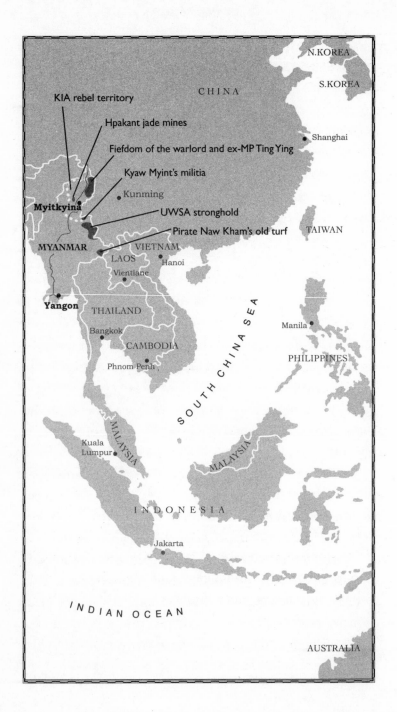

KIA rebel territory

Hpakant jade mines

Fiefdom of the warlord and ex-MP Ting Ying

Kyaw Myint's militia

UWSA stronghold

Pirate Naw Kham's old turf

CHINA

N.KOREA

S.KOREA

Shanghai

Kunming

Myitkyina

TAIWAN

MYANMAR

VIETNAM

LAOS

Hanoi

Vientiane

Yangon

THAILAND

Bangkok

CAMBODIA

Phnom Penh

Manila

PHILIPPINES

SOUTH CHINA SEA

MALAYSIA

Kuala
Lumpur

MALAYSIA

INDONESIA

Jakarta

INDIAN OCEAN

AUSTRALIA

CHAPTER II

Holy Revolt

Location: Kachin State, Myanmar

Where vigilantes rebel against narco-kings

What a fine night for a home invasion. The towns-folk are holed up in their dwellings, most of them driven inside by the rains that came lashing down earlier in the day.

Myitkyina's unpaved backstreets are a soupy mess. Walk ten steps and your flip-flops are slathered in mud the con-sistency of pancake batter. Who'd want to slosh around in this muck?

Not the police. They're probably drinking whiskey indoors somewhere. Not the workaday traders and farmers. It's nearly 9:30pm. They'll soon conk out on their floor mats. The streets are clear of witnesses and the night is given over to cicadas, chattering in the wet shrubs.

'The weather is our friend tonight,' says Naw Sam, a *Pat Jasan* mission commander. He's a squat, humorless man in his mid-forties.

'There should be very few bystanders out and about. That means fewer people who might alert authorities or otherwise interfere with our mission. With God on our side, our opera-tion should prove successful.'

That's how Naw Sam talks. Like a stodgy colonel. He even

dresses the part: woodland camouflage vest, a green helmet covered in mesh netting.

I've joined the commander inside a small, fenced-in compound located on the property of a Baptist church. We're in a two-room structure: concrete flooring, hatched rattan walls. The roof is wafer-thin steel. Earlier, when rain fell on this command post, it sounded like a kettledrum pelted by marbles. But now the skies are calm.

In his left hand, Naw Sam grips a walkie-talkie. He uses its metal antenna as an instructional pointer, tapping it against a large whiteboard. The board is all scribbled up with crude diagrams drawn in blue magic marker. He's sketched out a bird's-eye-view map of tonight's targeted neighborhood.

'These lines right here signify an intersection. Understood?'

Two subordinates in fatigues, huddled around the whiteboard map, are nodding along. One of these men will lead a small team of scouts on tonight's mission. The other will guide a six-person 'warrior' unit armed with bamboo sticks.

'Once the scouts locate and confirm the target,' Naw Sam says, 'your men will come up this road to secure the house. This area is lightly populated and the homes are far apart. But please, ensure that there are no neighbors outside before you commence.'

I peer through a window at the *Pat Jasan* foot soldiers, dozens of them, milling about in an enclosed courtyard. They're loading fresh batteries into their flashlights, doling out wooden sticks, conducting last-minute mission prep. They await Naw Sam's exit from the operations center. In a moment, he will bless tonight's raid.

I came here expecting a pack of disorganized young men

amping themselves up to rove around town and snatch up addicts by the collar. Instead, I've found an organization governed by strict hierarchy – and a commander planning out his mission like the Battle of the Somme.

Naw Sam oozes authority. When he finally steps into the courtyard, preparing to address his squadron, their chatter ceases. They instinctively form a semi-circle around their leader and bow their heads in unison.

'Oh, heavenly father,' Naw Sam says, eyes tightly shut, his forehead creased. 'How grateful is *Pat Jasan* to receive your blessing!'

As they pray, I sneak a peek at the vigilantes assembled in the courtyard. Most are clad in camouflage vests with a large seal stitched on the back: a poppy bulb, dissected with a red bar, like the Ghostbusters logo. This is *Pat Jasan*'s official crest.

Many wear open-toed sandals, their feet speckled with mud. But they've at least managed to scrounge up motorbike helmets to protect their skulls from concussive strikes.

'Lord, protect us on our mission,' Naw Sam says. 'We may not behave perfectly tonight, God, but we place our fate in your hands. Amen.'

'AMEN!' shout the vigilantes.

'Now,' Naw Sam says, 'if anyone here is drunk, confess now. You cannot join the operation if you've consumed alcohol.'

No one budges.

'Good,' Naw Sam says. 'I'm counting 28 heads. By God's grace, I want no fewer than 28 to return. Remember. We demand obedience. Scouts and warriors, listen to your respective leader. You shall not argue in the field.'

And with that, the vigilantes dash to a fleet of motorbikes parked by the compound's front gate. I can see Gideon's car idling on the dirt lane outside, just beyond the entrance. I sprint over and he cranks down the window by hand.

'They're ready to go,' I say. 'You gonna follow us?'

'This car can't keep up with a bunch of motorbikes,' Gideon says. 'They're going to be sneaking around on little backstreets. Too narrow for my car. Go without me.'

'That's too bad,' I say. 'What if we get stopped by cops?'

'Be friendly. But don't say much. Inform me immediately. I'll do what I can.'

There is a great din of motorbikes kick-started to life, and whooping from the cavalry.

'Just curious,' I say. 'Does *Pat Jasan* know you work with the cops?'

'Of course, they know,' Gideon says, laughing. '*Pat Jasan* is like the CIA. They know everything about everybody. They can trust me though. We're all Kachin.' And Kachin, Gideon tells me, are honor-bound to side with their own kind over the Burmese.

I feel hands grabbing at my forearm, dragging me towards an idling motorbike. I'm being tugged away by a *Pat Jasan* raider, the guy assigned to shuttle me around tonight. No time to chat, he says. We're going to get left behind.

As soon as I hop on the back, he twists the hand throttle, revving hard. We zip out of the compound. I can see the rest of the pack up the road, their rear lamps casting a red shimmer on the wet earth.

We race ahead to rejoin the swarm. The wind is beating on my ears, damp air fluttering my collar. My feet flail about, seeking the bike's rear foot pegs. When I find them, I dig in, stabilizing my body as we accelerate over puddles. My sneakers are soaked and I am exhilarated.

It's hard to fend off the intoxicating rush of running with a pride, charged with purpose, weapons at the ready. Most of the vigilantes are riding with two guys on one motorbike, the men on the back gripping bamboo staffs, their long weapons wobbling in the wind.

But my excitement is tempered by a sense of foreboding. It feels as if a dark spell has been cast – as if this mission is pregnant with violence. I fear the vigilantes are too eager to make someone bleed.

So far we've been racing down barren country roads. But now I can make out signs of civilization: power lines drooping above the path, farm huts topped with satellite dishes. We're approaching a tiny settlement.

There's an intersection ahead and, as we get closer, most of the raiders slow down, switch off their headlights and kill their engines.

But the five-man scout team doesn't stop. They shift into low gear and motor ahead, vanishing around the corner.

The rest of us wait in the darkness, basking in a symphony of chirping insects. The surrounding fields glimmer with silvery moonlight. The men speak in low whispers. I pity the driver saddled with me. Better to be paired with one of the rod-clenching bruisers, sucking on betel nuts, getting all psyched up to bring wrath upon the wicked. Not playing taxi driver for some clueless foreigner.

After about five minutes, a walkie-talkie squawks and the crew falls silent. The leader of the warrior unit pulls the device off his belt and presses it to his ear. The scouts are sending a dispatch through garbled static.

'Lights on at the target's house. Stand by for confirmation.'

From what I've gathered, the man they hope to abduct is named Lashu, an itinerant smoker of meth and opium in his mid-thirties. His habits have come to the attention of *Pat Jasan*'s extensive web of spies and snitches.

The vigilantes typically receive intel from two sources: churchgoers ratting out neighbors or captured addicts, beaten until they squeal on their drug buddies. None of these raiders seem to know or care how Lashu became tonight's target. His name is on *Pat Jasan*'s blacklist. He must be guilty of something.

More walkie-talkie chatter. 'He's here. Upstairs bedroom. Proceed.'

The men turn their motorbike keys all at once. A guttural roar resounds through the trees. The cavalry speeds around the corner and there it is – the target's simple two-story farmhouse, as depicted on the whiteboard map. The home is surrounded by dark fields. Light glows from an upstairs window.

The stick-wielding pillion riders do not wait for their drivers to park before leaping off and rushing to the house. Two warriors dash into the backyard, ready to tackle any potential runners. Four others bound towards the home's exterior wooden staircase, which leads to the second floor.

'To the bedroom! Go, go, go!'

The motorbike drivers veer onto the front yard – front tires gliding on the mud, brake pads whinnying. They dismount. Now everyone is stampeding towards the house. I'm sprinting to catch up with the warrior unit upstairs. They've already crashed through a door by the staircase and seized control of a small bedroom.

Inside, the lead warrior – an unusually tall and broad-shouldered man named Goom Li – is towering over three Kachin guys squatting on the floor.

The men on the floor look like three jittery puppies. They're sitting in a circle around their evening entertainment: one bottle of 'High Class' whiskey – a $3 rotgut local brand – and, also on the floor: a mound of fish curry and rice, piled atop a big green banana leaf instead of a plate.

There is no drug paraphernalia in plain sight. But we've clearly interrupted a boozy grub session. The men's fingers are sticky with rice grains and fish bits. Meth is an appetite killer. I'm not so sure these men are high right now.

Regardless, they're frozen in place, silent as stones, staring upward at their bedroom intruders – six guys in army helmets. What a terrifying buzzkill on a Saturday night. The air is sour with the vinegary musk of scared men.

I'm also not sure which guy is the sanctioned target. Two look like overworked laborers with sculpted forearms. The other is lean, a second-hand T-shirt that reads 'SINGAPORE' hanging off his thin frame.

I suddenly notice scores of eyes gazing upon me. The bedroom's walls are plastered with various images of a Caucasian Jesus with luscious amber locks. These are garish Christs with mournful Bambi eyes, blood-streaked palms, hearts glowing through transparent chests. No matter where you stand in this room, you cannot escape the glare of Jesus.

Less prominent wall space is papered over with a different sort of milk-skinned idol: dreamy Korean boy bands, gazing sultrily from posters. This could pass for the bedroom of a very messy and insolent Catholic schoolgirl.

'Perhaps you've heard of us?' Goom Li says. 'We're from

the church. We've come here to investigate. And if what we've heard is true, we are here to save you.'

There is a racket coming from downstairs – the clanging of pots kicked over and drawers yanked open. The other raiders are ransacking the kitchen in search of speed pills.

'One of you has a reputation for using drugs,' Goom Li says. 'So, gentlemen, please stand and strip to your underwear.'

The men wobble to their feet and obediently pull their shirts over their heads. Then they slide off their pants and sarongs and pass them to the *Pat Jasan* warriors. Not a single word of protest so far. They seem to have accepted *Pat Jasan* as a rightful arm of Kachin society, one imbued with an authority that emanates from the church.

Each garment is throttled to shake loose contraband. But this only yields a few grubby bills and a set of motorbike keys clanging to the floor.

A snippet of *Pat Jasan* chatter over the walkie-talkies:

'Guys downstairs – you find anything?'

'Still nothing.'

A few of the warriors tug rubber gloves onto their hands and start rifling through the bedroom's waste bin. Another *Pat Jasan* duo begins tearing apart the room. Literally. One has climbed onto a cabinet to pry loose ceiling planks, searching for a hidden crawlspace. His partner is trying to wrench up the floorboards.

This is starting to feel like a massive screw-up. En route to this location, the *Pat Jasan* crew buzzed with righteous zeal. How thrilling it is to race through the night, hunting down the wicked so that you might smite them down with rods.

But invading an innocent man's home and stripping him to his undies? Not very honorable.

Just as I'm wondering how 28 adrenaline-jacked vigilantes are going to handle this humiliating loss of face, the walkie-talkies crackle with news. Someone downstairs has discovered a partially-constructed meth bong and an opium ladle. Plus several empty plastic sachets — some with that methy cake-frosting smell, others scented with 'mouse shit' opium.

That will have to do.

Lashu is asked to step forward. He's the one with the 'SINGAPORE' shirt, the skinniest dude from the trio. His arms are ropey, his clavicle pronounced. His hair is parted to the side in an unkempt tuft. Neck limp, head downcast, he shuffles towards Goom Li in his tattered sarong. The man is utterly docile.

'It's your stuff, isn't it?' Goom Li says.

Lashu murmurs something in his defense. I can't make it out. I'm not sure it matters. We all know he's getting dragged out of here tonight.

And so it is decided: Lashu, resident of Myitkyina's fifth quarter, will be detained under the authority of *Pat Jasan*. His transgressions? Possession of paraphernalia. Contributing to the ruination of the Kachin race. Ungodliness. He will face trial before midnight.

The other two drinkers are allowed to get dressed and continue swilling their whiskey. Lashu is marched down the stairs and onto the muddy lawn. He is ordered to clasp his hands as if praying. One of the warriors produces a loop of plastic from his vest and cinches it tightly around Lashu's thumbs.

The warriors and evidence-scroungers and scouts all remount their bikes. Thumb-cuffed and compliant, Lashu straddles the back of a motorbike without being told. Headlamps glow, engines growl. Tonight, we will return to the operations center with 29 men.

God has favored the hunt.

⋊

Lashu is instructed to kneel on the concrete floor of the command center's main room. He is forbidden to sit on his rump. So what if his knees pulsate with pain? All the better. He is to meditate on his suffering and how he ended up here – facing the Lord's vengeance, meted out by a flock of men in fatigues.

There are rules here. Squirm too much and you get flogged. Grumble under your breath and you get flogged. Worst of all is to deny your transgressions. For those who proclaim false innocence, *Pat Jasan* reserves a punishment worse than flogging. They will hand you into the clutches of the beast.

Naw Sam has cleared out the command center, wiped clean his maps, closed all windows and latched them shut. He will now turn over the proceedings to a *Pat Jasan* tribunal.

There is a fluorescent bulb overhead, dive-bombed by fat moths.

Lashu is told to kneel beneath the light.

He faces a table arrayed with evidence confiscated from his home. Seated at this table is a vigilante judge, a rotund and bespectacled man in his late fifties. The room is otherwise emptied of furniture except for a few benches in the back for warriors who wish to observe the trial.

The judge is wearing an ill-fitting army helmet bearing the *Pat Jasan* emblem. So are his two adjutants: an interrogator, standing to the right of the judge, and an enforcer, lurking in the back, leaning on his bamboo cane. This headgear serves no practical purpose – Lashu is too tame to retaliate against his captors – but crested helmets help confer a sense of martial authority to this illegal courtroom.

'State your name,' says the judge in an irritated rasp. With his oversized helmet and doughy cheek fat, he looks like a grumpy turtle.

'Lashu. Thirty-three years old.'

The judge's pen scratches noisily into his ledger.

'And what is your clan?'

'Laphai Nuk Hpwi.'

'When did you first use drugs?'

'Seven years ago. At the mines in Hpakant. Long time ago.'

'Tell us your government identification number.'

'It's MKN, like Myitkyina, followed by zero-five-three. The rest I can't recall.'

'Unbelievable!' screams the interrogator, flashing stained teeth. He's a sinewy guy in his mid-forties with the uncharitable disposition of a drill sergeant. The interrogator leaps explosively towards Lashu, raising a fist as if to slap him, but it's a bluff. Lashu braces for the blow. Five seconds elapse before he dares to unsquint his eyes.

'Do you understand how this is going to work?' the interrogator asks. 'You will tell us the truth. Lies get you flogged.'

'See, at first: we talk to you nicely,' the judge says. 'When that doesn't work, we beat you. Now tell us your education level.'

'It's, um, eighth standard.'

'Let's talk about the stuff we found at your house,' the interrogator says. 'I'm an expert on drugs and paraphernalia. And I see we've got a water bottle with a hole in the side. This is what you've been using to smoke your meth. It even reeks like chocolate.'

'Next we've got a packet of instant coffee mix. Only it doesn't smell like coffee. It smells like opium. You like to hide your opium in coffee packets, don't you?'

'Coffee packets?' Lashu says. 'I don't know anything about that.'

The interrogator leaps forward and mashes the plastic sachet into Lashu's nose. I am reminded of a cat owner angrily pressing his pet's face into a piss stain on the rug.

'Smell it! Tell me what it smells like!'

'I don't know. Opium?'

'You're a drug addict and you don't know the smell of opium?' the interrogator says. 'Are you pretending to be foolish?'

An awful cracking sound echoes off the concrete floor. It is the enforcer's bamboo rod, wailing into Lashu's bony back. The strike causes his body to shudder. Sweat beads at his temples. His eyes flash like a scared rodent.

After the whack, the brawny enforcer returns to the back of the room, standing just beyond Lashu's peripheral vision. There is a bulbous lump in the man's cheek. He's gnawing on betel nuts and rocking back and forth, eager to thrash Lashu once more.

'How long have you been smoking meth?' says the interrogator.

'Honestly,' Lashu says, 'I don't really smoke meth.'

'Oh, Lord!' says the interrogator, addressing the ceiling. 'Can a drug user ever tell the truth? It's rarer than lightning striking on a sunny day!'

'I want to see your tongue,' says the judge. 'Stick it out.'

Lashu complies. The judge produces a flashlight and leans forward, shining its beam into the pink wetness of Lashu's oral cavity. Then he grunts with disapproval.

'Your tongue is very strange. It has become strange from all the meth smoke.'

'That's not true,' Lashu says, 'because the last time I smoked meth was more than a year ago. My tongue is like this because I'm a heavy cigarette smoker.'

'Just write down that he smokes meth,' says the interrogator. 'Now, Lashu, who is your dealer? I want names.'

'Well, see …'

'What about those guys in your bedroom?'

'No, not them,' Lashu says. 'They just like to hang out and drink whiskey.'

The interrogator pulls a cheap Chinese mobile phone from his jeans. 'I've got your phone. Tell me the password.' Lashu mutters some digits. The interrogator punches in the code and begins scrolling through the saved contacts and recent calls.

'I see the name Laphai. Is he your dealer? Who the hell is he?'

'He's just a guy who likes getting drunk and singing karaoke. Laphai is clean. He ran off to join the KIA.'

'So where do you get your drugs then? Do they rain from the sky? Just tell us which one is your dealer. We'd like to pay him a visit.'

When Lashu hesitates, I see the enforcer's calf muscles

tense up. The judge nods. This second strike is nastier than the first. There is a sickly thud, like a dull blade whacking raw chicken.

'You think you're some sort of commando, don't you? I've got an idea,' the interrogator says. 'Since you won't confess properly, we can just take you to the police. We'll show them all the evidence we salvaged from your house. They'll test your piss.'

'Fifteen years in Burmese government prison,' the judge says. 'How does that sound?'

Terror washes over Lashu's face. I can't discern whether or not this threat to involve the police is sincere. It doesn't make much sense. I've watched *Pat Jasan* rack up a slew of misdemeanors and felonies tonight: kidnapping, larceny, assault. Lashu's most serious crime appears to be possession of some odd-smelling coffee packets and a water bottle with a hole in the side.

But the threat seems to break Lashu's spirit. I sense that the judge was holding it in reserve the whole time, saving it up in case Lashu proved too stubborn.

'No, please,' he says, addressing the judge like a pleading child. 'Not that. I wish to remain in the care of *Pat Jasan*. Guide me, brothers, and teach me how to live a better life.'

He spends the next ten minutes blubbering out the name of every friend – or friend's friend – who has ever sparked up a meth bong or sucked on a ka-boom. The judge scribbles down a half-dozen names and addresses in his ledger.

The blacklist expands. *Pat Jasan*'s cavalry shall not want for targets.

Once the judge is satisfied, Lashu is ordered to inch towards the table on his knees, dab his thumb in ink and press it onto some official-looking document. This is a confession detailing his history of drug abuse as determined by the tribunal. *Pat Jasan* owns him now.

'Send him to the stocks,' says the judge. 'But first we must sentence him to five additional lashes. Remember, brother. We're not flogging you. We're flogging the drugs inside your body.'

The enforcer grabs Lashu's collar and tugs him to his feet. He is led out of the operations room and into the courtyard. I follow close behind.

My eyes adjust from the overly bright interrogation room to the gentle blackness of night. Frogs are honking in the bushes. Bats careen over our heads, swooping low to snatch up insects in their teeth. Peering beyond the gate, I can make out Gideon's sedan. He's been waiting there for hours. Probably dozing in the driver's seat.

Lashu is marched over to a wooden post. Hug it, says the enforcer.

He then whistles, summoning an idling warrior who has already swapped his vigilante fatigues for a knock-off blue Chelsea football jersey.

The warrior stands opposite Lashu, grabs his wrists and pulls his body flush against the post. Lashu's face is mashed into the wood, hard enough to put splinters in his cheek.

'Why did we bring you in tonight?' the enforcer slurs through a mouthful of betel.

'Because I use drugs.'

'And why am I about to flog you?'

'You're not flogging me. You're flogging the evil drugs inside me.'

'Now shout out this phrase: "I shall never use drugs again!"'

'I shall never use drugs again!'

The enforcer throws his entire back into the swing, nearly throwing himself off balance. Compared to this beating, the earlier flogging was a tender caress. Lashu releases a guttural squeak.

Now I understand why the warrior in Chelsea gear is tightly gripping Lashu's wrists. He's holding him upright so that Lashu doesn't collapse into a whimpering puddle.

'Shout it again!'

'I shall never use drugs in my life!'

The second and third strikes are even more ferocious. I find myself wincing and rubbing my lower back in sympathy. I feel ashamed of the quick blast of dopamine I felt hours earlier as we careened towards Lashu's home.

After the fifth brutal whack, Lashu is guided to a different chamber in the compound. This appears to be a dual-purpose room: both a holding cell and a storage space for the church's Christmas decorations. There is a life-sized Santa Claus mannequin propped up in the corner. But the center of the room is dominated by medieval stocks made from hardwood.

The stocks, resting on the floor, are only about a foot-and-a-half tall. The enforcer crouches down, unfastens a latch on the side and opens up the stocks. Lashu drops to the cement and slides his feet through the footholds. The enforcer then makes the contraption whole again, lowering the top beam over Lashu's ankles. The two halves are re-latched and secured with a padlock.

Lashu – now seated on his rump, feet jutting through two holes in the wooden stocks – looks as drained as any person I have ever seen. It's as if his dignity has been sucked out of his soul with a vacuum.

His eyelids droop and he begins to recline. But when his stinging back touches the floor, he jolts upright, wincing through gritted teeth. If only he could turn over and lie on his belly.

The enforcer switches off the lights and spits into the courtyard. He's on guard duty tonight. That means he must stay here until sunrise. He should manage about five hours of sleep before waking for Sunday morning service.

)(

Back in 1839, when the British Empire was flooding modern-day Myanmar's shores with black-booted riflemen, a man sat down to compose a letter.

He was far from Burma – nearly 2,000 kilometers, in fact. But like the Burmese, the man was vexed by Britain's conquests across Asia. His name was Lin Tse-Hsu, and he was a scholar who wore ankle-length robes and a beard the color of snowfall. Lin was a foreign relations officer with the Qing dynasty of China.

The letter was addressed to England's Queen Victoria. It lamented that her seafaring subjects were running a lucrative and deadly drug syndicate.[1] At the time, British merchants produced opium in India and, each year, shipped 40,000 chests full of the narcotic to the Qing dynasty's port cities. Chinese addicts numbered in the millions. British magnates were earning obscene amounts of silver while foreigners bore the social costs.

China's 'celestial empire' was fed up. First they burned the opium chests or chucked them into the sea. Then they decreed that any outsider trafficking drugs into their homeland would be hung or decapitated.

Lin's letter to Queen Victoria sought to justify these violent punishments. 'A murderer of one person is subject to the death sentence,' he wrote. 'Just imagine how many people opium has killed.'

'As months accumulate and years pass by,' he wrote, 'the poison they have produced increases its wicked intensity and its repugnant odor reaches as high as the sky. Heaven is furious with anger and all the gods are moaning with pain!'

Lin pointed out that, in London, the queen outlawed opium dens. And still she permitted her merchants to infect the Chinese people with this stupefying drug? Such hypocrisy was hard to stomach.

British opium traders, Lin wrote to the queen, 'are so obsessed with material gain that they have no concern whatsoever for the harm they can cause to others. Have they no conscience?'

Fast forward more than 150 years to the present day. To make sense of their woeful condition, the Kachin must study this historic feud and ask similar questions of Myanmar's army.

So says a man named Tu Raw.

Tu Raw is the admiral of all *Pat Jasan* units in Myitkyina – an underground force of roughly 10,000 men and women. I have come to meet this gruff vigilante chieftain on the outskirts of town. He's agreed to chat outside a stone church painted eggshell white.

Two days have passed since the *Pat Jasan* raid I attended. With Gideon's help, I've set up this meeting with Tu Raw in the hope of hearing a rationale for *Pat Jasan*'s more sadistic tactics.

When I arrive, the rain has abated, so the two of us decided to take a stroll around the church's mossy grounds.

Gideon, who seems a bit suspicious of Tu Raw, opts to hang by the car.

Our conversation begins awkwardly. As I introduce myself, Tu Raw – bald, bespectacled, but still beefy in his fifties – whips a smartphone out of his sarong and aims it directly at my face. The loud beep lets me know that he's recording video.

He maintains a wooden expression while quizzing me about my background – where I'm from, who I know, what I think of the military he so deeply despises.

I patiently answer his questions, waiting until his arm grows tired. Once he's done sizing me up, Tu Raw slips the phone back into his waistline and veers into his spiel about the Opium Wars.

Tu Raw explains that the predatory relationship between the Imperial British and the Qing dynasty is similar to the Burmese exploitation of the Kachin. In both cases, powerful outsiders deliberately infect a weaker populace with drugs – not only to generate wealth but to debilitate their rivals.

'This drug war against the Kachin?' he tells me, 'It's ten times worse than the opium war in China. I'll bet the Chinese never suffered like this. Like the British, the Burmese are using narcotics to weaken the minorities who oppose their rule. They are brutal.'

'Perhaps,' I say, 'but your group is also quite violent. You're raiding homes and beating up drug users. Is that really necessary?'

'No one looks to me for permission to whip people,' Tu Raw says. 'I'm not sitting here in a palace giving out orders. Our *Pat Jasan* units have independence. They deliver justice as they see fit. That can include beating suspects.'

'Or turning them over to police?'

'Yes,' Tu Raw says. 'That's our last resort.'

'But aren't the police your enemies?'

Tu Raw explains that dumping a drug user on some police station's steps, along with copious evidence and signed confessions, is actually a means of shaming the cops. It sends a message: you, the police, may tolerate crime but Kachin Christians will not.

'That's bold,' I say. 'I'm surprised you're so willing to antagonize the cops.'

'We have no choice,' he says. 'They are engaged in ethnic cleansing. In cold blood.'

'Now let me ask you a question,' Tu Raw says. 'Have you ever been to Hpakant?'

'No, I haven't,' I tell him. 'But not for lack of trying.'

Hpakant is a jade-mining district more than 100 kilometers to the east of Myitkyina. It's forbidden to foreigners, save for Chinese gem brokers. The two-lane highway to Hpakant is lined with endless checkpoints – and, rumors have it, the roadside is so heavily mined that truckers won't even step out of their vehicles to take a leak.

The state has good reason to quarantine Hpakant from outsiders' eyes. It is one of Asia's most blighted corners: a grim vortex, sucking in men with the allure of riches and regurgitating meth and heroin addicts.

By the thousands, men descend into Hpakant's stadium-sized quarries each day. Those who find jade stones can sell them to middlemen at the rim of the mine. The miners are then invited to spend the proceeds in an open-air bazaar selling speed, sex and heroin.

Recovering addicts tell me that drugs in Hpakant are sold

as freely as cabbage. They say that its flimsy meth dens, con-structed of plastic tarps and bamboo, are blatantly operating under the auspices of plain-clothes police.

Hpakant, Tu Raw says, is the crucible in which *Pat Jasan* was forged. Some of the group's early calls to arms rose from Hpakant in 2014. For years, Tu Raw says, the Kachin have helplessly watched government corruption transform their towns and villages into open drug markets – and they fear more places will become just as dystopian as Hpakant.

'That's why we must take a hard stand,' he says. 'I've got something exciting to show you.'

Out comes the smartphone again. Tu Raw cues up shaky footage of skinny men whipped, *Pat Jasan*-style, before a jeer-ing mob. The topography behind them is the unmistakable wasteland of Hpakant – an ochre moonscape where jade-rich hills are scraped down to muddy pits.

Tu Raw is even more proud of a second clip, also filmed in Hpakant. It appears to show a uniformed police officer partially stripped to his underclothes. 'This cop was taking bribes from meth traffickers,' he says. 'Now watch this.' A man barely in frame cocks back his hand and smacks the officer across the face.

Tu Raw has made his point. *Pat Jasan* is now ready to dole out violence against agents of the state. The holy war is intensifying.

'The other night, you saw the first stage of our mission,' Tu Raw says. *Pat Jasan*, he says, is now graduating to stage two: confronting both the feckless police and the drug syndicates head on. The vigilantes have even begun to raid various deal-ers' stash spots. He claims they've seized half a million meth pills so far.

'Soon we will go after the drug lords directly,' Tu Raw says. 'But it's not easy for us to march into their terrain, which is heavily guarded by armed men.'

Still, the vigilantes are experimenting with a new tactic, he says. They'll deploy an overwhelming number of raiders – several hundred or more – into a drug lord's poppy fields. Then they'll hack down as many stalks as they can until the goons show up.

He boasts that *Pat Jasan* recently completed a trial run against a relatively small militia in Kachin State's Hukawng Valley. The vigilantes managed to ruin a few acres of poppy before gunmen emerged from the foliage and let off rifles. The raiders escaped unscathed.

'That's bold. But you're talking about remote fields,' I say. 'What about a well-defended meth lab?'

'If we need more firepower, perhaps we'll call on the KIA. We have to fight back somehow. We can't let the Burmese slowly torture us to death.'

On that cheerful note, I shake Tu Raw's hand, wish him well and head back to the car. Gideon fires up the engine. Before we've pulled out of the church lot, he tells me the source of his suspicion towards the *Pat Jasan* leader.

'I think a lot of these *Pat Jasan* guys are actually former KIA rebels,' Gideon says. 'I've got nothing against the KIA. But I know ex-KIA officers when I see them. The way they move. The way they talk. The way they watch everything you do.'

'Gideon,' I ask, 'what are the cops going to do next? They've got a militant Kachin organization growing inside almost every church. Possibly backed by the KIA, you say. And now they're talking about all-out revolt.'

'The Burmese police have no idea what to do,' Gideon says. 'They're intimidated by *Pat Jasan*. It won't stop growing.'

'What I don't get,' I say, 'is how *Pat Jasan* can beat up addicts and dump them at a police station without getting in trouble. Aren't kidnapping and assault serious crimes?'

'The police don't care about Kachin beating up Kachin,' Gideon says. 'They just care about *Pat Jasan*'s threat to their bottom line. If the vigilantes really go after the big dealers – the guys who pay monthly bribes – then that will force the police to really confront *Pat Jasan*.'

At this point, I'm really not sure what to believe. My mind is whirling in history lessons and gossip, conjecture and ominous threats.

Hanson, the missionary, once observed that Kachin speak in 'high-flown poetic ideas'. I might add that, these days, many Kachin also speak in conspiracy theories. This is a land aswirl in rumors and radical allegations. But this is a tempest of the state's own making.

Until the recent glasnost, the state maintained a total stranglehold on information. The press was severely censored for five decades. Even today, it's still muted by fear. The army is still known for siccing agents on anyone who speaks openly about government abuses.

So the Kachin, in search of truth, turn to pastors and rebels and upstart radicals like Tu Raw. In lieu of relying on government statements, they cobble together their own narratives from whispers and rumors.

I worry, however, that I'm now a bit too saturated in the Kachin counterstory. Inflected by rage, it sees a Burmese plot in every shadow. My brain is roiling in the words of jungle clerics and opium stoners and vigilante chieftains, their wild allegations told between hallelujahs or bong rips.

To what degree is the military entangled in Myanmar's multifarious drug trade? That is the question I'm still committed to answering. I've peeled away many layers here in Kachin State. But to reach the core, I will need to travel to the low-country, the crux of Burmese power.

There, I might find army insiders willing to talk.

)(

Travel to the former capital Yangon from Myitkyina by train and you may see the sun set twice. The 1,200-kilometer trip can last more than 24 shuddering hours. Riding on particularly derelict stretches of the rail system, that were first laid in Queen Victoria's time, you may bounce around your cabin like a rag doll in a dryer.

But the view justifies the jostling.

Along the downward-sloping ride, as you cross the tropic of Cancer, the hills flatten. Greenery melts into amber-colored plains. Stone church steeples give way to golden spires, scintillating on the horizon. Keep going and the palm trees appear – their bladed fronds waving like seductive fingers.

As Yangon approaches, the plains cede to emerald-colored paddies. The distance between villages shrinks and shrinks, until settlements coagulate into small towns and, eventually, loud concrete cities. These are Myanmar's southern lands, fertile and populated, drenched by hot rain for half the year.

All rail lines lead to Yangon, Myanmar's only real metropolis. The city rises from a delta, a confluence of two rivers.

Near Yangon's downtown, the streams join currents for 50 kilometers and then empty into the Andaman Sea.

From landscapes such as this – where crops grow easily and the sea-adjacent rivers act as gateways to the world – big civilizations are bound to arise.

This delta has seen many kingdoms rise and fall. But for more than a millennium, life here has revolved around a 99-meter-tall gold-plated spire called Shwedagon. Located in Yangon's heart, it lends historical gravity to a city that, in recent years, has changed at warp speed.

In the first years of the 21st century, Yangon still felt like a city trapped in amber. Flying from one of Southeast Asia's booming capitals into Yangon was to travel back in time – to a place where, for 99 per cent of Burmese people, the internet never happened and mobile phones had not been invented.

A paranoid vibe permeated the city. In the mid-2000s, as Facebook trained Westerners to spew their every whim into the public sphere, Yangonites were still closely guarding their thoughts. Not only was 99 per cent of the population offline but exhibiting opinions remained dangerous. No one wanted to draw the attention of government spies.

It's not so Orwellian anymore. The surveillance state in its most extreme form was largely dismantled starting in 2012 – a truly transformative benefit of the military's reboot. These days, the government mostly targets noisy provocateurs. It's still ill-advised for a citizen to, say, post a Facebook poem about tattooing the president's name on his penis. Such a ditty landed one Yangon man in prison as recently as 2016.[2] But slagging off the army in a tea shop, which was downright dangerous just a few years ago, is no longer so risky.

How this city has changed. For those who knew pre-transition Yangon, a stroll through its downtown is now disorienting. The bleep of mobile phones, flashes of pasty tourist thighs, the groan of cranes as they piece together the newest high-rise condo – it's enough to trigger vertigo.

All the foreign cash sluicing around the city has even sprouted patches of nascent hipsterism. There are yoga studios and mixologists and a cat cafe. There are foodie joints selling artisanal *mohinga* – Myanmar's unofficial national dish, a succulent fish broth – for twenty times the street price. The adult children of well-to-do Burmese exiles are returning ('repats', they call them) like the avant-garde who flocked to Prague after communism collapsed.

None of this is bad per se. Deluxe *mohinga* is really tasty. But this new influx of elite hipsterdom can feel jarring in a broken nation where the GDP is smaller than the economy of Jacksonville, Florida.[3]

Foreigners and Burmese elites – if they choose – can now easily drift around Yangon inside an opaque bubble of upscale shops and eateries. The affluent can sip cocktails in rarified air, quarantined from the spectacle of poverty playing out on the street.

Yangon has also seen a renewed fetishization of the British imperial era – that long and ugly chapter of subjugation. Tourists are particularly drawn in by the romance of refurbished Victorian-era hotels and servile waiters in butler-ish attire. They can be found ordering gin and tonics at The Strand Hotel, playing out a Rudyard Kipling fantasy, toasting a freer Myanmar while basking in colonial chic.

Myanmar now takes in more than 4 million tourists per year – a six-fold increase over 2010.[4] Once they arrive, they're unlikely to hear much about the military's ongoing civil wars. Ethnic cleansing is terribly off-brand. Even among the small-but-expanding expat scene – a mix of academics, business types, starry-eyed wanderers and NGO workers – many regard the northern war zone as a separate planet.

But the fact remains that Yangon – Myanmar's nerve center – is where officials determine the fate of the hinterlands. That's why I'm here. I've arranged a meeting with an ex-military officer named Thura, who I am told to address with the honorific 'Master'. He is a recent retiree from the dreaded Military Security Affairs agency.

Not too long ago, this agency – better known as 'military intelligence' or MI – was nothing short of a gestapo. Anyone who emitted a whiff of dissent could be dragged off by MI agents and tortured. Though partially defanged by reforms, it is still reviled.

Our encounter has been arranged by trusted intermediaries. I am told that Master Thura, a veteran of MI's narcotics division, fell out with his superiors on two fronts. For starters, he is not Buddhist (which is unusual among high-ranking officers) and his refusal to convert proved toxic to his career. Secondly, his conscience had become noticeably afflicted over his bureau's treatment of minorities.

And so he has agreed to tell me what he knows. Communicating through a mutual contact, I ask Thura to choose our meeting place. He suggests a trendy new coffee shop. In the Lonely Planet guidebooks, the place is described as a 'chic cafe bar' with a rooftop where 'you might just glimpse the tip of the Shwedagon'.

Had it been up to me, I might have chosen some greasy tea joint. But I think Thura is on to something. Better to hide in plain sight amid the chattering foreigners. We agree to rendezvous in the middle of the day, when most Burmese are at work, and the coffee shop is filled with backpackers.

I find him wearing a crisp polo shirt and shades, sitting at a table in the back, sipping on a fruit shake.

※

One of the greatest perks of a police state – for those running it, at least – is the pleasure of confabulation. When the truth chafes, officials can simply compose an alternate reality and force-feed it to the public. The citizens and the press, fearing a future in leg irons, will just nod along.

Myanmar's military has lied so hard for so long that, even in the reform era, its officers still make absurd promises that practically no one believes. But one diktat stands out as especially fantastical:

By 2019, Myanmar will be 100 per cent drug free.

Thura tells me that this 'drug-free Myanmar' pledge is a joke among narcotics detectives. 'I'm not saying we don't have guys who are serious about working drug cases,' Thura says. 'We do. But not nearly enough.'

'What about the rest of them?' I ask.

'They're in it for the money,' Thura says. 'Most of the time, if you see a senior officer chasing down a drug lord, he's not trying to arrest him. He's trying to get on his payroll.'

As Thura explains it, Myanmar's borderland police essentially run a protection racket for narcotics traffickers. All of the incoming bribes are pooled within each department. Low-ranking grunts get a small piece of the action while higher-ranking officers receive larger shares.

No one in the precinct can take an ethical stand and refuse to participate. Everyone must earn.

'The drug bribes are their actual salary, not the salary you see on paper,' Thura says. 'Officially, a colonel makes about $600 per month. But if he spends just one year in Hpakant? He'll have enough money for a BMW and three concubines.'

'That's why everyone wants to work in Kachin or Shan State,' he says. 'You have officers begging their superiors, "Please, send me to the border." And the chief will say, "Look, I myself want to go to the border. Get in line!"'

'What about the addiction crisis?' I ask. 'Are they at all sympathetic?'

'Not really,' Thura says. 'In their eyes, every Kachin is KIA. They're seen as insurgent gypsy people.'

As Thura describes it, many police officers in Kachin and Shan areas are practically employees of the meth traffickers. This explains how transporters and dealers can move product around the frontier zone with such ease.

But this does not adequately account for the rise of narco-militias – the organized criminals who actually produce the drugs. They run swaths of the frontier zone with near dictatorial control – seemingly unimpeded by a military that is, above all, obsessed with dominating terrain.

'I still don't get it,' I say. 'Are these drug lords paying off the army to control little pieces of Myanmar?'

'It's not like that,' Thura says. 'They're not merely bribing the army. They belong to the army. These drug-producing militias are children of the military.'

What Thura goes on to illuminate is a conspiracy that is, frankly, a feat of strategic brilliance. It is a pragmatic means of extending army tentacles into rebellious places – all at practically zero cost.

This is how it works.

The army extends a standing offer towards all rebel commanders: abandon your revolution and we'll give you a stellar benefits package. The terms are simple. You keep your weapons and guerrilla fighters. The army will stop attacking your positions. You will maintain day-to-day control of your terrain.

But if you agree to the deal, you are now holding that turf on the army's behalf. You must act as the army's eyes and ears in the black zone, monitoring nearby rebels and feeding intel back to the beast. And when given the order, you will turn rifles on your ethnic kin and fight for the state.

Typically, this pact does not include many hard gifts from the army such as bushels of cash or drums full of ammo. What it confers is much more valuable: an unwritten license to engage in the black market with total impunity.

Want to fell endangered trees and sell them to Chinese traders? Traffic desperate peasants to Thailand for cash? Tax every truck winding through your turf? Go for it. Best of all, each militia is given carte blanche to synthesize meth, grow poppies or traffic drugs – tapping into a regional narco-economy worth more than $31 billion.[5]

Variations of this arrangement have existed since the 1960s. The most prominent warlord to take this deal was Khun Sa, a poppy kingpin who ruled over patches of Shan State like a feudal prince.

Like Pablo Escobar, he touted himself as a great liberator of the peasantry while stockpiling cash. Heaps and heaps of cash. In the 1980s, Khun Sa ran a global empire that deluged

New York City with heroin. The DEA maintained a $2 million bounty on his head.[6]

During Khun Sa's heyday, he vacillated between resisting the army and cozying up to its top brass. But ultimately the warlord kept coming back to a stark business calculation: cooperating with the army is more profitable than diehard resistance.

Hunted both by American agents and its allied Thai forces, Khun Sa ultimately had to capitulate and dissolve his militia, known as the Mong Tai Army, in 1996. By this stage he feared foreign mercenaries would come for him in the night. When he died in 2007, Khun Sa was living well in Yangon, under state protection.

From Khun Sa and others, Myanmar's generals learned a valuable lesson: warlords spouting revolutionary rhetoric will betray their ideals for greed.

Khun Sa died in the years preceding Myanmar's big perestroika. But even then, the generals were already desperate to re-enter the global market with America's consent. However, they felt that, before welcoming attention from the outside world, they should bring more order to their insurgency-wracked nation.

The army's plan was to cripple the insurgent groups from within. (Or in stultifying junta-speak: 'to crush internal and external destructive elements hindering the stability and progress of the State through People's Militia strategy'.)

In the late 2000s, the army began courting rebel brigades across the borderlands, wooing them with dreams of heroin and meth profits. They hoped to flip as many rebel battalions as possible.

The army lavished extra attention on brigades within

large rebel forces such as the KIA. Flipping a battalion within the KIA – or other fearsome rebel armies, such as the Karen National Liberation Army – was a doubly attractive venture. Not only would the army slide a new tentacle into hard-to-reach minority lands but morale-sapping chaos would also infect the entire rebel organization.

This turncoat campaign was successful. By 2009, Myanmar's military had created 35 new militias wielding a combined 10,000-plus militants.[7]

These new armed units were divided into two categories. Factions with more than 300 personnel became 'border guard forces' containing small detachments of Burmese army advisors. Smaller units were called 'People's Militia Forces' (or *Pyi Thu Sit* in Burmese) and given a longer leash.

(The two types of groups are scattered all around the borderlands – and I've brushed up against both. The pair of guys that squeezed Gideon and me for cash in the backwoods of Kachin State belonged to a People's Militia Force. The armed clan that had forced a teenage Hawng Dai to tax meth truckers? That was a border guard force.)

Take in the cleverness of this plan. The army boosted its borderland forces with no major financial outlay. Moreover, all the social costs are borne by ethnic minorities and foreigners. The former must contend with newly powerful drug lords in their backyards. The latter are all drug users located in China, Thailand and other export markets.

This army campaign has injected growth serum into the meth trade. The effect was felt almost immediately in towns and cities abroad. From 2008 to 2016, authorities in China and Southeast Asia have seen meth pill seizures increase by a whopping factor of ten.[8] Pink pills have flooded through Bangkok and Kunming, Kuala Lumpur and Phnom Penh.

The region's authorities now seize more than 300 million pills per year. But that's a mere fraction of the total volume churned out in frontier labs. UN anti-crime officials believe 90 to 95 per cent of the meth rolling out of Myanmar is never seized by authorities and reaches the streets.[9]

'The militia commanders are now extremely rich,' Thura says. 'They use the money to buy more weapons, more businesses, more political connections. They're like little kings.'

'I'm just wondering,' I say, 'if any journalist has ever directly confronted the military about these drug militias.'

'I don't think so,' Thura says. 'The Burmese press wouldn't dare.'

'Let's presume I wanted to ask them myself.'

'You'd have to go to the Central Committee for Drug Abuse Control [CCDAC],' Thura says. 'They're sort of like America's DEA.'

I'm familiar with this bureau. Jointly run by the army and police, they're the same institution vowing to eradicate all drugs in Myanmar by the decade's end. This agency was once a laughingstock. But in recent years, it has enjoyed regular contact with its counterparts in the West.

Now that sanctions are gone, Western governments seeking influence in Myanmar have competed to aid and befriend sectors across the government. With great zeal, they've rushed in to advise the military's dubious 'peace' talks, mentor upstart politicians and train cops on proper riot control.

This has led to strange outcomes. Among them: both the US and European Union now fund and train the CCDAC's narcotics agents. Ties are so cozy that the agency asked donors for half a billion dollars to help achieve its dubious 'drug-free Myanmar' pledge – a request that was ultimately rebuffed.[10]

Though thirsty for foreign donations, the agency remains opaque. It appears unwilling to publicly discuss the narco-militias. 'There's no point in contacting them,' Thura says. 'They're not going to talk to a foreign journalist. They're certainly not going to let you ask hard questions.'

But in the margins of my notebook, I jot a reminder to myself: file a formal interview request with the CCDAC. I will brace myself for a time-sucking exercise involving unanswered faxes, evasive secretaries and, ultimately, rejection. But I've come too far to forego the attempt.

✳

Following Thura's big divulgence, I begin shoring up more contacts with insight into Myanmar's state-backed drug lords. If I can gather enough intel, I might defy the odds and cajole military officers into acknowledging this murky nexus – if I ever manage to secure a meeting.

Seeking a panoply of sources, I turn to two men who've fought on opposite sides of Myanmar's drug war.

One is John Whalen, a burly former DEA agent, recently retired after a 26-year-career spent mostly in Myanmar. By the time he left the agency in 2014, Whalen was heading the DEA's Myanmar bureau. He has gathered evidence on the nation's rebels and militias for decades.

The other is Khuensai Jaiyen, a septuagenarian whose thick-lensed spectacles lend him an owl-like appearance.

This benign look belies his past within the most infamous

drug syndicate in Southeast Asian history: Khun Sa's Mong Tai Army, which was once backed by 20,000 fighters, Soviet surface-to-air missiles and a patronage network including scores of officials. Khuensai was the warlord's personal secretary – and he's still busy collecting information inside Myanmar's black zones for civil society groups opposed to army dominance of ethnic lands.

From Whalen, I hear many of Master Thura's claims corroborated. 'The army is involved in various areas of the drug trade,' he says. 'Absolutely. Are they producing drugs? No. But they are providing tacit approval for drugs to be produced in their areas ... and they fund their militias through the trade. The army needs them as force multipliers, guides, maybe cannon fodder.'

'All of these "People's Militia Forces" are involved in the drug trade at some level,' he says. 'It might be acquisition of methamphetamine precursors. It could be producing or tableting meth. Or maybe taxation and security. But all of the militias are intimately involved.'

Militias typically specialize in one link within the meth supply chain, he says. Some will focus on smuggling in drums of pseudoephedrine – meth's key ingredient – from India or China.

Others will prioritize logistics, running trucks through the gauntlet of army checkpoints throughout the borderlands. Some rent themselves out as hired guns protecting drug caravans sneaking into Thailand on foot.

The militias' most valuable commodity of all is a secure patch of land – free from state intervention – where meth refineries can safely crank out pills. This is the army's greatest gift to its allied militia. Any warlord with untouchable turf will soon hear from a criminal-minded investor who'll pay a premium to rent some land and open a drug lab.

From Khuensai, I learn that many (if not most) narco-militias are financially sustained by joint ventures with Chinese mafia. Militias are adept at jungle ambushes and managing local clan politics, he says. But they're not always great at managing capital investments and export outflows. They often require assistance from Chinese mafia – based in Yunnan province as well as Hong Kong and Macau.

The new wave of militias birthed by the army, Khuensai says, has sent shockwaves through the drug trade. Foreign financiers have pulled out of rebel turf – which is vulnerable to army strikes – and shifted to terrain run by People's Militia Forces.

'Think about it,' Khuensai says. 'If you're an investor in drug refineries, where would you set up shop? You'd go to the safest place, not rebel areas.'

'It's not that rebel groups don't produce drugs,' he says. 'They certainly do.' But Khuensai estimates that the ratio of drug production, between army-created militias and rebel groups, is now 'about two to one'.

Myanmar's meth trade wasn't always so complex and diverse. In fact, it was once monopolized by a proto-state known as the United Wa State Army or UWSA. In fact, no examination of Myanmar's meth trade is complete without acknowledging the UWSA's role. They are the godfathers of *ya ba*.

The Wa, unlike most of Myanmar's minority groups, have managed to fend off foreign invaders, Burmese and British alike. They're a tribe numbering 600,000 people in Shan State, clustered by the Chinese border.

British colonials and Christian missionaries knew them as 'head hunters' who could not be subdued through force. Nor were the Wa swayed by promises of material comfort. In 1947, as the UK prepared to leave the country, a British official asked a Wa emissary: 'Don't you want education, clothing, food, good houses, hospitals?'[11]

The Wa responded: 'We are very wild people and don't appreciate all these things.'

The Wa are wild no longer. In the 1960s, they were finally converted to a Western ideology: Marxism, not Christianity. They absorbed this doctrine from Maoist China and, with Beijing's help, assembled themselves into the prime border-land fighting force of the now-defunct Communist Party of Burma. When the party collapsed in the late 1980s, the Wa held onto their guns and became the UWSA – an independent force bound together by racial identity.

Today, they operate a semi-independent territory about 700 kilometers southwest of Kunming. The UWSA is essen-tially a client state of China. Its leadership speaks Chinese. Its people trade in Chinese yuan, chat on Chinese mobile phone networks and can easily cross back and forth into China.

Historically, their heavily-armed statelet has been one of the most prolific speed producers – not only in Myanmar but the world. Though perpetually at odds with Myanmar's army, the UWSA has proven too formidable to take down militarily.

The Wa have amassed the toughest minority-run armed force in Southeast Asia. Their 30,000 troops defend ter-rain the size of Belgium and possess light tanks, missiles and helicopters. This rise to power was made possible both through Chinese backing and profits from a billion-dollar methamphetamine trade.

In the late 1990s, many of Myanmar's rogue armed groups (including the Wa) were busy farming poppies. But the Wa had grander visions – of pink pills, sold on the cheap, containing 20 per cent methamphetamine and padded out with caffeine and other fillers. They were the first to synthesize the pills en masse and the first to firmly establish complex meth smuggling routes abroad.

But birthing Asia's great speed epidemic brought infamy to the tribe. For more than a decade, the DEA has sought to capture ranking members of the UWSA, and both US and Thai agents have long fantasized about catching the UWSA's meth production mastermind – an adroit businessman in his sixties whose name is Wei Hsueh-kang.

In a gambit to snare this drug lord, the DEA once passed out beer-bottle coolers bearing Wei Hsueh-kang's photo around Bangkok's brothel districts – where he was alleged to enjoy quick getaways. The coolers (those foam sleeves that keep cans and bottles cold) were printed with a DEA hotline and a promise to pay $2 million to anyone whose tips led to the drug lord's capture.

'We actually got a few decent tips,' Whalen says. But the cooler scheme never panned out. Wei Hsueh-kang remains as free and rich as ever. He's even expanded his business interests into construction and mining.

In more recent years, Wa kingpins appear to have diversified their statelet's economy away from the drug trade. They've become huge players in the global tin business and have replaced many of their poppy fields with rubber plantations. Evidence suggests that Wei Hsueh-kang is now more fixated on Kachin jade than pink meth.[12]

Once the Wa's meth monopoly was cracked, state-backed militias rushed in to fill the void.

⋊

For the dozens of army-aligned militias now freckling the borderlands, their territories are worlds unto their own. Whether their commanders control 50 or 1,000 men, they rule over zones sealed off to outsiders by checkpoints and mines.

Yet a few militia commanders have generated reputations beyond their fiefdoms – often through forays into politics.

These drug lords aren't just tolerated by the government. In a few cases, they literally *are* the government. A few have even sat in parliament alongside Aung San Suu Kyi or represented their government in the US Capitol.

Let's name some names.

The most prominent warlord in Kachin State is Ting Ying. Heavyset, and bald as an egg, he presides over a syndicate that – according to Khuensai and other sources – is flush with profits from jade mining, poppy fields and meth trafficking.

Ting Ying is no ideologue. Through the decades, his politics have ping-ponged all over the map. He began as a KIA revolutionary, later defected to join a cabal of communists and eventually snuggled up to the military government. In 2009, he agreed to bring his 1,000-soldier militia under the army aegis – and threatened to 'wipe out' his former KIA allies for good measure.[13]

Ting Ying's armed faction was so large that the military

⋀

broke it up into three units and embedded each with Burmese advisors. His fealty to the state paid off big in 2010. That was the year he was allowed to join parliament through a rigged junta election.

Fast forward to the fall election of 2015. Aung San Suu Kyi's party members were rallying for seats across the nation. Ting Ying was seeking re-election. When Aung San Suu Kyi's party members showed up to canvass on Ting Ying's turf, he dispatched armed men to ambush their campaign team, smacking them around and smashing their equipment. Ting Ying then circulated a letter among officials calling the campaigners 'invaders' and 'public enemies'.

By knocking out his competition with brute force, Ting Ying held on to his seat. And when Aung San Suu Kyi's National League for Democracy won the general election, filling parliament with idealists and former political prisoners, she and her faithful were forced to work alongside this unrepentant warlord.

In the West, this naked act of sabotage was drowned out by a giddy jubilee. Then-Secretary of State Hillary Clinton quickly proclaimed that the election proved the 'indispensable role the United States can and should play in the world'.[14]

Ting Ying wasn't the only one who'd wriggled into this US-praised parliament.[15] The deputy speaker of Myanmar's Lower House is Ti Khun Myat, a man who rose to power by commanding hundreds of fighters in Shan State's poppy-growing borderlands.[16]

Unlike Ting Ying, Ti Khun Myat actually enjoys warm ties to Aung San Suu Kyi's camp. He was even tapped to lead a delegation that flew to America to meet senators inside the US Capitol building.

Yet another parliamentary warlord is Kyaw Myint, who in 2010 joined a state-level government in Shan State. He rules over peaks and vales that were traditionally covered in tea plantations. But according to Thura, Khuensai and many other sources, this commander prefers to grow poppy.

Kyaw Myint did not stand for re-election in 2015. Perhaps he was distracted by the rebels in his midst. Honoring his deal with the army, the commander was forced to spar with a guerrilla faction known as the Ta'ang National Liberation Army or TNLA – a feisty band of fighters who've gathered photographic evidence against Kyaw Myint. They possess hours of footage showing guerrillas hacking down poppy fields that allegedly belong to this commander. The rebels also claim they've blown up one of his suspected meth labs with an RPG.[17]

Details about these three men are known only because they've dared to seek political office. But the typical army-allied militia commander in Myanmar remains nearly invisible, obscured by two or three false names, with operations hidden away in places barely touched by the internet or even paved roads.

Outside of these fiefdoms, their faces are practically unknown – and most have good reason to remain in the shadows.

〤

Notoriety can bring great risk to a militia chief. No one evinced this more than the dreaded river pirate Naw Kham – among the most notorious 'People's Militia Force' commanders in Myanmar's history.

Even in death, Naw Kham reminds other kingpins that,

while Myanmar's army will condone endless predatory violence, its more powerful neighbors may not.

In the early 2000s, the military permitted Naw Kham – a Khun Sa protégé – to conquer a key section of the Mekong River near Thailand and Laos. Barely literate but ruggedly handsome, he led the Hawngleuk Militia, a company-sized unit of killers armed with M-16s and RPGs.

The pirates raked in millions by extorting cargo ships and trafficking bundles of meth. Their reputation resounded throughout the Golden Triangle, spooking every boat crew who plied Myanmar's stretch of the Mekong.

But in 2011, Naw Kham made an error that would lead to his death. He dispatched his crew to attack more than a dozen Chinese sailors who were shipping oil, apples and garlic down the Mekong. The victims' alleged offense was failing to pay protection money. For that transgression, they were shot dead and mutilated.

Beijing's officials were irate. China seldom brings its forces to bear on criminal syndicates operating within allied nations – but those syndicates seldom murder a dozen innocent Chinese nationals in a bloodbath. Breaking form, China commenced a manhunt for Naw Kham on foreign soil. They even pursued the warlord with a drone rigged up with remotely detonatable TNT.

Myanmar, feeling the heat from China, had officially disavowed Naw Kham before the search began. But by all accounts the militiaman was still protected by regional army officers and police. Even while on the lam, Naw Kham and his men splashed money around to riverside hamlets, sustaining a Robin Hood-esque reputation, buying the silence of potential snitches and old army pals.

'Naw Kham was close to military intelligence until the end,' Thura tells me. 'Even on the run, he was always very careful to stay under the military umbrella.'

Ultimately, Chinese officials did not assassinate Naw Kham with flying dynamite. Their task force caught Naw Kham on the ground. He and his militia did not go down quietly. A Chinese narcotics officer, speaking on television, relayed that 'the guy was equipped with very modern weapons – exceeding what we'd expected.'[18]

Captured alive, Naw Kham was eventually hauled up to China. He was charged with murder, kidnapping, drug trafficking and hijacking. In 2013 – aged 44 years old, and leaving behind him an estate worth more than $60 million – Naw Kham was executed by lethal injection.

Naw Kham's big mistake had been to run afoul of Asia's most powerful nation. But all signs indicate that, if he hadn't angered the Chinese, Naw Kham and his pirates would still be terrorizing the Mekong with the blessing of Myanmar's officials.

※

The Yangon headquarters of the Myanmar Police Force is a four-story cement slab built with Stalinesque simplicity. Much of the building is hidden from the public by high gates and palm fronds ringing the perimeter.

Today, I'm headed inside this imposing place – into the nucleus of an institution that historically regards journalists as enemies of the state.

To my astonishment, a barrage of calls and e-mails to the Central Committee for Drug Abuse Control has paid off. I've secured an afternoon interview with Colonel Myint Thein, a top-ranking police officer within this military-run agency.

There is a caveat. They insisted that I submit a pre-approved list of questions. My plan, admittedly unsophisticated, is simply to veer off this list as much as possible.

Myanmar's anti-narcotics officials typically avoid the press like rabies. So I'm not entirely certain why the colonel consented to this interview. I suspect it has something to do with his agency's hunger for American aid.

Both Myanmar and the US, it seems, are eager to revive a relationship steeped in scandalous history. Through most of the 1970s and 1980s, America was actually the prime financier of Myanmar's counter-narcotics campaigns. Over fifteen years, the US doled out $80 million – along with dozens of planes and helicopters.[19]

This American aircraft was meant to help surveil and rain pesticides on poppy fields. Instead, the military used it to grind down rebellious minorities. According to one former American official, the US-supplied aircraft transported soldiers and weapons to the front lines, where they were pitted against ethnic guerrillas – including factions with no ties to the drug trade.[20]

This flow of cash and planes finally ended with that bloody 1988 crackdown, which turned Myanmar's junta into a pariah. The ensuing cold spell lasted more than two decades. But recently, in 2015, the US began quietly funding and training Myanmar's anti-narcotics officials once again.

Let that sink in. The CCDAC is essentially a wing of the army. Its stated purpose is to rid Myanmar of meth and heroin – the same drugs that are cranked out by the same army's own militias. This is like Kellogg's vowing to rid the world of Corn Flakes.

Yet the US government insists upon lending cash and prestige to this muddled mission. Myanmar's anti-narcotics officials now fly to America (or US-run facilities in Thailand) for training. US trainers also operate inside Myanmar. In coming years, they're expected to provide non-lethal gear such as night vision goggles or maybe even aircraft.[21]

So far, the US is easing back into this relationship gently. The new wave of funding amounts to roughly $1 million per year – totaling $2.1 million from 2016 to 2017.

That's not much, of course. The federal government will spend $2 million to provide security for Melania Trump during one weekend in New York City. But this aid matters greatly to Myanmar. The backing of the world's most powerful nation lends badly-desired credibility to an otherwise ignoble agency.

The State Department was once more clear-eyed about Myanmar's role in the drug trade. In 2008, US officials accused the army of offering 'the criminal underground immunity from law enforcement'.[22] Earlier still, in 1997, then-Secretary of State Madeleine Albright said Myanmar's drug traffickers were becoming 'leading lights' in the nation's economy and that 'drug money has become so pervasive in Burma that it taints legitimate investment and threatens the region as a whole.'

The US still concedes that 'credible reports' show 'mid-level military officers and government officials are engaged in drug-related corruption.'[23]

But America's zeal to build influence in Myanmar is overpowering its concerns about subsidizing dodgy drug agents.

In fact, the US now subverts its own laws to prop them up. Under the 'Foreign Assistance Act', the US is explicitly forbidden from aiding nations that have 'failed demonstrably' to rein in narcotic production on their soil – a category that clearly includes Myanmar.

To undermine this policy, the president must sign a document stating 'it is in the vital interest of the United States to grant a national interest waiver to Burma'. Obama signed such a 'vital interest' waiver five years in a row. Nothing indicates that President Donald Trump's administration will change course.

The colonel I'm about to interview is involved in the agency's donor relations. He likely views our meeting as an opportunity to pitch for more US aid. It doesn't hurt that I'm American. Officials in this part of the world often view reporters as intermediaries for their home governments rather than independent seekers of truth.

I arrive at Yangon's police headquarters in the late afternoon. The entrance is crowded by dozens of police officers. All are clad in gunmetal gray uniforms, floppy trousers and non-regulation flip-flops. Their unabashed gawking suggests that foreign visitors are rare. I'm soon spotted by one of Myint Thein's subordinates and escorted to his office upstairs.

From within, the building feels far less imposing. The center of the structure opens up into a leafy courtyard garden. The decor of the hallways is rather like a bomb shelter – exposed plumbing, concrete walls speckled with mold stains, flickering fluorescent lights overhead.

When I enter the colonel's office, I see that he's built like an oil drum, his black flat-top flecked with pewter streaks. He shakes my hand firmly and we take our seats, facing one another in heavy wooden chairs. His men rush over with a tray topped with mugs of ready-mix instant coffee.

At last, I am face-to-face with a proxy for an institution feared from the Bay of Bengal to Myanmar's frosty peaks. For weeks, I've been hearing Kachin sources castigate officers at Myint Thein's level as masterminds of oppression.

And yet I can detect from his tight smile that – to my surprise – the colonel seems afraid of me. Only now does it occur to me: any missteps during an interview with a foreigner could bring wrath from his superiors.

And then we are cast into darkness. A power outage has killed the overhead tubular lights and, in the absence of their loud hissing and humming, the room is unnervingly quiet. The contours of the colonel's face catch a bluish dusky gleam from the window. The vibe is strangely intimate for a few moments and then, somewhere within earshot, a diesel generator coughs to life.

The light returns and we recommence.

I begin with a vanilla question from the sanctioned list, a peace offering to unfurl the tension.

'Colonel, what exactly is your agency hoping to gain from the US?'

His answer is clearly rehearsed: Myanmar's officers want to train with cops in America, learn how to spy on poppy fields with satellites and use cutting-edge demographic techniques to count the number of addicts in Myanmar.

'How far do you want to take this?' I ask. 'Would you like to bring a full-on American-style drug war to Myanmar?'

'Well,' the colonel says, 'that would be difficult. Look at our geography. Consider all of those armed ethnic groups. We've got drugs pouring out of areas where state authority is difficult to enforce. High mountains. Dense forests.'

This is the military's stock answer. Once they've subdued these drug-producing insurgents through peace treaties, the state will valiantly rush in and destroy the meth trade. 'We have to secure the peace first,' he says. 'Then we can take action.'

'So even in your own country, there are large areas where you don't conduct drug investigations?'

'Legally, we can go anywhere,' the colonel says. 'But in reality, there are far-away places where we're still negotiating for peace.'

Time for an off-script question. 'What about your own state-backed militias – such as the *Pyi Thu Sit*?' I ask. 'Are they involved in drug production?'

'Well, yes, we do believe these groups are involved in the narcotics business.'

Now I see why the agency wanted a scripted Q&A. This is what happens when a government criminalizes critical reporting for decades on end. Its officials forget how to properly lie under questioning.

Realizing the implications of his unsanitized answer, the colonel tries to recover, squirming a bit, conjuring ways to soften this admission. The real masterminds, he points out, are foreign mafia figures – namely from China – who set up refineries on the militias' turf. He's making it sound like militia commanders are bullied into hosting meth labs.

'You see, outside syndicates take advantage of our complex political situation,' he says. 'Those militias, they're often just levying a tax on the foreign traffickers. The syndicate actually does most of the work.'

'So,' I say, 'it appears that one wing of the government is going after drug dealers. And then there's another wing of the government that's actually propping up militias that produce drugs. Doesn't that seem kind of senseless to you?'

The colonel stiffens, fidgeting with his thumbs.

'I don't want to answer that question. Sorry.'

'Is it dangerous to answer that question?'

'No. It just doesn't relate to me directly.'

Translation? You're going to get me fired. Or worse.

As we move on, it becomes clear that Myint Thein is not going to screw up twice. With each answer, he anxiously recites the party line, bracing himself against my attempts to nudge him off course. As with all my interviews, I end by encouraging him to expound on any subject I've neglected to raise.

'I'm pleased to invite you here to ask me questions,' the colonel says. 'In the past, people have written one-sided stories about us. I'm sure they've never believed our words. So thanks for allowing me to speak.'

'My pleasure, colonel. Anything else?'

'Yes. I recently learned that Bolivia is receiving nearly $100 million to fix its drug problems. What about Myanmar? We're getting much less. Our drug problem spills into many other nations. But we alone are fighting it here – and we have very scarce resources. We need help.'

I had expected this appeal for cash. I had not expected it to sound so sincere.

I'm sure *Pat Jasan* would love to give this colonel a good flogging. But it's possible that Myint Thein belongs to a small strain of relatively uncorrupted officers. Maybe he's pleading for foreign assistance because his investigative narc units are truly neutered by the army and starved of cash. Perhaps, like Thura, he too is troubled by the army's cruelty.

I can't glean the colonel's intentions. But I am grateful for his acknowledgment – however fleeting – that the state is enmeshed in the world's largest methamphetamine trade.

It seems those conspiracy theorists in the hills are not so delusional after all.

⋎

In the minds of many around the world, the word 'Burma' elicits visions of valiant rebellion.

They conjure scenes from 1988 or 2007, years defined by monks and college students and acolytes of Aung San Suu Kyi mobbing the streets in defiance of Southeast Asia's cruelest regime – and often paying with their lives.

These were the events that forged Myanmar's reputation as a land where the downtrodden stoically resist their tyrants.

Then, in February of 2016, Myanmar saw its largest civilian uprising against the military in nearly a decade. But this time, practically no one cared. The international media shrugged it off. America's president did not stand before the UN and proclaim that 'Americans are outraged by the situation in Burma' as George W. Bush had done in 2007.

The protesters were not Buddhists, nor were they terribly jazzed about Aung San Suu Kyi. They weren't crying out for democracy per se. Their demand was more crystallized. They called for the demise of army-backed narco-militias. And they too were willing to die for their cause.

This uprising was organized by *Pat Jasan*, which now claims 100,000 adherents. Bearing rods and sickles, a special corps of 3,000 vigilantes – including women and teens – marched into terrain controlled by the hated warlord Ting Ying.

They were hell-bent on destroying his poppies.

Their numbers were so overwhelming that police didn't attempt to thwart the mission. Instead, a small detachment of cops actually tagged along to keep an eye on the mob.

The outcome of this mission was terribly predictable. Militiamen, seemingly appraised of the siege, emerged from the bluffs to mow down the vigilantes with machetes and rifles while also lobbing grenades.

Dozens were injured, many seriously. Mobile phone footage shows young *Pat Jasan* raiders scrambling for cover as bombs erupt and vehicles burn. One nineteen-year-old vigilante was shot dead. He was later buried as a martyr, lowered into the earth wearing his *Pat Jasan* fatigues.

This death was not *Pat Jasan*'s first – drug traffickers had previously stabbed two raiders to death in Hpakant – but the loss of such a young commando compelled thousands to flood Myitkyina's streets.

Many waved signs condemning Ting Ying and his cadres by name. They surrounded his estate in Myitkyina, chucking stones at his windows. The more hardline *Pat Jasan* warriors vowed to hunt down the warlord like a boar.

History suggests that this will end in disaster. The uprisings in 1988 and 2007, which welled up from Yangon, were crushed with obscene violence: protesters and monks shot in the chest, their comrades dragged into torture cells.

But unlike the low-country protesters, who are largely

Burmese, the Kachin are a people inured to war and possibly supported by KIA rebels. They are even less likely to shrink from violent retribution. This could portend a fresh gyre of bloodshed in the hinterlands.

Pat Jasan is best understood as a primal howl – not only in defiance of meth and heroin but against the military that holds the Kachin people in a state of chaos. *Pat Jasan* is an ugly symptom. The disease is institutional plunder and neglect.

The cure that Aung San Suu Kyi offers involves Myanmar's armed minorities dropping their weapons, cooperating with the army and embracing 'democracy'. But the Kachin are not that gullible. The primary threat to their lives – the military and its pet militias – will not be voted out of existence.

There is a path out of this morass. But it requires listening to the Kachin. Through the KIA and the church hierarchy, they've repeatedly presented the same demands. First off, they want army boots off their necks. Secondly, they want a chance to benefit from the mineral wealth that is buried under their toes.

Kachin State is not some wasteland doomed to poverty. Its inhabitants are the rightful heirs to a great natural bounty, including the finest jade deposits on the planet. If the military ever wanted to do right by the Kachin – a very big 'if' – perhaps it could stand aside and let the Kachin fund their own spectacular rehabilitation.

In 2014 alone, Kachin State jade generated $31 billion, according to Global Witness, a London-based environmental watchdog group. That's roughly half the GDP of Myanmar. It's the nation's health care budget times 46. Imagine if that sum were taxed and plowed back into social welfare schemes – not just in Kachin lands but the entire nation.

Managed properly, jade profits could be used to modernize schools and hospitals from the mountains to the shores. Kachin State could conceivably prosper like a Qatar-style petro-state. Instead, the bulk of that wealth is funneled into secret accounts belonging to generals and their cronies.

There's no reason to stop at jade. The frost-nipped hills of Kachin and Shan – an area roughly the size of the United Kingdom – are notorious for sprouting poppies. Must this be a curse?

The West's favorite lab-created prescription opioids – Hydrocodone, Morphine, Oxycodone – are synthesized using a key ingredient: the pain-relieving sap of the poppy. The major conglomerates that produce these drugs, such as Actavis and Purdue, rely on poppies grown in Turkey, India and the Australian island of Tasmania.

Myanmar is deemed too chaotic to enter this well-regulated slate of approved suppliers. But this is largely the fault of the army, which would rather its militias control poppy fields than any transparent, taxable companies. That results in $16 billion – the value of mainland Southeast Asia's Myanmar-centered heroin trade – funding warlords and mafia instead of roads and clinics.[24]

There isn't a single panacea that can heal Myanmar's long-suffering borderlands overnight. But no set of solutions will ever gain traction until the government and its foreign allies start speaking honestly about the state-backed narcotics trade.

You might assume that, in the era of Western-backed reforms, foreign diplomats and donors would push the government to dismantle its pet militias – or at least acknowledge their role in the trafficking meth. But most treat the drug trade as a sideshow. It's a taboo undermining their 'New Myanmar' narrative.

Instead, Western powers direct their calls for disarmament towards ethnic minorities, not the meth militias. This message is purveyed through a 'joint peace fund' that is now soaking up $100 million from the EU, the US and other state donors.

The work of this group (and other foreign-led 'peace' efforts) is drenched in jargon about 'jointness' and 'empowerment'. But ultimately, it is a government-steered attempt to talk the rebels into standing down.

For this task, the peace fund's foreign executives will earn salaries ranging from $150,000 to $200,000 – 120 to 180 times the typical Myanmar citizen's annual pay.[25] But don't expect these well-paid Western arbiters to aggressively root out the army's worst abuses. Not once do the fund's stated principles mention drug-trafficking militias.

As far as the influential foreign corporations go, they're also in sync with the lightweight peace-and-democracy narrative. After US sanctions were dissolved, Hillary Clinton proclaimed that Western investors should do business in Myanmar as 'positive change' agents whose investments 'support reform'.[26]

This helps explain why Coca-Cola's CEO has gushed that Myanmar feels like Berlin after the wall fell. Or the influential finance guru Jim Rogers proclaiming that Myanmar is the best investment opportunity in the world. 'If I could put all of my money into Myanmar,' he says, 'I would.' Seldom has Wall Street sounded so effervescent about an economy utterly corrupted by drugs.

On paper, Myanmar's top exports are gas, precious gems

(wildly undervalued at $2 billion) and dried legumes. But this is a joke. Forget the beans. The real top exports are meth, jade and heroin – all derived from the war-wracked hinterlands. Meth shipments alone are almost assuredly worth more than $12 billion, the combined annual value of all legal exports.[27]

This black market taints almost every corner of Myanmar's economy. On Obama's final visit to Myanmar in 2014, he slept at the Kempinski – a hotel co-owned by a firm that was caught shipping heroin bricks to Taiwan.[28] And while Coca-Cola crowed about Myanmar's reforms, it also hired an executive who was secretly invested in Hpakant's ghastly and exploitative jade mines.[29]

Not to be outdone, the Fortune 500 company Caterpillar – which manufactures mining machinery – recruited the front man for a firm owned by Wei Hsueh-Kang, the jade-and-meth kingpin wanted by the DEA.

Caterpillar even paid one of the drug lord's lackeys to tout Myanmar's potential around the world. He was flown to the UK, Spain and finally France, where he purchased a Rolex worth more than $50,000. That's four decades worth of income for the average person in Myanmar.

For now, most Western attention on Myanmar swirls around Aung San Suu Kyi's failures as a humanitarian and her party's antipathy towards the Rohingya. This spotlight seldom drifts towards the state-sponsored drug trade. But her government might not be able to play down this massive black market forever.

Some estimates suggest Myanmar's drug trade is the world's largest – possibly churning out more narcotics and generating more cash than the cartels in Mexico. More boom times are ahead, thanks in large part to the narco-militias' proximity to China, soon to become the world's largest economy.

Yet the West could not seem more aloof. Many diplomats and foreign executives in Myanmar still struggle to articulate how the drugs are funding chaos in Myanmar. Their ignorance only goads the army to keep nourishing this narcotic behemoth.

This is a scandal. As long as the narco-fiefdoms exist, the people of Myanmar will never be free.

※

It is the fall of 2015, monsoon season in Kachin State. On one of my last days in Myitkyina, before boarding a train bound for the low country, Gideon and I ride over to *Pat Jasan*'s operations center. I'm keen to check on Lashu before my departure.

As we bump along Myitkyina's cratered backstreets, Gideon emanates cheeky mischief. 'Hey, brother,' he says. 'I've got to tell you something.'

'What is it?'

'I've joined *Pat Jasan*.'

I can tell from his pleased expression that I look utterly bewildered. The Christian vigilantes, who so revile drug users and cops, have taken in a police agent who spends his afternoons in opium dens.

'I can't believe it,' I say. 'You always told me *Pat Jasan* is crazy.'

'Well, they had a recruitment drive at my church,' Gideon says. 'The neighborhood was pressuring me to join. So was my wife. It's a Kachin thing, you know. I couldn't refuse.'

'I'm impressed. You're cool with cops, criminals, pastors and vigilantes. Is there anyone you can't charm?'

Gideon's face is aglow with a troublemaker's glee. 'They even gave me a helmet and wooden baton.'

When we arrive at *Pat Jasan*'s command center, the front gate is unlatched and the courtyard is empty. Just a few nights ago, this place was seething with dark mojo.

I recall dozens of young men amped up before the hunt, thunder in their bellies. They were miming bamboo baton strikes in the night air – just like golfers practicing their long drives. Now it is morning and sunlight has cooked off the menacing vibe.

We find Lashu in a barred chamber, one leg still in the stocks, the other tucked beneath him. He is sitting upright, wearing the same T-shirt. They've given him a Burmese-language newspaper.

'Hey, Lashu,' I say, 'how they treating you in here?'

'They have been kind to me,' he says, sounding genuine. 'I feel relief, actually. They've taught me to cut the bad things out of my life.'

The site commander, Naw Sam, walks in and greets us with a nod. He tosses a fresh polo shirt to Lashu. A guard unfastens the stocks and instructs Lashu to change clothes and report to the ad hoc courtroom. There, he will receive his final sentence.

Several minutes later, Lashu is being judged before yet another *Pat Jasan* tribunal. This time, he's allowed to sit in a chair. The local church's pastor is present, which helps the proceedings feel a bit less martial. I decide to loiter outside, eavesdropping as Naw Sam plays the role of vigilante warden.

'After three nights and two days, we have concluded that

you are not a hardcore drug user,' Naw Sam says. 'You have shown no signs of severe withdrawals. Rehab camp is unnecessary and, in a few moments, you will be released.'

'However,' he says, 'know that we have eyes and ears in the community. The next time you use drugs, your punishment will be more severe.' Naw Sam then lowers his voice to a threatening whisper, warning Lashu that repeat offenders are referred to KIA rebels.

'But that shouldn't prove necessary,' he says. 'We have faith in you, Lashu. Just remember always that only those filled with the gospel can truly repent.'

Out in the courtyard, a few *Pat Jasan* grunts are building a flaming altar out of bricks, steel grating and lumps of charcoal. The pastor rises to his feet and beckons Lashu out of the courtroom. He is instructed to come before the altar and complete a ritual of contrition.

Obeying the pastor's commands, Lashu kneels on the pavement. He is told to smash his opium ladle with a stone. Then he is handed the rest of his paraphernalia – a half-constructed meth hookah – and told to feed all of it into the holy flames.

The spoon shards char and crackle. The plastic bottle shrivels and turns liquid. The preacher orders Lashu to bow his head.

'Oh Lord, our Kachin have fallen under Satan's command. This man and his peers? They have pursued a false happiness. In Christ's name, we shall cleanse all of this wickedness from the land.'

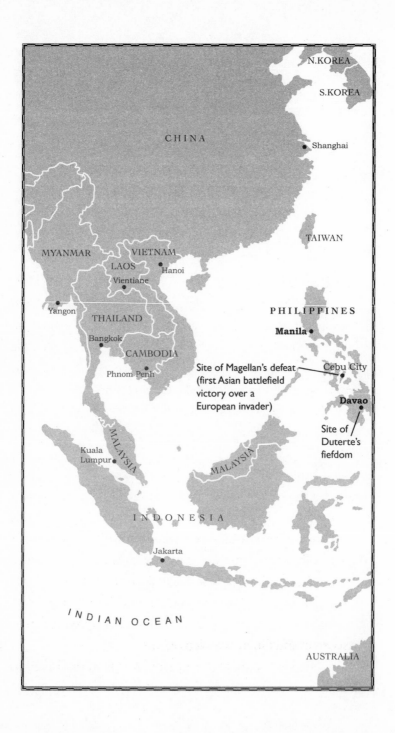

CHAPTER III

The Devil's Cocktail

Location: Manila, the Philippines

*Where a female-run crime ring
sells forbidden elixirs*

Manila is crowded.

I'm not talking New York City's wait-two-hours-for-good-pizza crowded, nor London's can't-find-a-seat-on-the-tube crowded. Manila's human density is seven times that of New York and thirteen times that of London. It is, by some measures, the most jammed-up city in the world.[1]

This is a crowdedness that is sensory, often tactile. It squishes you on all sides in the market. It dampens your shirt with other people's sweat.

In Manila, you can identify someone's status by noting how little time they spend outside in this hot crush of people. During daylight hours, those in society's higher tiers huddle inside steel office towers, and in the evenings, they flock to malls defended by armed guards. These places are air-conditioned sanctuaries, fortified against the maelstrom outside.

But the poor among this metro area's 21-million population inhabit a much rawer Manila – a riot of poured concrete, rusty steel and flimsy wooden planks.

In vast slums, there are people everywhere, forced to do private things in public: bathing under alleyway spigots, brushing their teeth over gutters, hanging clothes on electric cables. The city's lower classes live in an unstable world, made fearsome by literal pitfalls. They must sidestep holes in the sidewalk big enough to swallow absentminded pedestrians and plunge them into black sewage.

Those who can't afford a tenement room may stake out small areas on the sidewalks and make them their own, building lean-tos out of refuse and tarps. These shelters, sometimes outfitted with pirated electricity, can become semi-permanent homes for families of six or more. But even this counts as luxury for the mothers who sleep further up the block on scraps of cardboard, often cradling infants, their bare feet stained black.

Manila doesn't quarantine its poverty into little pockets. Slums lap at the edges of the glitzy quarters. Ragged squatter camps seep into middle-class neighborhoods. As one of the Philippines' most beloved senators once put it: 'Gleaming suburbia clashes with the squalor of the slums. Here is a land of privilege and rank, a republic dedicated to equality but mired in an anarchic system of caste.'

That politician, Benigno Aquino Jr., was legendary for diagnosing his nation's troubles with fury and great eloquence. He believed that a prime cause of Philippine poverty was the nation's 'ballooning population'. Way back in 1968, he was already warning that, if the 'abjectly poor' masses grew too large, the nation would never achieve lift-off.[2]

When the senator sounded this alarm, the Philippine population stood at 35 million. It has since tripled to nearly 105 million.[3] Just try to imagine one third of the American population crammed into a space the size of Arizona. Now chop up Arizona into thousands of separate islands.

That is the Philippines, a crowded archipelago growing by 5,000 babies each day.[4]

This is an island chain crackling with talent and ingenuity. More so than any other Southeast Asian people, Filipinos are outward looking, English speaking and primed for the age of globalization. Yet many forces conspire to deny them their full potential.

City-smashing typhoons are high on the list. So are ravenous kleptocrats and a vicious legacy of colonialism. But any honest discussion of the nation's troubles cannot ignore the role of babies.

Yes, babies. Don't take it from me. Listen to the women of the Philippines.

Every five years or so – most recently in 2013 – Philippine government statisticians working with the US Agency for International Development will contact 15,000 homes across the nation and ask women about their reproductive desires.

Survey after survey indicates that Filipinas are having far more children than they want.

According to the data, for every three kids born in the Philippines, one of them is totally unplanned. Now sharpen your focus on Filipinas who never studied beyond elementary school. The average woman in this category can expect to have four or five kids – even though she intends to have only three.[5]

This epidemic of unwanted pregnancies helps explain why the nation has one of Asia's highest birth rates – a population expansion so fast that, by 2050, the Philippines will hold more people than Russia.

For working-class Filipino parents, extra children aren't just inconvenient. They make prosperity almost impossible. As many as 40 per cent of all Filipinos in the country scrape by on $2 per day.[6] That's barely enough for a couple bowls of vegetable-flecked porridge – and not nearly enough to feed four hungry mouths.

Parents in this predicament will sometimes starve themselves to feed their kids. Mothers, seen by society as primarily responsible for child rearing, are especially likely to go without food if their sons or daughters are hungry. They're a common sight on the streets of Manila, where I once interviewed a malnourished woman named Josephine. At 35, she'd had eight kids and was so depleted of calcium through breastfeeding that most of her teeth had fallen out. Skin sagged from her cheekbones and her limbs were skeletal.

Perhaps that's a more extreme case. Here's one that should sound more familiar to working-class women in, say, Dallas or Leeds. For any lower-middle class Filipino woman, a third child may drain household savings such that none of her children will be able to afford college – crushing the family's hopes of climbing into the educated class.

In the West, women facing these decisions were liberated decades ago by birth control pills. But when Filipinas reach for those same pills, they are too often called whores or even baby killers.

Worse still, they are thrust onto the losing side of the Philippines' longest-running drug war.

Hold that thought. Because I'm not referring to the drug war waged by state-backed death squads – that nightmare that keeps splashing photos of supine corpses across news sites worldwide.

That is the government's war on crystal meth. It pairs the righteousness of *Pat Jasan* with lethal firepower, and it is racking up a body count seldom seen outside large-scale land battles. The death toll has, by some estimates, already exceeded 10,000.

Led by President Rodrigo Duterte, this war deploys police (and allied hitmen) to exterminate meth smokers and deal-ers – all under the banner of restoring purity to a nation gone astray. As in northern Myanmar, outrage over meth addiction is proving to be a galvanizing political force. Filipinos are told by Duterte's camp that, once society's scum is all mopped up, the nation will at last become prosperous.

This ongoing massacre has come to define the modern Philippines, bleeding into almost every facet of life, but it is not the reason I've come to Manila. I'm here to explore a different drug war that, while far less notorious, has quietly proven just as devastating.

Orchestrated by an all-male priesthood, this other drug war seeks to eradicate any substance, ancient or modern, that might prevent or terminate a pregnancy. It is a crusade led by the Catholic Church, which in the Philippines is an institution nearly as mighty as the state itself.

While the president's campaign primarily kills poor men, the one orchestrated by the church targets poor women.

Indigenous herbs, birth control pills, homemade elixirs and chemical injections – any drug that Filipinas might use to exert control over their wombs is deemed ungodly and marked for suppression. Overpopulation crisis be damned.

Like the meth war, its dark twin, this anti-drug crusade is designed to exercise power over minds and bodies. Both rest on the claim that, upon victory, the Philippines will be cured of wickedness and hardship.

Yet in reality, both wars are driving families deeper into poverty. Worst of all, they smear millions of non-violent

Filipinos as monstrous criminals. Those who defy these operations are pushed deeper into a grim underworld, many of them singled out for humiliation, ruination or even death.

)(

Birth control pills aren't illegal in the Philippines. Not yet. Nor for that matter are contraceptive injections or implants. But they're increasingly hard to procure – particularly for the working-class women who need them most of all.

Filipinas scraping by on a few dollars a day generally get their health care from cheap, state-run clinics. Most of these mini-hospitals, however, refuse to stock birth control on ideological grounds. This is true even in Manila, the country's largest and most liberal city, which has largely banned state-funded contraception since 2000.

In decades past, this birth control void was filled from afar. For four decades until 2008, the US poured nearly half a billion dollars into spreading contraception throughout the Philippines. America's stated goal was to reduce family sizes and thus the burden of poverty.[7] All the while, Filipino priests condemned Americans for 'spreading their culture of death'.

But they need not fear the return of a US-funded contraception wave. That now-defunct aid campaign was nixed by former President George W. Bush, whose conservative camp preferred to promote abstinence overseas. It certainly won't be revived under Trump. His White House, seeking to shrink America's largesse around the world, hopes to cut all health-related aid to the Philippines in half.[8]

Until recently, the Philippines' pill shortage was mostly a problem for women too broke to shell out $7 per month for over-the-counter meds. But now scarcity is hitting the middle and upper classes, too. Each day, more Filipinas are told by pharmacists that their go-to brand of pill is out of stock and may never return.

These are the spoils of a new anti-contraception coup: one that has been deftly executed by the Catholic Church.

After many centuries, the church remains one of the island nation's most powerful institutions, second only to the government. The Philippines is Catholicism's main stronghold in Asia. Its priests don't just adjudicate the fates of Filipino souls.

They're also a guiding force for many of the nation's laws.

Many high-ranking politicians and attorneys are deeply beholden to the priesthood, and for decades, they've obediently decried using tax money to disseminate birth control, which in their view promotes degeneracy. This is the reason so many clinics in poor neighborhoods don't stock the pill.

But recently, in 2015, this powerful Catholic lobby pulled off a much greater triumph – one that would expand the fight beyond public clinics and into regular pharmacies. They convinced the Supreme Court of the Philippines to consider aligning itself with the Vatican by ruling that hormonal contraception is tantamount to abortion.

The nation's top judges have been deliberating this since 2015. They face a wrenching predicament. They could defy the Vatican, enraging powerful priests who would brand them as morally corrupt in masses across the country.

Or they could finally deliver the church's dream scenario, and rule that birth control pills really do murder embryos – which the priests see as being speck-sized humans.

If that happens, both rich and poor Filipinas alike can say goodbye to the pill forever. The meds would be deemed to violate the constitution, which enshrines protection for the 'life of the unborn'.

In the meantime, while the judges wring their hands, they've thrown up a birth control blockade to further satiate the church. The courts are effectively choking off the nation's supply of birth control drugs – almost all of which are shipped in from abroad.

Importing a brand of pill or implant requires a license that must be regularly extended. But now, under court orders, no brand will get its papers renewed until the judges have finished deciding whether these meds are homicidal to the seedlings of human life. This ethical quagmire could drag on for years more.

This leaves women to rely on a dwindling list of brands that still have a few years left on their licenses. But that menu is shrinking fast. Stockpiles are running low.

The Supreme Court appears to be running out the clock. If the judges don't stand up to the church and reverse this course, only condoms will be left on the shelves by 2020.

Seen by the Vatican as the least nefarious form of contraception — and the hardest to regulate because prophylactics aren't drugs — condoms will likely survive any religious cull.

But condoms are terribly unpopular in the Philippines and not always easy to find in stores. They're used by fewer than 2 per cent of married Filipino couples and, when unmarried Filipinas aged 25 or younger have sex, they're used only 8 per cent of the time.[9] Even Duterte mocks prophylactics, telling citizens 'don't use them because they don't feel good' and comparing condom use to eating a piece of candy 'without unwrapping it'.[10]

So if only condoms are left in the Philippines, the war

on contraception will essentially be over and the priests will declare victory.

This is not the future most Filipinos want. When polled, more than half say they want *more* cheap or free birth control, not some theocratic ban.[11]

Instead, they've seen these essential drugs grow stigmatized and scarce – a crisis leaving Filipinas with more unwanted pregnancies. These women aren't deviants. Many are otherwise doing everything right according to the church: getting married, going to mass and raising children. They just don't want (or can't afford) more kids.

Increasingly, there is no refuge for these women but the underworld. As the state further attempts to criminalize reproductive health care, it is inadvertently forcing more Filipinas to seek treatment from, well, criminals.

Those 'criminals' are the people I've come to Manila to meet.

I am pursuing a band of outlaw herbalists and pill dealers who operate in the shadows. They are almost entirely female, many of them middle-aged. These women are practitioners of an arcane trade: abortion by means of roots, leaves and illicit medications.

All of them risk imprisonment. The nation's church-inspired penal codes don't just threaten any woman who hopes to terminate her pregnancy. They also endanger those who help 'conceal her dishonor' by assisting with the abortion. Both dealer and customer can face up to six years in a crowded prison cell.[12]

To evade this fate, these underground herbalists operate like any other drug dealers. They disguise their speech with impenetrable slang. They rely on police bribes to evade arrest.

They obey a code of silence, never disclosing their customers' names.

But unlike the meth merchants, they're not violently exterminated by cops. Those who pay off corrupt police can ply their trade without much fear of violent retribution – for now, at least.

My mission is to find one of these dealers and unravel the mechanics of this trade. I'm told they congregate near a rather unlikely location: the Minor Basilica of the Black Nazarene. It's a resplendent old church by the Pasig River in a district called Quiapo.

There, they can be found peddling their sinful elixirs in the shadows of Manila's most exalted cathedral.

The interior of the Black Nazarene cathedral is as big as an aircraft hangar. There must be 2,000 people here for Friday mass, swarming the aisles, craning their necks to see the priest. He's standing on a far-away pedestal at the back of the room – a distant white-robed figure flanked by twin pillars of sacramental smoke.

The muggy air is swished around by three spinning fans fixed to the ornate ceiling. Their blades are big enough to lift an Apache helicopter.

Still, the thick air hardly circulates. There are just too many warm bodies smushed into this space. Some of the standing parishioners are holding their flip-flops in their hands, cooling their toes on the marbled floors. The tiles are gleaming, polished smooth over the years by thousands of bare feet.

I'm here with a reporting companion named Rica

Concepcion. I ask her what the priest is intoning into the public address system.

'The sanctity of marriage,' she says. 'He's against unmarried couples. He says that if someone who's in a relationship is dying, and they can't show a marriage certificate, he'll refuse to perform their last rites.'

How uplifting.

Rica is a veteran Filipina journalist with a reputation for tenacity. To my great fortune, she's agreed to team up. Exploring the black market for abortive drugs is light work for Rica. It's actually a reprieve from her main pursuit: documenting the president's war on meth.

In recent months, Rica has attended many funerals of fathers shot dead by masked assassins. She's spent late nights stepping over bodies at crime scenes. The victims' heads are sometimes wrapped in electrical tape and draped with handmade signs that read 'I'M A PUSHER. DON'T BE LIKE ME.'

Police at these scenes joke that she's a bad fit for this line of work. They say that Rica – with her practical shoulder-length hair and adult braces – is 'too much of a mom' for such a grim job.

Yes, Rica is a mother of three. She's also chased stories for three decades, more recently exposing a secret prison run by local officials. Fellow journalists know her pedigree. Rica is the widow of the highly-regarded documentary filmmaker Egay Navarro, and the daughter of a political prisoner who was persecuted under the regime of Ferdinand Marcos, the infamous US-backed dictator.

Rica knows journalism and state abuse intimately. She moves comfortably through the underworld. So she's an ideal partner for an American guy exploring an illegal trade run by and for Philippine women. I'm going into this with plenty of blind spots. I'm grateful that she's around to help cover them.

Rica is also a Catholic, and Catholicism, more than Buddhism and Islam, is a world in which I often feel utterly befuddled. I'm not sure what to make of the statues ringing this cathedral: of saints holding broadswords and standing on disembodied heads. Or the stone figurines, in garish robes, gripping daggers and flanked by grimacing falcons.

Rica and I start to wriggle through the steamy crowd to reach the exit.

When we near the front gates, however, I'm startled by a clamorous scene.

We've come upon a life-sized crucifix on a pedestal. It's surrounded by an agitated crowd. This Christ figurine is sculpted from what looks like black mahogany. His beard is woolly, his eyes agog, and he is draped in burgundy robes. There is a wig atop his head, a mess of permy blonde curls.

Worshippers fitfully clutch at his ankles. As I step nearer, I can see that they're rubbing white rags over his lower extremities. This non-stop rubdown has chafed Christ's shins and feet, wearing away the dark varnish in creamy white splotches. It looks like Jesus has vitiligo.

'Um, Rica?' I say. 'What are they doing?'

'Praying,' she says. 'Once the cloth rubs the statue, they think it's become holy.'

This statue in the vestibule is a replica of the cathedral's namesake: the Black Nazarene, a mesquite-wood Christ figure that was reputedly carved in 17th-century Mexico. It was bequeathed to the church in the early days of Spain's nearly 400-year occupation of these islands.

Each year, the Black Nazarene statue (or another replica,

so I hear) is marched through Manila in a mass procession of millions.

I've seen the parade on TV. It's an orgy of fanaticism. Waves of people climb on one another's backs to briefly touch the Black Nazarene as it moves through the streets.

They believe that grazing this statue with their fingers or swatches of cloth will bring them closer to God – a notion promoted by the Philippine priesthood. The Black Nazarene, they say, is a portal to the Lord. Catholics who can't wait for the yearly parade can come here to re-enact this ritual on a cheaper replica of the Nazarene.

Leaving the sacred statue behind, we make our way outside the cathedral to find a much vaster commotion. The chapel is surrounded by a loud bazaar – a maze of stalls selling holy oils and Virgin Mary statuettes, love potions and pocket-sized Christs splattered with fake blood.

The entire market smells of sizzling wax. As we push into the crowd, vendors beckon us to come and light prayer candles, each one color-coded by dreams and fears. Burn a green candle to escape poverty. Burn a red candle to find love. Burn a peach candle to ace your exams. Burn a black candle to bedevil your cheating husband's soul. It seems they've covered the full taxonomy of Filipino troubles.

As we slip deeper into the bazaar, I can see that this is much more than an emporium for holy kitsch. It's also a haven for entrepreneurial faith healers – a place where men and women are promised supernatural solutions to very real problems. Here, you can secure the services of an *albularyo*, who will exorcise your troubles using hot embers, candle wax and chicken feathers.

'An *albularyo* is like a witch doctor,' Rica says. 'You come to them with body pains or fears of being jinxed. Then out come the concoctions and the potions and the smoke. It's a Filipino thing. In the villages, Western medicine is far off and expensive. But the local witch doctor is always close by.'

These rituals are born from animism: spirit-worshipping beliefs that long predate the arrival of Christian priests in the 16th century. The Spanish crown reviled these 'heretic' beliefs. As in the Americas, its conquistadors tried to totally purge the rituals of indigenous people.

Here, as there, it looks like they failed.

Rica brings me to a vendor's table overflowing with polished stones: hundreds of amber-colored chunks, translucent purple gems and green pebbles the color of seaweed. This operation belongs to Erica, a rotund 25 year old with a sweat towel around her neck.

She looks up wearily, wearing the expression of a woman who spends hot afternoons listening to strangers' troubles. There's a sign over her head, explaining that her stones are magical, some christened with names such as 'Tooth of Thunder'.

I ask Erica to brief me on her inventory. 'Well, this one brings you luck when working overseas,' she says. 'This one brings you luck in gambling. This one brings you luck in school. And this one protects you from theft.'

Erica seems to have great faith in her anti-theft stones. She's placed a few of them atop a wad of Philippine pesos on the table. These are her earnings so far today. Any thief could easily snatch the cash and disappear into the bazaar. But the mound goes untouched.

'It looks like business is good,' I say.

'Oh, yes,' she says, holding aloft a tiny crescent-shaped

piece of rock. 'This one is really selling now.' She drops it into my outstretched palm. It's not much bigger than a splinter.

'It offers protection,' she says. 'From *tokhang*.'

Tokhang. That's a drug-war expression meaning 'knock and persuade'. This is how police are, in theory, meant to roust suspected meth users from their homes: urging them to get clean or go to jail.

But *tokhang* has become a twisted farce. Everyone knows that the cops and their allied kill squads don't knock. They kick in your door, drag you into a ditch and put two bullets in your skull. *Tokhang* is now the go-to slang for extra-judicial killings – or 'EJKs' as Filipinos also call them. These state-sponsored murders are common enough to demand a shorthand.

This tactic was named by Duterte, who launched the first 'Operation *Tokhang*' shortly after his 2016 election victory. His police campaigns have since taken on action-movie titles. There are signs all around the market announcing the latest iteration: 'OPERATION DOUBLE BARREL RELOADED'.

'You know about *tokhang*?' Erica asks.

'Yeah,' I say. 'Operation *Tokhang*. Duterte.'

'Oh!' she asks, 'then what do you think of our president?'

Like Trump in America, Duterte has become a cloud that hangs over everything in the Philippines – drifting into any conversation that goes on for longer than three minutes. He has radically reconfigured society, dividing the populace into a simple binary: upright Filipinos versus 'sub-human' lawbreakers. He blames 'criminals' for just about everything: poverty, rape, skittish foreign investment, you name it.

Erica's question is perfectly fair. Why wouldn't she want to know how the Duterte era looks through foreign eyes? But there's no way I'm answering her. Duterte has an approval

rating most US presidents would kill for. Criticizing his policies in a crowded market seems like an exceedingly bad idea.

'I've got no opinion, really,' I say. 'So how much for the
anti-*tokhang* stone?'

They go for 250 pesos. Roughly $5. She tells me each is
dug out of the ground in Mindoro, an island south of Manila
rife with wild pigs and fruit bats. 'When you are in danger
from *tokhang*, this little stone will make you bulletproof and
invisible,' Erica says matter-of-factly. 'Very useful.'

Erica doesn't put much energy into her sales pitch. She
doesn't need to. These rocks sell themselves. I hand over the
cash. You never know.

'How do I, um, activate it?' I ask.

'I'm going to wrap the stone in red cloth,' Erica says. 'You
must place it into your wallet, never removing it from the
fabric. Do you understand?'

I nod.

'I should tell you that, to receive the full effects of the
stone, I would need to place it inside your body.'

'And how might you do that?' I ask.

'I would take you to the island of Mindoro. Out on the
beach at night. I would give you a big bottle of rum to drink.
Then I would cut open your forearm and embed it under your
skin.'

Reading my thoughts, Erica adds: 'Don't worry, it's a very
sanitary procedure. I have rubbing alcohol and good surgical
blades.'

With a shout and wave of her hand, Erica beckons over a
friend loitering nearby. Up walks another twenty-something,
with a red leather purse swinging on her shoulder, her hair
dyed marigold blonde.

With the no-nonsense gruffness of a primary care doctor, Erica grabs the woman's forearm and begins pinching at the flesh above her elbow. There it is: a discolored lump the size of a marble.

'My friend here had big trouble,' Erica says. 'She needed protection from a bad man, a crazy ex-lover.' (So much for witch doctor–patient confidentiality.)

'He was stalking her with a gun and a knife,' Erica says, still gripping the woman's arm. 'Then I embedded this stone. He's no longer a threat. Isn't that right?'

The woman nods somberly.

'It really works,' Erica tells me. 'You just have to believe.'

X

Now that I'm feeling bulletproof, it's time to track down some drug dealers.

If you know what to look for, the outlaw herbalists aren't hard to find. They're a bit like weed dealers in Manhattan's Washington Square Park. They lock eyes with passersby who seem nervous and whisper names of their wares in strangers' ears.

I'd imagined them wandering all around the market. But the women actually have fixed stalls where they sell their herbs in open sight. Each is posted behind a wooden table spilling over with leafy plants and thick, ropey vines.

They're also prominently displaying glass bottles filled with amber liquid. Each has a crude, homemade label attached. Rica picks one up, squinting at the label. 'I can't even read these ingredients,' she says. 'This is in Visayan.'

Visayan is a language group from the central Philippines.

It's similar to Tagalog, the Philippines' dominant language, but they're not mutually comprehensible. Rica says many of the sellers rely on Visayan, allowing them to communicate somewhat openly about their not-so-legal activities. Few beat cops in Manila would know Visayan.

Still, you don't need to speak Visayan to figure out what they're selling. You only need to know two words, and they are printed in giant letters on the dealers' bottles.

'PAMPA REGLA'. *Pampa*, to cause. *Regla*, menstruation.

Like branding designer drugs as 'bath salts', or synthetic weed as 'incense', selling these concoctions relies on a clever legal dodge. It's sold as a natural supplement for women – sexually abstinent women, that is – whose periods are running late.

But everyone knows the deal.

The vendors are eyeing us suspiciously. We're trouble. They can smell it. Turning to one vendor, I ask: 'So how far along in a woman's pregnancy will this stuff still work?' She recoils, turning her face in the opposite direction.

'No, no,' she says, shooing me away. 'A pregnant woman can never drink this. That's against the law!' She's right, of course. Any woman who drinks this stuff to destroy her embryo could face years in prison – and so could her dealer.

I try a few more vendors but don't get very far. Some talk to me guardedly, as if I'm a narc. Some hide their faces behind Japanese-style hand fans. One women is quite direct: 'Young man, if I answer your questions, I'll get a visit from the police commissioner.'

Rica laughs. 'They probably think we're from some hard-core Catholic group,' she says. 'Like we're trying to gather information to shut them down.'

We do make a suspicious pair. She's past her childbearing years. I'm a guy. Not exactly the prime demographic for the Quiapo district's infamous abortifacient potions.

'There's no use standing around,' Rica says. 'No one will talk to us here in the market.' She'll have to come back tomorrow, alone, to arrange a clandestine meeting with one of the herbalists.

'Don't worry,' Rica says. 'I already have someone in mind.'

)(

Elsa the drug dealer is ready for her close-up.

'Look at me! Time for my big interview with Mr Patrick from America. I'm a superstar now!'

I've never met a criminal so eager for attention. Elsa is loud and hilariously brash with a raspy cackle like Roseanne Barr. She dresses simply: wearing her hair in a bob, denim shorts, and an oversized T-shirt depicting Sleepy from Disney's *Snow White and the Seven Dwarfs*.

We're sitting in the back seat of a sedan, parked in a backlot a few kilometers from the Black Nazarene cathedral. Rica sits up front. As requested, Elsa has brought her full inventory of herbs and elixirs. She carries it all in a shopping bag, looking every bit like an ordinary aunty headed to the market.

'Wait. Before we start,' Elsa says, 'are you even famous?'

Elsa doesn't give a fuck. I like her already.

'No,' I tell her. 'Not even a little bit.'

'Damn,' she says. 'Well, if you become famous, you must be wary. You are a good man, I can tell. But don't be gullible. People may try to exploit you as you gain fame. Even your best friends.'

'You know,' Elsa says, 'I have medallions that can protect you from these bad people.'

Sensing that gullibility being exploited, I quickly change the subject.

'How do you know so much about me, Elsa?'

Elsa is a self-proclaimed clairvoyant. Now in her fifties, she was born in Tacloban, a central Philippine city. It was demolished in 2013 by a tempest straight out of the Old Testament. Fortunately, Elsa was long gone by then. She's been dealing near the Black Nazarene for more than two decades – long enough to acquire godmother status among the other sellers.

'I see things. My third eye, it was handed down to me through genetics,' she says. 'I imbibed this talent from my mother.'

Elsa's mom was a *hilot*, a sort of indigenous Filipino chiropractor. *Hilots* are known for their ability to terminate a woman's second-trimester pregnancy through violent abdominal massage. For women in their first trimester, however, her mom had a less extreme cure: homemade abortive potions. That's how Elsa got into the game.

'She made people's problems disappear, either through black magic or herbs,' Elsa says. 'I'm the same. I just want to help out my fellow women.'

Elsa and her peers operate in a folk-healing realm where male mystics can't compete. 'There are very few men in this trade,' she says, 'and they get little respect. Why should they? They can't understand a woman's biology.'

I ask Elsa to dump her bag of illicit wares on the backseat for inspection. She turns it upside down, scattering an astonishing variety of plant life on the seat cushions. My eyes are drawn towards a gnarled root, the color of cabernet. It's coiled in a circle like a rattlesnake. I run my finger along its nubby skin.

'That's one of the main ingredients,' she says. '*Makabuhay*.'

Then she holds up a stem bristling with leaves that, when alive, will recoil to the touch. 'This is *makahiya*,' she says. 'The plant of shame.'

Finally, Elsa shows off bits of ginger-colored tree bark and a potpourri of dried green flakes. All of these herbs are packaged in little baggies. Just like grams of pot or speed.

'So,' Elsa says, 'you throw all this stuff in a pot, add water, make a tea. Give it to a woman who has missed her period for up to two months. Make her drink it three times a day. Tell her not to drink cold water with it or anything that's sour.'

'And what will happen?'

'The baby', she says, balling her fist above her stomach and flicking her hand, as if tossing away a tissue. 'Gone.'

'Right,' I say. 'But what will the woman actually experience?'

'All these plants are very bitter,' Elsa says. 'So bitter that the body can't take it. They'll make her blood come out. And the baby will come out with it.'

In other words? Miscarriage.

Elsa pulls out a pint-sized whiskey bottle labeled 'PAMPA REGLA', just like the stuff Rica and I saw in the market. The liquid inside is the aforementioned tea, pre-boiled and ready to drink. It's an abortion elixir for women on the go.

The appeal of this bottled brew is in its potential for secrecy. A married woman with her own kitchen might privately boil up a batch of herbs at her leisure. A high school or college student living at home, however, does not have that luxury. 'Think about it,' Elsa says. 'You come home and your mom sees you boiling all this stuff. She'll be like, "Are you pregnant!?"'

Elsa and the other dealers sell this bottled elixir at a premium over the dried herbs. It's a bestseller among teenage girls, she says, and a steal at only $5. I hold the bottle aloft, letting it catch the sun. The fluid inside looks like grape soda, frothing lightly around the bottle's neck.

Unable to restrain my curiosity, I unscrew the metal cap and bring the bottle to my lips.

Pampa regla tastes as bad as you'd expect. First comes a flavor wave of wet compost – like the liquid runoff from a fermenting batch of grass and pig bones. Then comes a jolting bitterness. My tongue feels like it's coated in wet chalk.

Elsa chortles, sputtering out something in Tagalog that gets Rica laughing too. 'Oh no!' Rica says. 'She says you're going to start menstruating.'

'It certainly tastes bad enough,' I say. 'Does it actually work?'

Yes, Elsa says. But there are caveats. It must be consumed within the first eight weeks of pregnancy. Dally too long after that, she says, and the potion may disfigure the fetus without killing it.

'I've had clients who've taken this too late. They'll have children with physical defects. Club feet. Or the heart is very weak,' Elsa says. 'So if you really don't want a baby, drink this stuff right after you have unprotected contact with a guy.'

And what about women in their second trimester? Ever the entrepreneur, Elsa has just the thing. She digs inside her shorts pockets and retrieves a metallic sleeve of medicine. I take it from her hand and inspect it closely. The foil reads 'CYTOTEC' in block letters next to the logo of its manufacturer: Pfizer.

I jab my finger into the blister pack and pull out a hexagonal white pill.

'Ulcer medication,' Elsa says. 'At least that's what you're supposed to use it for. But if you take a bunch of these, your pregnancy will terminate. Even if it's far along.'

Over the last decade, Elsa says, this Cytotec stuff has sent shock waves through the underground abortion trade. Desperate women skulk around the Black Nazarene church, asking for the drug by name.

Dealing Cytotec is a heavier crime than selling *pampa regla* herbs. Like the opiate Oxycodone or the methamphetamine Desoxyn, the pills are illegal to sell in the Philippines without a prescription.

The drug brings bigger risks for dealers, Elsa says, but it's easier to conceal and much more profitable. 'Now everyone around the church is selling Cytotec,' she says, sounding aggrieved. 'The girls selling flowers. The candle stalls. Even the tables selling rosaries. It's all a front for Cytotec!'

What a pity, Elsa says. The herbalists take pride in doling out counsel to scared women along with their illicit flora. They belong to a deeper tradition of folk medicine – an ancient sect of *hilots* and *albularyo* and other mystic healers native to the Philippine isles.

It was bad enough that Spain's Catholic empire tried to snuff out their indigenous knowledge, labeling it 'heresy'. Now their role is further eroded by some pill mass-produced by an American firm.

Still, the herbalists have to give customers what they want. Dealers buy the pills for $1.50 per tablet through a 'big boss lady' – a pharmacist, Elsa says, who imports via Pakistan.

'Is she tough?' I ask. 'Like a mafia figure?'

'No,' Elsa says, laughing. 'She's boring. Like a businesswoman.'

The herbalists try to sling the pills for $5 a pop. Customers often buy at least eight. That's a tidy profit of $28: three times Manila's daily minimum wage in one three-minute transaction. On a good day, dealers can rack up more than $100.

But there are operational costs too. The sellers are routinely shaken down by a rotating cast of cops. Elsa says there are three different departments within the local precinct that randomly squeeze them for $2 here, $3 there.

'They'll send over their plainclothes "strikers" [a term for police grunts dispatched to collect bribes] several times per week. The bribe price is always going up and up. But you have to pay. That's the only way to do your job without fear of arrest.'

Shaking down vendors outside the Black Nazarene might be a million-dollar business. The market contains an estimated 1,000 vendors. A single dodgy cop fleecing the sellers can conceivably rack up $200,000 per year – nearly 70 times the average Filipino's annual income.

Those figures aren't from Elsa. They come from a police captain who spoke to GMA News, one of the Philippines' largest media companies, back in 2009. I ask Elsa to verify the $1-per-day bribe prices cited by the captain. 'That's no longer accurate,' she says. 'It's gone up to $2.'

'Elsa, I have to ask you something,' I say. 'This is a Catholic nation. People may say you're a murderer ...'

She cuts me off with a squawky laugh. 'No way,' she says, 'I'm giving women their future back.'

She's heard it all before. Elsa has a local reputation. 'I'm vocal. I'm actually a front liner at the reproductive health rallies, arguing for our place in society. We have a right to sell herbs that help people.'

'But you're also a lawbreaker,' I say. 'Shouldn't you be more cautious?'

'I don't care. My bribes are paid up. No one's going to shut me down.'

'You know,' she says, 'I've had pro-life people come around. Talking about, "Where's that lady who kills babies?" Well, I'm right here. I say to them, "Don't come near me. I'm in a bad mood. I haven't killed anyone today."'

'Me? Killing?' Elsa cackles. How ironic. Her moralizing critics, she says, are often the same people who cheer on Duterte's murderous drug war. They support this purge even as it grows more chaotic, providing cover for all sorts of murderous score settling, its crosshairs threatening to widen until anyone at odds with the state can be killed without recourse.

'Now that's real killing. Killing parents. Creating a whole nation of orphans. It's in our psyche now – a joke almost. Kids running around shouting, "Look, I'm Duterte! Kill, kill, kill!"'

)(

If you really want to terminate your pregnancy, you should skip the potions and the folk medicine. Take the Cytotec instead.

This advice to Filipinas comes from Rebecca Gomperts, one of the world's best-known abortion doctors. I've called her office in the Netherlands to help cross-check some of Elsa's practices with established science.

That little white pill that emerged from Elsa's bag of illicit herbs is not nearly as dodgy as I first thought. Within five minutes, Gomperts has convinced me that it's a miracle drug – a medical breakthrough on a par with the birth control pill.

That drug, she says, has 'revolutionized women's right to abortion'. Just consider the old alternatives: knitting needles or violently pounding the abdomen.

The word 'Cytotec' is a brand name created by Pfizer. The drug's active ingredient is called misoprostol. It was first registered in the late 1980s as a gastrointestinal medicine that reduces stomach acid. But it turns out that misoprostol also causes a woman's womb to contract – so much so that, under high enough doses, it will reject a fetus.

'That's a miscarriage,' Gomperts says. 'And women don't die of miscarriages.'

'Is it dangerous in any way?' I ask.

'Well, let me put this into perspective. The risk of a fatal event is less than one in half a million. Yet roughly one in 20,000 men have a fatal event from taking Viagra.'

Misoprostol is actually safer than penicillin.[13] Going by US infant mortality stats, it's actually five times safer than giving birth in an American hospital.[14]

'Yet here in the Philippines,' I say, 'it's sold on the street like heroin.'

'It's sold that way in quite a few countries,' Gomperts says. 'It has nothing to do with proper health care.' Criminalizing misoprostol, she says, is a common government tactic to 'control women' and limit their reproductive freedom.

In America, misoprostol is doled out at Planned Parenthood clinics. It's also widely used in Europe, India and China. But in many religiously conservative nations – from Brazil to Ireland to Poland – its use as an abortion pill is strictly banned.

Governments that forbid abortion have good reason to hate misoprostol.

The pills really work.

Even the World Health Organization (or WHO) recommends their usage, citing studies that indicate roughly 75 to 90 per cent of abortion-through-misoprostol attempts are successful.[15] The WHO actually publishes a simple step-by-step guide for women who want to use the drug without a doctor's supervision.

The instructions are simple. If you're a woman with a pregnancy younger than twelve weeks, you put 800 milligrams (usually about three pills) under your tongue and wait three hours. Then pop another 800 milligrams under your tongue and, again, wait three hours.

Take a final 800-milligram dose and then prepare for your womb to expunge the embryo. That's it. For pregnancies beyond 84 days, cut the dosage in half but add two more rounds, each spaced out by three hours. Combine that regimen with another drug – mifepristone, also known as RU-486 – and the success rate shoots up to 98 per cent.

It's so easy, Gomperts says, that women can be guided to medically abort their own pregnancies over the phone. Her organization, Women on Web, does just that – in English, Arabic, Spanish, French and Tagalog.

Of course, women must first get their hands on the pills. This is where Gomperts' rebel ethos kicks in. She urges women to acquire misoprostol by any means necessary.

Don't like the law? Break it, she says.

This is the reason Gomperts is hated in pro-life circles and called a 'pro-choice extremist' by *The New York Times*. She is an unrepentant lawbreaker who earned her dissident bona fides through a series of rogue naval missions.

Since 2001, Gomperts and her team have sailed to seven nations that restrict abortion, with the goal of collecting pregnant women on shore, piloting them into international waters and performing abortions at sea.

Gomperts and her acolytes have been blockaded by warships in Portugal, waylaid by dockside army platoons in Guatemala and confronted by furious mobs in Morocco. She is undeterred – and currently experimenting with smuggling misoprostol across borders via drone.

'What about women in the Philippines?' I ask. 'How should they get Cytotec?'

Place an illegal order through an online distributor that uses discreet packaging, she says. Or try to fake a doctor's prescription. Her organization even advises women on forging hospital paperwork.

Get creative, she says. Find a male conspirator who'll fake stomach ulcers and get a legit prescription. 'Or find a veterinarian who'll help you out,' Gomperts says. 'Misoprostol is also used on pregnant dogs.'

And if that fails? Just find a dealer, she says.

'Honestly, I'm grateful for the underground market in the Philippines,' Gomperts says. 'I know how risky it is for them to sell this. But it's important for sellers to know the proper protocol.'

Many don't, however. Elsa, for example, will tell a pregnant woman to put four Cytotec pills in her vagina and just wait. That's subpar advice, to say the least. Worse yet, Elsa and other dealers also peddle counterfeit pills, which can be purchased on the cheap for bigger profit margins.

To thwart the counterfeiters, Gomperts has attempted to line up online sellers who can mail legitimate Cytotec to the Philippines. 'But the officials catch on quickly,' she says. 'They're getting pretty good at stopping those packages.'

'You don't sound too optimistic about reproductive care in the Philippines,' I say.

'I have no reason to feel optimistic.'

'Well, if women in the Philippines can't get Cytotec,' I say, 'should they find some herbs on the black market?'

'No, I would never recommend that to anyone,' Gomperts says. 'My work is based on science. And there is no scientific research showing that any of that herbal stuff is safe or effective. They should stay away.'

※

It's a Tuesday evening in Manila's outskirts. Rica and I have come to a stretch of strip malls and gas stations, their bright signage glowing against the dusk. The freeways are all hopelessly clogged. The night air is saturated in exhaust fumes and terrorized by mosquitoes.

Rica has brought me to the parking lot of a *Roy Rogers* burger joint. We're here to meet a woman named Karen.

Karen, Rica tells me, wanted to meet somewhere nondescript. She's been living on the run, and it shows. She walks up to our car in a frayed T-shirt with her ponytail unkempt, looking wan and underslept. Once we get past introductions, I ask her where she's staying these days.

'Here and there,' she says. 'I've got police trouble. It's a long story.'

And not exactly the story we've come to hear. Rica has

specifically summoned Karen to talk about her travails in the abortion black market. I've been eager to hear more about underground health care from someone who has actually consumed that bitter *pampa regla* brew and experienced the after-effects.

Karen is nearly 40. Raised in a family of fishmongers, she now scrapes by on about $5 per day. These are the proceeds from selling rice porridge on a rough block in Manila. For the past decade, this has been her most consistent job.

Karen was first swept into the abortion underground about seven years ago. At the time, she was in her early thirties and already facing her fourth pregnancy. She was, and is, married to a man who forbids her from using birth control pills.

'He says it's unnatural,' Karen says. Never mind the fact that her husband spends his days in a crystal meth fugue, manically bouncing around the neighborhood or sleeping off benders on the floor. 'There is no love between us,' she says. 'He treats me like a beer house girl.'

'A beer house girl?' I turn to Rica for clarification.

'Yeah, you know,' Rica says. 'A female servant. Like a concubine.'

Karen says she was raised to believe 'all children are blessings from the creator.' But when that fourth pregnancy came, the thought of those cells coalescing in her womb left her petrified.

After her third birth, doctors told Karen her uterine walls were dangerously thin and could rupture if she bore another child. On top of that, the pregnancy made her fear starvation – nor for herself, but for her young kids.

Her porridge stall could barely provide for three children. It definitely couldn't feed four. Not with her gambling-crazed, speed-smoking husband draining what little cash they tried to save.

This pregnancy wasn't just a burden. It was an existential threat. It had to go. Her aunt recommended she visit an *albularyo* working out of a plain-looking house in Quiapo, not far from the Black Nazarene's basilica.

Rica's go-to translation for *albularyo* is 'witch doctor'. But the woman who greeted Karen at the door could have passed for a middle school teacher: effusively smiley, roughly five feet tall, wearing culottes.

'She seemed really kind,' Karen says. The *albularyo* was so disarming that Karen didn't flinch when the woman led her into a tiny bedroom, ordered her to strip naked and had her lie belly-down on a mattress. 'She started tapping all over my back and on my butt,' Karen says. Then she felt the *albularyo* probing her insides with her fingers.

This amateur gynecology session went on for some time. 'It was like she was trying to pull something out,' Karen says. Finally the *albularyo* gave up. 'She was like, "You say you're three months along but I can't find it. We're going to have to do the *tawas*."'

'Tawas' is a chunk of potassium alum – a see-through crystalline substance that, when heated, liquefies quickly. 'Doing the *tawas*' involves heating this lump and letting it drip into a basin of water. This creates shimmery shapes on the water's surface that can be scrutinized like Rorschach blots.

For centuries, Filipino occultists have examined these floating blobs to discern the fates of nervous customers. A layperson might look in the basin and see an amorphous mess. But an *albularyo* will see magic dwarves, tree spirits or other creatures offering glimpses of the future.

The *albularyo*'s ritual would go down in a dedicated altar room – a chamber lined with doll-sized Catholic effigies. 'I saw so many saints in there,' Karen says. 'Santo Niño. Mother Mary. Three different Jesuses.' All of them were clad in fine robes.

The *albularyo* went all-out for the *tawas*. She lit a handful of leaves on fire, filling the room with gray smoke. She sniffed at the embers. She pawed at Karen's palms, seeming mesmerized by the lines. 'This woman had visible goosebumps,' Karen says. 'She was truly excited.'

The floating *tawas* blob, the scent of the smoke, the map of creases on Karen's hands –according to the *albularyo*, they all pointed to one conclusion. This pregnancy, if carried to term, would bring great fortune. The *albularyo* advised her to keep the baby.

'I was like, "Seriously?"' Karen says. '"No. I came here for an abortion."'

Have it your way, the *albularyo* said. The woman rummaged around in a back room, emerging with a bag filled with plants: *makabuhay*, mahogany seeds and the skin of a little grape-like fruit known as *lanzones*.

Karen was instructed to brew this stuff into a tea, drink it three times per day, and wash it down with RC Cola. On top of that, she was told to intermittently insert a few Cytotec pills in her vagina – just in case the tea proved ineffective.

Over the next few weeks, Karen drank this foul tea by the liter. 'It was so bitter,' she says, nearly retching at the memory.

'How did you get that awful taste out of your mouth?'

'Chocolate,' Karen says. 'I sucked on little pieces of chocolate.'

Weeks passed. Still no miscarriage. Panicked, Karen

guzzled more tea and sent her aunt out to score more Cytotec, taking one or two at a time vaginally – a regimen out of sync with medical guidelines.

'Even though I wanted a miscarriage, I was also terrified that I would bleed too much and have to report to the hospital,' Karen says. 'I thought they might run some tests down there. Something to prove I'd been using Cytotec. Then they could throw me in prison.'

The bleeding never came. Her worries about prison were soon replaced by a new fear. She imagined herself giving birth to a tiny, malformed child. 'I had been taking so much bad stuff,' she says. 'I thought I might have a blind baby or one with no teeth. Like those irregularities you see on television.'

One night, in her sixth month, Karen had a morbid vision. It came to her in a nightmare.

In normal conversation, Karen tends to speak with a rapid intensity, her thoughts careening from subject to subject. But in recalling this vision, she becomes even more difficult to follow.

In this dream state, Karen found herself wading into a sea of corpses. Then she was visited by the spirit of Senator Aquino's wife, Corazón, who served as president during Karen's childhood. 'Then came Papa Jesus, a great sacred-heart Jesus, who told me that I faced great disaster if I didn't repent.'

Karen woke up in a wild fever, as if possessed, and began scribbling out a message. 'I wrote down all of my troubles in great detail,' Karen says. 'I said, "Please God, save me, save us, save everyone who can be saved!"'

Now she was transfixed by a sense of mission. She knew what must come next. The annual march of the Black

Nazarene figure was nigh. She would plunge her pregnant body into the swarm of fanatics and deliver this note directly to Christ – or at least his earthly proxy, the one carved from Mexican timber.

'I couldn't stop talking about it,' Karen says. 'My family was like, "Just watch it on TV! You're pregnant! You'll never get close to it anyway."'

They were wrong.

The year was 2011. Karen, bulbous belly and all, managed to squirm through a crowd of more than 5 million marchers. She arrived barefoot, as all are instructed to do. Eventually she came within sight of the pedestal upon which Christ stood. He rode atop a gilded platform carried on the devotees' shoulders.

With all her strength, her body slick with sweat, she fought and pushed to get closer. And then suddenly she was airborne, lifted into the sky by fellow fanatics so that she could grasp at the Black Nazarene.

In those fleeting seconds, Karen managed to fulfill her mission. She crammed that handwritten note down the back of Christ's burgundy robes.

Karen felt herself start to descend, her bare feet returning to the asphalt. 'And then, for a moment, everything disappeared. The crowd vanished. Just for a second, there was no one there but me. I was in a trance, transported far away.'

'What happened next?'

'My consciousness returned to me,' she says. 'So I left.'

Karen returned home, back to her shabby apartment, back to her little porridge stall and her awful husband. She spent the next three months in misery, bracing herself to birth a child disfigured by her own sins.

※

Karen's moral landscape has been shaped by people who are utterly unlike her. Her Catholic faith is rooted in the diktats of long-dead theologians and saints. Most were male and European. The small ranks of women who've added to the Catholic canon generally never had sex, got married or raised children.

According to the Vatican, terminating an embryo smaller than a poppy seed is the same as murdering a toddler. It is an 'abominable crime' that 'cries out to heaven for vengeance'.[16] Anyone who receives an abortion needn't wait for a priest to banish them from the flock: God already knows. He excommunicates you on the spot.

This hatred for abortion goes way back to the days of tunics and gladiators. Not even one century after the death of Christ, a founding catechism known as the Didache stated: 'You shall not practice magic. You shall not use potions. You shall not procure an abortion.'

Yes, potions. As it turns out, Karen belongs to a long tradition of pregnant Christians drinking unholy elixirs.

Here's Marcus Minucius Felix, an early Roman Christian, writing in the first or second century: 'There are some (pagan) women who, by drinking medical preparations, extinguish the source of the future man in their very bowels … These things assuredly come down from the teachings of false gods.'

And here's Saint Jerome, writing circa AD 390: 'Some [women] go so far as to take potions that they may ensure barrenness … some, when they find themselves with child through their sin, use drugs to procure abortion.'[17]

In his next breath, Jerome rants about women who don

'cheap slippers', loosen their headscarves 'so as to leave the hair free' and wear tight shirt sleeves while 'drenching themselves in wine'.

The list goes on. Hippolytus, Basil the Great, the Council of Ancyra – all were early Christians subsumed by moral panic over herbal abortion. These were the men who installed the cornerstones of Catholic law, the same canon which now guides the modern-day Philippines.

I'll return to Karen's story in a bit. But first I want to trace the currents of history that sent this ideology, scratched into Mediterranean tablets, into a tropical Asian archipelago 10,000 kilometers from Rome.

Against the odds, these Catholic codes have reverberated through time and space to label women like Karen as wicked criminals.

※

The Philippines is named after a pink-skinned, blue-eyed guy named Philip who never set foot on the islands.

Philip II regarded the archipelago's inhabitants as inferior beings. Actually, he viewed most human beings as inferior – he was a Spanish king, after all – but the so-called 'natives' were especially depraved in his eyes. He saw them as primitive and ignorant of the world. Worst of all, they weren't even Catholic.

Many of these islanders actually knew a good deal about the world. Especially the Tagalogs, whose name means 'people by the river'. Their civilization converged around the mighty Pasig, the same river that now flows past the Black Nazarene church and snakes through the city of Manila.

Back in the year 900, when the land now called Spain was

known as Al-Andalus and was ruled by a Muslim emirate, the Tagalogs were busy building a kingdom. They called it Tondo. As the centuries unfolded, the people of Tondo engineered sophisticated sailboats, traded in gold ingots and kept records in their own indigenous script.[18]

More merchants than warriors, the Tagalogs of Tondo extended tendrils of trade to Japan, Siam and the Indian subcontinent. Their biggest mercantile alliance, however, was with the Ming dynasty in modern-day China. Tondo was the archipelago's exclusive importer of Chinese goods: tea, porcelain, silk and jade – all sold at a markup to smaller settlements in the nearby islands.

'Kingdom' isn't the best word for the Tondo civilization. That implies a sovereign lording it over subjects from a gilded throne. The Tagalogs (and their neighbors to the south, the Visayans) lived in a much looser confederation of mini-societies. It was organized enough to support specialists such as blacksmiths or sailors. But its people did not suffer under a European-style feudal order.

Nor did the Tagalogs expect women to be impossibly chaste. Sex before marriage? Whatever. Divorce? Fine.[19] In Tagalog and Visayan societies, religion did not suffocate women. It elevated them.

Each tribal unit would anoint a post-menopausal female to serve as its shaman. Her roles included advising the chief, sanctifying weddings and funerals and administering herb-based health care. She might also lead wild, drunken ceremonies, getting sloshed on ceremonial wine and decorating guys' faces in pig's blood.

These priestesses, known in Tagalog as *babaylan*, were considered guardians of ancestral wisdom. They were the human gateway through which everyday farmers, fisher-men and sailors could access the spirit realm or receive herbal healing. To purge a Tagalog village of its *babaylan* was to rub out its very soul.

So that's exactly what the Spanish tried to do.

✕

The first six weeks of Spanish occupation didn't go so well. Not for the invaders, at least.

It began on 16 March 1521. That's the day the explorer Ferdinand Magellan and his 235-man crew sighted a moun-tain rising from an island in Visayan territory.

When they realized the isles were inhabited, Magellan ini-tiated the usual colonial protocol: brandish guns, demand food and intimidate the nearest chief into swearing loyalty to Jesus. The first groupings of people he bullied didn't strongly resist Magellan – even as he barged ashore and ordered them to burn their idols. He even got away with changing one local chieftain's name from 'Humabon' to 'Carlos'.

Magellan's men had come upon a society that, by the Spaniards' own admission, was rather lovely. One of the crewmen was an Italian scholar named Antonio Pigafetta. In his journal, he described people with painted faces living in stilted bamboo homes, munching grilled pork and snack-ing on turtle eggs.

'These people live in justice,' he wrote, 'having weights and measures, and loving peace and are people who love ease and pleasure.' The women were all topless, Pigafetta wrote, 'and very beautiful and almost as white and tall as ours … having long, black hair and a small veil round their heads.'[20]

The conquerors even had time to take in a *babaylan* ritual that centered around a live pig. Pigafetta describes a joyous frenzy with blasting bamboo trumpets. It was led by an intoxicated priestess whirling about with a lit torch in her mouth. He watched the *babaylan* spear the pig's heart, dab its blood on all the men present (excluding the Spanish crew) and order her followers to roast it for the village.

The women ate first. The men told Pigafetta that this was standard. Pointing to their 'shameful parts', as Pigafetta put it, they also revealed another practice. Women, they said, generally refused to have sex with guys without decorative penis piercings. 'And those people do this,' Pigafetta added, 'because they are of a very weak nature and constitution.'

Some of the neighboring tribal units weren't so keen to party with Team Magellan. Particularly after he tried to terrorize the locals with a cannons-roaring show of force launched from his armada. One nearby chief, Lapu Lapu, became fed up.

When Magellan ordered Lapu Lapu to submit to Spanish rule, the chief led 1,500 warriors in a beach assault – overwhelming the Spanish with metal swords and flying iron-tipped spears.

'They charged down upon us with ear-shattering loud cries … so many [spears] rained down that the captain was shot through the right leg with a poisoned arrow,' Pigafetta wrote. 'The mortars in the boats could not aid us as they were too far away.'

Magellan's men scrambled towards their floating ships. The great navigator himself didn't make it. He was butchered on the white-sand beach by tatted-up guys with bamboo staves and pierced dicks.

Pigafetta and the others sailed off in defeat and eventually completed Magellan's mission: fleeing westward, rounding the southern tip of Africa and returning to Europe.

Though Lapu Lapu didn't know it at the time, he'd become the first recorded Asian to ever defeat Western invaders in battle. But the islanders would find that the next waves of strange-looking, armor-plated boatmen were not so easy to repel.

)((

In the late 16th century, after exploratory missions confirmed the islands were even more vast than Magellan imagined, Philip II began lobbing droves of conquistadors at the Tagalogs and the Visayans. Just as his empire had crushed the Aztecs and Incas, he hoped to seize this new chain of islands in the Pacific – establishing a Spanish foothold in Asia.

One by one, the islanders were overrun. The loose nature of their freewheeling societies was their undoing. They never managed to unite in concerted resistance. The Spanish also lost fighters but ultimately prevailed through superior organizational skills and weaponry.

Fresh from conquering American societies, the Spanish now had valuable experience in subjugating so-called Indians. Philip II told his most loyal military officers to install the same 'encomienda' system in the Philippines that had proven so brutally effective in New Spain.

The encomienda method is classic cutthroat colonialism: seizing land and forcing the locals to pay obscene amounts of tribute. The newly-christened 'Filipinos' (derivative of the king's Spanish-language title: Felipe II de España) were told to cough up gold, fabric, fruit, fish, pigs and slaves.

Spain soon established Manila as its capital in the Orient. The conquistadors reconfigured Tondo's ancient trading routes for their own ends. This supply chain would now inhale Oriental treasures by the ton and ship them back to the European motherland.

Using Filipino slavery, the Spaniards constructed massive new galleons, each built from thousands of trees. They were loaded up with Ming dynasty porcelain, ivory and silk and sent across the Pacific towards New Spain, specifically to Acapulco in modern-day Mexico. From there, this Asian exotica was lugged overland and sailed to Spain proper.[21]

These galleons would return to Manila loaded up with the Ming dynasty's preferred currency: silver. Much of it was mined in Mexico by other victims of Spain's rapacious empire: African slaves and indigenous serfs.

Also sailing westward to the Philippines was an army of friars.

Philip II was a burn-heathens-at-the-stakes sort of Catholic. As his empire expanded, he declared that, rather than let his new subjects worship as they pleased, 'I would lose all my states and a hundred lives, if I had them – for I do not propose nor desire to be the ruler of heretics.'

In the king's view, the Philippines was absolutely crawling with heretics. He bestowed these lands to his loyal officers with a major caveat. 'Take these islands,' he said, 'so that you may use and profit by them in your estates and commerce – provided that you indoctrinate [the indigenous people] and teach them in the things of our holy Catholic faith.'

Religious conversion drives can take many forms. Consider the subtle approach taken by the first missionaries to reach Myanmar's highlands, who arrived in the 1800s.

They came in with no weapons, studiously learning their targeted population's language and culture – all in the hope of gradually undermining native beliefs.

But the conquistadors of the Philippines favored a more ancient and brutish means of expanding their faith. Backed by musketeers, friars filtered throughout the islands to convert baffled Tagalogs and Visayans at sword-point. They also forced the islanders to fall in line with Catholic decorum. No more bare breasts. No more ornamental penis studs.

The *babaylan* tradition was swiftly criminalized. Female shamanists were told to mute their sensuality and start officiating somber Christian rites instead. Since invoking animist spirits was now forbidden, they had to adapt their rituals and call instead upon the powers of Catholic saints.

Many priestesses cooperated. But their identity was transformed and their political power was drained away. All of their ceremonies were made palatable to the church.

The diluted Catholic-style *babaylans* were now given a Spanish-language title: *albularyo*. This is derived from *herbalario* or simply 'herbalist', a title that strips away the suggestion of spiritual power.

Those sanitized shamanists still exist, carrying on occult rituals and dealing herbal concoctions to women. But despite being tolerated, they are still viewed with suspicion by the church hierarchy.

Today's Catholic priests would prefer that Filipinos stop looking for answers in *tawas* blobs and stroke their rosary beads instead. They are particularly disdainful of *pampa regla*, that witchy brew for women who can't resist temptations of the flesh.

If Elsa the dealer had been born 600 years ago, I bet she

would've made an excellent *babaylan*. Instead, she's reduced to slinking around a bazaar, squabbling with pro-lifers and bribing cops to practice her trade.

Meanwhile, her fellow *albularyo* operate secretly in Quiapo's back rooms, tending to desperate Filipinas like Karen, administering roots, pills and prophesies in secrecy.

Over the course of four centuries, Spain created what we now know as the Philippines, forging together a single political entity from thousands of islands and hundreds of distinct tribes. In a historical treatise, Senator Aquino summed up this bloody endeavor succinctly:

'With the cross and the sword,' he wrote, 'Spain stamped out the native culture, commerce and government. The people's codes and laws, their weights and measures, their literature and even their alphabet were destroyed. There were, of course, periods in Spain's 377 years of domination when liberal governors ruled. But in the main, Spanish rule was oppressive.'

In the last years of the 19th century, the Spanish were driven out by a brash new empire-in-the-making: America. The US acquired the islands – along with Puerto Rico and Guam – after triumphing in the Spanish–American war.

The conflict had been waged in large part to force Spain's decrepit empire out of America's oceanic backyard in the Caribbean. But the US – having already conquered lands all the way to its own west coast, as well as further afield to Hawai'i and Alaska – was also excited to gobble up even more Pacific terrain.

After wearing them down in a series of naval battles, the US forced the Spanish in 1898 to relinquish Puerto Rico, Guam and the Philippines for a mere $20 million, roughly half a billion in today's dollars. As the 1900s dawned, American lands stretched deep into the Pacific: from the Californian shores all the way to the Philippines: its largest-ever colonial possession.

Many Filipinos had early hopes that the Americans would prove themselves to be liberators, rather than just a different breed of foreign master. Among those welcoming the US was an anti-colonial force called Katipunan – a band of machete-swinging, friar-hating guerillas who despised the Spanish crown.

In their manifestos, this militia channeled a popular hatred of the Spanish. They railed against racism and classism, asserting that 'a person's worth is not measured by his or her status in life, neither by the length of the nose nor the fairness of the skin. And certainly not by whether he is a priest, claiming to be the deputy of God.'[22]

These rebels also articulated a widespread dream that the US, that nation of freedom-loving king haters, would uplift the indigenous people and snuff out the remnants of royal theocracy. But they were badly mistaken.

More than 120,000 US soldiers flooded into the Philippines. Many viewed their mission here as an extension of the brutal 'Indian Wars' at home – a campaign to ethnically cleanse native populations from US-claimed land.

Filipinos resisting their new overlords were waterboarded – the first widespread use of this technique in American military history.[23] Most rebels were simply gunned down. One popular marching song went: '*Damn, Damn, Damn the*

Filipinos … underneath our starry flag, civilize 'em with a krag.' (A *krag* is a speed-loading rifle.)

The conflict ultimately killed more than 4,000 American troops and 20,000 Filipino combatants, as well as 200,000 civilians dying from violence, famine and disease.[24] As one US general known as 'Pecos Bill' described the war's aims: 'It may be necessary to kill half the Filipinos in order that the remaining half of the population may be advanced to a higher plane of life than their present semi-barbarous state affords.'

Once all the bodies were buried, the US began remaking the Philippines in its own image. Americans built schools, courts and roads to service a new English-speaking bureaucracy.

The cathedrals, however, were left intact. By the early 20th century, most Filipinos were devoutly Catholic. The faith provided a common touchstone for the many peoples scattered among the islands. American leaders knew better than to uproot the church. So they merely prodded the Vatican to flush out the Spanish friars and replace them with US and Filipino priests.

The US also created a proto-congress with limited power. Officials promised that, one day, 'our little brown brothers' would use this system to run their country directly.

'Brown brothers' was a pet name for Filipinos favored by the American colony's top administrator: a portly, walrus-mustachioed official named William Howard Taft. (He would later become president of the US.)

The reins of power would never be handed over, Taft said, until the Filipinos 'showed themselves fit for it'. To this end, he built up an elite circle of Filipino bureaucrats.

Practically all of them were drawn from an existing ethnic and social class known as the *Ilustrados*: wealthy mestizos, many with mixed Tagalog–Spanish blood. They were an educated and landed gentry – their name meaning 'enlightened ones' – previously treated as a higher tier of natives under the Spanish crown.[25]

America helped cultivate these aristocrats into a new oligarchy of lawmakers and business magnates. As promised, this circle of Filipinos started running the country after the Second World War in 1946, the year of Philippine independence.

And for the most part, *ilustrados* have run the Philippines ever since.

Then and now, much of the nation's wealth is controlled by a small set of dynastic families in Manila. The halls of power are seldom occupied by people with Tagalog names like Diwata or Bayani. Instead you'll more often find Spanish-descended men with names like Manuel or José.

For decades, these oligarchs have derived prestige from their junior partner status with the US. Their moral authority, meanwhile, comes from a vow to uphold the majesty of the church. Despite its bloody history in the Philippines, Catholicism retains great sway over citizens' hearts.

But these aristocrats seem to have an awfully hard time upholding some of Christianity's highest ideals – particularly those pesky scriptures on lifting up the poor.

Filipinos have suffered through a bad run of rotten *ilustrados*, none worse than the infamous US-backed dictator Ferdinand Marcos. Though he was overthrown in a street uprising in the mid-1980s, Marcos racked up so much plunderous debt that Filipino citizens' taxes are still paying it down. They probably won't settle the dead tyrant's tab until the mid-2020s.[26]

Add to that untold billions in waste and corruption that have been piled up by a wave of kleptocrats since. Under the reign of these aristocrats, Filipinos have known crumbling schools, sidewalks overflowing with homeless moms and dealers selling crystal meth in broad daylight.

Their disaffection runs deep. Even in the late 1960s, Aquino described his people as being 'sapped of confidence, hope and will'. Filipinos, he said, lived in a nation 'consecrated to democracy but run by an entrenched plutocracy', their neighborhoods reeling under a 'wave of crime which has converted the country into a land of terror in time of peace'.

This is a fair description of the Philippines today. So is it any great shock that the masses have now handed power to a profane provincial brawler – a man promising to send kleptocrats and drug pushers to the graveyard?

X

Duterte doesn't come off like an *ilustrado*. He prefers to call himself a *probinsyano*. Translation: 'hick'.

Unlike his predecessors, Duterte doesn't drape himself in embroidered satin, mount podiums and issue stale appeals to justice and prosperity. He wears cheap-looking plaid button-ups and brags about the time he murdered 'scumbags' with his Uzi.

'I used to do it personally', Duterte proclaimed in 2016 from his presidential podium. 'Just to show to the guys' – meaning police – 'that if I can do it, why can't you?'

This refers to his murder of three kidnapping-and-rape suspects in the late 1980s. They were supposedly pinned down by cops in Davao, the largest city in the unruly southern island of Mindanao. Duterte, then mayor of the city, says he rolled up to the scene and finished them off.

Mindanao, like many provincial isles in the Philippines, often delights in scoffing at orders from Manila. This is where Duterte rose to prominence as the pistol-shooting, karaoke-singing mayor of Davao – a leader preaching the virtues of killing criminals without trial. For decades, he and his family have run this patch of the Philippines like a little fiefdom.

Duterte implies that he's shot and stabbed others. 'I'd go around in Davao with a motorcycle, with a big bike, and I would just patrol the streets, looking for trouble,' the president said in 2016. 'I was really looking for a confrontation so I could kill.'

These admissions are not accidental slips. This is classic Duterte. He is pure, bloody machismo on rocket fuel, a vigilante president wearing beat-up shoes.

Is any head of state as consistently shocking as this man? He's called Obama a 'son of a whore' for condemning the meth war and failing to apologize for America's colonial atrocities. He tells Philippine troops that he'll always have their backs – even if they commit rape.

Civilians who murder meth addicts, he says, should receive presidential medals. And if human rights advocates complain about all this? They'll be shot dead too.

To corrupt elites, he offers this warning: 'If I cannot put you in jail, I will kill you.' Sure enough, since Duterte's election, a series of bureaucrats have been mysteriously gunned down. This includes a Manila tax official, his body dumped on the curb beside envelopes stuffed with $7,000 in cash.

Yet there is one institution that appears largely immune to Duterte's poisonous threats.

It's not that Duterte hasn't *tried* to subvert the Catholic Church. He's called it the 'most hypocritical institution' in the world.[27] He also threatens to expose the sinners within its ranks. This has already included the priest who, according to Duterte, molested him as a teenage boy. Given this and other church crimes, the president says he's eager to have a debate with priests about 'whether or not you are still relevant'.

'Do not think you are the moralizing agents of our society,' Duterte has said. 'You're all pageantry.' He's even spit venom at the Vatican, calling the Pope a 'son of a whore' – his favorite slur – just for jamming up Manila traffic on a papal visit.

Duterte, like Trump, is a distinct breed of politician: the anti-authoritarian authoritarian. He is forever railing against the established order while promising to avenge its failures with brute force. But this iconoclastic streak can cause Duterte to support policies that many of the milquetoast aristocrats of the Philippines have been too scared to adopt.

No other Philippine president, for example, has so openly stood up for gay rights. And when it comes to the church's draconian birth control agenda, Duterte's policies can sound more reasonable than the priests who label women on the pill 'murderers'.

Duterte mocks the Vatican-endorsed 'rhythm method', which requires pencilling in a woman's fertile days on a calendar and abstaining from sex during that period. 'It doesn't work,' he says. 'You can't rely on a calendar like that. What are we doing here – playing bingo?'[28]

Duterte has even issued an executive decree ordering his government to stock public clinics with contraceptive pills and implants. Millions of women, he says, 'remain unable to fully exercise their reproductive rights'. His policy is to see 'zero unmet need' for contraception in the Philippines.

And yet, on the ground, not much has changed. His order is being rendered null by the courts, which appear more sympathetic to the priesthood. On this issue at least, this death-dealing president has faced the limits of his swagger.

The church, while inconsistent in denouncing the president's meth war, is united in its stance on contraception. It's hard to underestimate the determination that priests bring to their war against contraceptive drugs. It is now their raison d'être, a cosmic struggle for the souls of the unborn and a political battle to assert Catholic power in the 21st century. They seem to feel that this issue, more than any other, is worth fighting for.

And as badly as most sexually active Filipinos want birth control, I suspect that many of them – even those who dig Duterte's bluster – take some comfort in watching their leader being tamed by the church. In this era of mad upheaval, Catholicism offers a ballast.

This is still a nation where half the population faithfully attends mass each week. Fewer than 1 per cent of Filipinos born Catholic have totally abandoned the church.[29] I don't detect a citizenry desperate to see priests crushed under their president's fist.

Yet the people also love Duterte. Polls indicate he has the backing of roughly eight in ten Filipinos. To an anxious population on crowded islands – suffering from cruelties both old and new – Duterte has presented a vision. It is a dark vision, of course, but it is easy to grasp. It is the same tantalizing narrative that has so effectively galvanized the Kachin into violent rebellion.

It tells people that their poverty, their subjugation, everything that makes them feel impotent – all of it can be traced back to the evils of methamphetamine. Eliminate those under its spell, both smokers and pushers, and you shall be liberated from chaos, poverty and woe.

It's a wildly effective pitch. I won't be surprised if it keeps spreading, perhaps westward to the Islamic isles of Indonesia – another island nation struggling with addiction, poverty and orthodox politics.

But in the Philippines, this strident new doctrine cannot blot out Catholic traditionalism. This is a faith that, in its better incarnations, still promises redemption and hope. Even those who defy the church – Elsa and Karen and Duterte himself – still regard themselves as devoted Catholics.

Duterte might want to reconsider that debate on whether the priesthood is 'still relevant'. The man has overseen 10,000 deaths and got away with it. But he still can't manage to put birth control pills in the purses of broke Filipinas.

The white-robed clergy and their devoted flock simply won't allow it.

※

I'm en route to meet Rita Linda Dayrit, the face of the Catholic lobby's anti-contraception crusade.

Rita is president of Pro-Life Philippines, one of the country's best-known Catholic pressure groups. But she claims this job is secondary to her role as matriarch to a large family, which she considers a much greater achievement.

'I have five children, three grandchildren. I've been

married for 35 years,' Rita says. Her husband is an executive at a beer distribution firm. Prim, genial and fiercely traditionalist, she is the living incarnate of the church's feminine ideal.

Rita suggests that we meet at an upmarket shopping mall near the Pasig River. This is a pocket of Manila I've never seen before. The sidewalks are scrubbed clean and dappled with shadows from palm trees, each planted in neat rows. The lanes are filled with stroller-pushing moms trailed by nannies – all of them watched over by uniformed guards with batons and pistols.

I find Rita waiting for me inside a Dean & DeLuca franchise. After we settle into some tea and fruit shakes, Rita gives herself a proper introduction.

'When I got married, my priest asked me, "Are you willing to bring up the children that God will bestow upon you through this marriage?"' she tells me. 'I was, of course. But many other Filipinos have forgotten what we are taught by the church. That life must be valued. That marriage is between a man and a woman. That all children are gifts.'

Rita radiates maternal concern. She pauses to ask, in a fretful tone, if I've had time for lunch today. Were she to reach across the table and adjust my collar – or lick her fingers and tame one of my cowlicks – I wouldn't flinch.

But frankly, Rita and I share little common ground. One of us believes prodigious fertility under marriage is a heavenly command. The other spent a decade living out of wedlock before getting married in 2017. My wife and I are godless and childless.

Still, I feel that easy rapport that often comes easily between Americans and Filipinos. Rita reminds me of a Filipina June Cleaver from *Leave it to Beaver*. She's a TV-ready

1950s throwback with a porcelain smile. This cheery spirit makes her grim worldview that much harder to swallow.

'I've been reading your web site,' I say. 'It's full of articles that compare birth control to genocide.'

'Well, yes,' Rita says. 'Truly, there is mass killing through contraception.'

'Help me understand this,' I say. 'A 19-year-old college student on the pill – she's a potential murderer?'

'It's difficult to imagine,' Rita says. 'But it's true.'

'But there are more than 500 million women on the pill,' I say. 'That could mean birth control is responsible for more killing than the Second World War.'

'And we lament the deaths of people from war,' Rita says. 'But as Catholics, we must also grieve for the deaths of the unborn. We lament that women's wombs, which are meant to safeguard our future generations, have become such an unsafe place. This is worse than a terror attack.'

What a dark notion – that human life is routinely extinguished in numbers exceeding the Holocaust, a daily churn of pharmaceutical mass murder.

Let me concede the obvious. I'm biased against this idea. I'm also generally skeptical of any religious institution that claims dominion over women's bodies. That said, I'd like to approach her argument in good faith.

This is, in short, the birth-control-is-murder rationale that Rita's Catholic lobby wants to enshrine in Philippine law.

The Vatican says that conception occurs when a sperm wriggles into an egg to create an embryo. From that 'first instant, the program is fixed as to what this living being will be: a man, this individual man, with his characteristic aspects already well determined. Right from fertilization is begun the adventure of human life.'[30]

That's scientifically accurate and artfully put.

Hormonal birth control pills (and injections) make it difficult for sperm to ever reach the egg. They thwart them in two ways. Firstly, their chemicals tell ovaries to stop releasing eggs altogether. Then they make the narrow channel through which sperm must swim all goopy.

Every so often, however, the chemicals fail, an egg is released anyway and it is found and fertilized by sperm. Just how easily this can happen while women are taking birth control pills is a matter of debate. But groups such as the American Association of Pro-Life Obstetricians and Gynecologists argue that it is not exceedingly rare.[31]

Still, for women on the pill, this is no huge deal. The pills have yet another defense against rogue embryos. Their chemicals turn the womb into an inhospitable landing pad. This prevents tiny embryos from sinking into the womb's walls to start growing into a fetus.

The embryos are just sloughed off instead.

But wait! Hadn't those embryos already begun the 'adventure of life'? Though microscopically tiny, each one has the biological coding that could determine a potential person's wit, beauty, capacity for joy – everything that makes a human unique.

Instead, the adventure of that embryo – nay, that human, says the church – ends with a flush down the cervical drain.

'You see, it just disintegrates,' Rita says, looking forlorn. 'That means you just killed your baby.'

Here's the thing: wombs of sexually active women who *aren't* on the pill naturally reject embryos too. It happens all the time.[32] But I don't want to dwell on that. I'm trying to see how a full embrace of the church's beliefs would stoke a burning urgency to banish contraception from the earth.

For the most part, I get it. Given that so many lives are believed to be at stake, Rita and the priesthood she serves feel that their request is modest. They just want the Supreme Court to prove beyond any doubt that birth control pills in no way contribute to the termination of embryos. After all, if these drugs really do kill embryos, wouldn't that violate the constitution's promise to protect the 'life of the unborn from conception'?

But that is an awfully tough bar to meet. Hormonal birth control isn't infallible. It ranges in effectiveness from 90 to 99 per cent – and that's just a measure of women who become pregnant while taking the pill. Surely the number of pill-taking women conceiving embryos that *don't* implant is even higher.

This is the spiritual conundrum that the Catholic lobby has deftly forced the Supreme Court to confront. If the judges turn heel, and offer citizens full access to birth control, they will be excoriated by priests. The war would not end there. Rita says 'we will find another way' if the judges defy them. After all, she says, millions of embryonic Filipino lives hang in the balance.

'But many Filipinos,' I say, 'would tell you the country is already burdened by too many people.'

'We disagree,' Rita says. 'Our population is a good thing. Filipinos are a gift to the world!'

'We have so much reproductive wealth,' she says. 'If Filipina mothers had no access to contraception, we would have 2 million additional kids. Now imagine they are educated, well fed. They would become the next doctors and engineers, paying taxes, spreading out into the world – flying out to all the places in the world that need our manpower.'

'But Rita,' I say, 'we're sitting here in a nice shopping mall. If we take a walk further into the city, we'll see women with babies sleeping in boxes.'

'It's true,' Rita says, wagging her head ruefully. 'We have failed to take care of farmers, the very people who feed us. So they bring their children into the city to beg. There are so many children. Dirty, hungry children everywhere.'

'But I believe,' Rita says, 'that the Philippines is a rich country pretending to be poor. I know we have money. If there was no money, what would the politicians steal?'

That trove of pilfered wealth, she says, must be recaptured from the corrupt politicians and splashed about the country-side – sprinkling new schools and hospitals among the meek.

How utopian. I find it difficult to weld this optimistic political dream to her more dystopian view of humanity. Namely that every Filipina on the pill – roughly 20 per cent of all married women – is a potential baby killer in defiance of the Lord.[33]

'In the meantime,' I say, 'what would you say to poor women who are terrified of having another child?'

'If you want to plan your family, we have a solution,' Rita says.

It is – you guessed it – the rhythm method.

This technique requires male partners to forego sex for roughly ten days per month. To the Philippine Catholic lobby, this is more than just a Pope-sanctioned family planning rit-ual. Rita describes it as a cure-all that can instill discipline across a disorderly nation.

'If you're on the pill, you're like 7-Eleven! You're open 24 hours a day,' Rita says, covering her laughter with her hand. 'We must teach our husbands to wait! This is training in patience, training in virtue. It teaches obedience. Men must learn to fall in line.'

The rhythm method could flourish, she says, if it weren't for the influence of America and its culture of instant gratification. 'Your TV ads say, "Just be who you are! Don't care what people think!" We are so influenced by your way of life.'

'You know, my generation of women had about four children,' Rita says. 'My children are just having two. And, well, I notice that in America, young couples are just getting dogs now.'

'Actually, dogs are too much responsibility,' I say. 'Many of us prefer cats.'

As Rita continues moralizing – lamenting the brashness of gay couples these days, speculating about a secret Western agenda to depopulate Asia and steal its resources – I slide a free hand in my backpack and start fishing around. It takes a minute but, finally, my fingers scrape against a foil sleeve I've hidden in a zippered compartment.

When she finishes her thought, I pull it out – the sleeve of Cytotec I copped from Elsa a few days ago. I place the packet next to Rita's drink.

'Do you know what this is?'

'I believe so,' she says. She's eyeing the pills cautiously, like I've just dropped a dead lizard on the table.

'I bought it near a church …'

'In Quiapo!' she interjects. 'Of course.'

'That's right,' I say. 'It's a strange place to buy an abortion pill.'

Rita rocks her head back in laughter. 'The look on your face!' she says. 'I suppose there are many things you will never understand about the Philippines.'

'I bought it from a dealer in her fifties,' I say. 'And I've met women who've taken this drug too. They're nice people. All of them say they're devoted Catholics – just like you.'

'They are victims of poverty, perhaps,' Rita says. 'Victims of corruption too. I'm sure the police profit from this business. That's how it goes around here.'

'So you have sympathy for them?'

'Yes,' Rita says. 'Ignorance brought them to a bad place.'

'How should they be punished?'

'Life in prison,' she says brusquely. 'Not the death penalty, of course. I respect life.'

'How about in the afterlife?' I ask. 'What awaits them there?'

Rita sighs, brushing back her hair, absorbing the question. 'He is a God of justice,' she says. 'Everyone must face the consequences of their acts.'

'Err, sorry, Rita. I'm not really sure what that means.'

'Well, I cannot judge them myself. But perhaps these women will spend time in purgatory – a place of purging and repentance,' Rita says. 'Much, much longer than I will. When I die, I will face my God knowing I have obeyed.'

※

For Karen, purgatory came early.

No, her soul isn't roasted by holy flames that, as the saints describe it, glow hot enough to melt gold. But she is reeling through a suffering state of in-betweenness, unmoored from the family life she fought so desperately to preserve.

Karen can no longer go home. She sleeps rough, on the floors of friends and relatives, in the spare rooms of churches that will have her. She slips from place to place like a fugitive. That's basically what she is – a woman hunted by the state, albeit a subterranean wing controlled by Duterte's police.

I'm getting ahead of myself. Let's rewind a bit.

Karen had the child. She named her Miracle, a fitting name for a daughter who, as a fetus, survived an onslaught of acrid herbs and misoprostol that could have snuffed out her existence.

Miracle is now six years old. She's super cute. Nothing indicates the little pig-tailed kindergartner suffered any lasting mental or physical impairments. According to her teacher, she's one of the brightest kids in class.

Perhaps Miracle was spared by Karen's erroneous use of abortion drugs. Maybe her soul was protected by the Black Nazarene. It doesn't matter now. She's here.

The child did not appear to bring the 'great fortune' promised by that *albularyo*. But the mere mention of Miracle's name zaps Karen out of her fatigued haze and restores the glow to her cheeks.

'She is my strength,' Karen tells me. 'Sometimes I can barely stand to look at her, knowing I have so little to give. No rice, no milk, no new clothes. But she is still my little Miracle.'

Karen has boundless, ferocious love for Miracle. Once born, she could not imagine a world in which the child was never conceived. Yet the fears that preyed on her mind during pregnancy – that a fourth child would usher in turmoil, shattering her already fractured home life – all came true.

After Miracle's birth, Karen's porridge stall income was stretched impossibly thin. When food for the children grew scarce, Karen skipped meals, depleting her body of strength. Soon enough, her breast milk ran dry. 'I had to put something in Miracle's bottle,' Karen says. 'All I could afford was instant coffee mix.'

'Wow,' I say. 'Did she ever sleep?'

'Funnily enough, yes. It wasn't much of a problem. We were always so tired.'

As the family's privation worsened, Karen's husband grew ever more useless, hoarding what little money he scrounged from odd jobs for gambling-and-speed sprees. He grew even more dull witted and remote – a tumorous appendage on an already sickly home.

Karen needed pesos. Bad. She started scrounging tire scraps, selling to refineries that melted them down into crude oil. But that didn't cut it either.

Screw it, she thought. I'll start selling meth.

From a neighborhood supplier, Karen would buy a couple grams for $60 and break the crystalline powder into sachets that she could sell for $5. On a good run, she could double her money. There was no shortage of customers.

'Did you ever use any yourself?' I ask.

'No, never. I was mostly selling to neighborhood steve-dores, guys who carry heavy stuff down by the docks,' Karen tells me. 'Normal guys with wives and kids. Not zombies, not addicts like my husband. Just people who do physical labor and need help getting through the day.'

In Karen's mind, meth was always a temporary hustle – a

regrettable foray into the underworld, justified by the sight of her four kids, bellies full of rice, heading off to school in their clean uniforms.

So when a gruff presidential contender named Duterte came along in 2016, promising to dump dealers' corpses in Manila Bay until the 'fish grow fat', Karen started looking for an exit out of the drug game.

Once elected, Duterte unleashed the wolves. Meth dealers began dying in droves. Police would, without fail, insist that the people they shot had attacked officers first. Practically no one bought this line, not even the drug war's supporters. But Duterte seemed to relish in the lawlessness, vowing to protect the cops from any charges of abuse.

Duterte proclaimed that this cleansing wave of death would spare the next generation from 'perdition'. That is a Catholic netherworld, described by saints with the subtlety of North Korean propaganda. As Saint John Eudes said in the 1700s: 'Get out of the filth of the horrible torrent of this world, the torrent of thorns that is whirling you into the abyss of eternal perdition.'

Duterte also invoked a more contemporary sort of hell: 'Hitler massacred 3 million Jews ... and there are 3 million drug addicts. I'd be happy to slaughter them all.'

Any previous American president, Republican or Democrat, probably would have condemned the Philippine massacre as an affront to human rights – a core US foreign policy ideal that has been promoted for decades.

Instead, this chilling pronouncement was followed by an endorsement from the White House. Trump, also newly elected, phoned Duterte to 'congratulate you because I am hearing of the unbelievable job on the drug problem. Many countries have the problem, we have the problem, but what a great job you are doing and I just wanted to call and tell you that.'[34]

The response from Duterte was: 'Thank you, Mr President. This is the scourge of my nation now and I have to do something to preserve the Filipino nation.' As Trump was praising the drug war, it had already piled up roughly 6,000 bodies – often literally, under bridges and in back alleys. Sometimes victims' heads were wrapped in packing tape like mummies.

Karen didn't want to die. Not like that.

The government appeared to offer a way out. Officials were calling on all users, traffickers and dealers to cease their lawbreaking and register with their local police department. Come surrender, officials said, and spare yourself from the purge. We'll take you off the kill list, maybe get you into rehab.

Karen cooperated. She joined more than a million Filipinos in signing papers admitting complicity in the drug trade.[35] Some were arrested, overfilling the prison system by 500 per cent. Others were told to simply go home.[36]

Then, in late 2016, Duterte appeared on television with a bulging sheaf of papers. 'This is it,' he growled. 'This is the drug industry in the Philippines.' The registry had been a trap.

The government wasn't erasing names from the kill list. It was expanding it. Duterte had tricked Filipinos into feeding themselves into the *tokhang* meat grinder.

'I thought, OK, you surrender and that means you won't be killed. I put faith in that,' Karen says. 'But it was just a way to get our names and addresses. The guys on motorbikes started showing up at the beginning of 2017.'

The assassins came in packs, helmets obscuring their faces. One day, neighbors spied some men lurking near a basketball court around dusk, asking about Karen's whereabouts. Fortuitously, they peeled off just before Karen arrived home from a shopping run.

On another evening, some guys tried to enter Karen's home while she was readying dinner. But they happened to barge in just minutes after she'd stepped out to grab more cooking fuel. Dumb luck had spared her life twice. It wouldn't protect her forever.

'I don't go home much anymore,' Karen says, rubbing her eyes. 'I just move around.'

'What about your husband?' I ask. 'Is he on the black list too?'

'No,' she says. 'He was too lazy to register. He's still getting high. My oldest kid is fourteen. She runs the house now.'

'How often do you see them?'

'Not often enough. I stop by at odd hours. But I can't stay long.'

Karen tells me that life is like a wheel. 'Sometimes you're riding on top,' she says, 'and sometimes you are spinning to the bottom.'

'When were you last on top?'

'Hard to say,' she says. 'Perhaps when I was a teenager.'

Karen is sure, however, that she's now as low as she's ever been. She has become a casualty of both drug wars: one ancient and insidious, the other new and explosive.

The first is waged by the same institution that turned her Tagalog ancestors into Filipinos – and now claims dominion over their wombs. In seeking to deny women the fruits of medical science, the priesthood slowly drove Karen into an abasing poverty, overloading her with children in a post-agricultural era that is inhospitable to large families.

This is a slow war of attrition, waged in courtrooms, clinics and the hearts of well-meaning Catholics. It makes villains of mothers like Karen. It is the force that drove her into the underworld.

And then there is the meth war, fought in flashes and bangs.

The president has fallen short of his original promise to create 100,000 corpses within his first six months in office.[37] But he need only double his current body count of 10,000 to match the number of Filipino fighters slain in the American colonial invasion.

I've been unsparing towards the church's crusade against contraception. So let me, at the same time, praise the Filipino priests who have railed against Duterte's purge. Listen to the words of a Manila-based archbishop named Socrates Villegas. In the summer of 2017, after cops killed an unarmed seventeen-year-old 'drug suspect' and dumped his body in a pigsty, he had this to say:

'Why are we no longer horrified by the sound of the gun and blood flowing on the sidewalks? The country is in chaos! The officer who kills is rewarded. And the slain get the blame.'

There is a common thread between the two drug wars. Both are ripping through the lives of the poor. Generally spared are the 21st-century *ilustrados*, whose children can get high without much consequence or fly abroad for abortions. Meanwhile, Karen, the child of wharf merchants, is spun violently towards the bottom of life's wheel. How much longer, I wonder, until she is flung off and crushed under its weight?

I ask Karen to tell me about her next steps. She ignores my question and veers into an unrelated soliloquy about her youngest daughter. Her eyes look skyward, chattering on as if to herself. I sense she is far away from Rica and me and all the other strangers loitering around this *Roy Rogers* parking lot.

'One time,' Karen says, 'the teacher at Miracle's school gave her some markers and paper. So she made a sign for me. It was like those placards people in the movies bring to the airport. You know, the ones they hold up for their loved ones when they arrive.'

'She tells me, "Mommy, one day you'll ride on a real airplane. I'm going to join a children's TV show and make some money. I'll pay for you to travel somewhere. Believe me, Mom!"'

Up until this point, Karen has recounted her life in a straightforward sort of way – remarkably so given all the talk of blood and drugs and panic and hunger. But now some sort of emotional wave has crested and collapsed behind her brown eyes. Her chest shudders and tears streak her face, soaking into the ragged collar of her T-shirt.

'My God, I cannot give her anything,' Karen says, head drooping, pinching the bridge of her nose. 'I just want to shield her from the world. Just to let her dream for a while longer.'

Rica shoots me a look that says we're done here.

'Come on, Karen,' Rica says, squeezing her wrist and lightly shaking her arm. 'Let's go have a cigarette.'

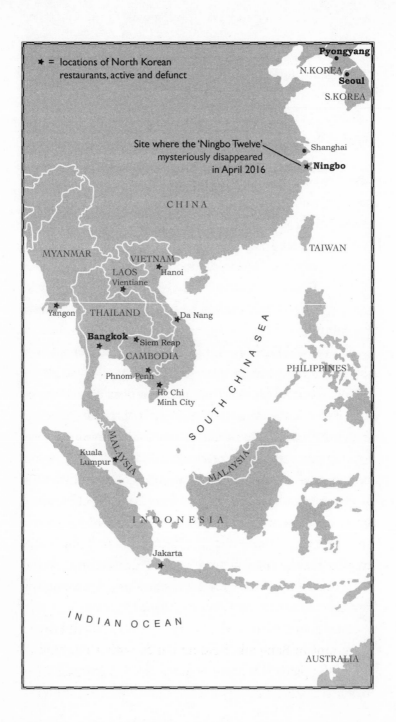

★ = locations of North Korean
restaurants, active and defunct

Pyongyang
N.KOREA
Seoul
S.KOREA

Site where the 'Ningbo Twelve'
mysteriously disappeared
in April 2016

Shanghai
★ Ningbo

CHINA

TAIWAN

MYANMAR
VIETNAM
LAOS   ★ Hanoi
Vientiane
★

Yangon
★   THAILAND   ★ Da Nang

Bangkok ★ Siem Reap
★
CAMBODIA

Phnom Penh
★ Ho Chi
Minh City

SOUTH CHINA SEA

PHILIPPINES

Kuala
Lumpur ★
MALAYSIA

MALAYSIA

INDONESIA

Jakarta
★

INDIAN OCEAN

AUSTRALIA

CHAPTER IV

Pyongyang's
Dancing Queens

Location: Bangkok, Thailand and Seoul, South Korea

Where customers pay to cavort with North Korea's regime-trained hostesses

H er fingers feel delicate in my grasp. Her palms are cool as porcelain. We are waltzing and, when she lifts my hand into the air, I pirouette sloppily.

My North Korean dance partner is a portrait of composure. Sadly, she is leading around an inebriated klutz. I'm flush with *soju*, my face splotched pink, feet scraping the floor.

I hadn't meant to get this sozzled. But the other waitresses, her colleagues, kept up-selling bottles of Pyongyang-manufactured rice wine. It's high-octane stuff, flavored with acorns, that torches your esophagus.

As we waltz or foxtrot or whatever we're doing – all I know is that she's playing the male lead, spinning me around like a debutante – I can feel the booze sloshing around my insides.

I am frankly astonished to be here, in a North Korean restaurant in Bangkok, holding hands with a representative of the planet's most anti-social regime. On past visits to North Korea's state-owned eateries – which are scattered from Myanmar to China to Vietnam – my interaction with staff has been terse.

Once seated, I'm inevitably asked: 'Where are you from, sir? Germany? Russia?' Some pointless sense of principle always compels me to tell the truth. I immediately out myself as an American, a citizen of the imperial United States, some Yankee dog whose cities, we are told, deserve nuclear immolation in a 'sea of fire'.

It's usually downhill from there. The waitresses' spines reflexively stiffen. Their lips curl downward ever so slightly. This is often the only spontaneous emotion I can coax from a North Korean waitress – a minor betrayal of her inner thoughts. They are otherwise perfectly composed.

But tonight, in the Pyongyang Arirang Restaurant in Bangkok, the waitresses don't seem fazed by the Yankee barbarians in their midst. It just so happens that I've brought along my father and his partner – on their first trip outside of North America – along with a large group of friends: a few Thais, one Bangladeshi and several other Yankee jackals.

Sequestered in a gated compound, this restaurant is quite small. Other than a few beer-buzzed Chinese guys, we're the only customers. I've actually never been to this particular North Korean joint. But before we arrived, I felt safe in promising my dad a spectacle of maximum kitsch.

As I explained to him earlier, you don't come to these restaurants for the overpriced bibimbap and noodle soup, which can be charitably described as mediocre.

The waitresses are the star attraction. After dishing out sizzling beef, they don spangly gowns and twirl about the dining hall, moving in perfect concert like a school of fish. Then they converge into rock bands – one on guitar, another on bass, a third on electronic drums – and jam out Western pop and rock 'n' roll.

You might hear the schmaltzy *Titanic* theme song. Or 'Ob-La-Di, Ob-La-Da' by The Beatles, sometimes punched up with an accordion solo.

They also do John Denver's 'Country Roads', sung in soaring operatic vocals. Once, in Yangon, I got to see North Koreans in cocktail dresses performing Frank Sinatra's 'My Way' on dueling flutes.

But in my half-dozen visits to various overseas North Korean restaurants, I've never witnessed any physical contact between the waitresses and the guests – and certainly not with any self-avowed Americans. Thus my shock when one of them glided over to my chair and beckoned me to dance.

It happened just moments ago. After the rock band disassembled, all of the waitresses vanished behind a curtain in back. There's a tiny stage at the front of the restaurant. For a moment, it was empty but for an assemblage of amps and drums and, inexplicably, two twinkling Christmas trees.

Then out came a woman in traditional Korean costume. She sashayed by herself for a bit. Then she seized my wrist and lifted me to my feet.

Now we are spinning around the room, her hand in mine. She sings beautifully as we whirl. With her left hand, she holds a wireless mic to her lips, crooning a Korean folk tune over a synthesized keyboard track.

The waitress is resplendent in her silky *hanbok*, a Korean dress that, from the waist, opens up and stretches down to the floor like a massive bell. It makes the wearer look like a human thimble. Hers is the color of pink peonies with floral vines stitched into its overflowing fabric.

We are grace and gracelessness intertwined. My beat-up Nikes are squeaking on the tile floor. Her footsteps are silent and unseen beneath her voluminous dress, its hem lightly caressing the ground. She appears to float above its polished surface.

Let me be perfectly clear: our impromptu coupling is about as sensual as a middle-school dance. As I spin clumsily, I can hear my dad guffawing. I can also feel the eyes of my friends' smartphone cameras upon us, collecting top-notch blackmail.

The North Koreans are recording us too, of course. The ceiling is studded with little orb-shaped cameras. There's one in each corner, scanning every vantage point, capturing every conversation and gesture. As with all North Korean restaurants, this joint is thoroughly bugged.

After a few more embarrassing spins, the waitress guides me back to our table and mercifully releases me into my seat. I notice that, during our dance, one of her colleagues has refilled my *soju* glass. I down it all in one go.

An upbeat synth track blares over the speakers and, when I look up from my glass, I can see that my dance partner has multiplied. No, it's not the alcohol. There really are three ladies standing there in identically pink *hanboks*, with identical bangs, and identical glittery heels.

Behind them, a screen lights up with idyllic scenes of the North Korean countryside: hulking mountain ranges and dazzling snow drifts, each image photoshopped to crisp perfection.

Vivid circles of color begin to flash upon the tile floor. They're beamed down from a bank of rotating disco lights mounted overhead. Now the women are yanking all of us from our seats – everyone from our table plus the three other Chinese diners.

We're being arranged into a conga line.

We grip one another's shoulders, snaking around the dining room. The waitresses are clutching mics, belting out a Korean anthem in warbling soprano. One performer has grabbed the left hand of Wesley Hsu – one of my American friends – and held it aloft to create an arch. Our conga line ducks to wind underneath their arms.

The waitresses' voices are melded in a flawless harmony. We can't understand a word of their singing. But everyone is tipsy and giddy and clomping their feet to the techno jam. It sounds like a stiff, martial version of 'The Final Countdown'. I'm half-expecting red confetti to flutter from their ceiling.

I glance up at the projector screen to see a funny-looking map of Asia. It's dominated by a glowing red nation that I don't immediately recognize.

Then it hits me. The nation is Korea, a fictional version where the two halves are married as one – all under the reign of the Kim clan. This imaginary country is depicted at an outsized scale. In reality, the Korean peninsula is just a bit larger than Florida. On this make-believe map, it looks as big as Brazil.

Block letters begin to flash underneath:

KOREA IS ONE!

KOREA IS ONE!

KOREA IS ONE!

That's my final lucid memory of the night.

I wake up the next day feeling like I've been dosed with acorn-flavored polonium. My phone has been bleeping all morning. It's now filled with highly regrettable photos, pinged over by my friends.

This causes me to reflect on all those cameras positioned overhead, gathering high-quality images for the state's surveillance apparatus. What a nice package last night's festivities could provide for the *Rodong Sinmun*, Pyongyang's premier propaganda outlet: AMERICANS REJOICE IN GLORIOUS SPLENDOR OF DPRK!

There's a slip of paper peeking from my wallet on the nightstand. I unfold it with dread. It's the bill. It seems that, in a gesture of drunken generosity, I charged the evening's entertainment ($262.40) to my Mastercard.

So now the Kim regime has my credit card number. Fantastic.

ᛒ

North Koreans.

Are there any other people on earth ridiculed by the West with such abandon?

Let's start with the Kim dynasty and its inner circle. In American pop culture, they're depicted as cartoonish villains on a par with Darth Vader. We're told by major news outlets that the ruling scion, Kim Jong-un, once fed his uncle to 120 starving dogs.[1] More cruelly still, he forces college kids to imitate his bouffant hairstyle.[2]

Oh, and did you hear about that time the government announced it discovered a lair of unicorns?[3] Or that human flesh is routinely served in North Korea's upcountry markets?[4]

Never mind that none of these stories are supported by good evidence. When it comes to North Korea, all skepticism is abandoned. There is seemingly no tale too diabolical to merit our disbelief.

The reclusive state is a boon for online tabloids. They're free to misinterpret events or regurgitate bad rumors, secure in the knowledge that their gossipy reports will go unchallenged. Pyongyang officials seldom bother to refute outlets such as the *Guardian*, let alone the *Huffington Post*. Who'd believe them anyway? They're North Koreans!

Most of these bogus North Korea stories swirl around the despotic Kim clan. Mocking one of the world's vicious dynasties is fine but not when the basic facts are misrepresented. This can only lead to bad policy.

That isn't what really bugs me though. I'm far more unnerved by our gleeful mockery of the North Korean people, those 25 million human beings who are unfortunate enough to live under what amounts to a sadistic monarchy.

This is how the late polemicist Christopher Hitchens famously described North Koreans in his caustic 2010 article 'A Nation of Racist Dwarfs':

'Unlike previous racist dictatorships, the North Korean one has actually succeeded in producing a sort of new species. Starving and stunted dwarves, living in the dark, kept in perpetual ignorance and fear, brainwashed into the hatred of others, regimented and coerced and inculcated with a death cult.'

This is the tone we often use when talking about North Koreans. They're a different species. Dangerously stupid. Possibly prone to cannibalism.

According to Hitchens, they're actually six inches shorter than their genetic siblings in prosperous South Korea.[5] Again, this isn't quite right. The actual height difference, according to proper studies of defectors, spans one to three inches.[6] But there's almost nothing we won't believe about North

Koreans. They are a people understood almost entirely through Hollywood parodies and viral online news stories.

For most people around the globe, the odds of ever meeting an actual North Korean are vanishingly small. Most are trapped in their home provinces, frozen in place by one of the planet's most oppressive states. Attempting escape risks years in a gulag.

Those who slip over the border usually get stuck in China where they must live in hiding. Only a thousand or so each year will make it to South Korea, where defectors are given cash, job training and a new life. It's a negligible number that ever makes it to America or Europe.

In any given year, only ten to twenty North Koreans are accepted as refugees in the US.[7] An American told to fear other 'rogue states' – such as Syria or Iran – might actually end up living near a family of Syrian or Iranian immigrants. The percentage of Americans who bump into North Koreans at the grocery store, however, is close to zero.

The result: North Koreans are, in the minds of Westerners, among the most exoticized people on earth. For many around the globe, encountering one of them is a truly novel and perhaps even sought-after experience.

Pyongyang, for its part, understands quite well that rarity breeds value. Its officials have figured out that curious foreigners will pay for proximity to the citizens they've so cruelly isolated. So they find nations willing to host regime-themed restaurants where tourists can indulge in a rare thrill: nights out with a cheery troupe of North Koreans.

There are now more than 100 of these eateries scattered around Asia. Most are in China. But the second-biggest market is Southeast Asia, a tourism magnet attracting

100 million annual visitors from around the world. There are now Pyongyang-run eateries across Cambodia, Vietnam, Myanmar, Indonesia, Laos and Thailand.

The female servers at these restaurants aren't just any North Koreans, mind you. Almost all of them are exported from the regime's artist class – an elite clique of singers, instrumentalists and dancers. Each has been trained from childhood to regale the Pyongyang upper class. They've been diverted from their official role – musically venerating the Kim regime – into tourist traps overseas.

As Professor Sung-Yoon Lee of Boston's Tufts University, a top expert on North Korea, tells me: 'They could be very competitive students at any leading conservatory in New York.'

'They're very talented, very pretty,' Lee says. 'But they aren't only selected based on looks. The regime also looks at the allegiance of their families. They must go through an intense selection process.'

In other words, the woman who slow-dances with gangly foreigners in Hanoi or Bangkok may be the daughter of a North Korean colonel. Her high-class lineage, however, does not guarantee a life of ease. These women work under conditions that, if replicated in London or Los Angeles, would land their employers in prison.

The singing waitresses don't report to work. They live at work. At each restaurant, they all bunk together in dorms, located above the dining hall or in rented buildings nearby.

Their movements are strictly controlled. Though posted near some of the world's top tourist sites – Bangkok's temples or the ruins of Angkor Wat – they are forbidden from leaving their restaurant's immediate vicinity without close supervision.

The women are constantly surveilled, both through recording devices installed around the property and by their own colleagues. Each woman is trained to report any protocol breach – say, a colleague's secret addiction to South Korean soap operas – to regime-appointed minders. All are subordinate to a manager, usually male, who rigorously controls their waking hours, toilet breaks and communication with the outside world.

'What's interesting,' Lee says, 'is that restaurants are an entrepreneurial enterprise. So you may ask, "How is that allowed by an authoritarian regime that bans free enterprise back home?" It's because this regime desperately needs foreign cash. They'll do anything to acquire it.'

North Korea's government, Lee says, 'operates like a giant criminal syndicate'. Its ruling party officials may proclaim themselves the guardians of a sacred Marxist revolution that will one day liberate all Koreans from 'capitalist hell'. But they actually function more like a transnational mafia – one that now happens to own a hydrogen bomb.

The reality of North Korea, as it turns out, is far more intriguing than phony tales of unicorns and cannibals.

※

In the parlance of economists, North Korea's central command is financed by 'rent-seeking enterprises'. That's a fancy term for financial schemes that suck value from a society and offer nothing in return.

North Korea is indeed starving for foreign cash. Its own currency, decorated with atomic symbols and stoic peasants, is an over-manipulated and semi-worthless mess.

The nation's on-the-books economy, which produces coal, steel and fish, is under strict global quarantine. Crushing sanctions imposed by the US, EU and UN target its imports and exports. Each new embargo is a knife twist, intended to inflict so much pain that the regime surrenders its nukes.

There's a reason the Western-led world order is fixed on this approach. A similar strategy successfully coerced Myanmar's junta to scrap some of its more North Korea-like strictures on society: laws that obstructed the masses' access to mobile phones, for example, or punished even the meekest grumblings about ruling officials. It even nudged the military cabal towards holding elections – if not a legit transfer of power to civilians.

But Kim Jong-un is not budging. Like his father, Kim Jong-il, he'd rather absorb economic agony than loosen his stranglehold on power or, more importantly, give up the most powerful weapon known to mankind. This inflexible position has forced the regime to plunge into global black markets where sanctions don't matter.

Since the 1990s, regime cadres have maintained a vast complex of state-sponsored underworld ventures. They've made a strategy of shamelessness, seeking a market advantage by spitting on international laws that other nations are too proud to break.

These enterprises have included bootlegging cigarettes, counterfeiting US dollars and Chinese yuan as well as smuggling weapons. More recently, North Korea has pulled off impressive cyber-heists – looting $81 million from a Bangladeshi bank and raiding online troves of bitcoin from South Korean servers.[8]

North Korea has also become a sanctuary for meth labs

– most them run, it is believed, by state-linked operators supplied with chemicals via Chinese mafia.[9]

Here we have a direct parallel with Myanmar's black zones: a pariah state, withered by American sanctions, utilizing its sovereign turf as an untouchable haven for drug production. In both cases, China is a primary target for export.

North Korea's meth output, however, is just a trickle compared to the tsunami of meth roaring out of Myanmar. Perhaps the Kim regime, mindful of the madness in Myanmar and the Philippines, realizes a speed epidemic would make its population more difficult to control.

Of course, Pyongyang's officials deny the existence of any transnational crime ventures. But no one believes them. Even their supposedly legal overseas operations are stained by scandal – and none more so than their guest worker program.

North Korea has deployed an army of roughly 100,000 workers around the world, mostly to Russia and China but also across Asia and the Middle East. These workers are used as cheap labor to build skyscrapers, stitch clothes, cut down trees and assemble goods.[10]

They get around. Qatar is relying on North Koreans to build infrastructure for the World Cup in 2022. In Zimbabwe, Robert Mugabe hired artists from Pyongyang to build statues in his likeness. But no matter where they go, these workers toil under conditions the UN describes as 'forced labor' or 'slave like'.[11]

Living in packed dorms, they're often poorly fed and can be ordered to work for up to eighteen hours straight. The pay is obscenely low. Quitting is not an option. But North Korean workers dare not complain.

From birth, the regime 'terrorizes them from within', says a UN panel assigned to investigate these foreign labor units.[12] Even while abroad, these workers fall under Pyongyang's Orwellian eye, which 'permeates the private lives of all citizens to ensure that virtually no expression critical of the political system or of its leadership goes undetected'.

Collectively, these overseas workers are believed to generate up to $2 billion per year for the government – a critical source of foreign currency for the regime.

The Trump administration is hell-bent on cutting off this cash pipeline flowing back to Pyongyang. The administration has repeatedly pestered China and Russia to deport all North Korean guest workers as punishment for Kim Jong-un's nuclear ambitions. But it's unclear if they'll comply. Both Beijing and Moscow seem to care more about keeping the regime stable and solvent than backing the White House's erratic anti-North Korean agenda.

Counted among North Korea's 100,000 overseas workers are legions of dancing waitresses. However, these elite-born women have little in common with their other foreign-deployed comrades – especially those sawing trees in frigid Siberian forests or welding hot steel under an Arabian sun.

Nonetheless they all serve the same purpose: shoring up dollars, yuan and euros for their masters in Pyongyang.

Thanks to high-ranking North Korean defectors, we actually know how money flows from these far-flung enterprises back to the regime.

Day-to-day operations are usually run from the nearest North Korean embassy. From there, cash is sent by diplomatic pouch or courier back to Pyongyang – namely to secretive departments known as Bureau 38 and Bureau 39, according to Curtis Melvin, a Johns Hopkins University economist specializing in North Korea.

'Their offices are located inside the Worker's Party of Korea compound in central Pyongyang,' Melvin tells me. 'They keep their money inside Taedong Bank,' a financial institution situated in one of the capital's downtown riverside districts.

'It's not a bank in any sense that we'd understand it,' he says. 'It doesn't have investing shareholders. It doesn't lend money. Its main job is to hold hard currency for the party.' Exactly what the Worker's Party does with all that cash is harder to nail down, Melvin says, 'but the money can do whatever the leadership wants it to do.'

The US Treasury has imposed sanctions on this pseudo-bank, calling it a 'key component' of North Korea's 'dangerous and illicit activities', namely money laundering and drug trafficking.

But the South Korean government goes one step further than this. Eat at a North Korean restaurant overseas, Seoul's officials warn, and you are inadvertently funding the construction of a nuclear warhead that could one day obliterate your family.

That's a stretch, Melvin tells me. North Korea's restaurant chain is a decent earner, clocking an estimated roughly $10 million per year, according to South Korean intelligence estimates.[13] But if they all shuttered overnight, the nuclear weapons program wouldn't fall apart.

'A North Korean restaurant,' Melvin says, 'is not some huge goldmine.' Nevertheless, the South Korean media fixate on the waitresses' minor role as shadow fundraisers for Kim Jong-un's nuclear weapons program.

That argument doesn't really excite me either. My fascination with these restaurants has little to do with ICBMs. I am instead driven to understand the inner lives of North Korea's singing waitresses.

Here are women molded from childhood to embody the North Korean feminine ideal. They are socialist show-girls with interchangeable smiles, emissaries from a self-proclaimed utopia. Any trace of individuality is hidden away behind masks of practiced perfection.

According to the UN, these women are also victims of 'forced labor'. But I wonder if this phrase accurately captures their experience. In Southeast Asia, forced labor is a crime that flourishes in the worst border-town brothels and isolated shrimp farms. Forced labor doesn't usually stand on a stage, under disco lights, playing 'Dancing Queen' on the accordion.

Perhaps I'm deluding myself. Maybe I've been indulging in some glammed-up slave trade all along. Are these women like captive songbirds, their masters charging admission to their cages? Or do they feel honored to carry out their sworn duty – glorifying their homeland abroad, generating funds to fortify their party against a foreign menace?

The answer, I suspect, lies between those extremes. Seeking clarity, I decide to return to that North Korean restaurant in Bangkok – not to dance but to chat. This time, I'm bringing an interpreter.

※

Four months have passed since my *soju*-fueled jamboree at Pyongyang Arirang Restaurant in Bangkok. Now I'm staring at its darkened facade through a locked gate, secured with an iron chain. Its garish signage is unlit. All of the windows are blacked out, even on the second-floor dormitory.

I jangle the chain against the gate's steel lattice. This rousts a uniformed Thai guard inside the restaurant compound.

'Closed!' he shouts.

'Since when?'

'Couple weeks ago. They all went back home.'

'Shut for good?'

'No clue. They never tell me anything.'

I fire off a quick text to two of my friends: Maher Sattar, a journalist originally from Bangladesh, and Mina Rhee, a human rights activist from South Korea. They're in a taxi, en route to join me for dinner.

'It's SHUT DOWN! But come anyway. I have a back-up plan.'

I'd half-expected this place would be shuttered. This really isn't the best time for North Koreans to host conga parties. Just three weeks prior to this, the regime suffered its most humiliating loss of personnel in ages.

On 5 April 2016, North Korean agents overseeing regime-run eateries in China had to notify their superiors with alarming news. A dozen waitresses had vanished from a restaurant in Ningbo, a Chinese port city, 200 kilometers south of Shanghai. Their manager was missing too. They'd left behind seven scared female staffers who claimed the others just walked out.

The missing waitresses and their manager soon resurfaced in South Korea. Officials in Seoul boast that they're all brave defectors. These high-class servants of the North Korean regime supposedly hatched a daring escape plan that involved flying from China to Seoul via Malaysia.

This narrative, pushed by intelligence agents in Seoul, says that even the daughters of the North Korean elites will risk it all for a life in South Korea, a bastion of liberty and opulence.

What pushed these young waitresses to their collective breaking point? Soap operas. Or at least, that's the claim from South Korean intelligence. Through clandestine viewings of South Korean TV dramas, the waitresses witnessed the hip splendor of Seoul. Their communist indoctrination unraveled. Then, with their manager's help, they pulled off the largest North Korean defection in the 21st century.

North Korea has a rather different take on the so-called Ningbo Twelve. The regime insists the waitresses were abducted by South Korean secret agents in a 'heinous terrorist act'. These women, they say, were 'talents who grew up in happiness while learning under [sic] their heart's content under the care of the DPRK.'[14] (The nation's formal title is the 'Democratic People's Republic of Korea'.)

Pyongyang's propagandists have even trotted the waitresses' parents out in front of TV cameras to wail and sob and demand fiery retribution. In one North Korean video clip, the father of a missing waitress appears pink faced with rage.

'Our daughter is incapable of treason!' shouts Kim Bok Nam, clad in a pastel button-up, a red badge bearing the face of Kim Jong-il pinned to his chest. 'Nothing, not even blowing up the South Korean president's home, will calm my hatred … Resist them a bit longer, my dear child. Our nation will rescue you. All of heaven cries over your fate!'

And so it goes: both sides claiming dominion over the waitresses' hearts, while their actual desires remain as opaque as ever. Ideally, I'd fly to South Korea and speak to some of these women directly. But even Seoul's most cunning tabloids haven't managed to track them down. They've been hidden away by South Korea's National Intelligence Service (or NIS), purportedly for their own good.

In the aftermath of the Ningbo Twelve case, Pyongyang keeps recalling its servers to come home from posts around Asia. Eateries are shuttering left and right – perhaps to reel in would-be defectors, perhaps to protect women from future abductions.

All I want to do is to find a North Korean restaurant and, with Mina's help, attempt a conversation with a server. In fact, that's the extent of my plan: a simple, light-hearted chat. I hope to gain some small insight into a waitress's daily life through a series of questions that, if asked of any other foreign-born server in Bangkok, would seem utterly banal.

Have you found time to see the local tourist sites? Are you on social media? What's your favorite song on the radio these days? The questions are pedestrian, even a bit dopey. But if answered by a North Korean performer, they might hint at the contours of her invisible cage.

Now I just have to find a Pyongyang-run restaurant that still has its lights on.

A lime-green taxi slows to a halt outside the abandoned North Korean restaurant compound. I spot Maher and Mina in the back. Hopping in the front seat, I tell the driver to head towards Ekkamai, a busy nightclub district just five kilometers away.

'So apparently there's another North Korean restaurant nearby,' I tell them. 'Maybe it's closed too. But let's give it a shot.'

'Bangkok has two?' says Maher.

'Yeah,' I say. 'This other one opened last year. Probably trying to soak up cash from all the South Korean tourists in Thailand.'

My heart jumps when we pull up to the address. There it is: Pyongyang Orkyu Restaurant, its signage framed by red neon. We're in luck. This joint has survived the cull.

But perhaps just barely.

When we step inside, I notice that there's no gaggle of female staffers greeting guests by the door. There is no soft mood lighting that precedes nightly performances. All the overhead fluorescent bulbs are switched on, their glare illuminating every corner for the cameras.

The stage is cleared of instruments. The small dining room is quiet, save for low-volume Russian opera playing on a wall-mounted TV.

We are seated by a lone waitress. I'll call her Jong Ae. She is 25 at most, silky hair pulled back in a ponytail, fetchingly dressed in a pink robe with navy blue trim. She sets down our menus, which are as thick as the Yellow Pages.

I flip through the laminated photos of seafood pancakes and beef soup. For the most part, this place serves the same fare you'd find at any Korean eatery – north or south – only the prices are doubled and the quality is cut in half.

'Please,' Jong Ae says, 'you must try our cold noodle soup. It is a symbol of Pyongyang, our capital.'

Mina translates. Sure, I reply, we'll have a large bowl of cold soup to share. Plus some slices of boiled pig's head. Maher adds some bibimbap. Mina wants fried dumplings.

'Excellent choices,' Jong Ae says. 'And some *soju*? I do apologize that I can only serve South Korean brands. We're currently having difficulties importing our own North Korean alcohol.'

'No soju, thanks. Say, we're just curious,' I say. 'Where are most of your customers from?'

'Many are from Thailand. Many from South Korea.'

'And how about Americans like myself?' I ask.

'Oh, I'm really not sure,' Jong Ae says, perfectly unruffled. 'To be frank, Europeans, American, British – they all look the same to me. I thought perhaps you were Russian. My job is to provide perfect service to our guests, no matter their background.'

Jong Ae bows ever so slightly, gracefully walking in reverse for a few steps so as not to turn her back on our table, and then slips into the kitchen in back.

'Wow,' Mina says. 'She's good.'

'No kidding,' I say. 'She mentioned that a lot of South Koreans come here. What do you think draws them in?'

'We come for a variety of reasons,' Mina says. The South Korean government forbids its citizens from interacting with North Koreans – anywhere on earth – unless they've properly defected through Seoul and experienced three months of deprogramming. Any South Korean defying this edict risks an uncomfortable round of questioning by police.

Cavorting with a real, unprocessed, Kim Jong-un-allegiant North Korean, Mina says, is sort of a naughty thrill. 'Most people are just curious,' she says. 'Or maybe concerned. We think it's sad that they lack freedom even when they're abroad.'

'I once brought my mom to a North Korean place in Cambodia,' Mina tells us. 'She kept giving them huge tips. I was like, "Mom! You're just giving more money to the regime!" But she said, "Mina, these girls are your little sister's age. Maybe they have a cash quota to reach. We have to help them however we can."'

Jong Ae soon reappears with the customary tray of *banchan*: a collection of nibbles including tiny salted fish, boiled sprouts, garlicky potatoes and, of course, kimchi. Each table visit offers a brief opening for questions. I don't want to waste a single opportunity.

'So what do you think of Bangkok?' I ask. 'Have you gone to see the temples?'

'No, not yet. My work schedule is quite busy. But I'd like to see them in the future.'

'What do you do in your free time?'

'I'm free to do whatever I want. I watch TV and practice singing and dancing with my colleagues,' she says, placing sets of metal chopsticks beside our plates. 'Please enjoy.'

Jong Ae is a hospitality droid, cordial but never too chipper. A few minutes later, when she returns with a sizzling clay pot full of bibimbap, I step up my questions.

'So you're a performer, right?'

'Yes,' she says, 'but I must apologize. Our performances are temporarily on hold while many of our staff are away.'

'No worries. Where did you learn to sing and dance?'

'We enjoy many years of training in Pyongyang.'

'That sounds nice. Were you trained by the government?'

I can detect a slight tensing in her neck. Her hands – busy stirring rice, eggs and beef in the clay pot – begin to quicken.

'Music is in the Korean people's DNA,' Jong Ae says. 'Training is joyful for us. Throughout hard times, Korean people have learned that singing and dancing will sweep away sadness. It helps us get by.'

She has totally parried the thrust of my question. The word 'government' seems to have put her on the defense. I attempt one more query before she retreats.

'So do you like all types of music – even American songs?'

'No, no. I am disinterested in American music. My country has everything I will ever need. When you begin to look into a culture outside your own, that is a worrying sign. Why would I look elsewhere when I have so many beautiful Korean songs to sing? Such behavior reflects a flaw in one's political mindset.'

And with that, Jong Ae spins around and speed walks away.

'More good answers,' Mina says. 'Pyongyang would be proud.'

'Definitely,' I say, 'though I feel like she's talking to the cameras instead of us.'

'If they've let her stay on during the big staff recall,' Mina says, 'then she must be deeply trusted. I do think we're making her nervous though.'

'Yeah,' Maher says. 'Don't look now but she's whispering something to her manager.' In my peripheral vision, I can see Jong Ae in the back, conferring with a waifish, serious-looking man in thick glasses. I swallow hard. Their tension is contagious.

Soon enough, Jong Ae returns with a platter of dumplings and a massive bowl of noodles, swimming in crushed ice, cucumbers and a kimchi-flavored broth. This dish completes our food order.

'Sorry to ask so many questions. I've never met someone from your country before,' I say. 'Do you miss home?'

'Of course,' she says, polite but unsmiling. 'But this

restaurant is an extended territory of Pyongyang. My colleagues are like family members. I feel that, right now, I am at home.'

'How do you keep in touch with friends back home? Do you ever use Facebook?'

'No,' she says. 'I know about the internet but I don't enjoy using it. It's a waste of time. I have better things to do. Now please excuse me, I'm a bit busy. Enjoy your dumplings.'

Jong Ae retreats, her heels clicking hard on the tile. We don't see her for the remainder of our meal. Once we've finished off the noodles and dumplings, the manager approaches with our bill.

I pad it out with a large tip. Perhaps the added wad of Thai baht will purchase a few wires and screws in the next intercontinental ballistic rocket. At this point, I don't care. I had naively hoped for a pleasant exchange. I hope our waitress isn't too upset.

'My questions were pretty vanilla,' I say to my friends. 'Did I come off as pushy?'

'You sound a little too curious,' Maher says, laughing. 'They can tell you're up to something.'

As we leave, the manager personally walks us out of his empty dining hall and directs us towards the door. Feeling confessional, I blurt out that I'm a writer interested in learning more about North Korea's overseas restaurants. Mina begins to translate but he cuts her off in competent English.

'So you want to interview us?'

'Actually, yes,' I say. 'That would be great!'

'Well, we don't accept interviews. If you're curious about our country, you should go speak to my embassy.'

'Embassy? No, I'm not interested in politics,' I tell him. 'I'm curious about North Korean restaurants. They're some of the only places Americans like me can spend time with people from your country.'

'Actually, you do like to ask political questions, don't you? Facebook? Do you miss home? Government training? We don't want to be involved in your story. The American news, they're liars. They don't know anything. You just make stuff up and put it on CNN.'

The manager looks as if he might be in his mid-thirties, like me, though his head comes up to my shoulders. His gruffness doesn't come naturally. I sense that this confronta-tion pains him. His jaw is lightly quivering. Like the waitress, he seems to be performing for an invisible audience, viewing us from afar.

'You know what, man? I'm sorry,' I say. 'I didn't come here to start trouble.'

'There's no trouble at all,' he says, sounding utterly uncon-vincing. He gestures for Jong Ae to emerge from the back. She lightly bows and then stares at the floor. 'See? We're fine. We just have our personal reasons for not giving you an inter-view. If you're still curious about our culture, you should go visit our country.'

This is the part where I should just thank him and walk out. Instead, I keep going – grasping in vain for some sort of connection.

'I hear you. I really do. But you know I can't easily fly to your country. That's why I came here. I just want to know more about the lives of North Koreans. Talking about social media and music – these are just friendly questions, no?'

A tight smile creeps across his face. 'Friendly questions?

This is a business,' he says. 'You're just a customer. We're not friends!'

The guy has a point. Maher is howling with laughter. Mina mutters a final apology in Korean. We shake hands with Jong Ae and the manager and bid them goodbye, doorbell jangling as we leave. Then we walk up the street a bit, away from the restaurant's windowed facade, and convene under a street light.

'That guy is a smooth operator,' Maher says. 'He wiped the floor with you.'

'They're under a lot of pressure right now,' Mina says. 'Maybe this was a bad time to do this.'

'Yeah, that was a disaster,' I say. 'I feel like shit.'

'Look,' Mina says, 'Facebook, missing home – these are red-alert phrases for her. I also feel bad for making her nervous. But don't worry too much. The responses were perfect. Her trainers would be very impressed.'

We hug goodbye and hail separate taxis home. I can already sense that tonight's debacle will join the roster of lay-awake-and-cringe moments that enjoy plaguing my consciousness as I try to fall asleep.

Chatting up active-duty North Korean performers is clearly a failing strategy. So perhaps there's another way to learn about their mindset. Maybe there are women raised in Pyongyang's song-and-dance academies who've since escaped – and now have the power to speak freely about the world in which waitresses are nurtured.

The obvious place to start looking is Seoul.

'Are you going to ask me about human rights?'

This is one of Han Seo-hee's opening remarks, right after we shake hands. The former North Korean singer extraordinaire has agreed to talk about her years in the top echelons of the Pyongyang performance circuit. She's even open to discussing her private recitals for Kim Jong-il and his coterie.

But first she wants to suss out my intentions. Honestly, I'm not sure how to answer her question. Neither is Sona Jo, a filmmaker and friend who has arranged this sit-down in one of Seoul's upscale enclaves. The three of us have found a quiet place to talk inside an office tower near Han's neighborhood.

'Um,' I say. 'Do you *want* to talk about your human rights?'

'No. I'm tired of all that.'

I think I get it now. She's asking if I've come here to wildly sensationalize her life story – tweaking every detail until she comes off like an enslaved lounge singer from some nightmare kingdom. That would be the classic media approach.

'Honestly, Seo-hee, I'm just here to understand the lives of North Korea's professional vocalists,' I say. 'I do want to hear about the bad times. But I want to hear your happy memories too.'

At that, she nods and brushes back her well-conditioned auburn locks. 'Good,' says Han, her shoulders relaxing. 'Because it actually wasn't all that bad.'

Han was born in the early 1980s to what she calls a 'noble class' family from Pyongyang. As in the USSR and China, communist ideology hardly rid the nation of class hierarchy. From the start, status in North Korea has been determined by proximity to the Kim clan.

Fortunately for Han, her family lived among the upper tiers. Her father was high up in a state-run conglomerate. Her mother belonged to a women's union that was responsible for intensifying female indoctrination.

Their 'nobility' was tarnished, however, when an uncle was accused of grumbling about the all-powerful Worker's Party while boozing with friends. He was promptly locked up. Favoring collective punishment, the regime shunted the rest of the family to a province 700 kilometers away.

That's how Han ended up in Musan, a mountainous northern outpost shrouded in clouds, known as North Korea's iron-mining heartland. Disgraced, the family was desperate for any shot at redemption. It came in the form of a talent scout who was combing primary schools for little girls with stand-out looks.

At the age of eight, Han was plucked from her classroom and asked to sing a few bars. The scout approved. It was decided: unlike her peers, Han would not spend her afternoons scrubbing bowls or yanking up radishes on a collective farm. She would instead devote her adolescence to exalting the fatherland through song.

'It was a high honor,' Han says. 'My mother was thrilled that her daughter would become an artist.'

The implications were huge. The state doesn't allow kids from irredeemable families to venerate the Kim clan. 'To perform for the government, you can't just be talented. You must hail from an upright background. So despite my uncle's track record, they clearly believed the rest of us were still worthy.'

Each day, after school ended at 2pm, Han would report to a four-story cement rehearsal hall. Inside, there were drab hallways with practice chambers lining the left-hand side.

Each room was devoted to a different skill: dancing, choral singing or learning instruments. They often trained until 9pm, hours past sunset.

'Now that I look back, it was kind of scary – all those long, dark hallways. I'd call to my friends, "Where are you!?" We couldn't see each other. There was no electricity, no lights. But at the time, I thought it was wonderful.'

It didn't take long for the young performers to notice that they all looked alike: slender, milk-skinned, eyes like fawns. 'That's how girls get selected,' Han says. 'You need big eyes, a fair complexion and a round face. Appearance is as important as musical aptitude.'

This is the raw genetic material required of all North Korean female performers – the orchestral sopranos and waltzing waitresses alike. 'Plus a voice that's very high-pitched and clear,' Han says. 'There are also specialty students. For example, if they need more piano players, they'll go scout for girls with long fingers.'

'When I imagine your trainers,' I say, 'I always picture someone really strict.'

'They're serious. They have to be,' she says. 'But my favorite coach, she was also very forgiving. She had an intense job. Every day, she had to train us – seven girls – to sing with a single voice.'

The goal was flawless synchronicity. North Korea's artistic style is steeped in socialist idealism. Their many voices were meant to resound as a single, unwavering one. There is no room for flashy soloists, no place for prima donnas to distract from the Kims and their righteous saga.

'In America or South Korea, girls have attitude. In North Korea, forget it. You're not there to be creative or steal the spotlight,' Han says. 'And if one person makes the slightest mistake during training, everyone starts over from the beginning. You don't go home until you're perfect.'

Throughout her teens, Han poured more than 10,000 hours of her life into vocal training. She sung of the nation's glorious peaks and its resilient peasantry. She lionized Kim Il-sung, the God-like revolutionary founder who 'severed the chains of the masses' when he sent America's army scurrying south in 1953.

Han and her fellow singers were akin to a choir exalting a strange religion – one that reared them to musically praise gods both living and dead. The holy father of this faith is Kim Il-sung, who passed away in Han's youth. Entombed in a glass coffin, he remains the 'Eternal President of the Republic' whose utopian visions must be carried forth by male heirs: first his son Kim Jong-il, now his grandson Kim Jong-un.

In state-issued scripture, the Kims are compared to celestial bodies. Kim Il-sung is likened to the sun. His birthday – the 'Day of the Sun' – is an annual gift-giving holiday on par with Christmas in the West. Kim Jong-il is the 'Lodestar of the 21st Century'. And Kim Jong-un – sure to accumulate ever more grand titles during his reign – is a 'great person born of heaven'.

Just as Filipino Catholics grovel before the Black Nazarene, North Koreans crouch reverently before portraits of the three Kims and even speak aloud to them, begging for their grace. These expressions of gratitude are embroiled in strict ritual.

Every citizen must display an image of Kim Il-sung and Kim Jong-il inside their home. By state decree, all portraits of the Kims are hung above the head so that they gaze down upon their subjects. Those who allow dust to collect on their visages can be fined.

Han, like all elite North Korean students, never left home without wearing a red lapel badge bearing the eternal president's face. This is a sign of devotion – like a cross worn around a Catholic's neck – that is subject to draconian codes. All pins must be worn over the heart, for example, but never pinned to a winter coat.

Han's devotion to this faith paid off. She was even tapped to study the *oungum*, a pear-shaped lute supposedly invented by Kim Jong-il himself during his college years.[15] Finally, at the age of seventeen, she was accepted to the Pyongyang University of Music and Dance.

This is North Korea's Juilliard or Royal College of Music. Her admission to this conservatory was so prestigious that it helped scrub away the old stain on her family's reputation. Han was allowed to move to Pyongyang and, with the regime's blessing, her parents and brother followed.

The family was noble once more, back among the elites in their pulsing nerve center – a capital where countless stone obelisks extol the Kims as deities and billboards depict the White House in flames.

But in the capital, Han noticed that there was a perceptible change in tenor from her home province. In China there is a centuries-old expression: 'The mountains are high and the emperor is far.' Same goes for North Korea. At a kingdom's periphery, subjects can more easily disobey their ruler.

'Back in Musan, I would occasionally hear people blaming the government for their hunger,' Han says. 'But you can't talk like that in Pyongyang. Not for a second. You're so strictly monitored that you can't even *think* badly about the government.'

'Did you truly believe in the greatness of the Kim clan?' I ask.

'You make it sound like a choice,' she says.

'What do you mean?'

'If you want to survive, you believe. You don't let your imagination wander. Especially when you're a performer in Pyongyang. The degree of loyalty there is so extreme.'

After more intensive training, Han was recruited to join an orchestra under the Ministry of People's Security – a domestic surveillance apparatus that also runs a network of brutal labor camps.

Yes, in North Korea, the Stasi has its own singing ensemble. In fact, many of the most powerful organs of state are sponsors of performance troupes. In a land where the government holds a monopoly on expression, the commercial market for music barely exists. The loftiest dream for any North Korean performer is not to sell albums but to gain an audience with the all-powerful leadership.

Han was like an artisan in a royal court. As in medieval times, the monarch's wealthy retinue are patrons of the arts, cultivating beautiful women to pay homage to the kingdom. This is an esteemed role for any young North Korean. (Kim Jong-un's wife, Ri Sol-ju, is herself a former orchestral singer.)[16]

The chief patron of Han's orchestra was Jang Song-thaek, then one of North Korea's top commanders and a brother-in-law to Kim Jong-il. Jang was so trusted that, upon Kim Jong-il's death, he was tapped to shepherd his young nephew, Kim Jong-un, when he took over the controls.

But this arrangement ended nastily.

After some mysterious power struggle, Kim Jong-un's regime labeled Jang 'despicable human scum' who 'perpetrated thrice-cursed acts of treachery'.[17] Then, if you believe the Daily Mail, they served his nude, screaming body to ravenous dogs (although they probably just shot him).

But Han is one of the few elites who knew Jang when his stock was still high. In the early 2000s, Jang decided to honor Kim Jong-il – the nation's 'Dear Leader' – with a twenty-member personal orchestra. It was a supergroup of sorts. Han was tapped to regale the supreme commander with her *oungum*.

'We were secretly taken to one of his summer palaces to perform. Always at odd hours,' Han says. 'We had to wear our best make-up and costumes.'

Before her first recital for Kim Jong-il, Han was stricken with anxiety. At last, she would come face to face with the infallible deity whom she had worshipped for years. 'I was so nervous. My friends told me, "If you just look upon the face of our Dear Leader, you will feel no fear." But I was completely freaked out. During the first performance, I just stared at the wall behind him.'

'And the second and third time?' I ask.

'I eventually got used to it,' she says. 'I realized, "Oh, he's just a human being." We played for him a total of four or five times over a period of two years.'

'What would have happened if you'd screwed up?' I ask. 'Something really bad – like dropping your lute on the floor?'

'Well, it's not like they'd kill me,' Han says. 'I'd probably get kicked out of the group. I'd definitely be humiliated in a group condemnation circle. I'd lose a lot of my food perks.

But that fear never came to me. How can you make mistakes when you've trained since childhood?'

'I'm embarrassed to ask this question,' I say, 'but what do you know about the *Kippumjo*?'[18]

Han laughs, somewhat wearily. I get the feeling she's been asked this question 1,000 times. *Kippumjo* refers to the Dear Leader's supposed teams of virginal dancing girls. Rumors about these groups have titillated headline writers for decades. They've been called a 'Pleasure Brigade' or, more creatively, North Korea's 'Joy Division'.

'Ninety per cent lies,' Han says. 'Some performers wore sexy clothes but nothing you wouldn't see on a Western TV channel. Women were happy to dress like this because it meant they were trusted to wear outfits banned from public view. It made them feel modern. The government didn't want common people to become intrigued by capitalist music styles.'

'As for the sexual rumors,' she says, 'every country has problems with sexual harassment, right?' Han says she never saw evidence suggesting the existence of a singing sexual service squad – at least not in her troupe.

'We were serious, skilled performers. Not some "Pleasure Team". All these rumors come from defectors who just speculate about what happens at the highest levels.'

'I'm the one who really met Kim Jong-il,' Han says. 'Not them!'

The early 2000s were Han's golden years. The good times abruptly collapsed in the middle of the decade. Once again, her life was turned upside down by a male relative's defiance.

This time it was her brother, a promising young man with a grad school degree. He'd endangered his future by falling in love with a woman from a disgraced family. His paramour's entire clan bore a black mark after one of them defected south.

Han's parents were outraged. They couldn't believe their son would put the family's hard-won resurgence in jeopardy. Then one day their worst fears came true: Han's brother and his girlfriend mysteriously vanished to South Korea where they could live in peace.

'My mom and dad panicked,' Han says. 'We feared the security forces would show up any day and throw us all in prison.' At great risk, Han's parents lined up a broker and escaped into China. 'I finally made it to South Korea in 2006.'

Today, Han is 35, married and raising a young child. She could easily pass for a woman in her mid-twenties. Dressed in an understated but hip maroon dress, her hair expertly braided, she looks like she's stepped out of an Anthropologie catalogue.

Han is now known in South Korea as a stylish defector, popping up in a new genre of variety shows and reality TV-style programs, which star attractive North Korean refugees. These shows mix lurid confessionals with exhibitions of 'northern beauties', often fetishized by South Korean guys as virginal and uncorrupted. It's a huge media fad.

'The TV appearances are a bit tiring,' Han says. 'I'm always having to talk about my artistic past in a sensational way.'

I ask Han to tell me one of her fonder memories from North Korea. She begins rattling off the gifts she and her fellow singers would receive from Kim Jong-il: 'Big pieces of luggage. They were filled with nice things: imported cosmetics, expensive evening wear.'

'How was the dinner spread at his palace?'

'Oh, the food! By North Korean standards, we always ate well – even when we weren't performing for the leaders. Other artists wanted to join my special orchestra just for the food.'

'So what did you eat?'

'Bananas!'

'Bananas?'

'Oh, yes. My cousins were so jealous.'

Pause here on bananas.

This detail might seem insignificant. But anyone raised in North Korea will know better. In that frigid, totalitarian nation, eating tropical fruit is a revealing mark of status.

Han's diet of bananas – 'and apples and pineapples too', she says – indicates she had reached the apex of North Korea's state-run 'public distribution system' or PDS. In fact, she'd climbed above its highest tier, where the state rewards supreme loyalists with rare imported food and goods.

Understanding this PDS and its spectacular dysfunction is essential to fully grasping the story of North Korea and its descent into criminality. This is a country that, in its founding years, promised its citizens a cashless utopia, a refuge from the capitalist forces amassing cannons at their borders.

The PDS attempts to put this rhetoric into action. It comprises the veins and arteries of this Leninist dream. It will ostensibly dole out everything a citizen needs in order to live: corn, pants, soy sauce, farm tools and so on. The system isn't designed to merely supplement the market. The PDS *is* the market.

Or at least it was.

Let's rewind to the days before the PDS fell apart, back when it legitimately nourished all of North Korea, not just the banana-eating elites of Pyongyang.

The PDS arose from carnage. When the US–Korean war ended in 1953, North Korea was a smoldering wasteland. Throughout the three previous years, America had pummeled the Korean peninsula with more than 600,000 tons of explosives plus another 30,000 tons of napalm – more than all of the ordnance dumped on Germany and Japan combined during the Second World War.[19]

This is how Air Force General Curtis LeMay, one of America's more flagrant war criminals, described the destruction:

'So we went over there and fought the war and eventually burned down every town in North Korea … we killed off – what – 20 per cent of the population of Korea as direct casualties of war? Or from starvation or exposure?'[20]

Twenty per cent. 'Every town.' Another commanding US general, Douglas MacArthur – who'd overseen America's brutal invasion of the Philippines – conceded after the war that: 'I shrink with a horror that I cannot express in words at this continuous slaughter of men in Korea.'

'I have seen, I guess, as much blood and disaster as any living man,' MacArthur said. 'And it just curdled my stomach the last time I was there. After I looked at the wreckage and those thousands of women and children and everything, I vomited.'

Despite this sickening bomb campaign, the US–South Korean alliance never managed to kill North Korea's Soviet-backed commander: Kim Il-sung. Once the war reached a stalemate, he crawled out of his bunker and proclaimed battlefield victory over the world's most powerful empire. Then he set about rebuilding his ruined country.

Kim Il-sung was a protégé of Joseph Stalin's regime. Its apparatchiks had scouted him when he belonged to a Marxist guerrilla organization based in northeast China near the Korean peninsula. They instructed him in Soviet ideology, armed him and his comrades and ultimately secured his path to power.

From this Stalinist tutelage, Kim Il-sung emerged as a totalitarian maximalist. Your job, what you ate for dinner, your portion sizes, the color of your shirt, the design of your house, even your thoughts – all of it, he decreed, would be controlled by his almighty state.

By the late 1950s, all market transactions – even buying and selling rice – were outlawed. Practically everything the North Koreans swallowed was provided by the government via PDS distribution hubs. Hard-laboring miners got 800 grams of rice, barley or corn per day. College students got 600. Housewives got 300.[21]

During the 1960s and 1970s, North Korea was the least capitalistic nation on earth. For the most part, there was only one employer: Kim Il-Sung's government. Farmers, machinists and soldiers could go for many years without touching dirty cash.

Still, for the proletariat, perks were rare. In advance of holidays – such as Kim Il-sung's birthday – commoners could pick up one bottle of *soju* and three bottles of beer, according to the scholar Andrei Lankov, among the most authoritative experts on North Korea.[22] (Lankov, born in Russia, attended

Pyongyang's Kim Il-sung University in the 1980s. He's now based in South Korea.)

Luxuries such as major appliances were acquired only by the lucky few who got hold of special coupons. They were as coveted as one of Willy Wonka's golden tickets. One neighborhood might receive a single voucher for a TV. Scoring a refrigerator was like winning a free sports car.

But Lankov says there was yet another channel through which officials acquired deluxe items:

'The most prestigious items were presented to North Koreans as gifts from Kim Il-sung. This might sound pompous but most of these gifts were quite simple.'

'Soldiers in a military unit were given oranges, for example ... officials and high-level military were given watches, TV sets, fridges and record players ... it implied that Generalissimo Kim Il-sung, in his magnanimousness, was taking care of a particular North Korean, providing her something as a token of his love.'[23]

In the summer of 1994, Kim Il-sung, the 'Great Leader', died from a heart attack at 82. A mass wail resounded through Pyongyang. The capital's broad avenues were swarmed with his sobbing, red-faced subjects – many convulsing in near-epileptic spasms of grief.

Those in the outer provinces had even better reasons to weep. The veins of the PDS system were frazzling. When millions of North Koreans showed up to their local distribution hubs to collect food, they were staring in horror at empty shelves.

These were the years following the Soviet Union's collapse. Critical Russian aid had faded away. Europe's Eastern Bloc, which North Korea relied upon for trade, had also imploded. Pyongyang was struggling to profitably export the machinery and crops churned out by its work units.

Factories were shutting down. Harvests were plummeting. The beginnings of a long famine, which would eventually wipe out more than 2 million lives, was creeping across the frost-bitten hills.

The Great Leader's paternalistic social contract went up in smoke. It was swiftly replaced by a new unofficial credo: fend for yourself or starve.

This famine was most dire in the hinterlands bordering China. In Seoul, I heard about this era firsthand from one of its survivors: Kim Ah-ra, now 25, a North Korean who defected to South Korea in 2009.

During the 1990s, her father was a miner and her mother toiled on a collective farm. She still remembers the frantic days when North Koreans, unaccustomed to money, resorted to primitive bartering to survive.

One of Kim's earliest memories is her father, shriveled from hunger, selling off her childhood home. 'The price was ten kilograms of corn,' she says. 'From there, we picked up our corn sacks and moved into a leaky shack infested with bugs.'

Around 1997 – the famine's deadliest year – Kim was a scrappy six-year-old girl. She didn't go to school. She scrounged. Her job was to collect anything remotely edible: grass, roots, bugs or acorns.

'We'd make grass soup,' Kim tells me. 'You put a spoonful of rice in a pot, mix in the grass and herbs and pour in boiling water. That creates a dark-colored porridge that four people can share.'

'I would wander the village, staring at the ground, hoping to spot a dropped noodle or chicken head,' Kim says. 'One time, I spied a single pumpkin seed and instantly swallowed it. It was bitter and smelled of shit. I quickly realized it had passed through a dog.'

North Korea's high society – those linked to the ruling party, police, army or military-industrial complex – was spared from such degradation. They could still cling to the PDS, which by now had withered down to a life-support system for essential state personnel.

Since the 1990s, the PDS has vacillated between near-total collapse and spasms of stunted revival. These days, the system still exists but just barely. A modern North Korean farmer might get 200 grams of corn per day.[24] That's the amount Kim Il-sung handed out to toddlers. Hard-working adults will need double or triple that lest they keel over in the fields.

So the North Korean government now grudgingly tolerates markets where citizens can trade rice, wild-caught rabbits, toothbrushes, second-hand shoes and other basic goods. Without a little bare-bones capitalism, famine would sweep the countryside once again.

There is a North Korean currency – called the 'won' – but the masses don't trust it. How could they? The ruling party is prone to shock policies that can render money worthless overnight.

For example, in 2009, the government declared that all existing won was defunct. It ordered citizens to hand in their cash for a brand-new series of redesigned bills.[25] The catch was that each person could only trade in $40 worth of old money. The party's goal was to take down savvy entrepreneurs who'd grown too rich for their liking. But it also wiped out millions of families' savings.

In such a precarious economy, peasants and elites alike crave stable cash: either Chinese yuan or better yet US dollars, the currency of their imperial tormentor. The legality of these bills, however, is murky. In 2012, the gestapo-like Ministry of People's Security (the same agency that backed Han's singing troupe) released a decree: circulation of foreign exchange among citizens is potentially 'punishable by death'.[26]

Yet enforcement is spotty. In Pyongyang, US dollars are commonly used and are all but required for big-ticket items: property, cars or appliances. This legal blurriness forces the most allegiant citizens to break the law, hiding $100 bills in cupboards and gardens. Even these loyalists, according to the letter of the law, can be tried and executed.

North Korea, smacked around by foreign powers for centuries, was founded on a principle of self-sufficiency at all costs. To the central command, its reliance on foreign money signals great failure. But this cash, tainted by the faces of Mao Tse Tung and Benjamin Franklin, is the country's economic lifeblood.

The Great Leader would be appalled. But since his death, his acolytes' wild scramble for foreign cash has never let up. This is the backdrop to North Korea's bank hacks, meth labs and kitschy themed eateries in Southeast Asia. Each is like a straw through which the regime sucks up money from afar, hoping to sustain its weak pulse.

Ж

In the years following the famine, some enterprising Pyongyang cadre had an epiphany. All those dazzling artisans trained to venerate the regime weren't doing much to bail out the fatherland. But perhaps they'd have commercial value abroad.

Pyongyang's first overseas restaurants opened in China during the late 1990s.[27] They have since expanded as far as Moscow, Dubai, Mongolia and Nepal. Though the majority of these 100-plus eateries have sprouted up in China, much of the recent expansion has focused on Southeast Asia.

The region is attractive for two essential reasons.

For starters, it's crawling with tourists. But Southeast Asia is also largely run by authoritarian governments that have adopted China's air of permissiveness towards dubious North Korean business ventures. They don't seem to mind hosting eateries that, according to the UN, rely on 'forced labor'.

To be clear: forced labor, in UN speak, need not involve bullwhips and leg irons. It refers to 'situations in which persons are coerced to work through the use of violence and intimidation – or by subtle means such as accumulated debt, retention of identity papers or threats of denunciation to immigration authorities.'[28]

But I'm not sure if that wording encapsulates the unique circumstances of a North Korean waitress. These women aren't so much 'coerced' as inculcated, from birth, in a Stalinesque cult that structures their entire lives.

Under the UN definition, forced labor sounds like a temporary predicament, brought about by some criminal boss who can be brought to justice: the overseer of a secret brothel exploiting teenage girls in Thailand, for example, or a ruthless boat captain abusing Burmese captives. If these slave drivers are nabbed by police, they can face long prison terms.

But for most North Koreans – overseas waitresses included – their eternal boss is an all-powerful state, totally immune from prosecution. Only government collapse would spare them from servitude.

Forced labor can also imply that workers are not paid. That's not true of performing waitresses, who do receive cash handouts. In fact, they earn far more than their colleagues stuck on the Pyongyang performance circuit, where vocalists largely survive from gifts and PDS handouts. Of course, the servers' wages are criminally low. But shutting down every North Korean overseas restaurant and eliminating their jobs would no doubt leave them even poorer.

When considering these restaurants, it helps to think of North Korea as a human resources company. The regime seldom owns the building itself. It prefers to partner with a non-Korean entrepreneur – usually an established local business person – who can provide the space. Pyongyang is paid to furbish the eatery and supply singing servers. The local partner pays out a set price per waitress.

The pay of an overseas waitress will vary wildly by restaurant and host city. Her income reflects many factors: the earning potential of the eatery, the negotiation skills of her manager and the vitality of the host country's economy.

But it's safe to speculate – based on the accounts of defectors and reports by intelligence analysts – that a foreign-deployed North Korean server would make not much less than $150 per month and possibly as much as $400. (Evidence suggests any overseas North Korean worker should expect to make no more than 75 per cent of the local minimum wage.)[29]

Those figures assume that Pyongyang has already taken its cut. This can range between 30 and 70 per cent of the set wages paid by the local business partner.[30] The money usually flows to government cadres back in North Korea first and, from there, a smidgen of cash is doled out to the servers – or sometimes handed directly to their parents for safekeeping.

So let's assume that a waitress might collect a measly $2,000 to $3,000 annually. That's a fortune by North Korean standards. It far exceeds the $600 that the average Korean citizen scrapes together in one year, and they wouldn't even have to toil in a corn field.

According to Lankov, North Koreans sent abroad for just two years expect to make enough money to keep their families comfortable for up to five to ten years. This is equivalent to an American racking up $250,000 to $500,000 for a couple of years toiling overseas.[31]

Still, anti-regime activists tend to regard these women as 'slaves'.[32] Human Rights Watch says their 'lack of liberty meets the international legal definition of trafficking'.[33] The women are described as being servants to a secretive, criminally-minded organization, one that mocks local labor laws and basic workplace decency.

That's essentially true. But I wonder: is that how these women see themselves?

I put this question to Han. Her answer is an unequivocal no. These women, she says, hail from the same privileged arts-and-propaganda scene that reared her from childhood. They are not slaves, she says. Nor are they desperate.

They're banana eaters.

'I knew girls who went abroad to the restaurants. They did so eagerly,' Han says. 'The average performer in Pyongyang lives off little gifts and rations, making very little money. These waitresses earn more than they could ever dream of earning back home.'

'What was your official salary in Pyongyang?' I ask.

'It was terrible. I got 750 won per month.' (Back in the early 2000s, during Han's heyday, this was equivalent to about 50 cents.) 'It was enough to occasionally buy some very cheap shoes.'

'So did you ever long to sing in a restaurant overseas?'

'I was never asked.'

'But would you have wanted to go?'

'That's not relevant. In North Korea, you have no personal choice,' Han says. 'Besides, I knew they'd never send me away. The officials don't deploy their best performers overseas.'

'So what type of women are chosen?' I ask.

'Girls who were selected as children but don't grow tall enough. Performers who can't fully develop their skills. These restaurants are a good way to make use of our not-so-talented people. But they must have total ideological purity. They must come from unblemished families. That matters more than anything.'

Before deployment, Han says, waitresses undergo a three-to-six-month regimen of ideological strengthening. Their minds are fortified against the evils that lurk beyond North Korea's borders – including the 'filthy wind of bourgeois liberty' blowing through modern China.

They're also divvied into groups of two or three and instructed to routinely assail one another with criticism, a daily recounting of sins that breeds guilt and compliance. 'We would hold self-criticism sessions back in Pyongyang too,' she says. 'But it's more intense for performers overseas.'

'So what might one of these waitresses think,' I ask, 'if she encounters an American customer?'

'Well, if you don't reveal where you're from, they'll never know. We can't tell European-looking people apart,' she says.

'But if they figure it out? They'll be afraid. We're trained to see you as jackals and barbarians.'

I ask Han to interpret my waltz with the *hanbok*-clad singer back in Bangkok. She's skeptical that the woman was fully aware of my Americanness. This could be the case. That night, when the dancer's colleague (a fellow waitress) asked everyone at my table about our origins, we answered with a jumble of different nationalities. Perhaps my nationality didn't register.

'But the dance routine itself is not strange,' Han says. 'On special holidays, like Kim Il-sung's birthday, people gather in a town square and dance to folk songs. If a foreigner showed up, they would dance with that man to exhibit their kindness. Your waitress was trained to replicate this gesture in the restaurant.'

'So,' I ask, 'you don't think the waitresses I've met are unhappy?'

'Hardly,' Han says. 'They are the envy of their friends and the pride of their families.'

X

Suggesting that North Korea's waitress brigades are happy is quite provocative – and not just in human rights activist circles. It's a counter-narrative at stark odds with the South Korean government's position.

Officials in Seoul have long depicted North Korean restaurants as human zoos. In their view, the waitresses are no freer than the hoop-jumping orcas at SeaWorld. The smiles are fake and every patron is complicit in their enslavement.

This has become the dominant narrative about North

Korea's eateries – not just in South Korea but around the world. Much of it is constructed by South Korea's NIS, which was officially titled the 'Korean CIA' until the early 1980s.

It has long claimed intimate knowledge of the restaurant chain through a web of spies and defectors. Then along came the Ningbo Twelve: living, breathing proof, it would seem, that North Korea's restaurants truly are dens of misery.

By escaping North Korea's grasp, the twelve women have effectively undercut their masters with a damning political statement. It goes something like this:

We, daughters of the elite, are so tormented by your oppression that we would trade lives of so-called luxury in Pyongyang for obscurity in South Korea, the land you have reared us to vilify through song. Seoul's television dramas have shown us how the other half truly live. Given half a chance, we chose to betray you for a future of our own making.

That's the storyline pushed by South Korean officials anyway. As for the performers themselves? They haven't uttered a word, at least not in public. They remain under NIS protection in undisclosed locations.

Millions of people, myself included, would love to hear the Ningbo Twelve speak. A number of parties are actively clamoring for a face-to-face meeting to verify their true wishes.

This includes the North Korean government.

The North Korean regime has actually offered to shuttle the women's parents through a heavily-guarded opening in the DMZ, all the way to Seoul, to meet their estranged children.[34]

Gather up the daughters, Pyongyang says. They plotted

this escape all on their own? Let them tell it to their mothers' faces.

Then there's *Minbyun*, which is known in English as 'Lawyers for a Democratic Society'. They're a South Korean left-leaning consortium of nearly 1,000 lawyers working to 'protect basic human rights and attain social justice'.

Based in Seoul, this activist alliance rose out of South Korea's public backlash to the US-backed military dictatorship in the late 1980s. They have a long history of rankling any government wing with authoritarian tendencies, especially South Korea's conservative intelligence apparatus.

They too demand a meeting with the women – an opportunity for the ex-waitresses to declare, once and for all, that they were not brought to South Korea against their wishes. *Minbyun's* agenda is clear. They hope to expose their government's secret agents as meddlers who, through risky spy games, are sabotaging hopes for future peace on the Korean peninsula.

The response from South Korea's National Intelligence Service? Go away. The women don't want to see any of you. They're doing their best to assimilate into South Korean society. Leave them be.

Assailed by doubters, the NIS has allowed one of its go-to attorneys, a woman named Park Young-shik, to repeatedly check in on the Ningbo Twelve. She has emerged from each visit assuring the public that the women desire total privacy. According to Park: 'They believe their families' lives will be threatened if they openly testify that they fled the north of their own free will.'

Frankly, I never expected this scandal to take on so much geopolitical gravitas. The question I've pursued for more than a year – what do North Korean waitresses really want? – is now the subject of a full-blown international feud.

Here we have two heavily-armed nations – bomber jets all gassed up, rockets on standby – arguing over the true desires of a dozen college-aged singers. The women are being used as a proxy clash for an unthinkable war, one that could blanket the peninsula with bones.

Are the Ningbo Twelve defectors or prisoners? Other than the women themselves, there are very few people who know the answer.

One of them is Heo Gang-il, their former manager.

※

Back in Ningbo, Heo was the waitresses' prime conduit to the mothership. He was the keeper of their passports and the orchestrator of their every move.

None dispute that Heo is a traitor to the Kim regime. He alone had the wherewithal to hustle a dozen subordinates through a series of airports until they finally arrived on enemy soil.

Heo, like the rest of the Ningbo Twelve, has since adopted a false name. He now lives in seclusion somewhere in South Korea. As in his homeland, he is heavily monitored – this time by NIS agents.

And yet, in late 2016, he managed to defy his handlers and secretly meet with a *Minbyun* attorney. I've come to *Minbyun*'s headquarters in Seoul to meet that lawyer. His name is Chae Hee-joon.

The offices are inside an unassuming building next to a hot-pot joint. This modest facade belies *Minbyun*'s notoriety.

Operating mostly pro bono, the lawyers count two liberal presidents among their alumni. One of them is South Korea's current leader: Moon Jae-in, a president known for his dovish politics. He's also a former paratrooper and the son of war-era North Korean refugees.

Minbyun's lawyers are notorious aggravators of the right-wing intelligence services. They're also prone to taking politically-charged risks. They've even declared themselves the rightful representatives of the waitresses' grieving parents in North Korea.

This is a strange and bold assertion. Under South Korean law, the lawyers are forbidden from speaking to any North Korean citizen – especially loyalists tight with the regime.

As best I can tell, this law has been honored. No *Minbyun* lawyer has ever directly communicated with any of the parents. They've instead resorted to interpreting their wishes by studying North Korean propaganda dispatches.

Minbyun adamantly supports Pyongyang's claim that the Ningbo Twelve are abductees, not defectors. In most countries, asserting common ground with North Korea, a regime notorious for torture and lies, is taboo. In South Korea, it's seen as borderline treason. But *Minbyun* is feisty – and confident that they're unraveling a truly appalling scandal.

Inside *Minbyun*'s offices, I find Chae. He's a harried-looking man in his forties. We sit down inside a brightly lit conference room. Its walls are lined with tomes on international law. It's now after dinnertime and Chae is still here – taking a break to speak with me before a 10pm meeting with colleagues. Such is the South Korean work ethic.

Chae and his legal team have been investigating the Ningbo Twelve case for more than a year – a journey that has taken him all the way to China to collect clues. Most of his evidence has been hard won, he says. 'But my meeting with Heo Gang-il? That was a lucky break.'

In late 2016, months after arriving in South Korea, the ex-manager had a spat with his NIS handlers. For reasons that aren't perfectly clear, Heo was blocked from seeing the former waitresses – his former subordinates. This made him livid. So he decided to link up with *Minbyun* – South Korea's equivalent to the ACLU – to piss off his secrecy-obsessed minders.

During their clandestine meeting, Heo allowed Chae to question him for four hours. 'What did you make of the guy?' I ask.

'Let's just say that Heo Gang-il is a troublemaker,' Chae says. 'He never refers to the waitresses as colleagues or partners. He calls them "*saeggi*".'

That's a Korean word for newborn animals. Rough translation? *Bitches.* Heo sometimes paired these insults with violent outbursts. Back in China, according to Chae, he once grabbed a senior waitress and shoved her against the wall.

'He enjoyed total control over the staff,' Chae says. 'Think of the relationship between a commander and his soldiers. You obey his orders or else.' This temper may explain why South Korean agents separated Heo from his former underlings.

'From what you've gathered,' I ask, 'do you think the waitresses were miserable?'

'Actually, no, I don't think so,' Chae says. 'It wasn't some extreme prison-like situation.'

I'm a little taken aback by this answer. By all accounts, Heo has the disposition of a slave driver. But Chae contends that the waitresses' 'working hours and break times were pretty reasonable. They were even allowed to keep a little money to buy stuff around the neighborhood.'

'When you talked to Heo Gang-il,' I ask, 'was he pretty straight with you?' No, Chae says, his answers were often cryptic. Despite his show of defiance, Heo still seemed wary of venturing too far from a script approved by his NIS handlers. Nor did he concede to Chae's most incendiary claim: that the ex-manager was recruited as a South Korean intelligence asset while working in China.

In Chae's version of events, Heo was an easy mark for South Korean spies seeking to turn a North Korean manager against his regime. He'd vexed his superiors in Pyongyang by hoarding Chinese cash for himself – a severe violation that could land him in a gulag. Heo likely feared that, at any moment, he'd be caught and dragged back to North Korea for punishment.

So South Korean spies flipped him, offering safe passage to Seoul. There was one major caveat, Chae says. He'd have to bring some young waitresses along for the ride.

'I don't believe these waitresses had any idea they were bound for South Korea,' Chae says. 'They were told they'd relocate to a new restaurant in Kuala Lumpur, Malaysia.' This detail was brought to light by the restaurant workers who were left behind in Ningbo – a group of women who, once they returned to Pyongyang, addressed the public on television.

What happened afterwards is not in dispute. Once Heo and the Ningbo Twelve flew from China to Malaysia, the South Korean government supplied them with travel documents and escorted them straight to Seoul. It was immediately touted as the biggest defection under the reign of Kim Jong-un.

Within days, a South Korean government official came forth to explain why such a large group was emboldened to escape:

'These workers learned about the reality of South Korea through Korean television programs, dramas, movies and the internet while living overseas – and so discovered the fakeness of North Korean government propaganda. That helped them decide on a collective escape.'

'Heo Gang-il tried to convince me of the same thing,' Chae says. 'He says the women all loved South Korean dramas. But they supposedly feared Pyongyang would find out and drag them away. He said that, if the government found out about the soap operas, they'd have all of them killed.'

'Do you believe that?' I ask.

'No. It sounds ridiculous. That's why I kept pressing him about the soaps. Eventually, he tells me, "Fine, we'd probably just lose our jobs. The girls would have black marks on their records. They'd have trouble finding good husbands." That's it.'

'Now ask yourself this,' Chae says. 'Would that potential punishment over soap operas make twelve waitresses abandon their families for the rest of their lives?'

X

The alternate storyline put forward by *Minbyun* seems plausible enough. But I can't say whether it truly squares with reality. I'm cognizant of the group's agenda: scoring points against the right-wing intelligence apparatus, a cabal derided as dangerously war-like by South Korean liberals.

There's also the fact that *Minbyun*'s top source is a moody North Korean turncoat, formerly allegiant to a state that obfuscates reality as a matter of policy.

But Chae is definitely right about one thing – that soap opera story is pretty wacky. This is by far the fishiest link in South Korea's official chain of events.

I've seen quite a few South Korean soaps. They fill the day-time programming hours of TV channels across Southeast Asia. The shows are equal parts saucy and melodramatic: lots of hungry looks, face slapping and lovesick sobbing.

These dramas, according to the South Korean government, were the hooks that yanked back the waitresses' heavy curtain of indoctrination.

So tantalizing were these soaps that twelve women supposedly risked torture to watch them. Amazingly, despite their indoctrination, none of them reported this habit to Pyongyang. We are told that, in unison, they all gravitated towards an inevitable conclusion: somehow, this lavish city on our screen must become our new home, our parents be damned.

This is a spectacular claim. But for South Korea, it's essential. It transforms the waitresses, subject to a regime-appointed manager, into willing conspirators. How else to explain a dozen intensely-vetted loyalists suddenly becoming traitors all at once?

Seeking a second opinion, I track down another defector named Choi My Kyung in Seoul. Now in her late forties, with close-cropped hair and hands studded with shiny rings, Choi was once an acclaimed dancer and gymnast in Pyongyang. She's well acquainted with the impact that foreign dramas and music have on the mindset of Kim clan devotees.

Choi was raised within the same performance regimen that churns out singing waitresses. Her father, she says, was a military officer close to Jang Song-thaek, the former top commander.

'We lived well,' she says. 'They let my dad drive a Benz. They gave us a black-and-white Hitachi TV. So back then, I was extremely loyal. When I'd perform, I wouldn't necessarily think about whether my parents were proud of me. It was more like, "I wonder if Kim Jong-il will hear about the good job I'm doing?"'

That wasn't such a far-fetched dream. Choi used to dance with the Wangjaesan Light Music group, which was among the top bands in North Korea. Created by Kim Jong-il in the early 1980s, Wangjaesan is still around. Its catalogue includes hits such as 'Streets of Victory,' 'Thunder from Jong-il Peak' and 'Light from the Central Party Committee'.

Wangjaesan doesn't keep a steady lineup. Like the Mickey Mouse Club, members are rotated in and out. Choi joined one of the earlier iterations, back when Kim Jong-il first permitted Wangjaesan to secretly experiment with foreign dancing styles.

'We were attempting disco, samba, rhumba,' Choi says. 'This was an era when shaking your butt was really censored. The musicians even got hold of electric guitars and keyboards imported from Japan. But our music was only for the upper class in Pyongyang. The authorities believed that, for the masses, this sort of art could spread interest in foreign, capitalist culture.'

'Were you any good?'

'At dancing? Yes,' Choi says. 'At electronic music, no. The musicians had no idea what they were doing.'

According to Choi, North Korean aristocrats – its artists, party stalwarts and weapons engineers – have a long tradition of peeking out at global pop culture from their nest in Pyongyang. 'We're not as isolated as people think. We know Switzerland makes a good watch. We know that Japan makes a good TV,' Choi says. 'We even know your American singers.'

'Like who?'

'Michael Jackson,' Choi says. 'Back in the 1990s, the moonwalk was popular among Pyongyang's upper class.'

'No way,' I say. 'You were listening to Michael Jackson in North Korea?'

'Of course,' Choi says. 'Especially people in the arts world. We've always had access to foreign music. Common people believe they'll get executed for listening to this stuff. But for us, it's basically OK – as long as you keep it inside your house. We read your books too. Like that one about the red-haired woman from Canada.'

'Pippi Longstocking?'

'No, that's Sweden,' she says. 'I'm thinking of *Anne of Green Gables*.'

Choi, who defected in the early 2000s, tells me she's been eagerly tracking the Ningbo Twelve case. She was particularly wowed to learn that one of the waitresses is the daughter of Choe Sam-suk, a beloved female soprano singer. Her tracks include 'A Snowy Night Behind Enemy Lines' and 'We are College Factory Students'. Back in the 1980s, Choe Sam-suk had Barbra Streisand-level name recognition in Pyongyang.

'It's astonishing. These women are really from top-tier families – just like me,' Choi says. 'For singers sent abroad, the top requirement isn't talent. It's loyalty. They undergo intense mental training for half a year before they deploy.'

'So,' I ask, 'do you think their loyalty could be compromised by watching Korean dramas in China?'

'Who knows?' Choi says. 'But I can tell you this. You don't need to go to China to watch South Korean soaps. Loads of people are privately watching that stuff in Pyongyang.'

)(

My first visit to a North Korean restaurant took place in Vientiane, Laos, back in early 2010. I showed up with a friend: Austin Bush, an American photographer and food writer who has lived in Thailand for two decades. The outing had been my idea.

To be honest, I wasn't drawn into that restaurant by some high-minded journalistic pursuit. I was really no different than any other customer attracted by the sheer novelty of exchanging a few words with a real-life North Korean. They were, until that day, abstractions created by menacing headlines and absurdist comedies.

'So where should we say we're from?' Austin asked as we approached the entrance. 'How about Sweden?'

'What would be the fun in that?' I said. 'I'm going to tell them we're American.'

Honestly, I don't remember much about that meal in Laos. But it set a precedent for me: I never lied about my home country to a waitress from Pyongyang. Part of me enjoys the mischief of declaring myself American on de facto North Korean soil, amid personnel raised to believe we are jackals, vampires and even cannibals. (For some reason, accusations of flesh eating are rife on both sides of the DMZ.)

A more idealistic (or perhaps narcissistic) part of me feels that, in some small way, I might counter their anti-Yankee programming by acting really polite, cheerful and non-cannibalistic in their presence.

The conceit of the North Korean restaurant experience – for Americans and South Koreans anyways – is that you are coming face to face with someone from a world in total opposition to your own. Their casts of heroes and villains, their sagas of good versus evil, are a photographic negative of the storyline baked into our heads.

But in this sense, we are both utterly different and inextricably linked. It was my grandparents' generation that snuffed out as many as one in five North Korean lives, while the waitresses' grandparents – if they survived – were the ones stumbling through towns reduced to cinder, gathering up charred limbs to bury.

Then, it was my parents' generation that taught me to believe all North Koreans are mindless slaves to tyranny – one-note characters starring in a wintry dystopia. Meanwhile, the waitresses' parents taught them revenge anthems: violent operatic fantasies conjuring a world where my own home-land, in lieu of theirs, gets bombed to ashes and darkness.

To be honest, I'm not at peace with my experience in North Korean restaurants. Not because I worry my kimchi-and-*soju* feasts will fund the nuclear incineration of Guam. I'm more uneasy with the fact that these waltzing waitresses have no right to hang up their *hanboks* and walk out. Even an unapproved stroll through the nearest park is an act of heresy.

That is plainly indefensible. The governments of China, Thailand, Indonesia and other nations that allow these eat-eries to operate on their soil should force North Korea to pay these women the local minimum wage – at least – and allow them to move about freely during their off hours. This goes without saying. And to know about this degree of mistreatment and eat there anyway makes me complicit in their suffering.

That said, my meals in North Korea – by way of Vientiane, Yangon and Bangkok – have also given dimension to a people I've been trained to regard as pitiful.

Here's the thing: I don't want to pity the performing waitresses of North Korea. I don't think that's what they desire or need from us. Han and Choi have shown me that there is dignity in what they do – their triumphant singing, their immaculate synchronicity, even their ripping drum solos in the middle of 'Country Roads'.

Nor do I believe all of them are severely anguished. Plenty of them surely are – especially those ruled over by sadistic managers. But as banana eaters, they likely enjoy a feeling of status and many material comforts denied to millions of other workers across Asia.

I have to wonder if Karen, dodging killer police in Manila, might actually envy the life of a perfumed North Korean dancing in an air-conditioned dining hall. Both have been ill-served by their respective faiths, which demand female purity and promote subordination. But the North Korean waitress is safer, healthier and, among her fellow citizens, treated with more esteem.

The true purpose of this journey from Southeast Asia to Seoul and back was to get some sense of the North Korean waitresses' inner lives: their actual desires, hopes and goals.

On that front, I'll concede a measure of defeat. I've tried to scrub my analytical lens of the political and cultural gunk accumulated over the years. My time with high-status defectors, who were incubated by the same regime, did at least bring a great deal of clarity.

But I'm probably incapable of truly understanding what it's like to grow up as a North Korean – to have my thoughts probed ceaselessly, to live a life deprived of choice, to absorb a siege mentality as a sort of religion.

As I write this, in late 2017, North Korea has been threatening nuclear war against America, South Korea and Japan on an almost weekly basis. Statements from Pyongyang, seething on the mildest days, have turned to ever-more violent metaphors.

We are told that Kim Jong-un's forces will 'cut the windpipe of the US imperialists' with his 'nuclear force, an almighty treasured sword'. Trump responds with his own threats of 'fire and fury like the world has never seen', a phrase containing all of Pyongyang's bombast but none of its peculiar poetry.

All this reckless taunting drowns out a smaller drama playing out between the Koreas – the ongoing saga of the Ningbo Twelve. From a mid-sized scandal, expected to blow over in a few months, their case has since been welded to the larger nuclear crisis.

South Korea's president – Moon Jae-in, the former *Minbyun* lawyer – has staked his reputation on peace talks that will bring Kim Jong-un back from the 'bridge of no return'.[35]

His ultimate goal is the fusing together of Korea's estranged halves into a singular nation, just as East and West Germany were once made whole. In the summer of 2017, he flew to Berlin to elucidate this dream – one pursued by South Korea's Ministry of Unification, which was established in 1969.

However distant this outcome may seem, reunification remains the official policy of Seoul – and the same is true of Pyongyang. When North Korea's overseas restaurants flash the words 'KOREA IS ONE' on projector screens for foreign diners, they are reflecting the state's official position. Leaders in both Koreas promise to glue the country's parts back together, though each half imagines itself reigning over the peninsula.

Moon, for his part, proposes a series of collaborative projects, each more complicated than the next, that will force the Koreas to collaborate.

Step one: joining forces to briefly reunite the 'separated families and relatives' living on opposite sides of the DMZ. This is not as far-fetched as it might seem. The two Koreas have pulled off cross-border family reunions multiple times, mostly recently in 2015.

North Korea's response? You can't be serious. You just abducted a dozen of our most loyal women. You've created twelve more estranged families – heaping pain atop our 'tragic national division'. And now you bring us this 'highly illogical' proposal?[36]

There are no two nations more desperately in need of peace talks than North and South Korea. This is not an Asia problem. It is a global problem – one with the potential to stoke conflict between the United States and China, which control the two most powerful militaries ever assembled.

I don't mean to overdramatize the Ningbo Twelve case. But future peace negotiations could be complicated by twelve women who, until recently, were twirling and singing in a Chinese port city, and whose subsequent fate – however it actually played out – has infuriated Pyongyang. They are now bona fide geo-political chess pieces.

Here's the good news. For now, in lieu of lobbing artillery shells, the two sides are feuding over the contents of a dozen ex-waitresses' hearts.

The former waitresses, like so many North Koreans before them, have been turned into symbols rather than people. To Pyongyang, they are evidence that Seoul will go to cruel lengths to keep the peninsula divided, whereas to South Korean officials, they are proof that the Kim regime's elites are keen to revolt against their masters.

Only the Ningbo Twelve (plus Heo and a small circle of spies) know whether they've truly forsaken their homeland.

They rest of us can only wonder.

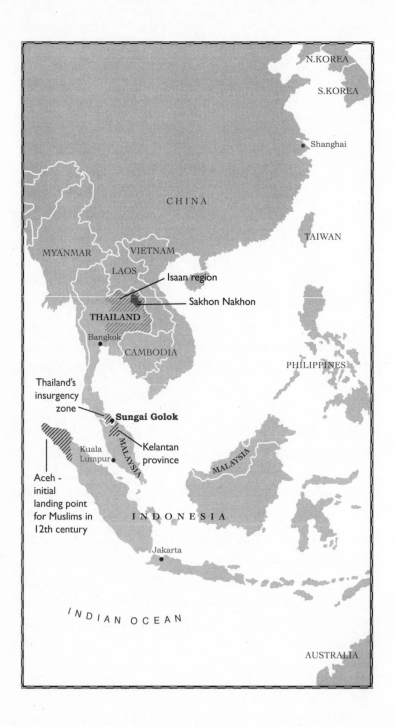

CHAPTER V

Neon Jihad

Location: Sungai Golok, Thailand

*Where Islamic rebels terrorize
Asia's strangest party town*

Her breath smells of menthols. Her ragged denim shorts are damp with spilled beer. She will not stop laughing.

I suppose her forced cackle is supposed to convince the men in this bar – myself included – that we're all having outrageous fun tonight. Yet that flutter in her voice betrays an inner panic.

Pin is 35 and slender with a copper-blonde dye job. She's liberally spritzed with perfume, strong stuff that puts a chemical tang in your sinuses.

Pin is manic. She can't sit still. She is the opposite of the North Korean waitresses gliding from table to table with immaculate poise. Pin careens around the bar, moving jerkily like a marionette, all elbows and knees.

She really should not be here right now. Nor should I. This entire strip – a row of open-air bars – should be cleared out. After all, the city is currently under attack from jihadi bombers.

Again.

But Pin and I and a few other customers remain in this

gritty bar. It's one of many lining the red-light promenade in Sungai Golok, one of Thailand's southernmost cities.

This is about as stripped down as a bar can get: one room, three walls, every surface painted lavender. There's no facade. Electro-pop blares at a skull-rattling volume.

The only decorative touch is a web of twinkling Christmas lights stapled to the ceiling. There's no cocktail menu here, just a selection of beers bobbing inside a plastic cooler. Customers who ask for the toilet are directed to a nearby alley.

Pin serves the standard Thai lagers, Leo and Chang, along with the occasional Heineken. But her real focus is on generating cash by pressuring men – most of them past their prime – into Cancun-style speed drinking.

She hops from lap to lap, tousling hair, draping an arm over customers' sweat-moist necks. Every three and half minutes, she purrs 'Cheeeeeers!' into their ears and clinks her glass to theirs.

Drink it all up, she says. Now how about another?

Pin's technique is quite effective. Some patrons are totally stupefied by booze. They seem oblivious to the fact that, just an hour or so ago, a bomb exploded roughly 300 meters from their heads.

Pin wobbles over to my table with the tools of her trade: cigarettes, a tin pail full of ice cubes and a bottle opener. First, she refreshes my beer with ice, a technique that keeps lager cool in the equatorial heat.

Then she grabs my Heineken bottle off the table. Pin drains half of its contents into my glass. The other half goes down her neck in three hard glugs. In this town, hostesses help themselves to the customers' beer. It's a Golok custom.

'Cheeeeeers!'

Pin is awfully thirsty tonight. 'One more?' she says.

This sounds like a question. It really isn't. Before I can respond, she's back on her feet. The plastic cooler squeaks open and then comes the hiss of a loosened bottle cap. Another 120 baht (about $3.50) is added to my tab.

When Pin returns, fingers gripping the neck of a fresh beer, I urge her to sit down for a bit. Unlike most guys on this street, I'm not here to flirt or get stumbling drunk. I've come to Golok to understand how sex workers cope in a town where they are routinely targeted by rebels.

Tonight's attack went down within earshot of this strip. It was a shrapnel bomb, hidden near a phone booth, detonated just three blocks south of here.

'Surely you heard that loud explosion?' I ask her in Thai.

'Of course. I was right on that stool, eating some *Mama* (a brand of instant noodles) when BOOM! You could feel the ground shake.'

'And you know that the bomb killed someone?' I say. 'Some terribly unlucky woman blown right off her motorbike.'

I heard, Pin says. Word spreads quickly.

Well then, I ask, why are you still here? Aren't you afraid?

'Look, I'm really scared,' she says. 'But I'm also kind of drunk.'

Pin says her boss is adamant about keeping the bar open during attacks. So she just douses her fear in cheap lager and gets on with it. 'That's all I can do,' Pin says, offering up another unconvincing laugh.

Leaning in, I tell Pin that I've just returned from the murder scene. I expect her to ask why the hell some foreigner would loiter around the flaming aftermath of a terror attack. But Pin is more observant than she lets on.

'Yeah, we know you were there,' she says. 'I saw you looking at photos of a dead person on your phone. And you keep writing stuff in that notebook.'

'Right. Well, I'm a journalist from America. I live in Bangkok.'

'Oh,' she says. 'Can I see those photos you took?'

I cue up the pictures on my iPhone and pass it over.

'This is horrible,' she says. The sing-song affectation has vanished from her voice – as if she's placing her party-girl act on pause.

'What happened exactly?'

I explain that I was lazing in my hotel room around 8pm when I heard a percussive boom. Peering over the balcony railing, I saw a street corner, maybe 250 meters distant, awash in orange flame.

Within minutes, I was jogging towards the fire. Cops and soldiers were also rushing in to establish a perimeter around the blast site.

'You shouldn't run towards a bomb scene,' Pin says, sparking up a cigarette. 'There could've been more explosions.' It's a fair point. Jihadis will sometimes use one bomb to draw first responders to the scene and then ignite a secondary bomb hidden nearby. Sometimes they get lucky and level a whole platoon.

I arrived at a street corner smothered in black haze. The curb was showered in glass shards and bits of scorched plastic. Soldiers were sweeping for explosives. For my own sanity's sake, I wanted to tap into their emotional frequency. Vigilant but cool. Greeting horror with nonchalance. One of the grunts politely told me to hurry up, get what I need and zip back to my hotel.

Then I saw her – a woman, supine on the road, her manicured hand splayed towards the sidewalk. A detective stood over her, aiming a camera lens at her face. The pop of his flash bulb lit up the whole block. Another officer twisted gold rings off the woman's fingers and plopped each one into a ziplock evidence bag.

Then they pulled a cotton sheet over her body. The white fabric shone brightly against the black asphalt – all of it saturated in a peach-hued light glowing from street lamps above.

Pin interjects. 'The woman. Was she Thai Buddhist? Or Muslim?'

'She was wearing a hijab,' I say. Looked like a workaday Muslim woman, probably in her thirties.

I was eavesdropping on detectives sizing up the crime scene. They didn't think the victim was intentionally targeted. The jihadis probably wanted to strike the red-light zone but couldn't get close enough. Too many army checkpoints.

So it seems they settled for a bombing at the perimeter – a blast designed to kill any random person in the orbit of this sinful enclave. That's how this woman became the latest statistical uptick in one of Asia's grisliest Islamic insurgencies.

As I talk, Pin keeps flipping through my iPhone photos. Minutes have passed with no forced laughter. It's as if the images have drawn out her morose soul, a photographic negative of the lusty hostess role she's paid to perform.

'You know,' she says, 'I thought the bomb scene would be more gory.'

So did I. In the photos, the woman's face appears unscratched. The blast barely ruffled her hijab. The grimmest image shows the woman, wearing jeans and a T-shirt, in a macabre sprawl. Her right shoe is missing. Pin notices that her toes are painted strawberry red.

I tell Pin that, according to the detectives, the woman was likely killed by flying shrapnel – little screws or flecks of steel that lacerated her back.

'Does the victim look familiar?' I ask.

'Nope,' Pin says. 'Did you catch her name?'

Unfortunately, I did not. Got shooed away before I could find out.

As Pin returns my phone, I notice a heavyset woman looming at our shoulders. It's her boss. She's probably wondering how this foreigner suddenly made her hostess turn so sullen.

The boss introduces herself as Tip, the bar's 33-year-old manager. She has the brawny look of an enforcer: camo pants, butchy bouffant, wallet chain. Her forearms are raked with scar tissue. She excuses Pin with a flick of her hand.

So, I ask Tip, you've worked on this strip for a long time?

'Yeah,' she says, plopping down on a plastic stool and snatching my phone off the table. As she swipes through my photos, Tip explains her many roles: babysitter of tipsy hostesses, arbiter of barroom disputes, holder of the purse.

That last title is literal. All of the bar's cash proceeds are stuffed in a zippered pouch fastened to Tip's belt. I sense that reaching for this fanny pack would be a fantastic way to get choked out.

'I'm worried about your hostess,' I say. 'Is she OK?'

'She's just a little scared,' Tip says. 'But we can't shut down the bar every time there's an incident.'

'I really thought this whole strip would be emptied out

right now,' I say. 'I can't believe bombs go off and these guys keep drinking like nothing happened.'

Tip shrugs. Could be worse, she says. Back in 2011, a car bomb turned this entire strip into an inferno. Four people died. Nearly 120 were wounded.[1] Tip saw dazed survivors in the street, half naked, their clothing singed off by the flames.

Tip herself was grazed by shrapnel, she says, pointing to her forearm. She explains that, for veterans of this city's red-light trade – the sex workers and brothel keepers alike – experiencing an attack is practically a rite of passage.

Even after a devastating bomb, she says, men will start drifting back into the bars after a few nights. 'I've had to clean up blood myself,' Tip says. 'You just have to get used to it.'

I'm not sure how anyone gets used to innocent women being killed by bomb shrapnel. But that's how bad nights play out in Golok. It's one of the strangest party towns in Asia – if not the world.

※

Thailand's tourism authorities don't like to talk about Golok. This is not the sort of town you promote with glossy pamphlets. It's a little bit Tijuana and a little bit Kabul.

Sungai Golok literally means 'Sword River' in the Malay tongue. It's a dumpy little town on the border with Malaysia. Population: 35,000 or so. Distance from Bangkok: 1,200 kilometers by road, 22 bumpy hours by train.

Thailand is home to one of the largest flesh trades ever created by any civilization – and Golok is its most distant outpost. The town's red-light strip feeds a national prostitution industry that, while technically illegal, rakes in an estimated

$4 to $6 billion per year.[2] That's billions more than the nation earns from exporting rice – and Thailand is one of the top rice producers on the planet.

This behemoth industry is sustained by an estimated 250,000 sex workers. Officially, they're all considered criminals.[3] Under Thai law, those who 'gratify the sexual desire of another person' for cash are subject to a month in jail – and anyone who owns or supervises a 'prostitution establishment' can be put away for three to fifteen years.

These laws aren't widely enforced. But Thailand's junta is too obsessed with notions of 1950s-style piety to ever properly decriminalize such an icky trade. So these women are confined to an underclass devoid of basic labor law protections.

This is a gift not only to brothel-owning mafia, who can impose client-per-night quotas or twelve-hour days, but also to the police who squeeze brothels and nightclubs for payoffs. Legalizing prostitution would dry up torrents of cash flowing into Thai police departments. The cops would revolt.

So this black market – officially deplored yet tacitly upheld by the state – continues to operate not only in plain sight but under the vivid glare of hot-pink bulbs.

Sex is sold in every major Thai city and even in rural towns. But none of these places terrify sex workers quite like Golok. Even veterans fear this place. They may be well acquainted with threats from rough men. But only here, in the Thai-Malaysia borderlands, are insurgents conjuring up plots to kill them with bombs.

By day, Golok seems fairly harmless. Its downtown is a grid of streets fronted by cement buildings, their facades blackened by mold. Motorbikes grunt up and down narrow lanes. Ladies sell duck noodle soup from pushcarts. Come afternoon, female students in lilac-colored, school-issued hijabs walk home in giggling packs.

As in most provincial Thai towns, the golden spires of Buddhist temples jut above Golok's low-slung skyline.

But in Golok, they share that skyline with minarets.

At around sunset, the central brothel district begins to shake off its day-long slumber, and the families who live downtown start yanking their gates shut. They know what's coming.

Once the moon rises, noisy out-of-towners begin streaming into the city. Neon light drenches the streets. High heels clatter on the asphalt. Bad Top 40 music roars from the nightclubs. The air is filled with hoots and catcalls and thudding bass.

But if you stand outside the bars, and strain your ears, you can hear a few solemn voices – each straining to pierce the sonic thicket of high-decibel pop.

This is the sound of muezzins, crying out to Allah from nearby mosques. The prayer calls are a reminder that this pocket of vice intrudes into a land where more than four in five people follow Islam.

Here in Thailand's so-called 'deep south' – a cluster of provinces collectively the size of Qatar – most people are Muslim. But generally speaking, the Muslims are not in charge.

Buddhism is Thailand's official religion and, even in the Muslim-majority south, a small Buddhist minority holds almost all the power. They are the bureaucracy. They are the army and the police. They own the nightclubs and brothels that power this little town's economy.

Yet for all their power, the Buddhists here remain surrounded.

X

From the sky, Golok looks like a glob of concrete – gray as pigeon droppings – that has been splatted on a jade green canvas. The Buddhists congregate in that urban blob, a zone patrolled at all hours by troops. But the town is surrounded by lush farmlands and thick jungle, the domain of native-born Muslims.

Golok's southern border is Sword River, a ribbon of neck-high water that constitutes an international boundary. Beyond its shores is Malaysia: a nation of rubber trees, fish-head curries and even a few skyscrapers. It is a country where Muslims rule outright.

But the province across Sword River from Thailand is not the Malaysia of Kuala Lumpur, the nation's semi-cosmopolitan capital – a city filled with halal hipster cafes and Muslim mall rats.

Known as Kelantan, it's more like Malaysia's Kentucky. Rural and religious, Kelantan is controlled by an all-Islamic party. Its elders attempt to enforce Sharia law through squad-rons of morality police.[4]

This is a world totally at odds with Thailand's freewheeling culture of naughty fun. That means no extra-marital canoodling. No whiskey sodas. No spaghetti straps.

It means a woman with Pin's job – swigging beer, pouring herself into strangers' laps – will go straight to jail. In Kelantan, women who besmirch religious piety are punished by the state so there is no need for hardliners to strike from the shadows.

Even some of Kelantan's grocery marts are divided by gender. One cashier for the women, another for the men, lest the sexes mingle while purchasing mangoes.

In Kelantan, you marry young. You go to sleep early. You don't miss Friday prayers. Deviate from the script – perhaps by holding hands with your girlfriend – and the police can toss you in a cell.

And yet, on the other side of Sword River, everything that makes Thailand infamous is available in abundance.

Sword River divides these two worlds, but it's only a skinny band of brown water – a membrane too porous to stop men from slipping out of Eden and into Babylon.

X

'The beers, the booze, the ladies! Ohhh!'

So exclaims a white-haired Malaysian guy in an ill-fitting polo shirt. I've found him after nightfall in downtown Golok. He might seem grandfatherly if it weren't for the two young girls, squeezed into denim shorts, that flank him on both sides. The old man is radiant with glee.

'The nightlife here is fantastic!' he tells me. He is so enraptured with Golok's essence that he tries to kiss it – a wet, sucking smooch planted on the night air.

'Mamma mia!'

It's a weekday, around 10pm on Golok's red-light strip. I've planted myself on the town's busiest sidewalk. It links the largest hotel, The Marina, to a row of rowdy pick-up joints.

I've stationed myself here to talk to the dudes who love Golok. I'm not particularly eager to interrupt them as they tug women back to their rented rooms. But I have to know: why would anyone visit an insurgency zone as a sex tourist?

In the last dozen-odd years, the conflict swirling around this region has racked up roughly 7,000 killings.[5] That's more conflict deaths in the same timespan than in the Gaza Strip. In Thailand's deep south, weeks without a bombing are rare.

Thailand is a paradox. It consistently ranks among the world's top ten tourist destinations. Yet it has also popped up on a less-celebrated list: the US government's 'Ten Countries with the Most Terror Attacks' report.[6]

There, it sits alongside Syria, Iraq and other places that do not conjure thoughts of sunbathing or pole dancing.

Somehow Thailand has managed to straddle these two worlds – terror hotspot and tourist playground – without much of the planet taking notice. In fact, some of its world-famous crystal-sand beaches, favored by rich Westerners, are just a few hours' drive to the north.

On the Golok strip, I bump into Eddy, a goateed Muslim dad. He's chain smoking by the Marina Hotel's front steps. He's as curious about me – a fair-skinned foreigner in Golok – as I am about Malaysian sex tourists.

'Funny to see you!' he says. 'We almost never see *far-angs* around here.' (In Thailand, *farang* is a catch-all term for people with Caucasian features – no matter if they're from Tallahassee or Tbilisi.)

By day, Eddy works as an oil importer. He slipped across Sword River about an hour ago. Now he's soaking up the dark energy and amping himself up for the night ahead.

'You seem less drunk than most of the guys out tonight,' I tell him. Eddy says his vice isn't booze. That's *haram* – forbidden by the Quran.

But when it comes to women, Eddy just can't help himself. 'We're not angels,' he says. 'Look, religion can bring out the good in people. But everybody has a breaking point. Our Islamic government totally bans nightlife. So we have to seek our happiness here.'

His wife is at home in Malaysia. 'She's sleeping,' he says. 'Doesn't even know I'm in Thailand.' To slip into Golok, Eddy says, all you need is a little cash and a Malaysian ID. The journey across Sword River takes 45 seconds on a wooden motorboat. Just palm off some money to a boatman and he'll ferry you across. Even at odd hours.

Upon arrival on Golok's shores, you flash your ID at a Thai checkpoint and walk up the riverbanks into the red-light quarter. No one stamps your passport. There's no ink trail for suspicious wives.

'I don't know how we'd survive without this town,' Eddy says. He's giddily bouncing in place. 'No one cares where you're from in this town. We can all be friends!'

Eddy hugs me, a little too tightly, and then floats towards the sound of techno pulsating from nearby bars.

X

In Thailand, most foreigners seeking obscene thrills end up in one of two places. There's Pattaya, a seaside bastion of sleaze. And there's Bangkok, a metropolis with multiple red-light zones.

Like moths to neon, men are drawn to Thailand from across the world. On any given night, a single go-go bar in Pattaya might fill its barstools with guys from America, Japan, India and Russia. But Golok is dominated by sex tourists from a single country: Malaysia.

There are the Malay Muslims, Malaysia's primary ethnicity, who come seeking the pleasures that Islam forbids.
They're apt to slink around, betraying their faith discreetly in
hotel rooms – or at least the back booths of very dark bars.

Then there are ethnic Chinese Malaysians. Back home,
they form part of a well-to-do merchant class, amounting
to roughly one quarter of the country's population. Less
encumbered by religious stigma, Chinese Malaysians are free
to party openly like spring breakers – pompadoured twenty-
somethings and paunchy grandfathers alike.

After dark, Golok's sidewalks become a parade of male
excess. Guys retch into the shrubbery. They drink until their
legs turn to gelatin. Some have to cling to their newfound
female companions to stay upright.

Men with big appetites will greedily hire two women,
sometimes three, and stumble back to their hotels. Wait
30 minutes by the lobby and you'll see the same women exiting the hotel and straightening their bangs as they stroll back
towards the strip in search of new clients.

None of this behavior really distinguishes Golok from
Thailand's more notorious brothel districts. When they want
to debase themselves, men from Kelantan tend to act just like
guys from Berlin, Mumbai or Cincinnati.

What truly distinguishes Golok as a sex tourism hotspot
is the looming threat of violence. Those car bombs in 2011
– the attacks that killed four people and wounded Tip the
bar manager? They were detonated right here on this busy
sidewalk.

I flag down a Chinese-Malaysian guy ambling down
Charoenkit Road, the town's repeatedly-bombed main drag.
He's a plump 30-something, forehead dewy with sweat, with

a mop of messy black hair – and he exudes the scampish euphoria of a fourteen year old in a sex shop.

After a brief chat, I ask him if he feels scared in Golok.

'Um, why should I be scared?'

'Because,' I say, 'there's an Islamic insurgency here. Come on. You know that.'

'I know,' he says, tittering. 'But if you find a girl here, you won't be so scared.'

The more men I chat up, the more I hear some version of this answer. The aforementioned jolly grandpa in the polo shirt? He's equally unflappable.

'Not that long ago,' I tell him, 'there was a car bomb right here where we're standing.'

'Yup.'

'And you're not thinking about that when you go partying?'

'Nope!'

He rambles for a bit, gesticulating wildly in the air. The girls he's hired for the night stare down at their sparkly heels. Finally, grandpa arrives at something resembling a point.

'Look, in Malaysia, as an Islamic country …' he says, trailing off.

'You know? Alright? I don't have to elaborate more on that. In Malaysia, if I say this, I would be …' THWACK! He mimes shackles clamped around his wrist.

I think I get what he's trying to say. Living under Sharia law is so suffocating that guys will do anything for a night of boozy liberation. Apparently, even jihadi bombs can't drown out the siren call of Johnny Walker and anonymous sex.

But there's another reason he's willing to roll the dice on a weekend in Golok. This place is as fortified as it is raunchy.

In the shadows, whisker-lipped army recruits stand guard. They're posted up outside karaoke joints, in twos or threes, sweating inside their bullet-proof vests. Almost every bar facade, every dark corner, falls under the gaze of security cameras attached to light poles overhead.

About once an hour, a blast-resistant armored vehicle cruises the promenade. Half tank, half Hummer, it's a military vehicle produced in South Africa known as a REVA. It's popular with armies in Yemen and Iraq. From the REVA's roof turret, soldiers can scan the sea of boozers for suspicious activity. Their fingers rest on mounted machine guns.

This is what it takes to keep Golok's nightlife buzzing. It's more than just a red-light district. This is a Green Zone for men on the prowl.

$\displaystyle \text{)\!(}$

It's a nuclear-hot afternoon. I'm about an hour's drive outside Golok, baking in the back cabin of a REVA as it rumbles down a backcountry road. My skin is pink as a salmon and nearly as damp.

The interior of this vehicle is brothy with sweat-infused air – a rolling sauna filled with heavily armed men. I'm on bench seats, knee to knee with black-clad rangers. In Thai, these guys are called *tahan pran*. Translation: hunter-soldiers.

We've just entered a 'red zone' (not to be confused with a red-light zone). In Thai army parlance, a red zone is a district under the jihadis' sway. This is the sort of place sex tourists would never, ever visit.

Inside the REVA, the only whiff of ventilation comes through circular gun ports built into the bulletproof glass windows. If we're attacked, the rangers will thrust their M-16 barrels through these fist-sized holes. Then they'll return fire.

So will the turret gunner whose body juts through a roof hatch. He controls an Israeli Negev machine gun that can fire 1,000 rounds per minute. And what will I do if jihadis suddenly materialize from the jungle? Probably go fetal on the REVA's steel floor, shell casings raining on my face.

Frankly, I'm surprised to be here. It's not easy to score a ride with troops patrolling the most violent corner of the Thai–Malaysian borderlands.

The men who control access to this area – Thailand's military generals – are about as media-friendly as Freemasons. My previous attempts to embed with troops have crashed hard. Years ago, when I formally sought permission to tag along with an elite Thai bomb squad, a three-star general stepped in to squash the request. His rationale was that I might be a CIA spy.

The general threatened to eternally ban me from visiting Thailand's deep south – and warned he'd track me down if I ever tried. Needless to say, I didn't bother ringing him up to set up this ride.

In Thailand, as in much of Southeast Asia, faxing official requests to grumpy officials isn't the best way to gain access to sensitive places. It's much more effective to work back channels and personal networks. That's how I ended up here. A Thai journalist who's chummy with army officers knew that I wanted to go on this patrol. She made a few calls on my behalf and – poof! – I was in.

So here I am. Face pressed to a firing port, sucking in as much oxygen as I can. Watching the lushness stream by through bomb-proof glass.

Ж

We're bouncing down a skinny cement lane. The road slices through thick foliage, parting a canyon of greenery. Jurassic-sized fronds are tickling the windows.

There are a few small settlements here, half-swallowed by jungle. I see cinderblock shacks with tin roofs. Muslim moms in black *abayas* tend to roosters. Old men in sarongs burn plastic garbage by the roadside.

When we approach, the villagers tense up and lower their gaze. They're like children spotting a bully entering the schoolyard. I see a tiny girl in a bubble-gum pink hijab clutching at her mom's legs.

'How rough is this area?' I ask the soldiers. 'Do firefights ever go down around here?'

'Not so many prolonged back-and-forth firefights,' says a skinny ranger, hand resting on his rifle's wooden stock. The enemy, he says, prefers to ambush and flee. 'But we do get bombings and shootings every day. Especially on narrow roads like this.'

As if on cue, his Samsung phone bleeps. A bomb has just gone off in a neighboring province. Soldiers are circulating photos on 'LINE' – a messaging app popular across Asia.

'See?' he says, passing over the phone. Though his screen is badly cracked, I can make out a photo. It shows a tangle of blackened, twisted metal – the aftermath of a bomb wired up to a parked motorbike. It was detonated remotely by mobile phone.

Updates from fellow soldiers arrive via LINE with a series of alert tones. *DING!* Bike exploded in semi-crowded area and *DING!* looks like some injuries here *DING!* but no one killed.

Peering through bomb-proof glass, these men see alien terrain. Few of the Thai troops know much about the local faith, Islam, and even fewer speak Malay, the local tongue. Rangers tend to see every Muslim guy aged sixteen and up as a potential threat. In their eyes, every chicken farmer's shanty could be a jihadi safe house.

It's not like the troops are outgunned. Thailand's deep south is flooded with about 60,000 armed security officers. That's one for every 30 residents. This is a full-on Buddhist police state.

But many of these guys are draftees, dragged to the borderlands by force. Before they arrive, their only insight into this world comes from Thailand's sensational TV news channels. Ambushed convoys, bombed markets, farmers decapitated – it's all televised in revolting detail.

From boyhood, these conscripts have been told that the deep south is a violence-wracked ghetto. They're about as eager to fight tropical mujahedeen as American GIs were keen to fight the Viet Cong.

Many end up resenting the skull-capped boys chattering in Malay. They distrust hijabi girls whose whispers they cannot understand. And behind every village elder's eyes, they perceive sinister plots.

Meanwhile, back in Bangkok, Thailand's generals stand behind gilded podiums and proclaim that the enemy's defeat is nigh – a refrain they've been repeating for more than 100 years.

X

Suddenly, the REVA brakes. The rangers mumble into their

headsets. Then they motion for me to get out. I'm not sure why I'm the only one exiting the vehicle. But I nod and comply.

I struggle with the REVA's back hatch, which feels as heavy as a bank vault door. When it finally swings open, I gulp in a delicious rush of fresh air.

There's an older ranger standing outside, waiting for me. I instinctively clasp my hands in a 'wai,' the standard polite greeting in Thailand. He returns my wai and follows up with a crushing handshake.

Officer Kamphen has the bearing of man in charge. He looks like he's answering the casting call for 'grizzled jungle commander' in a *Rambo II* reboot. His face appears to have been chiseled from a flint rock. He's dressed in midnight black from his beret to his boots.

Yet this forbidding look is offset by incessant grinning. 'Never fear!' Kamphen says. 'The villagers here have pure hearts. They've joined hands with the army.'

I'm starting to realize why we're here, standing on a half-paved road in an empty village, mosquitoes sucking at our necks. It seems that Kamphen has been rustled up to take on my questions – lest some 22-year-old ranger in the REVA veers off message.

He's here to project the Thai army's official stance on this conflict. It will sound familiar to anyone who recalls US military propaganda during the terrifying heights of the Iraq War.

It's a recipe of absurdly optimistic talking points. It calls for a dollop of 'the enemy is nearly vanquished' with a splash of 'we're winning hearts and minds' and a dusting of 'you know, those insurgents aren't even *real* Muslims.'

'The future is bright,' Kamphen says. 'The Muslims used to think wrongly. Their eyes were closed. But now they get it.'

Given the subject matter, Kamphen is over-the-top chipper – especially for a guy who looks like he enjoys garroting terrorists. 'But wait,' I say. 'This is the "red zone". It can't be all that peaceful.'

'Well, sure, there's this underground force that dares not show its face,' Kamphen says. 'But it's just a small group clinging to the past. That ideology is still in their heads. It hasn't been completely eliminated. Not yet.'

'You know,' Kamphen continues, 'the Muslims, they never want to separate from us. They love the army. One hundred per cent of them.'

'Wow. Really?' I say. 'One hundred per cent?'

I'm struggling to hide my incredulity. What about the 'underground force' that he mentioned just 30 seconds ago? And if everyone loves the troops so much, why did we drive here in a blast-resistant vehicle?

But Kamphen's grin is unwavering.

'Yep,' he says. 'One hundred per cent.'

Ж

Back in Golok's downtown, I'm nervously pacing inside the Merlin Hotel – a local institution offering one-star lodging near the strip. Rooms here rent by the hour. I've slept here for several days.

I no longer notice the cigarette burns that blacken the bed sheets. I'm even getting used to the nightly sound of women faking pleasure, their theatrical moaning barely muffled by thin walls.

Λ

Carpet crud mashes into the pads of my bare feet as I circle the room. I'm hyping myself up for an important call. I mash +60 on my iPhone screen – the country code for Malaysia – and read the rest of the digits off from my notepad.

This number was passed to me by a local newspaper columnist. I was warned that it might be out of date and that, even if the guy picks up, he might be too skittish to meet in person. After all, the man I'm calling is an avowed separatist.

I hear a ringing tone. Exhale. At least the number works.

'Hello?'

'Yes, hello, is this Wan Kadir?'

Long pause. 'Yeah.'

'My name is Patrick Winn. I'm a journalist staying in Sungai Golok. I'd like to interview you. In person. Is that possible?'

'You sound like an American.'

'That's true. I'm from America but I live here in Thailand.'

'I see. Well, sorry. I can't meet you in Thailand.'

'I can come to Malaysia. Please,' I say, revving up the flattery. 'I'm writing about the insurgency. I need to speak to someone with great expertise. I think you're the only one who can help me.'

Another long pause. 'Fine. Why not?'

My brain releases a squirt of dopamine. Landing a slippery interview must be as exhilarating as cracking a safe. I scramble for my notepad as he starts giving directions. He wants to rendezvous near Kota Bharu, a dusty city 45 kilometers south of Sword River. That's deep in the heart of fundamentalist Malaysia.

The man I'll soon meet is named Wan Kadir Che Man.

He's an elder statesman of sorts for a shadowy cabal, its adherents sworn to wrench this southern chunk of Thailand free from Buddhist control.

Wan Kadir once helped lead a network called *Bersatu*, which means 'unity' in Malay. Now defunct, it was a formidable coalition of violent separatist cells. It included groups with onerous-sounding names. The Patani Islamic Liberation Front. The Muslim Mujahadin Movement of Patani. The Patani United Liberation Organization.

The coalition also included a rebel faction called *Barisan Revolusi Nasional*. In English, that means National Revolutionary Front. Despite having the blandest name, the insurgent group was orchestrating more violence than all the others combined – and this remains true even today.

This rebellion is disorganized by design. Its fighters aren't structured like the guerrilla forces in Myanmar's mountains: mini-armies with uniforms and flags, led by commanders with public personas, all of them assembled into a hierarchy of platoons and brigades.

There, ethnic groups are blessed with choppy terrain – a landscape of gullies and peaks that unwieldy government forces struggle to invade. But Thailand's far south is all low-lying flatness. The landscape is more easily dominated by a large military, especially one armed and trained by the United States.

Here, the jihadis can't hope to occupy and defend terrain. So they hide in plain sight. The insurgents do not wear uniforms. In lieu of holding ground, its guerrillas strike hard and then melt back into the population. In that sense, they're more IRA than ISIS.

Their leadership is diffuse. They don't answer to a single

Osama bin Laden-style firebrand or one centralized committee. The insurgency isn't one raging sun. It's a constellation
of little stars: dozens and dozens of militant cells swirling
around a common cause.

Many are outright criminals: gold shop robbers, extor-
tion specialists and contract killers. Some cells are deft at
acquiring *ya ba* or crystal meth synthesized in Myanmar and
trafficking it over the river into Malaysia. This gives Thai
authorities a pretext to deride the entire rebellion as criminality disguised under a veil of extremist Islam.

This is a crass oversimplification. The movement's core
organizing principle is jihadi separatism. Each cell is devoted
to a singular mission: liberating this Muslim region from Thai
Buddhist dominance. But to fully understand their struggle,
you have to dial the clock back to the 1200s.

Seafaring Muslims from Arabia and the Indian subcontinent
first began landing on Southeast Asian shores around the
13th century. With monsoon winds at their sails, Muslim
traders could launch from the Persian Gulf and arrive in just
a few months.[7]

They first appeared in Aceh, the easternmost point of
the Malay-Indonesian archipelago south of Thailand. Look
at a map and you'll see why. Aceh is a natural place for initial
contact. It's a spit of land, jutting into the Indian Ocean like
a hitchhiker's thumb.

The locals – Buddhists and spirit-worshipping animists
– were impressed by these sailors. Perhaps they were wowed
by their Middle Eastern exotica – pearls, dates or fragrant

myrrh. But the seafarers also brought something much more potent: their religion.

Islam slowly spread from Aceh across the Asian tropics, all the way through what is now Indonesia, a nation containing the largest Muslim population on earth. A string of Islamic mini-kingdoms sprouted up along the region's shores. The northernmost Muslim stronghold was called Patani – a sultanate that occupied what is now much of northern Malaysia and southern Thailand.

Patani was no dump. Founded in the 1500s, this maritime sultanate would eventually dominate an area larger than Denmark. It grew prosperous as it traded with nations as far away as England and Japan.

Patani was ruled by a succession of queens who lived in an ornate palace. The first queen, Ratu Hijau, known as the 'Green Queen', took the throne amid a bloody succession fight that put many of her male heirs in graves.

Female rule, though uncommon for any Muslim sultanate, was widely accepted by Patani's subjects – particularly after the Green Queen proved herself politically savvy and socially generous. Her rule coincided with a period of prosperity, bolstered by sea trade and irrigation projects that nourished farmers' crops.

Under the Green Queen, Patani's subjects ate well and enjoyed the respect of foreign powers. They were pleased when power passed down to her kin: a succession of equally impressive women known as the Blue Queen, Violet Queen and the Yellow Queen. Starting in 1584, these women presided over the pinnacle of Patani civilization.

In the 1600s, European seafarers who visited would come away raving over their lavish royal court and festooned elephants. The sultanate was surrounded by lush paddylands and a dizzying variety of fruit orchards – all defended by 4,000 soldiers. Its army wielded a cannon that, in the words of one Dutch explorer, was 'bigger than any found in Amsterdam'.[8]

Patani needed this army to ward off the Buddhist Siamese (now known as Thais) who controlled vast lands to the north. For a few centuries, the sultanate proved sturdy enough to fend off Siamese invasion. But as time dragged on, Siam's wealth and military prowess grew – and little Patani struggled against the Buddhists' might.

By the late 1700s, the Siamese royal army had ground Patani down. They'd looted much of its wealth. They'd executed its most combative leaders. They'd even stolen its finest brass cannon.

However, Siam had yet to formally claim this Muslim terrain. Though colonized, the people of Patani could cling to the notion that, officially speaking, they were not 100 per cent conquered.

But that final humiliation was inevitable. It would come in 1909 with the intervention of a Western naval superpower.

)(

Enter Britain: an empire with a nasty habit of redrawing borders in hot, faraway places. Patani was about to join a pantheon of lands, from Nigeria to Hong Kong, that would find themselves forever altered by some English cartographer's pen.

By the early 20th century, the British Empire was lurking at Patani's backdoor, having already exerted control over several Islamic sultanates to the south. The Empire was busy building what would become one of its most profitable colonies, British Malay, replete with two vital commodities: tin and rubber. Britain was seeking to expand this lucrative territory as far north as possible.

Rolling over Patani, however, would not be so simple. After all, this was the de facto turf of Siam, one of Britain's valuable trading partners.

In lieu of an armed takeover, the British simply bullied Siam into ceding much of Patani's land. The Empire also forced Siam to promise that it would stay out of the Malay settlements nearby which the Buddhist kingdom had traditionally squeezed for gold and other tributes.

But the Siamese were allowed to keep a chunk of land north of Sword River. Left with only a sawed-off piece of Patani, Siam decided to go ahead and formally claim it.

To further erase the Islamic kingdom's identity, they hacked it into three new provinces named Yala, Pattani (with two Ts) and Narathiwat. The once-mighty sultanate was disintegrated beyond recognition. Much later, it would be popularly known as '*sahm jangwat chai-daen*'. Translation: those three border provinces. This label may sound banal but, in Thai, it connotes a dark otherness.

As for that grand cannon, once a symbol of the sultanate's golden years, it's now used as lawn art in front of the defense ministry in Bangkok – a middle finger to the memory of Patani.

〤

Of course, no one asked Patani's Muslims if they wanted to become full-fledged subjects of a Buddhist kingdom.

Having spent centuries under Buddhist swords, they were not exactly thrilled. Remaining defiant, they would not grovel to their Siamese overlords – and neither will many of their descendants.

Today, Siam is called Thailand. But in the eyes of many Patani Malays, they're still facing the same old oppressors. Their go-to slur for Thais is *Babi Siam*, which means 'Siamese pigs'.

Muslims still chafe at Buddhist teachers who force their children to speak Thai. They resent Buddhist bureaucrats who run their homeland like a fiefdom. But most of all, they loathe Buddhist cops and troops – imported from afar to stop them from seceding.

In 'those three border provinces', the Thai military is omnipresent. The roads are strangled by a system of check-points. Muslims can't go anywhere without bumping into soldiers blocking their paths with M-16s and spools of barbed wire. These checkpoints are scenes of daily degradation for Muslims. They're often pulled out of their trucks, interrogated and locked up for no good reason.

The vast majority of deep-south Muslims merely grouse about their mistreatment. Their blood may simmer when soldiers march past their windows. But they grumble privately, inside their homes, lest the state brand them as radicals.

A sliver of the population, however, has chosen to violently resist.

Patani separatism has flared and waned for more than a century. As recently as the 1990s, attacks were relatively infrequent – and the Thai army thought the resistance might fade away. But as it turns out, the insurgency was quietly mounting the greatest backlash to Thai occupation since the sultanate's collapse.

In the early 2000s, the rebellion rocketed to new heights. Thailand was suddenly facing a new breed of fighters with a flair for shock violence. Insurgents who coordinated under *Bersatu* – the insurgent network once headed by Wan Kadir – began deploying more sophisticated attacks.

They learned how to build Baghdad-style car bombs. They looted armories, building a stockpile of heavy weapons. They started coloring their separatist screeds with the vernacular of 21st-century jihad. They even beheaded Buddhists by the dozens – monks included. Occasionally, they'd film these killings and post snuff films online.

To this day, jihadis appear along the roadside, like wraiths, picking off government employees. They park cars packed with TNT outside Buddhist-owned nightclubs, set the timer and slip into the night. Practically anyone connected to the state is on their kill list. They'll shoot policemen, municipal workers, even postmen and kindergarten teachers.

This terror campaign has proven effective, turning Thailand's centuries-old project to fully assimilate Patani's 2 million descendants into a bloodstained failure.

Buddhist civilians have hunkered down in cities or fortified jungle outposts. Their prime institutions – schools and monasteries – have been converted into makeshift army camps. Even their golden-spired temples are ringed with razor wire.

In Pattani province, one prominent temple is home to seven monks and more than 100 soldiers – a confusing mashup of serenity and martial force. Fearful of dismemberment, tangerine-robed monks ask troops with M-16s to guard their morning alms runs.

As for fellow Muslims deemed too friendly to the Buddhist

state? Insurgents will mark them as *'munafiq'* (traitors to Islam) and shoot them dead inside their homes.

A series of jihadi pamphlets, scattered around victims' corpses in the mid-2000s, lays out the chilling terms of engagement:

'Do not accept any help, money or gold from infidel officers because this is poison ... Do not go to see doctors in infidel hospitals ... Otherwise, you will be killed. If we kill you, we kill for Allah on high.'[9]

)(

These death pamphlets are menacing. But these days, the jihadis' most vicious taunts are posted on Facebook.

Millennial separatists now serve as an unofficial media arm of the movement. To demoralize the enemy, they upload photo after photo of murdered Thais. In one Facebook photo, an insurgent lifts a Thai soldier's severed head by the hair. In another, a charred corpse, barely recognizable as human, is tagged 'DIE, SIAMESE PIGS'.

'As long as I can breathe, we won't grovel at Siamese feet,' boasts one Facebook jihadi. 'It's better for us to die as martyrs than live for centuries under the power of pigs.'

Once parochial, this insurgency is now colored by the sort of ultra-violent threats common in ISIS propaganda. Across Southeast Asia, cell towers and smartphones have proliferated – even in Thailand's rebellious south – and foreign influences are coursing into these 'red zones' through this new digital pipeline.

But these anonymous provocateurs aren't just soaking up jihadist content. Their accounts are also littered with the detritus of globalized pop culture. On their Facebook timelines, decapitation videos mingle with wacky cat photos. Their 'likes' include pages devoted to Quranic scripture, Harry Potter, Israel's demise and Liverpool Football Club.

They also delight in exposing Buddhists' full names and addresses ('doxxing') and calling for their heads. It doesn't take much to get marked for death. One young Thai man's offense was sending online come-ons to cute Muslim girls. The jihadi response: 'Piggy shithead, never flirt with our girls … you live at [address redacted] and we'll be taking care of you real soon!'

Women are not spared. Here's a typical Facebook threat sent to a Buddhist policewoman: 'Hey dickless pig in a skirt! You're finished.' And another, sent to a Buddhist high school girl who was accused of mocking Islam: 'If any Patani warriors see this cunt, kill her on sight.'

That's how they talk about teenage girls who, at worst, slag off their religion. You can only imagine how badly they despise women who sell sex within their homeland. The militants are increasingly devoted to striking brothels, dodgy clubs and other perceived impurities.

Even the insurgency's old guard – men who once preached self-determination, not religious extremism – are now sounding more fanatical. This is how Abu Imad, a supreme councilman from the Patani United Liberation Organization, describes Golok's brothels:

'It's all a plot. The Thais want to destroy our young generation. Muslim men use drugs and go to a prostitution house … then they get HIV, go home and spread it to their wives. Prostitution? No, no. This is not our culture. This is *their* culture.'[10]

This war was once a conventional struggle over land and power. Now the movement is shaded by the morbid tenets of Middle East-style jihad. Its moral crusades are muddling legitimate grievances.

Is this what Patani's ancient queens would have wanted – men bombing random moms and hostesses in the name of Islamic purity?

Is there no one inside the movement with enough clout to tame the sadists?

〉〈

If anyone can answer this question, it's Wan Kadir. After all, he was helping steer the insurgency during its hard descent into ruthlessness.

Back at my musty room at the Merlin Hotel, phone in hand, I scribble down directions as Wan Kadir dictates into my ear.

I start to realize he's not giving me a precise address. He's describing some sort of clandestine meeting spot by a roadside in Malaysia. He says he'll be waiting for me there in three hours.

'I want you to know that I'm only meeting with you because you're American,' Wan Kadir says. 'See you soon.'

Not the sort of comment I'd expect from a diehard Islamic separatist. But there's little time to ponder Wan Kadir's odd remark.

I've got to put some pants on and skate across the border.

〉〈

Here in coastal Malaysia, the air is the same as in Thailand: sizzling hot and lightly scented with sea breeze. The atmosphere, however, is entirely different.

Gone is the nervous energy radiating from thousands of young, armed men. Tube skirts are replaced with formless *abayas*. Paunchy dads in white-cotton *taqiyah* caps lounge in hammocks strung between palm trunks.

While Golok screams, Kelantan murmurs. Golok prods you to party 'til dawn, while Kelantan says, 'It's noon already? Bet you could go for a nap.'

I'm in a clunker Toyota taxi, careening towards Khota Bharu on a two-lane road. It's sweltering in here. When I grab the seatbelt buckle, my fingers recoil. The sun-baked metal clasp is as hot as a steel forge.

'Sorry,' the taxi driver tells me. 'Air-con is broken.'

Perhaps I should apologize too. I'm puddling sweat all over his vinyl seats.

There are zero bars along the roadside but plenty of little cafes and seafood joints. And they're packed. Down here, this is what passes for sensual pleasure: gorging on curried crab or getting buzzed on milk tea.

This place, I suppose, comes closest to approximating the separatists' dream state. All of this land once belonged to an Islamic sultanate. It is now a territory governed by Quranic law, purged of any visible vice, where Malays run the show. And it is free of Buddhists with machine guns.

After more than an hour, we reach the rendezvous point that Wan Kadir has selected. I spot a car parked on the shoulder of a nondescript stretch of highway. Its license plate matches the number he relayed over the phone.

'Right there,' I tell the taxi driver. 'You can pull up behind that car.'

'So you have a Malaysian friend. How do you know each other?'

'Um,' I stutter, fumbling for a passable lie. 'It's a long story. Here's your money. No change. Thanks!'

Wan Kadir steps creakily from the driver's side to grasp my hand. In the Malay fashion, he follows by touching his palm to his heart. Then he hustles me into his car.

He's in his mid-seventies and looking more frail than I'd imagined. He has the ruffled look of a professor: bad-fitting trousers, untidy gray hair that appears charged with static electricity.

'So. You're American. I bet you don't know that I fought for your country. In the Vietnam War. I'll tell you all about it when we reach my house.'

That was really not the sort of greeting I'd anticipated.

'Um, I look forward to that,' I say. 'Speaking of which, you told me on the phone that you agreed to meet because I'm from the States. Why is that?'

'Because you can help convince America to get involved in this struggle. They're the only superpower in the world. Only they can sort out this problem for good.'

'Wait, seriously?' I say. 'You want America to come here?'

'Of course.'

'After the all the chaos we've started in the Middle East?'

Wan Kadir groans. 'You sound like a typical Muslim. Saying all America does is bad. What about the good things America does for Muslims? Supporting Kuwait! Saudi Arabia!'

'America is good people,' he says. 'America ain't never come and kill nobody round here!'

So now an Islamic revolutionary is lecturing me on the virtues of US intervention. We're off to a baffling start.

We soon arrive at Wan Kadir's home, hidden away in a jungle clearing. In a nearby canal, fishermen offload armloads of silvery fish from bobbing wooden boats. The trees surrounding his land are alive with songbirds.

I hadn't imagined he'd bring me to some grim underground lair. But this is downright charming. Within minutes, we're seated in his living room. His wife emerges from the kitchen and starts switching on electric fans.

'Here you go,' she says, smiling warmly and setting down a platter of sugar-dusted donuts. 'Would you like coffee or tea?'

☓

In his 1996 declaration of war against the West, Osama bin Laden decried military occupation in all the places 'where Muslims have been the victims of atrocious acts of butchery'.[11]

He namechecked a series of well-known war zones: Kashmir, Chechnya, Palestine. But he also mentioned the lesser-known battleground of Patani. Wan Kadir grins when I bring this up. He's pleased to hear his struggle ranked alongside the great Muslim rebellions of the world.

Well, I ask, has your insurgency ever thought about enlisting the help of Al-Qaeda or ISIS – or any other multinational jihadi organization?

His grin curls into a sour sneer. 'To hell with Al-Qaeda!'

I've stumbled over a political tripwire. Apparently, you never suggest to a proud Patani insurgent that he could use some help from the Middle East. I am treated to a rant about the arrogance of Arabs – how they view themselves as the purest caste of Muslim, rich and wise benefactors, occasionally deigning to toss a few coins at Islamic crusaders in some Asian jungle.

We don't need their charity, Wan Kadir says. 'As far as terrorists are concerned, we can be at any level. On par with any group in the world!'

And if international jihadi groups come here despite your wishes? 'We'll kick them out. You think we're scared of Al-Qaeda? Hell no!'

Wan Kadir's English is essentially fluent. It was honed during a youthful stint in the United States – namely Philadelphia, where he hung with African-American Muslims in the late 1960s.

This chapter of his life left behind some endearing linguistic residue. When Wan Kadir gets heated, he sounds a bit like Dolemite, the 1970s hero of Blaxploitation movies. 'We are the great fighters of Patani,' he says, his voice oozing swagger. 'Al-Qaeda can go bullshit with other people. But not with me!'

Born around 1941, in Thailand's Pattani province, Wan Kadir is the son of an imam. Now, just as then, his home village is a rough and impoverished place. Most boys born there are fated to fish or to farm rubber and never see the outside world.

Not Wan Kadir. His father, fearing he had 'too many Thai words in his head', sent him to study the Quran in Saudi Arabia. There, he hung with students from across the world – including an African-American friend from Philadelphia.

That friend once slipped an address to Wan Kadir and told

him, look, if you ever make it to the States, my folks might put you up for a bit. Then in his early twenties, Wan Kadir was bristling under the Middle East's extreme orthodoxy. This offer stoked dreams of a freer life. He abandoned his studies and scrounged up just enough cash for a ticket to America.

'I arrived at the family's door at night,' he says. 'I had no money and didn't really know English. They said I could stay three nights 'cause those are the Islamic rules. But no more.'

Fast forward one year and Wan Kadir had his own pad. He spoke passable English, knew everyone at the local mosque and survived by working odd jobs. Yet he was nervously eyeing his visa's expiration date.

Desperate to stay, Wan Kadir sunk his hooks into America the only way he knew how – by walking into a recruitment office and volunteering to fight in Vietnam. He barely passed the height requirement.

His two years in the army, from 1967 to 1968, were unremarkable. He was largely confined to store rooms on US bases in South Vietnam. But in his downtime, he took classes, eventually scoring the equivalent of a high school diploma.

When his tour ended, Wan Kadir was able to enroll in New Jersey's Rutgers University. His chosen major: political science. He arrived to a campus crackling with anti-war fervor. Wan Kadir was about to get his first thrilling taste of political rebellion.

'My classmates were all going to demonstrations. I said, "What about our studies?" "Forget your studies!" they said. "This is more important."'

'It seemed like people liked the guys protesting more than the returning soldiers,' Wan Kadir says. 'So I joined them. For good or bad, I was filled with this incredible energy.'

In the span of five years, Wan Kadir had been jolted from a Thai fishing village to the Arabian Peninsula to Philadelphia's inner city – then over to Vietnam and, finally, back to an American college campus.

A unique jumble of characters had taken turns molding his young mind: Saudi clerics and Philly dudes, American drill sergeants and hippie idealists.

What emerged was a complex man. He drew strength from Islam yet resented Arab chauvinism. He was fond of America yet wary of its imperial talons. College professors sharpened his political acumen. Anti-war agitators taught him the language of protest.

But Wan Kadir was done taking cues from foreigners. He felt the lure of home, where his own people had long resented outsiders' heels on their necks.

After graduation, in the 1970s, Wan Kadir left the US – turning down a path to citizenship – and returned to his troubled birthplace. He would go on to become an academic with the International Islamic University, a mid-sized school in Malaysia. He worked as a small-time political science professor fixated on a niche cause: liberating the occupied land of Patani.

※

Fast forward to 2004. That was the year Thailand's war turned really gruesome – as well as being the year that Wan Kadir was yanked from obscurity.

It kicked off with a daring January pillage: 50 Patani insurgents butchered Buddhist troops as they overran an armory and looted assault rifles. Before the month was over, a monk was hacked to death. Many government schools were torched.[12] Soon thereafter, the militants debuted one of their earliest anti-sleaze attacks: an explosion outside a Golok karaoke bar that bloodied nearly a dozen Malaysian fun-seekers.[13]

The Thai government panicked. First, officials declared martial law – a free pass for troops to crack heads with impunity. Then they began rounding up and torturing suspects: some guilty, some later deemed innocent.

This hysteria crescendoed with a massacre.

In April 2004, more than one hundred Muslim men and teenage boys attacked a series of Thai army outposts. They rushed at fortified camps suicidally, like Norse berserkers, many armed with nothing more than kitchen knives.[14]

Most were swiftly shot down. But one group, about 30-odd guys, managed to kill three soldiers and then flee. They found refuge in an ancient mosque, built in the 16th century by a Patani sultan. It was soon surrounded by furious army squadrons.

Cornered, the insurgents screamed insults at the troops – essentially tempting them to rush in and kill every last man. The Thai soldiers obliged. They mowed down the militants in a blazing assault. Those who survived the initial attack were finished off with bullets to the head.[15]

Thailand's top brass thought they could crush this rebellion with brute force. The generals (and their American military advisors) still perceived the guerrillas as sloppy bandits. But banditry can't explain why boys in their prime will run screaming into certain death.

These guys weren't a bunch of drugged-up criminals – a common misconception among Thai officials. They were the harbingers of a darkening ideology.

The young men slain in that historic mosque became martyrs, and calls to avenge their deaths worked as an effective recruitment drive. This was the origin of a more hardcore epoch for the so-called 'Patani Liberation' movement.

This new generation would delight in dramatic violence, designed to maximize terror in a post-September 11 world. The young militants started beheading their so-called colonizers. Their nightmarish attacks provided the backdrop for an astonishing confession.

At a glance, the confessor, Wan Kadir himself, appeared harmless – a scruffy-haired scholar, then in his sixties. He'd written a well-regarded book on Muslim grievances in Thailand, published by Oxford University Press, along with plenty of papers decrying the colonization of Patani.[16] But he was little known outside academic circles.

That was about to change.

Wan Kadir wanted the world to know he was more than just some subversive historian. At a public seminar in Kuala Lumpur, he proclaimed that he was, in fact, the leader of *Bersatu*, the ultra-secret umbrella network of armed separatists.

Yet his public debut was marked by an appeal to calm — an unexpected overture from a violent syndicate. From his scholarly perch in Malaysia, Wan Kadir proclaimed that the time had come for negotiation —— lest his long-suffering people suffer more army massacres.

This came as a surprise to the Thai army. Though Wan Kadir had a tiny public profile, *Bersatu* was infamous. The network condoned the murder of anyone linked to the Thai state – from the police chief to the middle-school janitor. They were not known to be negotiators.

They waved no flags and held no territory. They instead preferred to dissolve into villages after attacks, dissipating like ghosts. This gave the group an ethereal quality that exasperated the Thai officers ordered to hunt them down.

Worse yet, Thai intelligence suggested that *Bersatu*'s members were linked up with both Hezbollah and Muammar Gaddafi's Libyan regime. Some were allegedly cavorting with Jemaah Islamiyah, who were then Al-Qaeda's affiliate in Southeast Asia.

'Is that true?' I ask Wan Kadir. 'Were your people in touch with all of those international militant groups?'

Yes, Wan Kadir tells me. But the degree to which Patani fighters parley with outside terror syndicates is overblown. Then as now, he says, the insurgency is mostly self-reliant.

'We don't want money from Arabs. We don't need money from ISIS.'

A little help from outsiders now and then, maybe, he says. 'But when you take money, you have to do what they say. And we don't share the same objectives as outsiders.'

I'm still in Wan Kadir's living room. Plaques emblazoned with Quranic passages hang on the walls. The tea is getting cold and I'm on my second super-sweet donut.

At this point, Wan Kadir has already told me about the fallout that followed his self-outing as an insurgency chieftain. Naturally, he lost his professor gig. But he picked up a new role: negotiating with the Thai army. He was eager to represent the more pragmatic side of an insurgency that seldom agreed to sit down with the enemy.

The military, exhausted from battling ghosts, was relieved that a man with a verifiable history had given a face to the movement. Satisfied with his bona fides, the generals agreed to talk.

In his younger, feistier days, Wan Kadir would never have consented to peace talks. But his ideology was softening. He could see that the army would never retreat. Its troops would instead grow more aggressive following each jihadi attack. He also realized that his movement was morphing into something more overtly sinister.

Wan Kadir had come to see the depravity in maiming moms and kids with marketplace bombs. Moreover, these Al-Qaeda-style attacks weren't bringing them closer to liberation. If the Thais would only concede some degree of autonomy, he would help wind down the war.

'My friends and I used to talk about killing anybody who gets in your way: Muslim or non-Muslim. But throwing bombs into a market – what type of fighting is that?' Wan Kadir says. 'I don't think we're going to defeat a nation of 65 million by killing a few innocent people in a market.'

'I say to the jihadis, "You're just killing yourselves out there." And they say, "Well, if I don't fight, the Thais will kill us anyway. So I [had] better go down fighting."'

Thais will always view Patani militants as 'weak and stupid', he says. 'Stupid or not, we're never going to stop resisting. But we need to start fighting peacefully. With reason. Through negotiation.'

'We give up something, they give up something,' he says. 'Argue. And if you can't agree, go home and come back the next day. That way, no one has to die.'

To most, all this will sound highly reasonable – especially coming from a self-professed terrorist. But during negotiations, Wan Kadir came off as too strident for the army's liking. He started by requesting total amnesty for other insurgent leaders – a non-starter for generals who'd seen too many young troops carved up by the rebels.

Nor did they care for his suggestion that the US play referee at future peace talks. The implication for the generals was that Thais are too inept to mediate without their American big brother.

'Honestly, I'm still waiting for America to sort this out. They're the only real superpower,' Wan Kadir says. 'No one else is on their level.'

'But America keeps refusing to help,' he continues, his voice taking on a peeved tone. 'Why? Because America's scared that groups like Al-Qaeda will get involved.'

He's got a point. I've interviewed several senior US security officials about this war and they all agree that America should keep its distance.

American intelligence officials stick to a consensus: the US should only offer light guidance and training to the Thai army and nothing more. No playing umpire between the generals and the rebels. Nothing flashy enough to attract the gaze of Middle Eastern jihadi organizations.

As one senior State Department security official named Randall Bennett told me: any overt American meddling is 'inviting trans-national, global terrorism. It's completely the wrong approach.'[17]

Still, Wan Kadir thinks that the Pentagon would fairly mediate a summit between Thailand, one of its oldest Asian allies, and a cabal of Islamic guerrillas. It's an odd notion that reflects his soft spot for America. But these US-led peace talks are pure fantasy.

When I gently convey this to Wan Kadir, he deflates, sinking into his seat cushions. Then he snaps back upright with righteous irritation.

'But I told you! We're not bad like Al-Qaeda. If other terrorists try to come help us, we'll tell them, "Get out. The Americans are our friends!"'

※

Wan Kadir's wife makes a sumptuous chicken curry. It's delectably oily, just as I like it, with a cinnamon aftertaste.

We've moved to the kitchen table for lunch. It feels good to drop some real food in my belly. I need a good anchoring to offset the jitters from all that strong tea and donut sugar. As we eat, I notice that his wife is unveiled, her gray locks tucked behind her ears. Wan Kadir is downcast, picking lightly at his food.

'I've put my family though a lot,' he tells me. 'I have sons but they don't think like me. One is a doctor. Another does business.'

'They don't care about the struggle?' I ask.

'The struggle? Forget about it,' he says. 'They don't ask one word about the struggle.'

Wan Kadir's life of rebellion has forced his family to hop from country to country. Few nations are keen to learn they're playing host to an insurgent on the lam. So they've lived a life on the run – from Thailand to Australia to Sweden. Even here, in the Malaysian backcountry, I sense that the tendrils of war could come slithering into this home.

'Does inviting me here put you in danger?'

'Oh, yes,' he says. 'If they think I'm leaking secrets of the movement? That's a bad accusation.'

'Are you concerned that someone from the movement will visit you after I leave?'

'Maybe.'

Ideologically speaking, Wan Kadir is in a tough spot. His adventures abroad gave him a view of humanity in all of its glorious complexity. At this point in his life, that seems to help inoculate him against the worst forms of dogmatism. Some globe-trotting jihadis are hardened upon witnessing perceived excesses in the West but, for Wan Kadir, these experiences have made his mind more limber.

Yet the new breed of rebels sees flexible men as spineless. Wan Kadir's fondness for the US really doesn't help his case. 'If you're pro-America? Like me? They'll say you're a bad guy.'

That may be putting it mildly. The movement's young vanguard, he says, views his whole generation with suspicion. 'The young guys say: "To hell with you! You're shit! You just stay in your air-conditioned room!"'

'They've told me: "Shut up your mouth. You're the guy running from the war zone. Open the Islamic books. Those who run from the battlefield – what kind of punishment do they get?"'

Wan Kadir no longer has much sway over the young men who wire up car bombs. But he's still an intermediary for militants who want to convey messages to foreign cohorts or disparate cells. 'After a bombing,' he says, 'they'll call me and say, "You know who did that? Us. Spread the word."'

'You know what?' Wan Kadir tells me. 'This younger generation, they are better in many ways. More brave. More solid in what they do. They have only one aim, to fight, and they don't care if they're going to die.'

Sure, I say, but they're also gunning down innocent civilians. Their kill list was once limited to hard targets: cops and troops. Now they'll bomb some poor hostess trying to earn her daily noodle money.

I suddenly remember a photo I had snapped the previous night in downtown Golok. I pull out my iPhone and cue it up for Wan Kadir.

It shows two porky men standing outside a karaoke bar. Both are shirtless. An elephant towers above their heads. The guys are eye level to its fuzzy chin – and the entire scene is saturated in pink light.

The beast is being led through the red-light district in chains by a handler, who charges drunk men $2 to feed the creature by hand. Sex workers help the guys guide bananas into the elephant's wet maw. The photo almost perfectly captures the otherworldly weirdness of Golok.

'Look at this,' I say. 'Back across the river, in your homeland, you can see this sort of thing every night.'

'I know,' he says, sighing. 'And for anyone who just came back from Mecca, wearing their white clothes? This stuff is very unusual. Very un-Islamic.'

'How about the hardcore jihadis?' I ask. 'When they see nightlife in Thailand – the bar girls, the booze, the prostitution – what are they thinking?'

'They think this is against Islam! It's their duty to eliminate this!'

There's that hot-tempered swagger in his voice again. When I bring up housewives dismembered by bombs, Wan Kadir goes dovish. But when I ask about another type of civilian – sex workers – the sympathetic notes in his voice disappear. I'm sensing a glitch in his moral code.

'Let me try this again,' I say. 'For any group that does this extreme violence against regular civilians, is there any way to excuse this?'

'No,' he says.

'So you say they shouldn't be bombing markets. And they shouldn't be bombing teachers.'

'No.'

'And they shouldn't be bombing nightclubs?'

'See, now you're talking about nightclubs,' Wan Kadir says. 'That's another story.'

'So nightclubs can be a legitimate target?'

'Oh, yes!' Wan Kadir says, snickering.

I flash back to the woman killed in the street near Golok's nightclub zone. I recall Pin the hostess gulping booze to extinguish the terror burning up her insides. I really don't see how slaughtering women in a red-light district brings Patani one inch closer to liberation. But I'm curious to hear his rationale.

Instead, Wan Kadir clenches up. Perhaps he's heard the sinister inflection in his own laughter. I implore him to go on. But he remains silent.

'I will say nothing.'

⋊

To the insurgents, Thai sex workers are like voodoo dolls: defenseless targets that, when skewered, make all the other sinners spasm with fear. It seems that even Wan Kadir, despite his inclination for peaceful negotiation, can't bring himself to fully denounce attacks on brothels.

My time with Wan Kadir has helped me to see this vice war through jihadist eyes. But now I'm keen to hear more from the women in their crosshairs.

So I've returned to Golok to meet one of the insurgency's female targets. Her name is Bam, a twiggy, pony-tailed sex worker in her thirties. During her ten years in Golok, Bam has survived a bombing not once but thrice.

She first experienced the bite of flying shrapnel back in 2007. When that bomb exploded, she barely noticed the jags of metal lacerating her face. In fact, she felt nothing at all. Her senses were blanked out by a time-stopping shock. All Bam perceived was a searing whiteness.

But as seconds passed, little blips of reality dribbled back into her conscious mind. I am at work, she thought. Hostessing at a bar. In Golok. And that sound? It was an explosion. A big one. The other women are scrambling around the bar. Shit, we're being bombed, she realized. I have to run too!

In the space of a hazy minute, the drip-drop trickle of stimuli swelled into a horrible torrent of sights and sounds. Suddenly Bam was taking in everything: the stinging on her forehead, tabletops showered with glass, the pained screams, flames lighting up the strip.

But when she tried to flee, nothing happened. Her synapses were fried by panic. Her legs were stiff. It was like trying to will a mannequin into motion.

Her next memory was the sound of an ambulance's screeching arrival. Not a proper, state-run service, mind you. Thailand mostly relies on privately-run disaster squads. They're more like body snatchers than medics.

These pseudo-EMTs, who usually lack formal training, are often the first to respond to a shooting or explosion. They scoop up injured bodies and rush them to emergency rooms. Hospitals will tip them for bringing business in the form of mangled patients.

Fortunately, Bam wasn't severely wounded. So she just sat there watching the medics drag away scalded bodies. 'You know, I've been through several bombings since,' Bam tells me. 'Death has grazed me three times. I'm kind of used to it.'

'But back then, though, at my first bombing? I was just thinking, "Damn, I want to go home so bad."'

※

Let's rewind so I can properly introduce Bam.

She works at The Night Lady, a karaoke joint in Golok. It's located a few kilometers from the heavily defended central strip. This is a second-tier party street, lined with half a dozen open-air bars. Out here, the working women are all a bit older, hiding their age under thick smears of rouge.

I arrive during a monsoon. Raindrops lash the vinyl awnings slung over bar facades. Despite the elements, women remain stationed in front of the bars. Commonly known as 'bar girls', no matter their age, these women work as sentries, scanning the street for potential customers and inviting them inside.

Tonight, they look desperately bored. So do the soggy street dogs that are huddled by their stilettoes, seeking shelter from the downpour. It doesn't take long for the 'bar girls' to spot me – a lone male, pelted by rain, walking down the middle of the street.

I soon hear cries of 'Welcommmmmeee!' and 'Helllooooo!' Once the first cluster of women cries out, others down the lane are alerted to my presence. They snap to their feet, releasing more calls that cascade down the dark street.

Bam, however, isn't solicitous like her peers. In fact, when I step into The Night Lady, she barely notices I'm there.

Inside, the bar's decor is provocatively girlish. Its walls are painted dollhouse pink. The tables are covered in plastic matting decorated with Disney princesses. I feel like I've stumbled into a sleazy daycare center.

I find Bam with her head down, sitting at a table facing the street. She's obsessing over some sort of arts-and-crafts project. The table is littered with scraps of wrapping paper, which she keeps snipping with a pair of children's scissors. After cutting out neat ribbons, Bam will pinch the paper shreds into little shapes.

'What are you doing?' I ask, breaking her reverie. She looks startled – like someone caught singing in the shower.

'Oh, um, I'm making paper stars,' she says, matter-of-factly. By way of explanation, Bam drops a tiny origami star into my palm.

She gives me a moment to look it over before plucking it away. Then she drops it into a glass flower vase brimming with hundreds of tiny paper stars. This project must have taken hours.

'Slow night?' I ask.

'Yeah,' she says. 'You know, the rain. Would you like a beer?'

Bam hops up, returns with a bottle of Leo and sets it down on the table – right on the face of Jasmine from *Aladdin*. A few beers later, Bam is telling me about her first-ever bombing. Peering over those scorched bodies, she says, brought on a primal impulse to flee towards the comforts of home.

But Bam wasn't thinking of her local digs, a drab little room above The Night Lady's bar. She meant her real home, a village more than 1,600 kilometers away.

It's located in Thailand's northeast, a vast rice-farming region known as Isaan.

𝕏

The backstory of most working women in Golok begins in Isaan. Often maligned by the upper classes, the region is Thailand's aching backbone.

Isaan isn't well known across the globe. But if you've ever eaten at a Thai joint anywhere in the world, you've likely tasted rice grown within a few hundred kilometers of Bam's village. Thailand is among the world's biggest rice exporters and most of its rice stalks are pulled from the Isaan mud. The region's soil and toil keeps the national economy humming.

Bam is from Sakhon Nakhon, a poor province even by Isaan standards. It's the butt of many jokes. The teasing revolves around the province's reputation for grilling up stray dogs.

Buddhist Thais generally don't eat dogs. Actually, neither do most people in Sakhon Nakhon. But you *can* find vendors selling barbecued dog ribs up there – and it only takes a little bit of dog eating to work up a bad rep.

The province's taste for canine was brought over by waves of Vietnamese refugees fleeing 20th-century imperial wars. Many settled in Sakhon Nakhon, a remote place where they could rebuild their lives in peace. They eventually assimilated with the native Isaan farmers.

To this day, urban Thais like to mock Sakhon Nakhon's melange of refugees, field hands and dog eaters. They also laugh at them for eating crickets and field mice – fine sources of protein in an arid land. Bam knows that city folk sneer at her kind. But the villagers of Isaan are her people and she loves them all the same.

Isaan folks are known for their soulful music, bawdy humor and lilting dialect. They don't shy from long days, strong drink or tongue-melting chilies. Isaan's toughness is beyond dispute. One spoonful of a spicy local stew can turn a Green Beret into a mewling, red-faced mess. An Isaan toddler, meanwhile, will casually slurp it all up like pea soup.

In the 1960s, Isaan was shaken up by war tremors rippling across Southeast Asia's mainland. Thailand – then and now, a kingdom dominated by its right-wing military – was deeply fearful of a communist contagion creeping over from Vietnam.

Thai officials were mindful that America had thwarted the total communist takeover of the Korean peninsula roughly ten years earlier. So they allowed the US to expand its military empire into Isaan. The northern Thai hinterlands were a perfect rear base from which American jets could launch into the sky, soar over the craggy mountain spine separating Thailand from communist-run terrain and unload bombs on guerrillas' heads.

The US military complex also had plans for Thailand's urbanized center. It funneled tens of thousands of war-frazzled US grunts towards Bangkok and Pattaya – a policy that transformed quarters of both cities into playgrounds of vice. This practice was officially known as R&R (rest and relaxation) and it caused the demand for sex workers to soar.

The vacuum was largely filled by young women seeking an escape from hardscrabble villages in Isaan. They fanned out to the bars and brothels, becoming the work horses of a trade that, for five decades running, has made Thailand the butt of vulgar jokes worldwide.

It's not that the American war machine introduced prostitution to Thailand. Sex work in the kingdom is documented in centuries-old texts. But the surge of American troops revolutionized the trade, exploding it from a more discrete, haphazard practice into a mass commercial industry: a raucous, neon-lit buffet of young women, many of them showcased explicitly for foreigners.

To this day, Thailand's sex trade still has a distinctly American flavor. The bars usually crank out Western Top 40 hits or techno pop. Many sex workers are hyper-commodified with numbers pinned to their bikinis – 32, 14, 25 – like fast-food menu items. This helps inebriated foreigners more easily single out their favorite dancer and buy her time for a few hours.

Though the GIs are long gone, this prostitution trade has metastasized into a billion-dollar sector servicing locals and travelers alike. The sex industry's resiliency is owed to a mix of complex factors: a permissive streak within Buddhism, stubborn poverty in the upcountry, police collusion and, most of all, the profits to be made.

This gray-market empire now stretches from Bangkok and Pattaya to second-tier cities in Isaan – Udon Thani and Ubon Ratchathani, former sites of American air force bases – and then all the way down to the remote karaoke dens of Golok.

Before Bam arrived in Golok, she spent her days shin deep in paddy muck. On the farm, she says, you're always one wave of drought or pestilence away from stomach-gnawing poverty.

But selling sex in a border town is almost recession-proof.

Like many tens of thousands of Isaan women before her – dating all the way back to the 1960s – she calculated that brothel work might be preferable to toiling in the mud.

'Never again will I bake under the sun,' Bam says. 'Working in a bar beats slaving in a field.'

'But this is much more dangerous than farming,' I say. 'Is it worth it?'

'Well, yeah. There's shade in the bar. And beer.'

Bam's backstory – farmer turned sex worker – is extremely common in Golok's bars. The overwhelming majority of 'bar girls' around here hail from Isaan. They may prefer to work in Bangkok but lack the looks, connections or English-language skills to work in the country's safer red-light zones. Most women, Bam included, originally came to Golok at the suggestion of a friend who was already working in the deep south. Their presence here is self-sustaining.

'People may look down on us,' she says. 'They'll talk about dignity. They'll say my virtue is more important. Well, tell me this – can I buy food with virtue? Or will I need cash?'

)(

In the West, karaoke is a public spectacle. You take a few Jäger shots. You humiliate yourself over a MIDI track of Lionel Richie's 'Hello'. You earn a few pity claps and slink back to your barstool. There's nothing sexy about it.

But in Thailand, as in much of Asia, karaoke is often a more private affair intertwined with prostitution. It's the medium through which sex workers can feign intimacy with strangers. They cuddle and croon together, sharing drinks, until the guy decides to bargain for paid sex.

Bam's first priority is feeding her customers overpriced lager – and lots of it, because she gets a cut of each purchase. And like most Golok bars, The Night Lady is also outfitted with a karaoke machine, a few wireless mics and a wall-mounted TV.

Bam likes to pressure men into singing. That only inspires more and more boozing because, hey, who wants to sing Lionel Richie sober? Then she'll flirt hard, tracing fingers along a man's scalp while cooing about his magnificent voice. If the guy wants more of her attention, he can shell out $30 to take her back to his hotel.

During Bam's karaoke bar career, she's picked up a few pointers. Think of them as best practices for successful sex work in an insurgency zone.

▶ **You are too vulnerable to make enemies:**
'If you're friendly, you'll live longer. We have to be friends with everyone. Bandits. Cops. Bureaucrats. Even terrorists are welcome here.

'I'm not here to make enemies. I talk sweetly to everyone. This is key to my survival. Even if I knew a customer was a terrorist, I wouldn't say a word to anyone. Because that wouldn't be very safe for me, would it?'

▶ **You're not just a 'bar girl'. You're a late-night therapist:**
'Our job is tending to these men. Figuring out what they desire. Figuring out how to get their happiness back. If they want to gripe about their jobs or their wife, you just listen.

'We even get big shots coming in here, confiding in me about business deals. They ask me for advice! I'm thinking,

"Seriously? Go figure this out yourself!" But you just have to listen.'

▶ **Soothe jealous men or risk their wrath:**
'Most fights start over jealousy. One man takes a liking to a girl. Then later on she's sitting with a different customer and, well, watch out. I've seen men slashing each other with knives. You have to calm the angry guy right away. Feed him beer. Tell him, "Let's just have fun and be merry!"'

▶ **Politely enforce a no-guns policy:**
Cops or militiamen will often enter the bar with guns on their hips. 'So I'll ask gently, "Brother, why do you need a gun in here? Can't you leave it in your car?" I worry they'll get drunk and it'll go off.'

▶ **Learn how to sing in a foreign tongue:**
Bam excels at Thai-language country pop. But she can also break out a few Chinese and Malay ballads to wow customers from Malaysia. She learned these songs phonetically. 'I have no idea what I'm singing,' she says. 'Love songs, I guess?'

▶ **Sappy romantics are a waste of time:**
'Some of the regulars will say, "I love you, Bam." Oh, that's nice. Can I eat your love? Will it help me survive? Is it real? Pull it out so I can see it. Sorry, but I prefer the love of friends and family over men.'

▶ **Never display your political loyalties:**
'Personally, I like the troops. If they went away, this place would be nothing but bandits and druggies. But my

customers might be separatist sympathizers. So I never bring up stuff like that.

'I don't have a problem with Muslims. Some of them hate women like me. Most seem fair. Honestly, even the terrorists, I don't think they're so different from me. They're just doing what they've been taught by hardliners in their religion.'

▶ **Never tell customers if you're miserable or afraid:**
'This is a life of stress and struggle. But no one forces us to come down here. Keep your troubles to yourself. Don't complain to customers. Just steel yourself against the awfulness.

'In this job, you're forced to get close to strange men. It goes against your natural instincts,' says Bam, clinking fresh ice into our mugs.

'So I just think to myself, "Look, Bam. You're a woman. All you have is your brain. But you can do this. You can survive."'

)(

Outside, the monsoon rains have softened to a drizzle. Hours have passed without another customer. But out on the street, we can hear male voices resounding in the humid air.

In stumble two guys, trailing a gray fog of cigarette smoke into The Night Lady. It's go time. Bam excuses herself with a smile.

Ten minutes later, Bam and the boys are all piled into a booth, thighs and shoulders mashed together, clinking glasses and crooning rock-song choruses. The guys' forearms are blotchy with crude tattoos. They wear Chuck Taylors and scratchy black goatees. Bam, arms draped around their shoulders, is a woman transformed.

With me, she was introspective, dissecting the nature of vice and virtue while dithering with origami stars. Now she is wild and loud, bristling with feminine energy, taking hard pulls of beer.

I guess that's what these guys want from Bam: a lusty, goodtime girl. And what had I wanted out of Bam? A brothel philosopher, I suppose, offering raw reflections on life in Golok. I didn't come here for cuddles, but perhaps I was seeking a certain intellectual intimacy. Bam, a master diviner of male desire, appears to have sized me up perfectly.

The longer I stay, the more I'll distract Bam from her real customers. I don't want to do that. I like Bam. She seems refreshingly human – a peace-loving soul in a sea of horny, war-like men.

So it's time to leave The Night Lady. I wave her over, pay my bill and get up to leave.

'Wait,' she says. 'I want you to have this.'

Bam picks up the vase full of paper stars and presses it into my hands. 'Really?' I say. 'It took you forever to make this!'

'I can always make more,' Bam says. 'Be careful out there. It's dark.' She clasps her hands in a *wai*.

I return the *wai* and wander out into the street, sidestepping puddles. Rainwater is pooling in craters on the road. Each one is lit with an orange shimmer, a reflection of fairy lights strung overhead.

⋊

It's my last night in Golok. Before I leave this town, I decide to wander over to the bomb-charred street that kicked off this strange journey.

Just days before, this was a messy crime scene. There's little evidence of that now. Rain has washed away the victim's blood. Municipal workers have swept the shrapnel into a storm drain.

But when I crouch down, I see bits of shattered glass twinkling under the amber streetlights. Crouching lower, my face to the curb, I can still see scorch marks darkening the pavement.

When the traffic goes quiet, I hear techno roaring from cheap amplifiers a few blocks away. I start walking towards the noise.

As I head into Golok's throbbing downtown, pole-mounted loudspeakers crackle overhead. An upbeat female voice issues a pre-recorded warning: 'If you see unusual vehicles or people, please notify police. We seek to ensure your safety!'

There's a monstrous REVA idling on the corner. In the wake of the bombing, these blocks are reinforced with armed men from various branches. I see a medley of uniforms out tonight: cops in dull brown, soldiers in jungly green, volunteer paramilitaries in khaki pants and white T-shirts. They're all out in force to protect the men who love Golok.

Entering the strip, I spot Pin looking a bit hung-over, perched on a plastic stool. She's half-heartedly calling out to male pedestrians while munching skewers of Isaan sausage. Tonight, most guys seem to be drifting towards The Marina – a massive hotel complex that dominates the strip.

At $31 per night, it is the city's most expensive venue. That price buys lodging in a fifteen-story fortress of vice. The Marina contains an in-house massage joint and two raucous nightclubs. There's even a ballroom where diners are treated to a middle-aged crooner in Tammy Faye make-up butchering love songs.

The Marina Hotel is actually a footnote in Southeast Asian terrorism history. In 2005, the Patani insurgency's first-ever car bomb exploded right here – destroying the ballroom and claiming five lives.[18] The hotel's immediate vicinity has been bombed four other times.

And yet it's often packed.

I stroll through The Marina's lobby and up to its second-floor disco. At the entrance, a bouncer politely urges customers to deposit their handguns inside lockers mounted to the wall.

Inside, the club is cavernous. Nicotine storm clouds pool by the ceiling. The DJ is blasting some mutant breed of music: Western Top 40 songs sped up until the vocals whine like chipmunks. It's murderously loud. I can almost feel my intestines jiggling.

All of the club's tables face a stage showcasing a troupe of 'coyotes'. This slang term derives from *Coyote Ugly*, that cheesy American movie about tequila-drunk bartenders dancing on tables. Somehow, in Thailand, the word 'coyote' has come to mean an attractive Thai dancer paid to wiggle for male spectators. For an added fee, they'll drink tequila with you. Off-site services are negotiable.

I feel fingers clutching at my forearm. I'm being accosted by an older woman, an aunty type, dressed in a candy-purple pantsuit. Her blazer glows lilac against the darkness.

Aunty cups a hand to my ear and fills it with hot breath. She rapidly shouts instructions: 'You! Sit down over here. What type of beer do you want? Pick out your favorite coyote. Buy her lots of alcohol. Then give Aunty a big tip!'

Aunty is an aggressive matchmaker. She recommends a twenty year old named Benz. I see her on stage, dancing joylessly, with a Samsung Galaxy III stuffed into her bikini bottoms.

Aunty boasts that she's imported all of these 'coyotes' from her native Isaan. 'They're Khon Kaen girls. You know Khon Kaen?' I nod. It's one of the more well-to-do pockets of Isaan. 'Khon Kaen girls are light skinned!' Aunty says. 'Sexy!'

Now Benz is sauntering towards my table. Somehow, Aunty has summoned her, perhaps with an unseen flick of her hand. I didn't agree to this but, whatever, I'm keen to hear another woman's take on Golok. Benz approaches hesitantly, eases onto a stool and offers a meek *wai*. Aunty vanishes into the dark.

Benz will barely look at me. Her mood emanates mild dread. I get the feeling she'd sooner endure an endoscopy than a chat. When I start speaking in Thai, however, relief washes over her face.

'Oh, good,' she says. 'I was nervous 'cause I don't speak any English at all. We never get *farang* customers.'

Benz is all glue-on eyelashes and glittery lotion. Wearing vanity contact lenses, her irises are as big as nickels. I suppose she's meant to exude cutesy glamour. But when I ask about life in Golok, Benz sounds grim.

'For this line of work,' I say, 'you must have one of the better jobs in Golok. You're indoors. There are bouncers here. You're not out on the street.'

'Yeah, but the customers here are extra aggressive,' she says. Benz points to her thick, flesh colored leggings. The coyotes have to wear them, she says, to ward off probing fingers.

I take a look around the nightclub. There's a crew of three guys nearby, ensconced in cigarette smoke, slugging glasses of beer and 100 Pipers, a discount brand of whiskey.

They're all huddled around a miserable-looking coyote in a pineapple-yellow bikini. I see hands pawing at the woman's tights. One guy hugs her possessively. Another, looking spurned, is sulking. A third is so drunk that he keeps ashing in his friends' beers.

'Malaysians,' Benz says. 'In their country, everything is a sin. Everything guys do – chasing girls, drinking beer – it's all a big sin. That's why we're here. To help them release it all.'

Benz, looking bored, starts fiddling with her Samsung. I've had my fill of this place. I pay up and slink out of the club before Aunty can badger me for a huge tip.

Downstairs, in the hotel's ballroom, the atmosphere is less caustic but equally depressing. It's strewn with men eating at tables, taking a break after bouts of lechery. They're sucking on cigarettes between bites of mediocre Thai food.

In the corner, a plump female crooner belts out 'My Heart Will Go On' by Celine Dion. She appears to have applied an entire cosmetics aisle to her face.

But the singer is largely ignored. Crowd participation is limited to sympathy applause from Thai waiters, all lined up along the wall in unfashionable slacks. The only other entertainment is a TV mounted to the wall. It's running a local news program at low volume.

The screen flashes to an image that startles me. It's a photo of a dead woman, half covered by a sheet, surrounded by uniformed men. Her body is lit by flashlight beams.

I know her.

It's the woman who was killed just a few blocks away. I finally learn her name, presented in Thai script that scrolls across the bottom of the screen.

Her name is Sarika Mama.

Now the news program is running closed-circuit security footage of the bombing. They're playing the video on a loop. Everyone in the ballroom can watch Sarika die over and over. Her murder comes in a white flash that flings pixelated debris across the screen.

A few of the Thai waiters stare up at the screen. The sex tourists look bored. The lady on stage begins warbling through Eric Clapton's 'Tears in Heaven'.

Through the ballroom's windowed facade, I can see the strip, its pink lights blinking across the rain-slick road. This place will erupt again. It's just a matter of when.

Maybe a few months will pass before another woman like Bam is picking glass out of her hair. Golok might even go a whole year before the next Sarika is killed by an indiscriminate blade of shrapnel.

But when the next attack comes, I'll probably be somewhere else. Same goes for the other heavy-lidded patrons in this hotel. Less fortunate are the working women of Golok, reporting night after night to the barroom front lines – where the night brings threats from drunks and zealots alike.

= major dog-trafficking route

N.KOREA

S.KOREA

CHINA

Shanghai

Isaan region: traditional source of
free-range stray dogs
for Vietnam

TAIWAN

MYANMAR

VIETNAM

Hanoi Bắc Ninh

DMZ

Yangon

THAILAND   Nhi Trung village

LAOS

Bangkok

CAMBODIA

PHILIPPINES

S O U T H   C H I N A   S E A

MALAYSIA

Kuala
Lumpur

MALAYSIA

I N D O N E S I A

Jakarta

I N D I A N   O C E A N

AUSTRALIA

CHAPTER VI

Swamp Hounds

Location: Nhi Trung, Vietnam

*Where Viet Cong vets ambush dog
thieves under the starlight*

It's barely 9am and the dog butcher's boots are already slick with blood.

The interior of his brick-walled abattoir keeps accumulating cylindrical cages fashioned from metal wire. Each is about the size of a duffel bag and crammed impossibly tight with two or three live canines.

Snouts smush against steel wiring. Tails jut at cruel angles. Their imprisoned bodies heave and squirm, rattling steel caging against the concrete floor.

In one particularly overstuffed cage, it's difficult to see where one dog ends and the next begins. The three animals – or is it four? – have become a singular, grotesque creature with too many paws and too many eyes. All of its mouths gulp for air.

The butcher's name is Thu, a compact man in his early forties. He's clad in a zippered jumpsuit made from synthetic material, pant legs tucked into rubber waders. It's a pragmatic outfit, he tells me. 'The blood rinses right off.'

Thu keeps his black hair buzzed and a cigarette permanently smoldering at his lips. It's currently drooping ash. The butcher is too busy to stop and inhale. He's got dogs piling up at his feet. Some were dropped off around dawn. Others arrived just an hour ago. All seem to have figured out what this place is all about. The animals are trembling, too panicky to bark.

Thu zeroes in on a tawny dog, uncomfortably mashed into a cage with another mutt. It's a particularly fit-looking creature: muscled haunches, glistening black nose, with silky fur the color of egg nog.

The butcher towers overhead. The animal flinches in his gaze, trying to make its body small. 'That one,' Thu says. 'Just you watch. In a moment, that dog will be white as snow.'

I start to ask Thu what that means but my voice is drowned out by a motorbike horn. The butcher turns his head to see another one of his suppliers rumbling up the asphalt lane out front. The man's bike is loaded down with two more cages, both triple-packed with live dogs.

It's been like this all morning. Every time Thu goes to yank out a dog and give it the knife, he's interrupted by another visitor. This morning has brought a half-dozen sellers to his open-air slaughterhouse.

They come along every half hour or so, pouring in from the countryside. Thu's back-alley shop is located in Bắc Ninh. It's a province roughly 50 kilometers from Hanoi on the north side of the Red River. This is where the capital's industrial sprawl begins to thin out.

These visitors are dog wranglers, eager to sell their catch. Prime canine fetches $3.50 per kilo, triple the price of pork. But only if the quality is high. Thu tells me his suppliers are always trying to pass off low-grade animals with rashy stomachs and purplish gums. He must scrutinize each mutt.

Thu flicks his cigarette and walks out to inspect the man's offerings. He unfastens the cages from the back of the motorbike, weighs them on a plastic scale and then sets them on the ground.

'Let's have a look at those teeth,' says Thu, reaching for a wooden pole. He jabs each dog in the ribs, provoking snarls that reveal their gums.

I'm no dog butcher but, at a glance, this batch looks healthy. They certainly aren't the sort of lice-nibbled wretches you see nosing through garbage in most Southeast Asian cities. Their eyes shine, fur shimmers. They seem like pets. Some look well fed, as if they've known love.

As Thu and the wrangler haggle over pricing, I kneel by the cages, peering in at a dog with a khaki-colored coat. He's lovely, the sort of dog who'd get chosen from an adoption shelter in just a week or two. I inspect its neck and, sure enough, there's a collar.

The butcher usually keeps his exchanges brusque and businesslike. But I can hear him browbeating the seller, a man roughly Thu's age in a puffy coat, reeking of dog funk and cigarettes.

'Look at this little ten-kilo thing here,' Thu says, prodding at the oldest dog in the lot. I hadn't noticed before but its muzzle is streaked with a few silvery hairs. 'I'll take the other five,' he adds. 'But this one is too old and you know it. Get it out of here.'

The man nods sheepishly.

'Seriously,' Thu says. 'Why the hell would you even bring me a dog like this?'

The seller silently kneels down to unlatch his cages. With his wooden staff, Thu herds them into empty cages belonging to the abattoir. Then he lets out a shrill whistle that summons his wife.

A harried woman hustles out from the back, face concealed behind a cotton hospital mask. The sleeves on her knock-off Adidas jacket are rolled up. She fishes out a wad of cash, counts out the equivalent of $200 in Vietnamese dong and hands it off to the seller. That's damn good money in these parts. More than a rookie beat cop will make in one whole month.

Thu sends the guy packing and lights another menthol. Then he's right back on the slaughterhouse floor. Time to work through that pileup of mutts. There are so many animals cluttering up the shop that his wife is double stacking cages to save space.

'Februaries,' Thu says. 'They're always like this.'

These are the last weeks before *Tết*, the observance of a new lunar year. This is Vietnam's largest and most joyous annual celebration. It's also peak dog-eating season: a time when northern Vietnamese, mostly men, feast on canine by the millions.

Nothing, the old-timers say, chases away bad luck quite like a boozy dog meat session with your pals. For superstitious Vietnamese, it's a ritual of purification – and, by tradition, it must precede the arrival of *Tết*.

Dog eaters don't go for variety. No one eats Huskies or Dalmatians. Restaurants stick to a common breed that you see everywhere in Vietnam: dingo-looking mutts ranging in color from pecan to umber to coal black.

But those who fancy dog meat have to squeeze in this meal before the new year dawns so that they can emerge, cleansed of misfortune, into life's next chapter. The Year of the Horse ends in twelve days. Hanoi's dog-meat eateries will take every grade-A carcass Thu can offer.

He picks up his favorite wooden-handled knife and rakes it over a sharpening stone. Between now and the beginning of the Year of the Goat, he will plunge this blade into the necks of more than 200 dogs.

Egg Nog Mutt – the one Thu was preparing to butcher before he was interrupted – is next.

Thu disappears into some room in the back of the slaughterhouse. He re-emerges with a bulging cloth satchel.

'What's in the sack?' I ask.

'Car battery,' he says. In his right hand, Thu grips a long metal wand. There's a black cable running from the battery all the way up the pole's shaft. It's connected to twin metal prongs at the tip. They look sharp.

This is a DIY shock baton. Thu made it himself. With his jumpsuit and battery-charged zap wand, he looks like some sort of post-apocalyptic Ghostbuster.

The butcher hovers the pronged pole over Egg Nog Dog and then – with a hard thrust – sinks the electrodes into its neck. Two jolts turn it into a convulsing mess. Its body bucks inside the cage, flopping against the cage's other dog, which dares not risk a single yip of protest.

Shocked unconscious, Egg Nog Dog is lifted from the cage by its neck with a long iron clamp. Thu plops the animal down onto a wooden cutting board on the floor. He slides a little basin under its head.

Then he jabs the dog's throat with his blade. Blood torrents out like an open spigot. Even after I reflexively look away, I can still hear the sound of liquid pattering against the plastic.

And then – to my astonishment – the bloodied dog stands upright, zombie-like, and begins to slowly pad away. Thu gasps too, more in amusement than horror. He is impressed with the dog's half-dead defiance.

'What is this,' he says, 'some kind of mountain dog?'

The butcher reaches for an iron pipe. He'll have to finish it off the old-fashioned way. The brick walls resound once, twice, with the sound of steel cracking skull.

There will be no walking away from that.

Thu's wife appears from the back, grunting, dragging a vat onto the slaughterhouse floor. It's brimming with boiling water. Thu picks up the animal and dunks its body into the steaming tub.

Fur melts off in clumps. They bob on the water's surface. After a few moments, Thu lifts the dripping creature from the water for inspection. It is as smooth as a salamander, its flesh a much lighter color than I'd have imagined.

So *that's* what he was talking about earlier. Dogs boiled bald are a brilliant shade of alpine white. 'See that?' he tells me. 'It's as easy as bathing a child.'

Thu carries the dog's carcass outside to a roadside ditch and lays it upon a heap of straw. Then he pillows the dried rice stalks around its corpse. With a flick of his lighter, the pyre is lit. The dog's lips recede in the flames. Tail fat crackles. Its pliable, squishy, life-y qualities give way to a charred-and-rigored death pose, four feet skyward like an overturned ottoman.

I can finally look at the animal without feeling queasy. The dog no longer resembles a soulful pet. It looks like blackened meat.

Over the next few hours, Thu will kill and roast the rest

of the dogs one by one. As lunchtime approaches, sunshine will bake off the chill fog. The street in front of his shop will become busy with passersby.

Neighborhood guys in oil-spattered work clothes will stop by to bum smokes and gossip. Moms in slippers, kids toddling at their feet, will come chat with Thu's wife as she works. While her husband butchers animals, she will hack off dog paws, pulling out hearts and livers, showcasing her carvings inside an ice-packed display case.

No one, not even the kids, will seem bothered by the dogs shivering and bleeding at their feet. They've seen it before. Februaries: they're always like this.

I'm trying to imitate their nonchalance. I don't want to reveal my nausea. That could make me look fragile. Or worse yet, rude.

'Thu, I have a question,' I say, catching him on a smoke break.

'Go ahead.'

'Do you like dogs?'

'I actually love dogs!' he says, his voice graveled by cigarettes. 'I used to keep a few pets around the house. Beautiful dogs! Good playmates for my three children. But they all got stolen.'

'Does this work bother you then?'

'At first, yes, it did,' Thu says. 'But you get used to anything. Look, it's an ugly job. And I'll be damned if my kids follow my footsteps. They'd better stay in school so they can work in an office.'

'You know, in Vietnam,' Thu tells me, 'we believe any job that involves killing will bring bad luck. So I at least try to limit the dogs' suffering.' The electric baton, he says, is meant to deliver high-voltage anesthesia – frying their senses before the blade touches their throats.

'I used to just bash them all with pipes,' he says. 'I know better now.'

'Do you think people will still be eating dog when your kids are grown?'

Thu squints as if he's misheard me.

'I'm asking,' I say, 'because some people say dog meat is only favored by the older generation, not the young. They think Vietnamese people will eventually move beyond eating dogs.'

'Don't believe that,' Thu says. 'This is our culture. It's never going away. Besides, people nowadays know that dog is much healthier than beef or pork. It's safer too. Dog meat isn't pumped full of all of those chemicals.'

Thu isn't a monster. He's a man with a really shitty job. In fact, when he's not electrocuting dogs, Thu can sound like a new-age farmer touting the perks of free-range meat. After all, he says, the animals he slaughters roam free until the moment they're wrangled and caged.

You certainly can't say the same of factory farms.

Consider the lives of domesticated livestock, trapped from birth to slaughter in miserable confinement. Animals imprisoned in this system number in the dozens of billions. That's more than 500 million tons of living flesh – much of it belonging to pigs, believed to be as smart as (if not smarter than) dogs.[1]

Collectively, these industrial meat farms are the greatest source of suffering to sentient beings on earth. So while Thu's little abattoir is inhumane, the behemoth operations that put bacon on my plate generate anguish on a far greater scale.

So let me be clear: I didn't fly to Vietnam on a sanctimonious quest to expose the horrors of dog butchery. That story was beat to death and picked clean long ago by other foreign correspondents.

I came to Vietnam to pursue killers – and Thu isn't one of them. His slaughterhouse is just the first stop on what will likely prove to be a long reporting trail. I'm hoping it eventually brings me to a face-to-face meeting with a fiercely defiant strain of Vietnamese pet owner.

I'm not talking about the Hanoi activists who've absorbed PETA-style messaging from America. I certainly don't mean the Saigon socialites who push Shih-Tzus in strollers and campaign against dog meat in their free time.

I'm seeking out Vietnamese villagers who've proven they will do *anything* to spare their dogs from the misery I've just witnessed. Even pick up clubs and engage in armed combat.

As it turns out, many of the animals sold to these abattoirs are pets snatched from loving homes. Limb-snapping confinement, shock batons, boiling vats – this is what happens to abducted dogs in Vietnam.

I was dreading this morning at the slaughterhouse. That's why I got it out of the way early on. Though unpleasant, the experience was essential to helping me understand what could motivate a good-natured dog owner to go vigilante.

No one wants their pet to die like this.

There's a reason Thu doesn't ask too many questions of his suppliers. He knows better.

Travel to the source of Vietnam's dog-meat supply

chain and you will find a deeply despised breed of criminal. The trade is supplied in large part by motorbike gangs that prowl for pets. In fact, I'm quite sure a few of the guys supplying Thu's butcher shop belong to one of these criminal enterprises.

These abattoirs are gray-market businesses, complicit in the crime. They are the link between snatching gangs and the grilled dog restaurants that pervade Vietnam. When butchers receive a stolen pet, they toss its collar aside and roast the pet into an anonymous carcass, effectively laundering its origins.

In recent years, dog thieves have become some of the most reviled figures in Vietnam. Even among people with an appetite for canine, there is a broad consensus: pet snatchers are scum.

No one seems to care when one of these bandits gets besieged by a posse of pet owners. In recent years, attacks on dog snatchers have grown quasi-routine in Vietnam.

These attacks are often brutal. Some thieves are left twitching in the mud. Others are bludgeoned so hard they never get up. Like *Pat Jasan*, their weapons of choice are simple: bamboo staves, scythes or whatever blunt farm tool is closest at hand.

The vigilantism tends to go down in remote hamlets – patches where police protection is notoriously weak. Attacks can break out from the mountainous north down to the southern coast. The vigilantes include men and women alike, sometimes converging into a rabble of more than 100 people.

Thanks to Vietnam's ever-expanding network of cell towers, the entire nation has enjoyed an intimate view of these brawls. Mobs in Vietnam will often record ambushes on their 3G-enabled smartphones and upload the footage to stoke fear among their rivals – a tactic also skillfully employed by the far-more violent jihadis in Thailand.

These videos are a digital warning to any would-be thieves: prey on our village and we will prey on you.

In Vietnamese, dog thieves are called *trộm chó*. Go type that into YouTube. (An unaccented '*trom cho*' will suffice.) Now prepare to watch men dragged by the hair and kicked in the face, pleading for mercy through bleeding gums.

You'll also see guys bound with rope and marched through the streets, a procession of teenage boys lining up for a kick to the ribs. A handful of thieves have been draped in cardboard signs scribbled with these words: 'I'M A DOG THIEF. PUNCH ME, PLEASE.' Those caught with a dead dog are sometimes forced to lie down in the road and spoon with its corpse.

Collectively, these videos have been watched by tens of millions. Some of these recordings actually capture the last painful moments of a dog snatcher's life. Yet this brutality isn't turning the public against vigilantes. Even Vietnam's state-run press, typically loathe to nurture public disorder, often seems to side with the attackers.

The newspaper *Tuổi Trẻ*, the official mouthpiece of the Ho Chi Minh Communist Youth Union, writes sympathetically of 'canine avengers'.[2] *Thanh Niên*, an organ of the Vietnam United Youth League, portends a 'war against the reckless thieves and illegal abattoirs'.[3] These are two of the top-selling newspapers in Vietnam.

An online wing of the Ministry of Information sounds even more stridently pro-vigilante: 'Why shouldn't hard-working people, laboring in the fields all day, be able to exist in peace – protected by loyal dogs left to guard the household?'[4]

'What would you do if you returned home to find your dog gone and the children crying? ... This is a call for some serious penalties to deter the thieves. Otherwise, the problem will continue to be a blot on the Vietnamese way of life.'

Since 2010, by my count, vigilante attacks have killed at least two dozen suspected dog thieves and severely injured two dozen more. That's a conservative estimate culled from censored Vietnamese media. It seems that, every third or fourth month, another dog snatcher gets bashed.

This trend seriously challenges one of Vietnam's most enduring stereotypes. For decades, if not centuries, the nation's taste for dog has provided fodder for crass jokes.

Western tabloids and advocacy groups often use the dog trade to portray Vietnam or China as barbaric. Consider screaming headlines like this one in the *Daily Mirror*: 'Defenceless dogs scream in agony as they are boiled ALIVE for sick trade in meat.'[5]

'Don't for a minute excuse eating dog meat as a cultural prerogative,' says the Humane Society. It calls Vietnam's dog meat trade a 'crude, sickening enterprise' and the 'betrayal of a bond first forged between humans and dogs' many millennia ago.[6]

The most overwrought of these condemnations echo Christian missionaries decrying the 'uncivilized' practices of tribes in Myanmar or Magellan's crew cataloging the 'savage' traditions on the Philippine isles.

Western media and activist circles give the impression that Vietnam is the world's most despairing place for a dog – a country where few people will lift a finger to stop animal suffering.

How to square that with villagers bravely rising up to defend their pets?

To make sense of this phenomenon, I'll need to track down a posse of vigilantes and convince them to talk. However, I'm not entirely sure how to pull this off. Mob beatings generally go down in insular hamlets that aren't easy for outsiders to penetrate – particularly Americans nosing around about a communal homicide.

I've asked some media contacts in Hanoi for help. They've agreed to scout around for vigilantes willing to meet face to face. Apparently one squad in Vietnam's coastal midlands is amenable – if only we can reach them without upsetting local communist party officials.

In the meantime, I've got a phone number for one of their rivals: a pet-snatching outlaw biker. This dog thief's name is Hac. I'm told he lives just a few districts from Thu's slaughterhouse, right here in Bắc Ninh.

𝄆

At the outset of the human-canine union – perhaps around 40,000 years ago in Europe, give or take a few 10,000 years – dogs were not kept around for the snuggles.[7]

They were proto-dogs, bred from wolves. These swift-footed subordinates had specific responsibilities. When we hunted, they took the lead. Dogs would sniff out boar or other tasty beasts and harass them, gnawing their hind legs until humans could catch up and deliver the death blow by spear.

By night, the dogs' superior hearing picked up incoming threats from predatory animals and Neanderthals. In return,

⋀

they received a steady supply of picked-over bones – a feast of succulent marrow.

But these dogs weren't pets in the contemporary sense. They were merely alarm systems and hunting sidekicks. 'And when times got hard,' says Hal Herzog, a top anthrozoologist based at Western Carolina University in the US, 'you could eat them.'[8]

'It's quite possible,' Herzog says, 'that dogs were originally domesticated because they were tasty but could also do chores.' Evidence suggests that, from the start, hunter gatherers relied on their dogs as an emergency food source. Researchers sifting through mounds of prehistoric feces will sometimes find bits of dog skull – the remnants of a dog-brain dinner.

But while canines were prone to domestication, they were never fated to become livestock like pigs or chickens. Dogs are carnivorous predators, their jaws lined with flesh-ripping fangs. There's a reason Thu handles them with iron clamps. He's afraid of getting his fingers chewed off.

Dogs' aggressive instincts and weaponized mouths make them unsuited for mass farming. Put pigs, cows, chickens and other harmless plant-eaters in a pen and they'll get along. They're prey animals with nubby teeth. When frightened, they huddle together harmlessly instead of lashing out.

Throw a pack of dogs in a tight space, however, and you're staging a bloodbath. Like wolves, dogs are wired to establish a social order dictating access to food, water and females on heat. This hierarchy is hashed out through violence. Amid the bloodletting, rabies and other diseases spread with ease.[9]

Raising dogs en masse would also prove prohibitively expensive. Unlike pigs, they can't thrive on cheap grain alone. They're omnivorous, requiring at least a little meat or high-quality plant-based protein. All those expenses would be passed on to the customer. And who wants to pay $30 for a platter of dog ribs?

With a predatory animal, there's just no way to achieve the economies of scale that fill our supermarkets with cheap chicken, beef and pork. But that doesn't mean no one eats dog.

It's consumed in small communities from the Philippines to Nigeria. It's even been sampled by one of the world's most powerful men: Barack Obama, fed dog as a boy in Indonesia.[10] Generally speaking, dogs are cooked up informally by aunts and uncles in backyards and typically served during special ceremonies.

Among those who eat dog, few enjoy it more than once or twice a year. But if they do, the odds favor them living in the great dog-eating arc of mainland Asia. This is a crescent running from the Korean peninsula, southward through the plains of China and down into Vietnam.

This 3,000-kilometer area is an anomaly. Here, you can find proper dog meat cooks in dedicated eateries, preserving recipes that go back centuries. In total, humans consume an estimated 30 million dogs per year – and these nations supply the bulk of the appetite.[11]

But this habit puts millions of Asians at odds with Western sensibilities. At some point in the recent past, Americans and Europeans adopted a radical and uncompromising position: dogs are our 'best friends'. This is posited as a marker of civilization, separating the enlightened from the savage.

In *The New York Times*, you can now find op-eds with titles such as 'Dogs Are People Too'. The modern West (and, increasingly, affluent people in Asian cities) likes to pamper its dogs. People goo-goo over them like toddlers and invite them into their beds.

It is hard to understate how insane this looks to the rest of the planet. In much of the world, a dog is most certainly *not* a person. It is a mite-infested servant with shit on its breath. You feed it your leftovers so it will work as your household sentry. You may even adore the scruffy thing. But welcoming it into your sheets? You'd just as soon snuggle with a goat.

Not so long ago, the American view of canines was more in sync with that of the rest of the world. Flash back to New York City in the mid-19th century when the metropolis was overrun with strays. Back then, officials were paying locals 50 cents per head to clobber dogs to death. Mutts captured alive were piled into a steel cage and lowered by crane into the Hudson River.

An 1857 report from *The Times* describes this mass drowning as a 'confusion of howls, a gulping, bubbling, choking sound ... and when the water is drawn off, there are fifty dog corpses.'

'Apparently, they'd do this all morning,' Herzog says. 'People would come and watch. It was a form of amusement.'

※

Vietnam's dog-meat industry is the world's largest outside China. Each year, an estimated 5 million canines are fed into its supply chain.[12] Every dog served in a Vietnamese restaurant comes through three possible channels – and only one is free of criminality.

Consenting dog owners are the least controversial source.

Some rice farmers who've reared a litter from birth will decide to cash in on their superfluous mutts. Those who enjoy dog meat like to imagine that the flesh between their chopsticks once belonged to one of these happy farm dogs, which was free to chase field rats and loll in the sun.

The other scenarios are far more unsettling.

Source number two: international smuggling syndicates. Roughly 600 kilometers southeast of Hanoi lies a dog snatcher's wonderland. This is Thailand's upcountry, where a seemingly endless supply of unwanted mutts roam the territory called Isaan – the same rice-farming region from which so many Thai sex workers hail.

Isaan's dog glut is owed to a swirl of cultural forces. Thais generally don't eat dogs. But they do love to fatten them up. Many believe that feeding a stray is a way to *tam bpun* or increase karmic merit. Giving a stray dog excess chicken bones adds points to your karmic scoreboard – and may even improve your chances of a desirable reincarnation.

But well-fed mutts produce bigger litters, putting even more dogs on the streets. Exterminating them all is out of the question. Euthanasia goes against the mores of Theravada Buddhism, the religion's dominant strain in Southeast Asia. This is the reason that many parts of Thailand are aswarm with canine vagabonds.

For years, Isaan was a target-rich environment for the canine hunters who service the Vietnamese dog meat trade. They'd snatch them up by the thousands, pile them on trucks and ship them over a short stretch of Laos up to Hanoi – a bumpy twelve-hour ride.

This racket once earned an estimated $3 to $4 million per year for regional smuggling syndicates.[13] Back in 2009, during the zenith of this trade, I crept to the banks of the Mekong River to see this underground operation firsthand.

With my future wife, Pailin, I traveled to a riverfront cluster of villages called Bahn Pehng. By day, it seemed like just another forgettable farming settlement – the sort of dull Isaan village that women like Bam are so desperate to flee. Its air was scented with plowed dirt. We could see the scrubby shores of Laos across the Mekong through a silvery mist.

But we'd heard that, as midnight approached, the village would turn into a dog-smuggling hub. Locals told us that the shoreline would come alive with cargo trucks, riverboats and armed stevedores – all hustling in unison to move cages across the border.

Pailin and I staked out a hidden spot by the Mekong and waited for the sun to fall. We smelled them before we spotted them. There was no mistaking that nuclear-strength musk of piss, fur and frightened animal. It is a stench that singes your throat.

Then the freight truck came rumbling into view. It hauled cages stacked higher than a house – a wobbly tower containing more than 700 dogs. Once the truck parked, workers emerged from the village to begin offloading cages.

They heaped them on riverboats idling by the banks. I still remember how the workers' flashlights lit the dogs' incandescent green eyes, which twinkled like thousands of fireflies against the darkness.

If you can imagine a legal and humane dog-trafficking operation, this wasn't it. No fees. No inspections. No vaccinations. As a concerned Thai parliamentarian told me at the time: 'It's a mafia. There hasn't been a crackdown because the officials, the police, they all take bribes.'[14]

In the ensuing days, Pailin and I spoke to local officials who tolerated this trade. 'Come on. Stray dogs?' said the province's top cop, a general named Panamporn, when I told him what we'd seen by the Mekong. 'Are they actually taking something from us that we value?'

The mayor of Bahn Pehng was even more candid: 'Society says those who trade dogs are hooligans. Well, I say it's an honest business. It's like selling garbage to foreigners for a profit!'[15]

Then came the big crackdown. By 2012, Thailand's military was fed up with the dog-meat mafia.[16] Shame campaigns pushed by Bangkok's high-society dog lovers prodded troops to act. Riverine units of Thailand's Royal Navy led the charge, intercepting freighters piled high with thousands of caged dogs. The mafias' profits were quickly obliterated.

Meanwhile, in Vietnam, communist party officials were drafting a separate diktat that would disrupt the mafias. But they weren't motivated by a need to defend animal welfare. They were instead rankled by outbreaks of rabies in the north. Vietnamese animal rights activists, backed by the Humane Society, saw an opening – and pressured the party to ban those stinking disease-wagons that were inbound from Thailand.

Towards the end of 2013, Vietnam started blocking incoming dog trucks from crossing the border.[17] The transnational mafias were getting crushed on two fronts. The flow of dogs from Thailand slowed to a trickle.

This could not have come at a worse time for Vietnam's dog trade. Since the mid-2000s – when the nation enjoyed an economic ascent – the demand for dog meat has seemed to steadily increase. The nouveaux riches are keen on alcohol-fueled dog meat parties and, towards the end of the decade, many new eateries opened to soak up their cash.

But while dog-meat restaurants were full, the abattoirs faced a drought. When the flow of illegally imported dogs from Thailand stopped, they had to lean more heavily on Vietnam's third and most heinous source of live canines: biker gangs.

Pet-snatching crews had been a minor menace in northern Vietnam for many years. But when the supply lines from Thailand were cut, their services were needed more than ever. Butchers urged them to recruit new members and step up their snatching.

Pillaging hit a new high. The gangs hit poorly-defended farming hamlets the hardest. Across the countryside, pets started vanishing in ridiculous numbers – as if raptured into thin air.

But as the thieving intensified, provincial newspapers began to report strange murders: bodies immolated or speared with pitchforks, motorbikes torched to black shells.

The pet-stealing bandits had underestimated the resolve of their countrymen. They were finding that even the quietest villages could contain a dormant force: men and women still skilled in the art of repelling invaders.

I find Hac clutching a stainless-steel bong. He's lollygagging on the patio of his home, a two-story structure made of mildewing brick. It's an untidy place, strewn with piles of plywood and rust-eaten motorbike parts. But I can't knock his view.

Bắc Ninh means 'northern serenity' and now I see why. This neighborhood overlooks a valley of rice paddies submerged under thigh-deep water. The flooded fields have become a mirrored pond.

Wispy clouds glide above its reflective veneer. The water is beautifully undisturbed, save for a cream-colored buffalo clomping around at the perimeter. His hoofing sends concentric circles rippling across the surface.

'You want some of this?' Hac says, extending the bong my way.

'It's just tobacco, right?' I ask.

He nods, pinching a fresh plug out of a little ziplock baggie. He then squashes it into the bong's stem with his thumb. A gaggle of aunties, loitering by the front gate, turns their heads to take in the spectacle. Look, look. The foreigner is about to do something Vietnamese.

I grab the massive bong – it's as long as my shin – and take a burbly rip. It doesn't go down well. My throat is scorched with smoke. Now I'm pink-faced and sputtering like a freshman dweeb. The aunties are cackling. Still wheezing, I pass the bong back to Hac.

Hac is about my age – mid-thirties – and scrappily built, his lean frame suggesting a diet of instant noodles and stimulants. He's dressed pretty snappily by rural standards. His neon-blue Adidas jacket is either real or a deluxe knock off. Only his rubber boots lend him a country boy flair.

'You wanted to see this, right?' Hac says. He reaches into an empty rice sack and pulls out a steel rod. It's several feet long with a thick rubber loop dangling from one end. I immediately recognize the tool from online videos of dog thieves getting cornered by villagers. The outlaws are often getting this thing smacked out of their hands.

'A dog snare,' I say. 'Can you show me how it works?'

Hac whips the loopy bit around his left hand and jerks the wand. The rubber constricts, tightening like a noose around his wrist. It's basically a lasso.

Hac explains that dog hunters work in pairs. One guy pilots the motorbike. The other sits right behind him, core taut, stabilizing his body on foot pegs jutting near the rear wheel. He needs free hands to work the rubber lariat.

'It takes a lot of practice,' Hac says. 'You only get one toss before the dog starts going crazy. You've got to perfect your aim.'

A lasso man and his driver work in clean synchronicity, instinctively anticipating the other's movements. The man steering the bike has to manage his speed just so – cruising slow enough to give the snatcher a clean shot without stopping altogether.

Once the snare falls over the animal's head, the driver must gun the engine. The bike zooming forward will cinch the lasso around the dog's windpipe. It'll go airborne, legs flailing, carcass bouncing on the asphalt a few times before its vision fades to black.

As the bike zips along, the snatcher will retrieve the conked-out dog and wrap its snout in duct tape – an insurance policy in case the thing wakes up angry. Then he'll shove it inside a rice sack made of a plastic mesh too thick for claws to puncture.

'How many times have you snared a dog?' I ask.

'Recently?' Hac says. 'Not much. I'm actually trying to quit.'

'No, I mean your lifetime total.'

'Um, let's see. Nearly ten years in the gang. Going out a couple times a week, catching anywhere from three to twenty each time. It's hard to say. Hundreds? Thousands?'

Hac was born in the late 1970s, just a few years after the People's Army of Vietnam reunited the country. Those were weary but exuberant times. The communists had just spent three decades fending off French occupiers, Japanese invaders and, finally, American imperialists. The nation was whole at last.

Hac was raised by a family toiling on collective farms. He grew up poor but so did almost every kid in Vietnam back in those days, when the nation was mired in the gray stagnation preceding market reforms. This was the era when Vietnam and America were still bitter enemies – long before the Pepsi and Nokia factories came to Bắc Ninh.

Adolescence didn't get much better for Hac. He proved a poor student, often quick to fight. In his early twenties, he was palling around with misfits – rough men comfortable living in society's margins. Some belonged to a local dog-thief gang. They were seeking new blood. Hac proved an easy recruit.

'The first time they took me out, we caught four dogs,' Hac says. 'They divvied up the cash and I got almost a million dong. I couldn't believe it.'

A million dong. That's $45. More than Hac's old man could make in a week. Other than his speed dealer, he'd never heard of anyone clocking a million in just one night. Now he couldn't unsee it. Every dumb pooch snoring in the dirt was a potential score. There was money just lying around, scratching at fleas and lapping at mud puddles.

Stealing dogs felt like Hac's only shot at an exciting life. Consider his other options. Other out-of-work guys in Bắc Ninh had resorted to bonking field rats over the head for cash. The province was suffering a rodent plague and officials were handing out the equivalent of 30 cents for every severed tail.

What a bunch of suckers: Hac could make 100 times that much by stealing one fat dog. Best of all, the cops didn't seem to care.

The senior members of the gang broke down the law. Under the Vietnamese penal code, stealing property valued under 2 million dong ($88) is just a misdemeanor, seldom bringing jail time.[18] You'd have to haul around four dogs to hit that value – and thieves usually carried no more than three.

In general, police tend to treat dog thieves like petty shoplifters. You can usually get rid of them with a minimal bribe.

Hac thought he'd stumbled upon the perfect crime. But the more-experienced gang members had to cure him of the notion that dog snatching is without risk. There are rules to this game, they told him. Break them and you might end up in a ditch.

You never snatch dogs in your own district. People might recognize your face. Always ride into the next province over. You get spotted? Drop the dogs and flee. And no matter what, never get off your bike to confront an angry farmer.

'What about slaughterhouses?' I ask. 'Are they affiliated with gangs?'

'Not usually, no,' Hac says. 'That's another one of the rules. You must remain a stranger to these butchers. Don't chat too much. You show up, get paid and get out.'

'Do the butchers know your dogs are stolen?' I ask.

'Of course,' Hac says. Stealing is built into the pricing

scheme. Farmers selling their own dogs get the best price: $3.50 per kilo. Thieves get $2.50 per kilo. The lowest rate is $1.70 per kilo. 'That's what they'll give us for a dead dog.'

Hac would soak up this criminal subculture during late-night hangs. The outlaws had drawn him into a private world with strict codes and a deep distrust of outsiders. Silence, they told him, was critical. Never tell anyone you're a dog snatcher. Not your mom. Not your girlfriend. No one.

'They said people won't look at you the same once they find out you're stealing dogs,' Hac says. 'Everyone hates us.'

He also discovered that dog snatching is entangled in a slew of other crimes: drugs, larceny and underground vehicle modification to name a few. Before a hunt, practically everyone in the gang sharpens their senses with crystal meth. Then they mount a fleet of pilfered motorbikes, each outfitted with stolen plates. Some are illegally tricked out to race at terrifying speeds.

Dog thieves live on the fringe. So it's no coincidence that, for Hac's gang, their go-to hangout is a local *thịt chó* (dog meat) restaurant – a back-street dive that specializes in roasted canine.

In Vietnamese society, a dog-meat joint is a bit like an old-school Western saloon: a noisy space where booze is swigged and secrets are shared. Even among outlaws, there is an etiquette to dog meat dining. You don't eat it on the go. You never eat it alone. Dog meat is a shared experience, favored by men. As the month closes, guys will rally their pals to a *thịt chó* parlor, warning wives and girlfriends that they'll be home late.

Dog meat restaurants are perfectly legal in Vietnam. But these places exude smutty decadence. Walk into one of these joints, pull back a curtain and you'll see men sitting cross-legged in a back room. They're all swilling rice wine from tiny ceramic cups and surrounded by heaping piles of dark flesh. Meat spills from bowls laid out on greasy sheets of newsprint. The ambiance is strangely reminiscent of a strip club.

On a big night, someone in Hac's crew might tell the chef to cook a dog 'all seven ways'. This will summon a cornucopia of meat: oil-dark liver sausages, belly strips fried in lemon-grass, bamboo-accented dog broth, moist and gamey cold cuts, back fat steamed in galangal and more.

No dog feast is complete without a super-funky dipping sauce: a lemony, shrimpy, peppery goop that sticks in your palate for days. After a few swigs of rice wine, it tastes like fermented heaven.

There is a notion in the West that people in the Koreas, China and Vietnam – all pounded by war throughout the 20th century – have turned to dog meat out of starvation. Five minutes in a *thịt chó* restaurant should evaporate that myth.

Desperately poor people don't eat dogs. They can't afford it. Then and now, dog meat is pricey, the food of blow-out parties. A group dinner can run to more than $50. In Vietnam, that's one week's wages for a common laborer.

'We could afford to go often because we were making so much money,' Hac says. 'I wish I'd saved some of it. It was all spent on partying, booze and speed.'

Hac's gang will usually meet at a local *thịt chó* spot in the late afternoon. Over Crocodile-brand vodka, they'll swap intel on recent hunts and plan the evening route, taking care not to pillage one township too heavily. Once a strategy is in place, they'll break out into groups: two scouts taking the lead on one bike, a driver-snatcher duo following behind.

'Everyone must carry a sword,' Hac says. In recent years, according to Hac, they've also started passing around a K-54. It's a Chinese-made pistol with a rubber grip, a replica of the standard Soviet handgun during the Second World War. During Vietnam's war with the US, this was the go-to pistol for communist forces. Now leftovers are strewn around Southeast Asia's mainland.

'One of the guys bought the gun in Lạng Sơn,' Hac says. That's a border town up near China with a black market for heroin and firearms. 'We bought our tasers in the same place.'

These days, every dog thief also carries a taser gun. It's an electrified weapon, powered by motorbike battery, that looks similar to Thu's shock pole. But there's a bonus feature. This weapon can shoot its razor-sharp electrodes five meters through the air – just like a police taser. It relies on a trigger-based spring mechanism.

Hac and his gang will usually start hunting around dusk. Once a district is chosen, the crew will sprinkle crystalline flakes into a glass stem, spark it up and take in lungfuls of meth smoke. Then they'll mount their bikes, zipping out across the skinny dirt paths, crisscrossing once-communal rice farms.

Two scouts will drive in front. Hac and his driver will trail behind, chasing the ruby glow of their buddies' tail lights. They'll avoid main roads and large towns, preferring to strike farming villages where most inhabitants are exhausted from laboring under the sun.

It's easy to find one of these dim-lit specks of civilization. Just follow the power cables strung up across the rice fields on bamboo poles. They'll lead to clusters of shanties on stilts, little homes built of unpainted wood and sloping tile roofs – often dignified with a red-and-yellow Vietnamese flag. These are dwellings with no one important sleeping inside. They are all but forsaken by police and left to their own defenses.

In a Vietnamese farm house, the line between indoors and outdoors is blurry. Bales of straw pile up on the balcony. Teenagers may be sleeping under the stilted houses on hammocks slung above the dirt. The home's entrance is often wide open. Ducks can come bounding into the bedroom.

In fact, anything on legs – neighbors, piglets, visiting grandmas or thieves – can attempt to stroll right in at any time. Nothing will stop them except for the family mutt serving as round-the-clock bouncer. 'That's the great thing about these villages,' Hac says. 'Every house has a pet dog. Often two or more.'

After entering a hamlet, thieves don't have to track down dogs in the dark. Canine ears will instantly prick up at the sound of their motorbike engines. Once the throaty woofing begins, they just follow the sound to its source.

'When I find a large-enough dog, I have to make a decision: lasso or stun gun? It all depends on the environment. If I sense there are villagers nearby, I'll use the stun gun. It's more stealthy. You fire it into the dog's stomach and it shuts up immediately.'

'But the problem with the stun gun,' Hac says, 'is that you've got to climb off your bike to put the dog in the sack. I hate getting off my bike. That's when you're most vulnerable. So if at all possible, I'll skip the taser, lasso the dog and get out of there quick.'

Hac's paranoia is justified. Around 2010, his fellow snatchers started reporting scrapes with enraged pet owners.

Villagers would rush at their bikes with hoes and sickles. It started to feel inevitable: someone in the gang was going to get hurt.

'When it finally happened, I wasn't even surprised,' Hac says. 'One night, two of our guys got knocked off their bike by a mob. They were beaten with farm tools. One died right there in the fields. The other, he lived. But they'd stomped on his thigh over and over. His leg was amputated at the hospital.'

'Did you try to quit after that?' I ask.

'No,' Hac says. 'I was terrified but I kept going anyway. I felt stuck. This was my only job. I actually started taking bigger risks, smoking more speed and going out during the daytime. There was one 24-hour period where I caught more than 24 dogs – one per hour. That's my all-time record.'

That spree netted more than 17 million dong or $800. This is the monthly salary (on paper at least) of Vietnam's prime minister. Hac had matched the official wages of the party chairman, a political successor to Ho Chi Minh – all while blitzed on crystal meth.

But soon enough, Hac fell into an ambush himself.

It was just him and his driver that day, bouncing along a lane that sliced through a flat expanse of paddies. He recalls that it was chilly. They'd already scored one dog. He felt its body radiating warmth into his lap through the rice sack.

The thieves approached some huts congregated around an intersection. They slowed to round the curve. The next thing Hac remembers is the earth tilting beneath him, a metallic crashing sound, a shuddering realization that his feet were now on the ground.

'There were men screaming "*trộm chó*" and shoving us,'

Hac says. 'They wanted to put distance between our bodies and the bike.'

None of the farmers took a swing. Instead, they seemed intent on shoving the thieves backwards towards the rice fields. Paths that cut through paddies are always elevated, flanked on both sides by a two-foot drop. This prevents roads from going underwater when paddies are irrigated.

Hac sensed their intention. If he and his driver spilled off the road – tumbling into the mucky ditch below – they would never manage to climb out. They'd be stuck in a grid of thick sludge. The vigilantes would dominate the high ground.

'Did you think they might call the cops?' I ask.

'I have no idea. I would have loved it if the cops came,' Hac says. 'If the police show up, you live. If villagers catch you, you might die. I had no choice but to fight to the death.'

Neither brought the K-54 pistol. But both had long blades attached to cords slung around their waists. Heels nearing the precipice, Hac drew his sword. 'I took a few wild swings. I caught some guy in the arms and stomach. Everyone backed up for a second, long enough for us to run back to the motor-bike. We took off as fast as we could.'

'What happened to the dog?' I ask.

'They got it back, I guess. I don't know. I dropped my sack on the road,' says Hac, reloading his bong. 'You want some more?'

Hac is already helping himself, burying his face into the bong's mouth and sucking hard. There's a shrill, bubbly whis-tling noise each time he inhales. He makes it look easy. Hac politely tries to pass it over but I wave him off.

'I've quit hunting dogs for now,' Hac says. 'I can't stand the hatred. In the mornings, at the noodle shop, I can hear people talking about how much they despise dog robbers. I feel so guilty. I even broke down and told my girlfriend.'

'Isn't that a violation of the rules?' I ask.

'Yeah. But I'd been lying to her for two years, pretending to be a laborer,' Hac says. 'I was shocked that she didn't walk out after I told her the truth. Most women would have dumped me. We're actually married now.'

'So what are you doing these days for money?'

'I'm having trouble finding a legit job. The guys keep calling, pressuring me to get back out there. But my woman is scared I'll get killed. She keeps telling me, "Hac, please don't do it. No one will cry over a dead dog thief."'

⋊

I'm leaving northern Vietnam to locate the farming hamlet of Nhi Trung. On aerial maps, it looks tiny – a little murmur of a village located a few miles inland from the Gulf of Tonkin.

This settlement sits inside Quảng Trị, a province the size of Ireland's County Donegal. This is the slender waist of Vietnam. It's situated in the center of this serpent-shaped country, hugged between the sea and a mountain range bordering Laos

For a remote province in Southeast Asia, Quảng Trị has been visited by an extraordinary number of Americans. But I wouldn't call it a popular destination. Most came and went in the 1960s, pouring off warships and attack choppers with a mission: eliminate all communists.

As for me, I'll be flying coach. And my goal will be sucking up to the Communist Party of Vietnam – or at least the cadres running Quảng Trị. I'll need their permission to visit

Nhi Trung. Once virtually unknown, the village is now notorious for a double homicide: a dog thief ambush that helped inspire a wave of similar attacks across Vietnam.

The low-ranking commune chairman in Nhi Trung is already on board with my plan. He's agreed to gather up the vigilantes who orchestrated the ambush so they can tell their stories themselves. This chairman is more than a sympathizer. He's a vigilante himself.

But I can't just turn up to Nhi Trung with my notepad and audio recorder. Vietnam's communist party leaders are generally not fond of Americans digging into highly sensitive murder cases. Especially when the confessors are out on bail and the trial is ongoing.

So for my well-being, and that of the vigilantes, I've got to seek out the blesssing of higher-ranking provincial cadres before proceeding.

Thankfully, I've got a solid interlocutor: Hoang, a heavy-set, ponytailed former TV producer in his fifties. He is the son of a venerated colonel from the People's Army of Vietnam.[19] Throughout the 20th century, Hoang's father fought the French, the Japanese and the Americans. After the US war ended, he deployed into Cambodia to help topple the Khmer Rouge.

This life of heroism has infused Hoang's family with pristine revolutionary credentials. So while I'm technically hiring Hoang to translate, his pedigree is just as critical. His clout can open doors and offer an umbrella of protection in case anything goes wrong.

In Quảng Trị City, the nearest provincial capital, Hoang has arranged a dinner with party officials. They've requested a private room in the back of a mid-tier restaurant. 'When we meet them,' Hoang tells me, 'don't bring up dog thieves or murder trials. Let me handle all of that stuff.'

They show up five deep: three women, two men. We feast on wok-fried morning glory, garlicky ground pork, roasted eggplant slices and much more. The bowls of food keep coming. The lazy Susans on our glass table struggle to spin.

Until now, I've never enjoyed close contact with communist party officials. Frankly, they seem indistinguishable from the other Southeast Asian bureaucrats with whom I've dined. Lots of gold jewelry, conspicuous mentions of shopping trips to Hong Kong, phones incessantly bleeping with people seeking favors.

Once the vodka starts flowing, Hoang goes into stand-up comedy mode. He's annihilating the room. I can't understand a word but his lewd miming suggests R-rated material. I tune out for a bit until he raises his shot glass and gestures for everyone to stand up. I know what comes next: a gauntlet of alcohol that none can refuse.

Someone makes a toast, everyone takes a shot. Toasting duties pass in a clockwise circle around the table. When my turn arrives, I garble out something about harmonious relations between Vietnam and America.

Toast, shot. Toast, shot.

At some point, a black-blazered official jumps the queue and breaks the pattern. Now the table is devolving into toasting anarchy – a free-for-all in which officials shout grandiose tributes over one another.

Then, abruptly, everyone is slapping backs, pulling on jackets and saying goodbyes. I reach for my wallet but Hoang pulls me aside and tells me not to bother. 'They've already paid,' he says. 'Let them expense it.'

'That's very generous,' I say. 'So are we good to head up to Nhi Trung tomorrow?'

'It's all arranged. They will alert the township authorities and clear the way.'

'There's just one condition,' Hoang says. 'Before you fly back to Hanoi, you need to have coffee with the daughter of one of our provincial party leaders. She's a university student hoping to study media and journalism. She'd like to make some American contacts.'

'Sure,' I say. 'That's it? They're not uptight about us looking into murdered dog thieves?'

'Not really,' Hoang says. 'Seems like the farthest thing from their minds.'

)(

Quảng Trị was once the northernmost corridor of South Vietnam, that vanquished US protectorate. For Americans of a certain age, names of former battlefields in this province – Khe Sanh or Com Thien – can still bring shudders.

In 1968, when my father was a freshman at the University of North Carolina at Chapel Hill, he roomed with a Marine who'd completed a tour in Quảng Trị. He'd survived a stint at Cam Lộ Combat Base, just 30 or so kilometers from Nhi Trung.

At the time, this entire northern belt of South Vietnam fell under a US-protected zone called I Corps. These were the front lines defending terrain along the DMZ.

At the time, Quảng Trị was probably the most violent place on earth. The earth heaved with American bombs. Its blasts were powerful enough to knock eyes loose or reduce human beings to puddles. Napalm infernos roared higher than the tree line.

Communist forces retaliated with ferocity, killing enough US troops to prompt a conscription drive in the states. American men in college could request student deferments. But the rules seemed to constantly shift, churning up paranoia on university campuses. The Marine's advice to my father was unambiguous:

'Don't go. No matter what. If you have to, shoot yourself in the foot.'

By the end of the 1960s, vast numbers of US soldiers were realizing the Vietnam crusade was senseless. Many doubted the official White House rationale – that young men had to 'die in such a remote and distant place' to destroy the 'Asiatic dominion of communism'.[20]

This distrust was well deserved. In private, US Defense Department planners conceded that their core motivation was not to preserve democracy. The main driver – quantified at 70 per cent of the war's rationale – was preventing a 'humiliating defeat' that might cause the world to question American superiority.[21]

Robert McNamara, then-Secretary of Defense, secretly fretted that the war's futility would become obvious. In a confidential memo, he wrote that 'the picture of the world's greatest superpower killing or seriously injuring 1,000 non-combatants a week while trying to pound a tiny, backward nation into submission – on an issue whose merits are hotly disputed – is not a pretty one.'[22]

The war wasn't just ugly. It wasn't winnable – and they knew it. McNamara later admitted that the Vietnamese were undefeatable 'short of genocide'.[23] Yet he and his successors would continue to order more bombings through 1972, all while collecting a Medal of Freedom here, a Nobel Peace Prize there.

The US ultimately dumped more ordnance on the region than the Allies unleashed during the Second World War. The officers directing this mass slaughter echoed the same twisted logic espoused during America's invasion of the Philippines.

You may recall General William 'Pecos Bill' Shafter, who spoke of killing half of all Filipinos to elevate the rest to a 'higher plane of life'. Six decades later, a US army major, targeting the Vietnamese city of Bến Tre, infamously told a reporter that 'it became necessary to destroy the city to save it.'[24]

The communists returned the pain the only way they could – through scrappy guerrilla warfare. Vietnam's National Liberation Front, pejoratively known as the 'Viet Cong', terrorized the I Corps. Though hated, the guerrillas' tenacity was unquestionable. After one particularly vicious battle, a top US commander had to concede that 'they're the finest soldiers I've ever seen.'[25]

Viet Cong would materialize from the foliage, charging at platoons, fighting in tight proximity. This tactic robbed the US of its prime battlefield advantage: airborne bombs. To blast the Viet Cong, US officers had to call in air strikes so close that they risked killing their own men. My father's roommate said Marines were often as scared of 'that fucker on the radio' as the guerrillas.

My dad – an acid-dropping bassist in a rock band – was particularly unsuited to killing. He'd seen how guys came back from Vietnam edgy and hollowed out. So when he came up for conscription in 1969, he heeded his roommate's advice.

In lieu of blowing his foot off, my father exploited a short-lived loophole in the complex draft law. It was a legal scam – too tedious to describe in detail – that effectively scrambled the paperwork. The result: he was marked down as already passed over without ever actually risking selection.[26]

This draft-dodging technique boded well for my conception. I'm not sure my mom would have dated a guy with a missing foot, let alone carried his child. I was born roughly a decade later in 1981.

Though my personal link to the war is tenuous, the conflict has always loomed large in my imagination. My mind is aswirl with stories from my parents' generation. Add to that Hollywood movies depicting killer communists in black pajamas – phantoms spouting bad dialogue as they drive US grunts to madness.

Then there are the black-and-white images of Vietnamese corpses overflowing from ditches. Even as a teenager, I'd decided the war exemplified America at its sadistic worst. Quảng Trị and its environs received the full force of that cruelty. For a time, its name alone could conjure images of death.

And yet, these days, the province looks spectacularly alive.

Hoang and I have been driving north from Quảng Trị City for more than an hour. I've been gazing out the window, trying to square all that accumulated mental crud with the enchanting countryside before my eyes.

I see a vast carpet, colored an electric chartreuse, stretching towards every horizon. The paddies are chessboard flat. Men and women toiling the fields are visible only as conical hats, bobbing above an ocean of swaying blades – vanishing altogether when they stoop to cut away a fistful of stalks.

The houses here are plain, built of plywood or painted concrete. The most marvelous dwellings belong to spirits. Outside every village, grave shrines decorate the fields. Each is an original piece of art – a painted mini-pagoda with stone dragons clinging to the side and carved towers pointing towards heaven.

We've turned off a two-lane highway and into a narrow cement lane. It is graced with a stone arch overhead that reads *NHI TRUNG* in fading yellow paint. There is another tiny placard posted in the scrub grass nearby. I ask Hoang to translate.

"'No dog snatching in this village,'" he says. 'I doubt that sign is necessary. Thieves should know better than to come around here anymore.'

Hoang tells me the vigilantes will be greeting us at a community center up ahead. 'Just so you know, they don't call themselves "vigilantes",' he says. 'They say "village security team".'

'Got it.'

'The guys we'll be meeting are much older than you. More like your father's age,' Hoang says. 'Some are war heroes who served in the Viet Cong. The judges refused to put them in prison.'

This is not exactly what I'd imagined. I was expecting a clutch of rough, young farm boys. But as the vigilantes come into view – all of them waiting for us at a picnic table, teacups and snacks arrayed for guests – I see a bunch of men in their sixties.

No wonder that ambush was so effective.

It was hardly their first.

ᛞ

ᚪ

I'm greeted at the car by the commune chairman. He is Nguyen Van Thiet, a whiskery man with a smile discolored by age. Like a doting grandpa, he takes my forearm and guides me to my seat.

As we approach the table, five men rise from their seats. They're dressed for company: button-up shirts, starchy slacks and knee-high socks. Their leather shoes are piled up at the tile patio's perimeter.

Hoang introduces me with an introductory preamble in Vietnamese. The men nod along. They are lean, their bodies hewn by toil.

Though their faces are raisined a bit with age, most look quite vigorous. They've got a sinewy old-man toughness that's become uncommon in the overfed West. Other than the chairman – who has a bald spot – the rest are crowned with thick, panther-black hair.

Hoang must have mentioned my interest in the war because now they're going around the table, recounting their service records. Only Chairman Thiet – in his early seventies – was old enough to join the infamous Tet Offensive in 1968.

The chairman rolls up a sleeve to reveal a cavity on his left bicep. It looks like a ball of flesh was dug out with an ice-cream scoop. 'The fighting was intense,' he tells me. 'Our commanders told us to get close to the enemy – so close that we could see their eyes. Grab 'em by the belt, they said!'

I'm full of questions but, when it comes to war, I know not to prod. 'I have other injuries that I can't show you,' he says. 'When the weather turns, everything hurts.'

The others saw their fiercest fighting in the early 1970s. One of them – Nguyen Dang Huan, now in his mid-sixties

– survived one of the war's most punishing campaigns: the 81-day siege of an ancient citadel in Quảng Trị City.

This battle pitted communist forces against South Vietnamese troops who were backed by 80,000 tons of American ordnance. The communists fought unaided by sky-borne bombs. It was an unrelenting slog of mud and blood. There was no 'R&R' for them. Their nightmare was never broken by forays to red-light playgrounds abroad.

I take in Huan the war hero, a short-but-strapping man, his hair scraped into a tidy parting. The veteran is all grins, more mirthful than stoic. His name is familiar. I've read it in newspaper reports about the Nhi Trung murders. Though more than 100 people from this village joined the beating, the police only charged ten.

Huan was one of them.

As Hoang flatters the old soldier – 'He survived meat-grinder combat!' – Huan offers a handshake. His calluses abrade my palm and my hand feels embarrassingly squishy in his grip. Nearly twice my age, he also seems twice as virile.

Another vet picks up a ceramic teapot and refreshes our tea: strong stuff swimming with leafy bits. Talk of fighting glides easily into talk of dogs. 'You know,' Huan says, 'back during the war, we would name our dogs "John" for John F. Kennedy. Later on, we switched to "Nix".'

'But don't get the wrong idea,' Thiet says. 'We love our dogs here. I'll even let a dog lick my face!'

'Most people around here don't eat dogs,' the chairman continues. 'Maybe we'll try dog meat if we go up north. But we just don't have a taste for it in central Vietnam.'

'So you've never had it?'

'Only a few times in my life. I never cared for it,' Thiet

says. 'I believe the human–dog relationship is very intense. It can become more powerful than the bond between a man and his son.'

'How so?' I ask.

'If you beat your son, he'll run off for a while. Hit your dog and he's back the same night … Who's the first to welcome you at the door?' asks the chairman, twisting in his seat to address the entire table. 'It's not your wife, is it? It's your dog!'

The men nod along, some puffing cigarettes or munching on rice crackers. I'm noticing that Thiet likes to speak in proverbs. Now he's getting worked up, speechifying, relishing a fresh audience from out of town.

'There are no dog killers in Nhi Trung,' says the chairman, index finger raised skyward. 'We raise our dogs from pups. When they die, we bury them in a proper grave. We lay bowls of rice and salt on top of the earth to nourish them in the afterlife.'

Huan leans in, attempting to bring the conversation back to earth. 'Look, it's not like we worship dogs like cows in India,' he says. 'But we wouldn't know what to do without them.'

'I want you to take a look around,' Huan tells me. 'Do you see any metal gates around our homes?'

I don't. We're sitting on a tiny elevation, looking down on many of the village's 300-odd shacks and cement dwellings. I see open doors, shutters flapping in the breeze. Most houses sit empty all day, Huan says, while villagers slosh around in the paddies.

'Even at night, we don't lock our doors,' he says. 'Instead, we leave dogs outside to protect our families and our property. So if you steal my dog, you're basically stealing the key to my home. It's a serious violation.'

In 2010, these violations became unbearable. So many dogs were vanishing from Nhi Trung that the chairman started marking down each case in his ledger. By the fall of 2012, he'd counted more than 200. Thieves were raiding the village on a weekly basis.

Snatching gangs had tagged this hamlet as an easy mark. I can see why. Like so many farming hamlets in Southeast Asia, Nhi Trung is largely drained of youth.

Any teenager with a twinkle of ambition will try to escape the dead-end drudgery of farming. The lucky few make it to college or vocational school. Most end up in the nearest boomtown: swinging hammers, pouring beers or stitching sneakers for export. They leave behind parents with slow bones, defended only by their dogs.

Nhi Trung's vulnerability seemed to goad the bikers' sadism. Each veteran at the table takes his turn sharing an enraging anecdote: a taser waved in an elderly woman's face, grandkids hearing pets strangled with rubberized wire. The villains in these stories are always faceless, dehumanized behind visored helmets and cloth masks. But I can't help but imagine Hac.

As the pillaging mounted, villagers grew sleepless and twitchy. For those who'd known war, it was an old, unwelcome feeling.

'There are rules in combat,' Huan says. 'For example, when I was a soldier, we never shot captives. If someone surrenders, you accept them. Even if they've killed your comrades. But these dog thieves have no code of honor. They aren't worthy enemies. They don't care about life.'

'Huan,' I ask, 'how many dogs did you lose?'

'Seven total,' Huan says. 'The hardest loss was Rex.'

'Rex?'

'Yes,' he says. 'I named him after that German TV show about the police dog: *Inspector Rex*. He was the best dog I ever had.'

One evening, months before the ambush, Huan heard a motorbike rumbling outside his window. He rushed out to find Rex limp in the arms of a thief. There was a lariat around the animal's neck.

'I came towards the man with a flashlight but he didn't budge,' Huan says. 'That's what scared me. I sensed that he might kill me. The guy said, "What are you doing to do about it?" and strung up Rex right before my eyes.'

That was the night that hardened the ex-guerrilla's heart.

'Did you ever call the police?' I ask.

'Constantly!' Huan says 'They almost never came. They don't take dog theft seriously. We had to come up with our own plan.'

I am keen to begin talking about the double homicide. I'm also worried that pressing for explicit details about the case could end their bout of candor. But I decide to just go for it.

'Would you all mind showing me where the incident happened?' I ask.

'Right over there,' the chairman says. 'Let's walk.'

The vets stub out their cigarettes, down their tea and slip on their shoes. Minutes later, we're back on the cement entrance road, just a way down from the painted archway, standing over a grassy ditch.

This is the spot where these men battered two strangers until they stopped moving. I don't know what I was expecting. It's just a shallow irrigation channel. An unremarkable place to die.

Huan is now jabbering fast, skipping the setup, blasting straight ahead to the climax.

'This is where I cornered him,' Huan says. 'The guy gets off his bike with a bottle – like he's gonna throw it at us – and says, "Back off or I'll kill you!"'

Head down, I'm scribbling madly into my notebook. Then a veteran tugs at my wrist, motioning for me to put away my pad.

I look up to see some guy in black trousers zooming towards us on a motorbike, rear wheels whipping up grit. As he approaches, I see the face of a man who looks accustomed to tracking down strangers and ruining their day. The man slows his bike and aggressively noses the front wheel into our circle.

The vets stare down at the road like schoolboys caught smoking by a teacher. Everyone except the chairman, that is. He's grimacing defiantly. I don't know who this man is but I sense Thiet is outranked.

'Police,' he says. 'They only show up when you don't need them.'

※

We've retreated to Huan's home, a boxy cement structure on the village outskirts. Its main chamber is sparse but clean. It's decorated with a single piece of nice furniture: a polished wooden display cabinet. Huan's wife sets up plastic chairs and readies tea.

Getting rid of the plainclothes cop was easy. The guy clearly hadn't received the memo from headquarters. So Hoang made a show of pulling out his phone to call VIPs.

There was some initial chest puffing but the policeman ultimately demurred. In Southeast Asia and beyond, the best way to shut down a cop is by convincing him you're friends with his boss's boss's boss.

As a concession to save the officer's face, we cleared away from the scene and headed indoors. The other men sauntered back to their homes. This is for the best. I'd like to hear the ambush tale from Huan alone. He is infused with a soldier's matter-of-factness, his speech free of bloviation.

Before we begin, Huan excuses himself to go fetch his granddaughter from a back room. He returns holding an adorable infant and plops down in a seat across from me. Child wriggling on his knee, he's pulling her into a pink cotton onesie, swaddling her against the chill.

'OK,' he says. 'Where do I start?'

'Start here,' I say. 'At your house. Before you ran out to confront the thieves.'

It was after midnight on 29 August 2012. Huan was roused from sleep by his wife, daughter and son. They'd awoken to cries ringing across the fields: Dog thief! Come quick!

'My wife heard it before the rest of us. They say an old woman's ears are more sensitive than those of an old man,' Huan says. 'I would have slept through it.'

Still in his undershirt, Huan grabbed a flashlight and dashed into the muggy night. His son, Ha – then about seventeen or eighteen years old – followed close behind.

They could still hear the security squad's distress call. Huan knew exactly where to find them. They were posted around the underbrush by the village archway. Right where their elders had put them.

This position allowed the vigilante squad to dominate the main entrance road, a choke point through which any motorbike-borne intruder must pass. There is no other route of escape out of Nhi Trung. The rest of the village is essentially an island moated by waterlogged paddies.

The security team was commanded by dads and grandpas with military experience. But the tough work of waiting up all night and tackling strangers would fall upon the village's diminishing stock of young men. Four of them had been assigned to stake out the entrance road.

Huan and his son mounted their motorbike and raced towards the commotion – an 800-meter ride along dirt paths. The route was well lit. The moon was nearly full, bathing the fields in milky light.

Huan reached the cement entrance road, parked and steadied his flashlight on the trouble up ahead. The beams illuminated the contours of a showdown. He saw two dog thieves standing next to their motorbike. It appeared they'd already done a bit of snatching. His light shone on a bulging rice sack at their feet.

The thieves were desperate to escape towards the highway. But they were on the wrong side of four forward-deployed vigilantes, who blocked the exit with their bodies. Going off-road wasn't an option. Irrigation canals lined both sides of the lane.

The thieves, shouting abuse, failed to heed the group of men approaching from the rear. It was Huan and his son plus a few others alerted by that initial cry for backup. Now the bandits were encircled.

One thief lunged at the vigilantes, flinging chili powder towards their eyes. The other reached in his jacket and withdrew a glass bottle. He cocked back his arm. Come closer, he said, and I'll fucking kill one of you.

He didn't get the chance. From the surrounding darkness came the whoosh of a long stick, cracking the outlaw across the face. The glass bottle dropped and shattered at his feet. This attack from the flank stunned the thieves and the vigilantes pounced.

'The guy closest to me had his arms up, protecting his face,' Huan says. 'I gave him a shot in the ribs. Then another. That really hurt my hand so I started punching him in the belly.'

A kick sent the dog snatchers' motorbike clattering on the pavement.

'I kept screaming, "Where are you from!?" My son was punching him too. We were going to keep hitting him until he answered us,' Huan says. 'We just wanted to figure out who these guys were, tie them up and wait for the cops.'

After a few knocks to the head, the invaders were slumped in the dirt – subdued but still conscious. Someone in the scrum dialed the nearest police station and told them to come. Quickly.

Back in the heart of Nhi Trung, the ruckus had set off the dogs, stirring farmers from their slumber. The village was waking up mad. Huan saw porch bulbs switch on. Then the white coronae of flashlights growing larger. Then the sound of flip-flops smacking against the cement road.

The mob came in pajamas. They were pregnant women in bed shirts, a few octogenarians, teenage girls, Viet Cong vets with gardening tools. Others acquired weapons along the way.

'People were pulling up fence posts. Breaking off tree

branches,' Huan says. 'There were more than 100 of them and their rage was uncontrollable.'

Nothing could have stopped the thrashing that ensued. There was skull kicking, leg cudgeling, stomps to the chest. Everyone wanted to seize an opportunity for violent catharsis. By the time the villagers had finished avenging their slain pets, the thieves were motionless in the ditch. Blood puddled beneath their heads.

'When the cops finally arrived,' Huan says, 'they didn't do much. Just stood around. They didn't even give first aid. Someone in the village eventually hired a taxi to bring the thieves to a clinic five kilometers away.'

Both thieves died at the hospital. By sunrise, the cops had determined their identities: Nguyen Dang Cuong, 32, and Nguyen Xuan Trieu, 42. They hailed from neighboring Quảng Bình province, in a district 80 kilometers to the north.[27] Observing dog-snatcher protocol, they'd chosen hunting grounds far from home.

The police recovered the following evidence from the scene:

One damaged motorbike

Several baggies of red-flaked chili powder

Bottles filled with powdery filament extracted from fluorescent bulbs – often used by dog snatchers to blind attackers.

Several rolls of duct tape

A taser gun, wired up to the motorbike's battery

Fifty-two blunt objects: sticks, garden hoes, bamboo rods, many of them streaked with the victims' blood.

λ

Nhi Trung can't claim Vietnam's first dog-thief ambush. Nor was their attack the most vicious. That superlative probably belongs to a 2010 mob killing in the northern province of Nghệ An. There, a dog snatcher was speared through the torso with a pitchfork, drenched in gasoline and set alight.[28]

What really sets the Nhi Trung killings apart was the drama that followed.

It was one of the most peculiar cases the provincial police had ever confronted. When cops canvassed the village, they found an unrepentant murder suspect in every other house. Few people denied a role in the beating. They were united in defiance, many seeming rather pleased with themselves.

Locking up the entire village would be untenable. So the police settled on charging the first ten people who arrived at the scene. This included the four young guys who laid the ambush plus the first six men who answered their call for help. Both Huan and his son were named as defendants.

A merciful compromise, so the police thought. But this decision enraged Nhi Trung all over again. As the trial commenced, dozens of people including the chairman openly condemned the government for *not* charging them over the homicide.

'All of us answered the call of duty, did we not?' Thiet told his villagers. 'If they want to punish one of us, let them punish us all!' Forming a motorbike cavalcade, they descended on the local courthouse and turned over a letter confessing to murder.

It was signed by 68 people.

The stunned police chief called this 'unprecedented'. Even worse – from the authorities' vantage point, at least – this tactic proved infectious. Seemingly inspired by Nhi Trung, a mob in the northern province of Bắc Giang later stomped two dog thieves to death and promptly handed the police a mass confession. This one bore signatures from 800 households.[29]

Since the Nhi Trung incident, vigilante counterstrikes have only increased. Some dog gangs have been felled by well-planned surprise attacks. Others are caught in the act and killed in a supernova of mob rage. This vigilante trend isn't organized. It's viral. Bloody videos and images keep careening around social media – a relatively new medium in Vietnam – to let far-flung hamlets know that they too can fight the dog thieves and win.

In the press, police are catching grief alongside dog snatchers. As one party-sanctioned newspaper opined: 'Local authorities seem to be sitting back as dog thieves supply Vietnamese tables, furtively carrying out their nasty work. How, therefore, can the ordinary public be blamed for taking matters into their own hands?'[30]

Obsessed with social harmony, authorities nationwide have made a shrewd calculation. In the interests of deflating public rage, vigilantes are almost never charged as full-on murderers. They mostly receive light prison sentences, typically no longer than three years.

Nhi Trung helped establish this precedent. Most of its defendants – including Huan's son – caught only two to three years in prison. Huan spent almost no time in confinement. Judges cited his role in liberating Vietnam and sent him home on bail.

But for Nhi Trung, these gentle sentences came with two caveats. By court decree, Nhi Trung must pay blood money to the thieves' families. There is some grumbling about this monthly stipend. Some complain the victims' families get more than war veterans receive in pensions. But the cash is collected nonetheless.

Nhi Trung was also forced to invite relatives of the slain men to view the crime scene. On the morning of the visit, the deceased outlaws' parents arrived with police escorts. They were greeted by elders who promptly guided them to that fateful ditch.

Surrounded by their sons' killers, the parents knelt in the mud and sobbed.

※

There is a second front in the war on pet thieves. It is waged not by farmers gone commando but by Vietnamese urbanites and their Western allies. In lieu of machetes and bamboo sticks, they rely on online outrage.

Animal cruelty is a relatively fringe concern in Southeast Asia. The cause mostly attracts college-educated idealists from the upper classes. But while their numbers are few, they possess connections that village dwellers do not.

Throughout the region, this has enabled activists to – every now and then – successfully lobby authoritarian governments. Though they've had no luck coaxing Vietnamese police to break up dog-snatching gangs, they have sporadically pushed officials to take action against the dog meat trade's worst excesses.

Consider the achievements of the Asia Canine Protection Alliance. This is an umbrella group, backed by the Humane Society, including several activist organizations operating between Thailand and Vietnam.[31] Their members were the force that nudged Thailand to break up the transnational dog-meat mafia and goaded Vietnam to ban dog-hauling freight trucks.

The groups rely heavily on shame campaigns directed not at the domestic masses but towards English speakers at home and abroad. They've even convinced the US House of Representatives to debate a bill demanding that Vietnam and China totally ban dog meat on the grounds that it is 'opposed by many Asian people' and 'involves the theft of companion animals'.[32] The resolution hopes to affirm America's commitment to 'advancing the progress of animal protection around the world'.

The apparent goal is to embarrass these governments, stoking officials' fears of a dip in tourism or investment. To this end, the activists have also recruited major celebrities to denounce Southeast Asia's dog meat trade.

Among them are Ricky Gervais and Judi Dench. Both appear in a graphic public service announcement lamenting the region's 'dark and tragic secret' afflicting 'stolen family pets'.[33]

'I didn't know animals were caught up in this hideous crime,' says Gervais, staring hauntingly at the camera. His voice is overlaid with footage of dogs snared in wire cages and metal clamps. A glowering Dench laments 'innocent creatures crammed into cages so brutally that their bones often break.'

The video, padded out with stars from the British show *Downton Abbey*, has racked up more than half a million views. It's safe to say that few of those views come from the swamplands of Vietnam, where British period dramas have yet to catch on.

There are two fronts of this struggle against dog thieves:

one rural, the other urban. They are not necessarily at odds. But they have nothing in common. Nor do they interact. Championing farmers who knock thieves' teeth in the mud? That might be bad for the activists' brand.

This divide goes beyond political strategizing. These two worlds are deeply divided by class and culture. They don't even bring the same motives to this fight.

There is a deeply held belief, among the activists, that dog eating is a habit doomed to extinction. They contend that backward-thinking old men are sustaining the delicacy – and that Vietnam's youth will rebel against the old tradition.

This is probably wishful thinking. Sure, the dog-eating demographic skews older, but step into any *thịt chó* parlor and you're apt to see a huddle of young, boozed-up men alongside a table of gray-whiskered old timers.

And yet these campaigners portend a coming dog meat rejection, led by the youth, which will supposedly grow as Vietnam's society modernizes. All the campaigners need, they say, is one last push to drive this abomination into the shadows. That will finally scrub this humiliating stain from Vietnam's global reputation.

This mindset is unfamiliar to the veterans of Nhi Trung. They don't spend much time worrying about Western scorn. The opinions of people who've dumped napalm on their heads don't count for much. The vigilantes themselves aren't even morally opposed to eating dogs.

Just don't try to eat theirs.

These farmers don't coo over their pets. Or shampoo their fur. Or get them tested for worms. When their dogs grow exceedingly old or sick, they relieve their misery with blows to the skull – just like Thu the butcher, minus the shock-pole anesthesia.

They are compelled by a different set of principles. Central to their identity is a vow to never let invaders torment their people – no matter if they arrive on American gunships or Yamaha motorbikes from the next province over.

Nhi Trung's ambush was more than just an expression of pent-up fury. In a way, it was a political act. It sent a message not just to the biker gangs but also to police. Protect our turf. Refuse their bribes. Let not our hamlet become an anarchic preying ground for lawbreakers. Do your job or we will do it for you.

'I don't want to challenge the credentials of any specific officer,' Huan says. 'But we're still angry over the way this was handled by police. They forced our hand. They left us with no choice.'

'Do you regret killing the thieves?' I ask.

Huan inhales sharply, looking up and to the left. He seems to be scanning around his brain for a version of 'no' that won't sound too off-putting.

'I'm proud of how our village sticks together. I'm honored that people rallied around my son and me. It sounds strange but the incident actually brought a new spirit of closeness to Nhi Trung.'

'Right,' I say, 'but would you do it again?'

'Yes, I would,' Huan says. 'The time for patience had passed. But next time, I'd try a little harder not to kill them.'

Hoang and I bid goodbye to Huan and begin walking back towards the village entrance. We pass by the community center, where the veterans have reconvened. The cop's bullying didn't scare them indoors for long.

Nhi Trung, Vietnam

I'm touched by the sight of them all together: best friends, happily bullshitting on a Wednesday morning, bound by struggles old and new. I walk over to thank Thiet for welcoming me into Nhi Trung and for encouraging everyone to speak with such openness.

Then it comes tumbling out: an expression of grief that my country brought war into his life. 'Before I leave, I just want you to know something. Most Americans from my generation believe that the war was a horrible mistake,' I say. 'We know it was wrong.'

Thiet grins silently as Hoang translates and I can't help but feel a bit self-conscious. But then I feel the chairman's cold hand cupping the right side of my face, pulling my head towards his. I feel the scrape of his stubble as he softly kisses my left cheek. Poignance and weirdness collide. The vets at the table break into hoarse laughter.

Thiet stands, mumbles something into Hoang's ear and then tenderly pats my shoulder. 'Before you leave, he wants you to hear a poem,' Hoang says. 'He composed it himself.'

The chairman clears his throat, waiting for the others to fall quiet and get serious. He is summoning a solemnity from within.

Then he serenades us in a voice that is reedy but strong:

> Nhi Trung is filled with fine people
> Who toil the year round
> But calamity came calling
> Spinning us into a rage
> There were two men from Quảng Bình
> Who invaded our town, stealing dogs by night
> Oh, the troubles they'd brought us!

373

So we laid in wait
No matter young or old, boy or girl, woman or man
We all fell upon them
And those thieves lost their lives in the fray
All of our people: single, married, poor and rich
We are united as one, noble in our defense
Of Nhi Trung hamlet
May our young ones grow up in peace.

There is no mistaking the style and cadence of this performance. The chairman's delivery evokes the stern humorlessness required of an old-fashioned revolutionary fight song.

That's essentially what it is: a lyrical lionizing of the villagers' exploits, one delivered in the same tone that Vietnamese elders use to valorize those who fought off invading Chinese, French and Americans.

Through song, the chairman has crafted a narrative in opposition to the courts. To hell with the judges and cops and the laws they selectively enforce. Here, in Nhi Trung at least, the vigilantes will be known as heroes, not criminals.

Afterword

I n early 2017, I came to Bangladesh to witness the world's most rapid refugee exodus since the Rwandan massacres of the 1990s.[1]

A brutal pogrom of the Rohingya was underway. Across the Naf River, which divides Bangladesh's eastern marshlands from Myanmar, pillars of smoke gushed up from the horizon. These black plumes marked villages where Burmese troops were busy carrying out a scorched earth campaign – a case of 'textbook ethnic cleansing', according to the UN.[2] By the year's end, they would cast more than half a million Muslims from their homeland.

I had come to gather testimony from new arrivals. I found tens of thousands of them in a dire refugee camp called Kutupalong. Many had just completed a four-day slog on foot, with swamp muck up to their knees and visions of flaming huts fresh in their heads.

Through their accounts, I tried to piece together the Myanmar army's unwritten playbook: the strategies used to force Muslims into Bangladesh with such terrible speed.[3] In short, troops were going village to village, gang-raping women and killing the men who tried to intervene, corralling inhabitants, torching huts and shooting livestock.

These tactics are extremely effective. They save battalions the trouble of slaughtering an entire settlement. After witnessing all that hideous abuse, practically everyone will sprint towards the river border. Some hamlets preemptively clear out as soon as they hear army trucks in the distance.

Once the survivors crossed the Naf River, they would pour into these Bangladeshi refugee camps – if you can call them that. Food, medicine and even shelter were sparse. Upon arrival, the newcomers were pointed towards Kutupalong's outskirts: a flat expanse of bald earth resembling the surface of Mars. There, they could scoop up handfuls of ruddy clay and build a home out of dirt clumps, foraged tree branches and bits of plastic sheeting.

Documenting the army's ethnic cleansing tactics had been my primary goal in Bangladesh. But at the tail end of my trip, I'd allotted a few extra days to indulge my long-running obsession with the Southeast Asian meth trade.

In all my years of investigating Myanmar's *ya ba* exports, I'd focused almost entirely on the two largest markets: China and Thailand, both adjacent to terrain controlled by narco-militias. That other country on the western border – Bangladesh – was a distant afterthought.

Trafficking pills from the meth-producing highlands of Myanmar westward into Bangladesh always struck me as a logistical nightmare. First, you'd have to navigate through the Burmese central heartland. There, unlike the anarchic borderlands, the government tends to punish drug crimes severely. (In general, the army prefers to keep the nastier facets of Myanmar's black market up in the hills.)

From the heartlands, you'd have to keep trucking along the coast and into an army-run apartheid zone – swampy terrain riddled with outposts built to quarantine the Rohingya. This is one of the most militarized patches of land in all of Southeast Asia.

I assumed that even in Myanmar, a quasi narco-state, traversing this route would require an absurd degree of official collusion. The route from a Kachin State mountain lab to the Bangladeshi borderlands is more than 1,500 kilometers – and it is littered with checkpoints. By my reckoning, traffickers would have to pay off so many troops and rebel factions along the way that they'd never turn a profit.

But perhaps I was mistaken. I'd been reading reports of Bangladeshi officers intercepting massive shipments of *ya ba*, Myanmar's signature narcotic. I began to wonder if these sleepy Islamic hinterlands were, like so many other parts of Asia, becoming transfixed with speed.

So I arranged a visit with Lt. Col. Abuzar Al Zahid, commander of two Bangladeshi Border Guards units stationed near the Naf River. If meth shipments were beginning to surge into Bangladesh, I figured he'd know all about it.

I got my first indication shortly after stepping into Abuzar's headquarters in the border town of Teknaf. His officers were dragging two wild-haired Bangladeshi men into the station. The young captives' T-shirts were torn and their wrists were bound with knotted rope.

One of the men was unable to walk, his left foot gashed open and twisted sideways at a grotesque angle. Guards held him upright by his armpits. As they dragged their dazed prisoner down a hallway, he left a speckled trail of blood on the concrete floor.

In a backroom, I found Abuzar, a bear-like man capped with a green beret. He was flanked by subordinates wearing crew cuts and woodland camo uniforms. The colonel was cradling the suspects' captured bounty in his arms.

It was a waterproof plastic bundle, wrapped up in thick

packing tape, believed to contain at least 10,000 *ya ba* pills. One of his marine units had spotted the duo fishing it out of the Naf riverbed. Abuzar told me that this was an increasingly popular place to stash narcotics packages. They're planted underwater by men in boats, weighted with stones and scooped out when the coast looks to be clear.

After these traffickers dredged their bundle from the river, they were spotted by border guards hiding nearby. Once confronted by officers with BD-08s – domestic copies of short-stock AK-47s – the men fled into the bramble. They scaled a wire fence in flip-flops, scraping themselves badly, buying time for the unit to catch up, force them to their knees and haul the pair back to headquarters.

Back at the station, Abuzar and his men were unraveling the stash with great effort, noisily ripping off tape and tearing through seemingly endless layers of plastic. When they finally reached the payload at the center – a jumble of meth-filled baggies – the cement-walled room was pervaded by that sickly sweet aroma.

Abuzar popped open a baggie, cupped his large palm and filled it with tiny pink pills. Then he held it under my nose.

'That smell. It's quite alluring, isn't it?' Abuzar said in British-accented English. 'Like a sweet biscuit.'

'You must be pleased, colonel,' I said. 'That's a big seizure.' But Abuzar swatted the air as if to wave away the compliment.

'No, this is nothing,' he said. As his subordinates continued tallying up the tablets, he walked me into his office and guided me over to his laptop. Then he cued up evidence photos of confiscated *ya ba* pills. They spilled out of all sorts of crafty hiding places: gourds, chilies, candies, boat hulls, tail lights, shoe soles, mobile phones, laptops and furniture.

'It's coming over the border inside babies' diapers. Women in burqas are putting it in their female organs,' the colonel said. 'It's easy to carry, easy to sell, and more comes every day. We don't know how to stop it.'

When I asked the colonel for some hard figures, he presented me with statistics so unbelievable that I later had to confirm them with the central government.

As recently as 2008, Bangladeshi police were only seizing about 35,000 ya ba pills per year – an amount small enough to fit inside a backpack. But by 2016, the nation's speed seizures had soared to more than 29 million pills.[4]

Twenty-nine million. That's an increase of more than 80,000 per cent, enough meth to get every man, woman and child in Texas high. Yet those 29 million pills likely amount to just a small portion of the ya ba pouring into Bangladesh.

Consider that, over in Thailand, much better-equipped border police are believed to catch no more than 10 per cent of incoming narcotics shipments.[5] Bangladesh's security forces are far less vigilant. They're severely underpaid, poorly trained and, in some units, underfed. They may be catching no more than 5 per cent – leaving another half-billion pills to course through the country.

Bangladesh's police and troops are also notoriously corrupt – and by Abuzar's own admission, criminality in his ranks has worsened as a result of the meth boom. Not so long ago, his officers were preoccupied with confiscating bottles of whiskey from villages to preserve the Islamic moral order. (Alcohol is treated as an illegal drug in Bangladesh, where more than 90 per cent of the population is Muslim.)

Now policemen – many officially paid just $25 per week – are presented with irresistible opportunities to collude with traffickers. Those who accept bribes might squirrel away enough cash to buy a house in just one year.

The fallout, Abuzar said, is an addiction crisis and an 'entire generation of Muslims derailed'.

'It dries the cells of their brains. People go totally mad. They rape. They murder,' he told me. 'I have to save my nation from this enemy. More and more people in Bangladesh must realize that we are at war.'

The colonel's rhetoric felt dreadfully familiar. This is how Thailand's officials sounded before launching their bloody war on meth in the early 2000s. This is how Duterte sounds today.

The difference is that Abuzar's anger was not just directed towards anonymous 'pushers' or 'junkies'. The primary culprits of the meth influx, he said, are Myanmar army officials and their families.

They are complicit, he said, in the production of *ya ba* in the hills of Shan and Kachin – as well as in protecting drug shipments as they travel through the army-controlled territory that abuts the Bangladeshi border. 'We have concrete information on this,' Abuzar said. 'Everyday people can't just pass drugs from state to state in Myanmar. Impossible. The traffickers have permission. We've raised this with Myanmar officials so many times but nothing changes.'

'What about the ethnic cleansing campaign in Myanmar?' I asked. 'Surely that's slowing down the meth trade?'

But Abuzar told me the army offensives seemed to have had little effect. Worse yet, they'd produced a bumper crop of young, unmoored Rohingya refugees who could be hired as drug mules on the cheap. They're easily recruited, he said, into Bangladesh's existing trafficking gangs. 'These organizations are run by influential Bangladeshis. Their Rohingya are picked up as low-ranking members. They're cheap transporters or muscle men.'

Abuzar stood no chance of catching them all. Yet the torrent of ya ba is so heavy that his units were still racking up big seizures – so much so that they struggled to dispose of all the pills. 'But I have a system,' he said. 'I tell my men to dig a hole near the station.' Then he orders them to dump vats of hot-pink pills into the pit.

The border guards can't just bury millions of pills in the dirt, of course. That would entice any addict with a shovel. So Abuzar tells his men to gather all of the station's confiscated booze, smash up the bottles and rain alcohol and glass shards into the pit of ya ba below.

I would be incredulous had Abuzar not played a video clip of this bizarre procedure on his laptop.[6] Sure enough, I saw uniformed men standing above a hole filled with a viscous, candy-pink slurry of intoxicants. Once all of the steel buckets brimming with ya ba were emptied into the pit, and stirred into a pool of whiskey, border guard grunts would scoop up loose earth and fill in the hole.

This isn't just a cheap way to get rid of contraband. The colonel told me it doubles as a 'psychological operation' to instill feelings of revulsion among his subordinates. 'As they destroy these drugs,' Abuzar said, 'I want my soldiers to feel hatred.'

The goal, he told me, was to ritualize this hate fest, repeating it over and over until his men were so nauseated by ya ba that they would resist any association with the drug. Most of all, he hoped to fortify their minds against the temptations of traffickers.

'I don't know what else to do,' the colonel told me. 'The demand has now arrived in Bangladesh. The supply will follow. No matter what, it will come.'

⋊⋉

I'm wrapping up the book with this vignette for two reasons.

For starters, it evinces the expansive power of Southeast Asia's underground syndicates. Having saturated southern China and mainland Southeast Asia with *ya ba*, Myanmar's meth barons are now taking on bigger challenges.

Identifying Bangladesh as a lucrative *ya ba* market was prescient. Where most would see an impoverished sea of rice fields inhabited by devout Muslims, the drug lords recognized a meth dealer's demographic dream: an untapped nation of 160 million – roughly half the population of America – where one in three citizens are aged between fifteen and 30.

Never mind that the drug lords' production center is separated from this market by inhospitable terrain: a trail of cracked roads longer than the distance from Paris to Warsaw. They somehow charted a course, eluding or co-opting all the armed factions – rebels and army brigades alike – who control stretches of the route along the way.

This is a logistical triumph, one accomplished without summoning the sort of cartel-on-cartel killing sprees seen on the US–Mexico border.

Just imagine how well they'll fare once China makes it even easier to move people and packages around Asia and beyond. Over the next decade or so, Beijing is poised to spend more than $1 trillion to interlink more of the eastern hemisphere with good roads, fast trains and modern ports

– an infrastructure plan far more costly and ambitious than America's Marshall Plan, which rebuilt Europe after the Second World War.

As long as disposable incomes rise in Southeast Asia, and barriers to travel keep melting away, organized crime will be poised to thrive.

Bangladesh's meth boom also demonstrates the degree to which crime syndicates depend on corruption. This meth expansion relies on a) Myanmar's army providing a safe haven for meth labs and b) secure trafficking routes as well as c) corruptible police and troops in Bangladesh plugging into this existing matrix of criminal collusion.

State protection is vital for criminal operators of many stripes: narcotics transporters, human traffickers, brothel owners and many others. Moreover, authorities who devote time to protecting criminal rackets are distracted from the unprofitable work of, say, defending a poor hamlet from armed pet thieves.

Sure, the police will always pick off low-end lawbreakers, such as poor *ya ba* smokers. None of that matters as long as cops, judges and politicians provide a force field insulating the top criminal profiteers from legal danger.

What might dim that force field's power? Here are a few proposals worth considering:

Increase officers' salaries
Many in Southeast Asia will cringe at this idea. Using public funds to reward the cops who've been fleecing your neighborhood for years is an infuriating suggestion. But there's no way to cobble together a professional police force from officers who are paid like 7-Eleven clerks.

Any lasting corruption purge would force Southeast Asian governments to stop offloading personnel costs onto the underworld (and, to a lesser extent, preyed-upon shopkeepers and motorists). They'd have to finally pony up and pay cops middle-class salaries.

At the risk of sounding like a Pollyanna, I suspect most rank-and-file officers would prefer a steady, respectable paycheck to grubby envelopes of cash – even if their monthly income took a hit. Many cops feel ashamed of their public image and sincerely crave society's respect.

Decriminalization/legalization

In other words, drag certain dark sectors of the economy into the light – particularly those associated with vice.

Bam, the sex worker I met in Sungai Golok, works a hell of a lot harder than I do. But she is technically a lawbreaker and thus deprived of any basic workers' rights. If her boss refuses to grant holiday time, or if a customer refuses to pay, she can't just phone the labor bureau or the police. She belongs to a realm that operates on threats and bribes, not transparency and regulations.

Who benefits from this system? Exploitative bosses and the cops on their payroll. Decriminalizing sex work would amputate a billion-dollar sector from the black market and would sever a major pipeline of illicit cash flowing into police departments.

Contemplating the legalization of drugs – yes, including meth – leads into more radical terrain. Yet I can think of no other policy that would drain so much power from Southeast Asia's narco-barons, the reigning overlords of the black market. As it stands, their profits are trapped in a $31 billion netherworld. This untaxed fortune builds mansions for kingpins and police generals in lieu of rehabs, hospitals and schools.

Legalization is an incendiary proposal, one that would spark all manner of unforeseeable effects on society. I won't pretend that this is a popular idea in any Southeast Asian country. We are, after all, living in an era in which a Philippine president can urge police to 'slaughter' drug users, citing Hitler's massacre of the Jews as his inspiration, and still manage to hold an 80 per cent approval rating.[7]

Yet in Thailand – where a murderous drug war killed thousands circa 2003 – a surprisingly liberal idea now swirls around the highest ranks of officialdom. In 2016, the kingdom's justice minister proclaimed that 'the world has lost the war on drugs. Not only Thailand.'[8]

This is an astonishing statement from a general whose ruling junta constantly bellows about law and order. But he's right. In Thailand, hardline drug enforcement has created an undeniable human toll. Its prisons are packed with non-violent drug offenders. The nation's per capita incarceration rate is worse than in China (though not as bad as in the US, a world leader in locking up drug offenders) and officials are starting to admit that the American lock 'em up model is a failure.

In recent years, the military government has quietly held meetings to discuss a range of proposals from lenient sentencing to decriminalization and even legalization.[9] This phase of self-examination may ultimately fizzle without any profound policy changes.

Yet it signals fatigue with the global 'war on drugs' mindset propagated by the US – and maybe even a moral backlash to the cruel notion that 'junkies' are scum. People will always get high. Some of those people will sink into severe addiction and become a burden on society. But surely governments can come up with a better solution than locking drug users in cages or, worse yet, shooting them in the head.

Create a powerful anti-corruption squad

This is the UN's refrain to countries in Southeast Asia: set up anti-corruption agencies designed to root out thieving officials.

Many have complied, albeit in the most superficial of ways. Cambodia, one of the more corrupt patches of Asia, has an 'anti-corruption unit'. So does Myanmar. Duterte started one in late 2017 and Thailand founded one nearly two decades back.

Meanwhile, as I write this in January 2018, Thai social-media sleuths are scrounging up photos of the junta's deputy chief flaunting $100,000 watches.[10] Officially, this general earns a salary of roughly $43,000 per year. But like so many high-ranking 'civil servants' across the region, he is a millionaire – one who rocks 'Richard Mille' timepieces, a deluxe watch brand favored by Kanye West.

Thailand's 'anti-corruption' commission promises to investigate. But the prospect of this agency severely punishing an official of the highest order is hard to imagine. The same can be said for the other commissions scattered from Phnom Penh to Manila.

To varying degrees, Southeast Asia's anti-corruption commissions are themselves corrupted. In more insidious cases, they're deployed by ruling parties to attack political rivals. None of these agencies merit a great deal of confidence.

But the allure of this solution endures. Namely because it was an 'anti-corruption commission' that transformed Hong Kong from, as one academic puts it, 'a place where corruption was once a way of life … to one of the most corruption-free places in the world.' This example looms large over Asia and is often cited as a miracle worthy of emulation.

When Hong Kong's anti-corruption commission was founded in 1974, 'every part of the public service was infected,' according to one of its former commissioners.[11] Another former investigator recalled that 'the government was run like Bangkok or Manila.' The rot was so deep that firefighters would squeeze citizens for cash before spraying down their burning homes.[12]

Nevertheless, this anti-corruption commission assembled savvy investigators and endowed them with the awesome power to arrest cops. Within a decade, the squad had taken down loads of corrupt officers, wiped out police-protected heroin markets and even locked up the bribe-taking police chief himself.

Their success relied, in part, on tapping public frustration. They even beckoned street vendors and day laborers to report shakedowns – and actually followed up on their complaints. Suddenly, even society's least fortunate were empowered to strike back at once-untouchable institutions. This was a revolutionary upending of class dynamics, and it entrenched an anti-corruption norm that persists four decades later.

From Southeast Asia, modern-day reformers look to Hong Kong with a desire to recreate this miracle at home. But Hong Kong is incomparable to any other populous nation in ASEAN. It was, at the time, controlled by the United Kingdom and composed of a mere 4 million citizens, the vast majority of them hailing from a single Chinese ethnic group.

It's far easier to pivot an ethnically homogenous city than, say, the Philippines: thousands of tropical islands inhabited by 105 million people, not to mention numerous armed sects – all weakly governed by politicians that elicit little trust. The same goes for Myanmar, an equally fractured nation where a narcotics empire can easily tempt officers with inexhaustible cash reserves.

Among Southeast Asia's ruling cliques, the notion of handing real power to Hong Kong-style anti-corruption crusaders must seem like an act of self-harm. Almost none would survive a ruthless auditing of their behavior.

In fact, Southeast Asian governments and the US Congress are bound by the same tragic conundrum: the power to upend their entrenched system of payoffs lies with politicians who have everything to lose from its demise.

And so corruption endures.

Ignore anyone who claims that bribery in Southeast Asia is a modus operandi wedded to culture or tradition. Everyday people are utterly exasperated with malfeasance. The problem is that autocrats have become skilled at tapping this frustration.

Ironically, coup-architects and strongmen tend to wave the 'anti-corruption' banner highest of all. Thailand's junta seized power in 2014 proclaiming an end to corruption. Duterte used similar bluster to win the presidency. He promptly turned to the same 'corrupt' police he'd been castigating and granted them nearly unchecked killing power.

This tired pitch – give us extraordinary power and we'll clean up the filth – seldom delivers in the end. According to Transparency International, Southeast Asians report that corruption is getting worse and cite police officers as the worst offenders.[13] (Even Duterte admits that Philippine cops are 'corrupt to the core' and estimates that nearly half are entangled in crime.)[14]

There are no obvious paths out of this morass. But I can say this with confidence: salvation from corruption (and its miscreant offspring, organized crime) will not come from the United States, the traditional evangelist for 'human rights' and 'rule of law'.

I know that America's Foreign Service is still replete with people who believe in these values. Nor am I quick to dismiss the limited good achieved by American pressure on human trafficking – a force that, in Obama's words, leads to a 'debasement of our common humanity' and 'tears at our social fabric'.[15]

But for too long, the American approach to transnational crime has proven so erratic that its rhetoric fails to inspire. This is a superpower that scatters DEA agents across the world to propagate a militarized mindset against drug users. Meanwhile, America has backed narco-traffickers in Nicaragua, Pakistan, Vietnam, Laos and, more recently, Afghanistan – all to achieve clandestine CIA goals.[16]

As American imperium slogs through the Trump era, its contradictions and self-serving nature have only become more glaring. Americans spend more on candy than poverty-reducing foreign aid – and still White House officials clamor to slash what they see as overseas largesse.[17] Three in four people polled globally have 'no confidence' that Trump will 'do the right thing regarding world affairs' – an appraisal worse than that of Vladimir Putin or Xi Jinping.[18] These are not the vital signs of a beneficent empire on the rise.

In November 2017, as Trump toured Southeast Asia, I attended a panel discussion in Bangkok. Thai diplomats and policy experts were convening to make sense of the White House's strategy for the region. (Well, they tried at least. Most seemed baffled.)

Their collective sentiments were summed up by Thitinan Pongsudhirak, a professor from Chulalongkorn University – Thailand's Harvard equivalent – who specializes in US relations. The 'US-led, liberal, rules-based international order', he told the crowd, is shrinking away.

'So we've got to start taking care of ourselves. If you want to be a democracy, don't expect the US to help you. You're not going to get anywhere by dancing and crying for democratic values and human rights.'[19]

For diplomats and other elites in Bangkok or Manila – especially those who've benefitted from alliances with the US – America's imperial decline must feel disorienting. But out in the shadowlands, in those black zones and border towns, the mood is mostly unchanged.

These places are inhabited by people who never got the chance to enjoy a system you might call 'rules based' or orderly. Nor has geographic isolation spared them from the claws of foreign superpowers. After all, in the case of Huan, the world's most powerful military was once trying to obliterate practically everyone he knew.

But most Southeast Asians feel the rise, fall and clashing of empires in a less overt manner. When foreign behemoths stomp around their homeland, the tremors rattle society in all manner of unpredictable ways – sometimes warping lives for generations, long after that empire has crumbled.

Consider the Philippines, where the Spanish inculcated a

religious dogma that, centuries later, forces mothers such as Karen to seek basic health care from the black market.

Or Myanmar, where the British drew a border around a patchwork of ethnic groups, empowered one to rule them all and thus primed the nation for endless conflict – a tragedy that mires Gideon and his fellow Kachin in chaos today.

Or Thailand, where the US military gave rise to a massive vice industry designed to pleasure soldiers weary from fighting communists like Huan. The trade has since subsumed a quarter-million sex workers and expanded to the nation's ragged edges, careening women such as Bam into hostile terrain.

Today, even in the twilight of US empire, states such as North Korea that antagonize America are still choked off from the global economy. This can produce all sorts of knock-on effects: hacking, smuggling rackets and even songstresses waltzing with tourists – all to finance an outcast regime.

China's imperial ascendancy will transform the Asian tropics too – and as with previous empires, some groups will prosper and others will get trampled. This will no doubt shake up every facet of society from politics to religion to family life, as well as my pet subject: organized crime.

How this saga will unfold is still unknowable. But Southeast Asia's underworld is as complex as Southeast Asia itself, and I know that its players, large and small, will find ways to adapt.

More than anything else, my work has taught me that many of those labeled 'criminals' are no more inclined to cruelty than bankers, politicians, priests or police. For the most part, they wake up each day and make a series of well-reasoned choices to survive. They've been taking care of themselves all along – by any means necessary.

Notes

Prologue

1. 'Investing in ASEAN', report issued by ASEAN, 2017.
2. 'Protecting peace and prosperity in Southeast Asia: synchronizing economic and security agendas', report issued by UNODC, 25 February 2017.
3. 'Asia Infrastructure Needs Exceed $1.7 Trillion Per Year', report issued by Asian Development Bank, 28 February 2017.
4. Author interviews with UNODC and US DEA personnel in 2015 and 2017.
5. 'Bombs Over Cambodia', report by Yale University's *The Walrus*, 2006.
6. Secret memo written by then-Secretary of Defense Robert McNamara, 19 May 1967. Revealed via 'The Pentagon Papers', a cache of Defense Department documents leaked to *The New York Times* and other outlets in 1971 by former US military contractor Daniel Ellsberg.
7. 'Remarks by the President to the Clinton Global Initiative', The White House, Office of the Press Secretary, 25 September 2012.
8. 'Desperate Life at Sea', Public Radio International, 21 May 2012.
9. 'Remarks to US Department of State Employees', US Department of State, Rex Tillerson speech in Washington DC, 3 May 2017.
10. 'Press briefing by Press Secretary Sarah Sanders and National Security Adviser H.R. McMaster', The White House, Office of the Press Secretary, 2 November 2017.
11. Late 2017 estimates calculated by Human Rights Watch and the Philippines Alliance of Human Rights Advocates.
12. 'Trump Called Rodrigo Duterte To Congratulate Him On His Murderous Drug War: "You Are Doing An Amazing Job"', *The Intercept*, 24 May 2017.
13. 'Emerging and Developing Economies Much More Optimistic than Rich Countries about the Future', Pew Research Center, 9 October 2014.

Chapter I: Hot Pink Speed

1. Columbia University professor and neuropharmacologist Carl Hart has said 'methamphetamine and Adderall are essentially the same drug'. See his report 'Methamphetamine: fact vs. fiction and lessons from the crack hysteria', Open Society Foundations, 2014.

2. 'A potent new type of meth is named after Myanmar's pro-democracy heroes', Public Radio International, 15 November 2015.
3. 'Was Burma's 1988 Uprising Worth It?', BBC, 6 August 2008.
4. If anything, this is an understatement. Mainland Southeast Asia's entire meth trade is valued at $15 billion per year – and Myanmar-based syndicates are this regional trade's key players. Myanmar is conservatively estimated by the UN to churn out no fewer than 2 billion speed tablets (ya ba) per year – and perhaps as many as 6 billion. Street prices for one ya ba tablet range from around $3–$10 depending on the city in which they're sold. Now consider that many Fortune 500 companies, such as Dollar Tree or Hormel Foods, take in less than $1 billion per year in profits. See also the 'Regional Programme for Southeast Asia 2014 – 2017', United Nations Office on Drugs and Crime.
5. Panglong Agreement, 12 February 1947.
6. 'Who Killed Aung San?', The Irrawaddy, August 1997.
7. World Bank Data.
8. 'Myanmar labour force, child labour and school-to-work transition', Myanmar's Central Statistics Organization/International Labour Organization, 29 August 2016.
9. 'Deciphering Myanmar's Peace Process – A Reference Guide 2016', Myanmar Peace Monitor.
10. 'The Female Warlord Who Had C.I.A. Connections and Opium Routes', Gabrielle Paluch writing for The New York Times, 21 July 2017.
11. The death toll for Myanmar's civil wars since 1948 is incredibly hard to calculate. Other estimates place the death toll much higher than 150,000. This figure – which does not account for much of the insurgent- and state-engineered violence of the early 21st century, including the ethnic cleansing purges against the Rohingya – is informed by the Political Economy Research Institute, University of Massachusetts Amherst.
12. 'Remarks by President Obama at the University of Yangon', The White House, 19 November 2012.
13. 'President Obama and Aung San Suu Kyi Celebrate Progress in Burma', The White House, 15 September 2016.
14. 'Building the Tatmadaw', Institute of Southeast Asian Studies, 2009. 'Special Report: Myanmar Old Guard Clings to $8 Billion Jade Empire', Andrew Marshall for Reuters, 28 September 2013.
15. 'A Flea Cannot Make a Whirl of Dust', Global New Light of Myanmar, 26 November 2016.

16. 'Half a million Rohingya arrive in Bangladesh; UN agencies rush to provide shelter, clean water', UN News Centre, 29 September 2017.

17. State Counsellor Office Information Committee Facebook Page, December 2016; 'Myanmar's army is tormenting Muslims with a brutal rape campaign', Public Radio International, 7 February 2017.

18. Author interview with Jeremy Douglas, Regional Representative of the United Nations Office on Drugs and Crime for Southeast Asia and the Pacific, June 2017.

19. In 2015, Starbucks sold 671,396,071 cups of coffee, according to a public relations video on the corporation's Starbucks Partners page on Facebook, posted on 26 December 2016.

20. McDonald's has estimated that it sells 550 million Big Macs per year, according to the article 'Creator of McDonald's Big Mac dies at 98', CNBC, 30 November 2016.

21. Walmart's stated net income for 2016 was $13.6 billion. Pfizer's net income in the same year was $7.2 billion. This $15 billion methamphetamine figure is cited in 'Regional Programme for Southeast Asia 2014 – 2017', United Nations Office on Drugs and Crime.

22. Mexico produced as much as 28,000 hectares of poppy in 2015. Burma cultivated 55,000 hectares. Both figures included in the US federal government's Bureau for International Narcotics and Law Enforcement Affairs report titled 'International Narcotics Control and Strategy Report 2017'.

23. Author interview with John Whalen, former head of the US Drug Enforcement Agency's Myanmar office.

24. 'Patterns and Trends of Amphetamine-Type Stimulants and Other Drugs: Challenges for Asia and the Pacific', UNODC's Global SMART Programme, 2013.

25. Chinese National Narcotics Control Commission stats as reported in '"Breaking Bad" in China: how meth is spreading across rural heartland', Christian Science Monitor, 3 May 2015.

26. 'Thailand's "war on drugs"', Human Rights Watch, 12 March 2008.

27. W.C. Purser, Christian Missions in Burma, The Society for the Propagation of the Gospel in Foreign Parts, 1911.

28. Ibid.

29. Ibid.

30. Rev. O. Hanson, The Kachins: Their Customs and Traditions, American Baptist Mission Press, 1913

31. Ibid.

32. 'Release of 2014 Census Data on Religion', Myanmar's Ministry of Labour, Immigration and Population, 2016.

33. Myanmar Peace Monitor figures plus author interview with unnamed KIA officers.

34. 'Kachin State sees over 1,500 drug-related cases in 2016', Eleven Media, 1 September 2017.

Chapter II: Holy Revolt

1. Letter to Queen Victoria, Lin Tse-Hsu, 1839.

2. 'The Bizarre Trial of a Poet in Myanmar', *The New Yorker*, 2 March 2016.

3. Jacksonville's GDP was roughly $65 billion in 2015, according to the US Bureau of Economic Analysis. In that year, the GDP of Myanmar, according to the World Bank, was $62.6 billion.

4. Myanmar's Ministry of Hotels and Tourism.

5. 'Mekong region officials address drug challenge', UNODC, 22 May 2015.

6. Khun Sa: obituary in *The Economist*, 8 November 2007.

7. Figures provided by Myanmar Peace Monitor.

8. Data from UNODC, Southeast Asia Regional Programme.

9. Author interview with Jeremy Douglas, Regional Representative of the United Nations Office on Drugs and Crime for Southeast Asia and the Pacific, June 2017.

10. US Bureau for International Narcotics and Law Enforcement Affairs report: 'International Narcotics Control and Strategy Report 2017'.

11. United Kingdom's Frontier Areas Committee of Enquiry, 1947.

12. 'Revealed: How Southeast Asia's Biggest Drug Lord Used Shell Companies to Become a Jade Kingpin', Global Witness report, 2015.

13. 'NDAK Chief Bars NLD from Campaigning in His Kachin State Fiefdom', *Burma News International*, 24 September 2015.

14. 'Statement from Hillary Clinton on the Burmese Election', 11 November 2015.

15. Ting Ying is no longer in parliament. In the summer of 2016, he was forced to give up his seat by Myanmar's election commission after Aung San Suu Kyi's party members complained about his harassment of their campaigners. The warlord has kept his militia in Kachin State but the seat went to an independent runner up named Yaw Nar. See 'Kachin Warlord Loses Parliamentary Seat in Post-Election Tribunal', *The Irrawaddy*, 25 June 2016.

16. 'Drug Lords in Parliament', Shan Drug Watch, 2011.

17. Author interview with unnamed TNLA officer in 2015.
18. That would be Hu Zujun, Narcotics Control Bureau, Yunnan Provincial Public Security Department, speaking to CCTV (China Central Television) in October 2012.
19. 'Report to the Honorable Daniel P. Moynihan, US Senate', United States General Accounting Office, 11 September 1989.
20. Pierre-Arnaud Chouvy, *Opium: Uncovering the Politics of the Poppy*, Harvard University Press, 2009.
21. Author interview with John Whalen, former chief of the DEA's offices in Myanmar.
22. 'Burma and Transnational Crime', Congressional Research Service, 2008.
23. 'International Narcotics Control and Strategy Report 2017' by the Bureau for International Narcotics and Law Enforcement Affairs.
24. 'Regional Programme for Southeast Asia 2014–2017,' UNODC.
25. 'Peace Fund Scores $100 Million', *Myanmar Times*, 28 March 2016.
26. 'Remarks With Foreign Minister of Burma U Wanna Maung Lwin After Their Meeting', US Department of State transcript, 17 May 2012.
27. Myanmar's government officially valued its annual exports at $12.4 billion in 2015.
28. 'Profits of Drug Trade Drive Economic Boom in Myanmar', *The New York Times*, 5 June 2015.
29. 'Lords of Jade', Global Witness report, December 2015.

Chapter III: The Devil's Cocktail

1. Manila's population density is 71,263 people per sq. kilometer, according to 'Philippine Population Density (based on the 2015 Census of Population)', Philippine Statistic Authority. New York City's population density is 10,500 people per sq. kilometer, according to the NYC Department of City Planning. London's population density is 5,510 people per sq. kilometer, according to 'Land Area and Population Density, Ward and Borough', Greater London Authority.
2. Benigno S. Aquino, 'What's Wrong With the Philippines?', *Foreign Affairs*, July 1968.
3. World Bank data.
4. 'Live Births in the Philippines: 2014', Philippine Statistics Authority.
5. This data comes from the 'Philippines National Demographic and Health Survey', published by the Philippine Statistics Authority with the backing of the USAID, released August 2014. See also: 'Unintended Pregnancy

and Unsafe Abortion in the Philippines', Guttmacher Institute, and: 'One in three births in the Philippines is unplanned', Philippine Statistics Authority.

6. 'Philippines, Country Brief', International Labour Organization.

7. 'Philippines birth control: Filipinos want it, priests don't', *Los Angeles Times*, 22 July 2012.

8. See documents published in 'The End of Foreign Aid as We Know It', *Foreign Policy*, 24 April 2017.

9. Data from 'Philippines National Demographic and Health Survey', Philippine Statistics Authority, August 2014.

10. See recording of speech posted on YouTube by the Rappler media outlet: 'Duterte on population boom: use pills, but not condoms', 14 February 2018.

11. Pulse Asia Research polling agency data from October 2010 indicates 69 per cent of Filipinos support a Reproductive Health bill that guarantees 'universal' access to contraception.

12. Philippines Revised Penal Code, Title Eight, Articles 258 and 259.

13. Association of Reproductive Health Professionals data.

14. Maternal mortality in the US is 26.4 deaths per 100,000 births, according to *The Lancet*.

15. 'Safe Abortion: Technical and Policy Guidance for Health Systems', WHO.

16. 'Intentional Homicide', articles 2268 through 2275, Catechism of the Catholic Church.

17. 'To Eustochium', *The Letters of Saint Jerome*, written circa 383–384 AD.

18. See 'The Laguna Copper-Plate Inscription' Philippine Studies journal, Ateneo de Manila University.

19. Accounts from Miguel López de Legazpi, reprinted in *The Philippine Islands, 1493–1803* by Scholar's Choice in 2015.

20. Antonio Pigafetta, *Journal of Magellan's Voyage*, written circa 1525.

21. See William Lytle Schurz, *The Manila Galleon*, Dutton, 1939.

22. See the *Kartilya ng Katipunan*, a short set of guiding principles for the anti-colonial Katipunan group.

23. 'The Water Cure', *The New Yorker*, 25 February 2008.

24. 'The Philippine–American War: 1899–1902', Office of the Historian, Department of State, United States.

25. 'History of the Philippines', Department of Foreign Affairs, Republic of the Philippines.

26. 'Taxpayers to Shoulder Marcos Debt Until 2025', *GMA News*, 7 April 2007.

27. 'Duterte calls Catholic church "most hypocritical institution"', ABS-CBN News, 22 May 2017.

28. 'Duterte: Natural Family Planning Goes Against Biology', *Philippine Star*, 17 March 2017.

29. Social Weather Stations, First Quarter 2017 report.

30. 'Declaration on Procured Abortion', The Vatican, 1974.

31. 'The Pill: How it Works and Fails', Pharmacists for Life International, October 1998.

32. 'New study establishes when pregnancy starts', University of North Carolina at Chapel Hill, 1999.

33. 'Percent of currently married women by current contraceptive method, Philippines, 2011', by Philippine Statistics Authority.

34. Transcript by Philippines Department of Foreign Affairs, *The Intercept*, 24 May 2017.

35. Philippine National Police press release, December 2017.

36. 'COA: Philippines jails 511 per cent congested', *The Philippines Star*, 17 June 2017.

37. 'Rodrigo Duterte's Talk of Killing Criminals Raises Fears in the Philippines', *The New York Times*, 17 March 2017.

Chapter IV: Pyongyang's Dancing Queens

1. 'Kim Jong-un "watched as uncle killed by dogs"', Channel 4, 3 January 2014; 'Kim Jong-Un fed uncle alive to 120 starved dogs', USA Today, 3 January 2014.

2. 'North Korea: Students required to get Kim Jong-un haircut', BBC, 26 March 2014; 'That Viral "Kim Jong-Un Haircut" Story is Another Hoax', *The Diplomat*, 27 March 2014.

3. 'Unicorn lair "discovered" in North Korea', *Guardian*, 30 November 2012; 'No, the North Korean government did not claim it found evidence of unicorns', *io9*, 12 January 2012.

4. 'North Korean reveals cannibalism is common after escaping starving state', *Sunday Express*, 17 April 2013.

5. 'A Nation of Racist Dwarves', *Slate*, 1 February 2010.

6. 'Are North Koreans really three inches shorter than South Koreans?', BBC, 23 April 2012.

7. US Department of State – Refugee Admission Statistics.

8. 'Here's one dangerous North Korean weapon that's being overlooked', CNBC, 15 September 2017.

9. Andrei Lankov, 'Narco-capitalism grips North Korea', *Asia Times*, 18 March 2011; 'North Korea's Dollar Store', *Vanity Fair*, 8 August 2009; 'North Korean Production of Fake Cigarettes Run by the Government', *Daily NK*, 23 May 2006; 'North Korea evades sanctions with network of overseas companies: UN report', Reuters, 25 February 2017.

10. 'FACT SHEET: Resolution 2375 (2017) Strengthening Sanctions on North Korea', United States Mission to the United Nations; 'North Korea putting thousands into forced labour abroad, UN says', Associated Press, 29 October 2015.

11. United Nations Human Rights, Office of the High Commissioner statement on 16 February 2016.

12. 'Report of the commission of inquiry on human rights in the Democratic People's Republic of Korea', Human Rights Council, United Nations, 7 February 2014.

13. 'North Korean restaurants: like the country, suspicious and in crisis', Reuters, 14 April 2016.

14. Korean Central News Agency statement in April, 2016.

15. 'Oungum, Popular Musical Instrument', KCNA press release in 2006.

16. 'Kim Jong Un married in 2009, according to intelligence service', CNN, 26 July 2012.

17. 'Traitor Jang Song Thaek Executed', KCNA, 13 December 2013.

18. 'Kim Jong Un "pleasure squad" lives life as elite's servants', *Daily Mail*, 29 April 2016; 'North Korea's Pleasure Squad', *Marie Claire*, 2010.

19. Bruce Cummings, *The Korean War: A History*, Modern Library, 2011.

20. 'Strategic Air Warfare: An Interview with Generals Curtis E. LeMay, Leon W. Johnson, David A. Burchinal and Jack J. Catton', Office of Air Force History, 1988.

21. Fyodor Tertitskiy, 'Let them Eat Rice: North Korea's Public Distribution System', *NK News*, 29 October 2015.

22. Andrei Lankov, 'North Korea's Antique Food Rationing', *Asia Times*, 15 January 2005.

23. Andrei Lankov, 'Rationing System in North Korea', *The Korea Times*, 26 August 2012.

24. Data from Food and Agriculture Organization of the United Nations.

25. 'North Korea Revalues Its Currency', *The New York Times*, 1 December 2009.

26. 'The Death Penalty in North Korea', International Federation of Human Rights, 16 May 2013.

27. 'South Koreans asked not to eat at NK Restaurants', *The Korea Times*, 16 February 2016.
28. 'The meanings of Forced Labour', International Labor Organization, 10 March 2014.
29. Andrei Lankov, 'Dandong's other North Korean workers', *NK News*, 4 February 2016.
30. 'North Korea Gets Strict on Recruiting Workers to Go Abroad', *Radio Free Asia*, 19 July 2017; 'North Koreans in Russia Work "Basically in the Situation of Slaves"', *The New York Times*, 11 July 2017; 'A Prison With No Fence', Database Center for North Korean Human Rights, 2016 report.
31. Andrei Lankov, 'North Korean workers abroad aren't slaves', *NK News*, 27 November 2014.
32. 'Stop saying N. Korean overseas laborers aren't slaves', *One Free Korea*, 23 May 2016.
33. 'North Korea's Forced Labor Enterprise', Human Rights Watch statement in 2015.
34. North Korean Red Cross central committee statement, 23 April 2016.
35. Moon Jae-in, speech to Germany's Korber Foundation in July 2017.
36. 'KCNA Commentary Urges Earlier Repatriation of DPRK Women from S. Korea', *KCNA*, 12 June 2016.

Chapter V: Neon Jihad

1. 'Confusion over bombing motive', *Bangkok Post*, 18 September 2011.
2. Calculating the value of any underground industry is inevitably tricky. Thailand's sex trade is no exception. In 2003, Thailand's Ministry of Justice endorsed a $4.3 billion valuation of the industry though the trade has almost certainly grown since then. One decade prior to that, in 1995, International Labour Organization supported a whopping valuation of $22 to $27 billion – a figure including profits brought in by hotels, bribes and bars, not just the sex workers themselves. In that same year, the International Monetary Fund valued the trade at much smaller $2.8 billion.

    Much more recently, a private data collection firm called Havocscope – which specializes in black market statistics and claims law enforcement sources – clocked Thailand's sex trade at $6.4 billion. While I doubt this firm has cultivated any legit Thai police or underworld sources, this estimate sounds fairly reasonable. The truth is that no one knows the value of

Thailand's sex trade. Nor does every group size up this industry's worth using the same metrics.

'Sex Industry Assuming Massive Proportions in Southeast Asia', ILO report, 1998.

3. Again, the exact number of women working in this industry is hard to pin down. This figure comes from a Thai Ministry of Health estimate published in a report titled 'Transnational Organized Crime in East Asia and the Pacific: A Threat Assessment' by the UNODC in 2013.

4. The ultra-conservative Malaysian Islamic Party has largely governed Kelantan province since Malaysia's inception.

5. These widely accepted figures are issued by Deep South Watch, an independent analytical group associated with Thailand's Prince of Songkla University campus in Pattani city.

6. National Consortium for the Study of Terrorism and Responses to Terrorism, Annex of Statistical Information – 2012/2013.

7. Michael Pearson, *The Indian Ocean*, Routledge, 2003.

8. *Ghost of the Past in Southern Thailand*, NUS Press Singapore, 2013.

9. Leaflets collected by Human Rights Watch.

10. Interview with author in Kelantan, Malaysia, in April 2014. 'Abu Imad' is a nom de guerre.

11. 'Declaration of War Against the Americans Occupying the Land of the Two Holy Places', Osama bin Laden statement first published in the newspaper *Al Quds Al Arabi* in 1996.

12. 'No One is Safe', Human Rights Watch report, 27 August 2004.

13. On 27 March 2004, a motorcycle bomb exploded in front of a hotel and nightclub in Sungai Golok – an attack interpreted at the time as a small-scale version of the Bali Bombings in 2002, according to *Southern Thailand: The Dynamics of Conflict*, Institute of Southeast Asian Studies, 2008.

14. Duncan McCargo, *Tearing Apart the Land: Islam and Legitimacy in Southern Thailand*, Cornell Press, 2008.

15. 'Independent Commission on Enquiry into Facts about the Krue Se Mosque Case', Thailand government-appointed commission report, released in July 2004.

16. Wan Kadir, *Muslim Separatism: The Moros of Southern Philippines and the Malays of Southern Thailand*, Singapore: Oxford University Press,1990.

17. Interview with author in 2011 in Bangkok.

18. 'Car bomb kills 5, injures 40, in Thai tourist town', Reuters, 18 February 2005.

Notes

Chapter VI: Swamp Hounds

1. See *Sapiens: A Brief History of Humankind*, by Yuval Noah Harari, published by Harper in 2011. Harari writes that 'if you took all the people in the world and put them on a large set of scales, their combined mass would be about 300 million tons. If you then took all our domesticated farm animals – cows, pigs, sheep and chickens – and placed them on an even larger set of scales, their mass would amount to about 700 million tons.'

2. 'Canine avengers', *Tuổi Trẻ*, 15 July 2011.

3. 'Ongoing dog-related violence rips apart rural Vietnam', *Thanh Niên*, 26 June 2014.

4. 'Are dog thieves to blame for fatal vigilante attacks?', *Viet Nam News*, 19 September 2013.

5. That story was published by *The Daily Mirror* on 7 September 2016.

6. Wayne Pacelle, CEO of the Humane Society of the United States, 'Don't for a minute excuse eating dog meat as a cultural prerogative', *Huffington Post*, 10 November 2015.

7. See the work of American anthropologist Pat Shipman of Pennsylvania State University. Her findings are summarized in the article: 'How hunting with wolves helped humans outsmart Neanderthals', *Guardian*, 1 March 2015.

8. Author interview with Herzog in January 2015.

9. Author interview in 2015 with Rosemary Elliott, president of the Australia-based group Sentient: The Veterinary Institute for Animal Ethics.

10. Barack Obama, *Dreams from My Father: A Story of Race and Inheritance*, Broadway Books, 10 August 2004.

11. Estimate issued by Humane Society International.

12. This finding was published by The Asia Canine Protection Alliance, which also says that 'it is estimated that up to 5 million dogs are traded and slaughtered for this purpose in Vietnam each year; however, accurate figures and data are impossible to obtain as wherever it exists, the dog meat trade operates in breach of existing laws and regulations, and the slaughtering, sale and consumption of dogs is largely unregulated.'

13. According to my reporting in 2009, smugglers earned $10 per dog smuggled from Thailand across the Mekong River into Laos. Various sources told me that roughly 1,000 animals were smuggled each day, which would generate roughly $3.6 million per year. These findings were reported more extensively in a series of reports titled 'Dog Meat Mafia', originally

published in November 2009 by *GlobalPost* and now available online at: *www.pri.org*

14. His name is Phumpat Pachonsap and he formerly represented the Nakhon Phanom province in Thailand's parliament. Quote originally published by *GlobalPost* in an article titled 'The Dog Meat Mafia: Corruption' in 2009.

15. Ibid.

16. Kate Hodal, 'How eating dog became big business in Vietnam', *Guardian*, 27 September 2013.

17. 'Dog trafficking ban reduces illegal imports to a trickle', Animals Asia, statement released on 19 August 2014.

18. 'Communal mob attack fells dog thief in southern Vietnam', *Thanh Niên News*, 2 July 2014.

19. This colonel was interviewed by author Mark Bowden for his book: *Hue 1968: A Turning Point of the American War in Vietnam*, Atlantic Monthly Press, 2017.

20. Speech at news conference by President Lyndon Johnson on 28 July 1965.

21. Confidential memo issued by then-Assistant Secretary of Defense John McNaughton in March 1965. Revealed via 'The Pentagon Papers', a cache of Defense Department documents leaked to *The New York Times* and other outlets in 1971 by former US military contractor Daniel Ellsberg.

22. Secret memo written by then-Secretary of Defense Robert McNamara on 19 May 1967. Revealed via 'The Pentagon Papers'.

23. Interview with McNamara by *The Los Angeles Times* in 1995.

24. 'Major Describes Move', *The New York Times*, 8 February 1968.

25. That would be then-Major Charles 'Chargin' Charlie' Beckwith. His comments are captured in the PBS documentary *The Vietnam War*, released in 2017.

26. My father, Ronnie Winn, basically exploited a loophole in the draft law. He left the University of North Carolina at Chapel Hill campus, returned to our rural home county and, on one of the last days in 1969, walked into the local draft board office. He then asked a stunned and suspicious small-town bureaucrat to void his student deferment, rendering him fully eligible for conscription as soon as the army wished to call him up.

    My father had learned this trick from an ex-Navy vet who was then in law school. One of the peculiarities of the draft law was that young men were only threatened with conscription for one calendar year. The thinking was that, after your year came and went, you could rest easy and began planning the rest of your life. My father's year was 1969. When

1970 rolled around a few days later, he was marked as having already offered himself up during his designated conscription year – a window that had now passed. This loophole was soon discovered and closed to future scammers.

27. 'In Vietnam, nearly 70 confess to murder of dog thief suspects after trial', *Thanh Niên News*, 9 April 2014.
28. Calvin Godfrey, 'The Dog Thief Killings', *Roads & Kingdoms*, February 2016.
29. '800 households confess of beating dog thieves to death', *VietnamNet Bridge*, 13 September 2013.
30. 'Are dog thieves to blame for fatal vigilante attacks?', *Viet Nam News*, 19 September 2013.
31. The Asia Canine Protection Alliance includes the following organizations: Animals Asia, Change for Animals Foundation, Humane Society International and Soi Dog Foundation.
32. See 'House Resolution 401 – Urging China, South Korea, Vietnam, Thailand, the Philippines, Indonesia, Cambodia, Laos, India and all nations to outlaw the dog and cat meat trade and to enforce existing laws against the trade', 22 June 2017.
33. 'Ricky Gervais, Judi Dench and *Downtown Abbey* stars speak out against the dog meat trade', posted to YouTube by Soi Dog Foundation on 7 July 2014.

Afterword

1. 'The Rohingya refugee crisis is the worst in decades', *The Economist*, 21 September 2017.
2. 'UN human rights chief points to "textbook example of ethnic cleansing" in Myanmar', UN News Centre, 11 September 2017.
3. I recounted my findings in this report: 'Myanmar's army is tormenting Muslims with a brutal rape campaign', Public Radio International, 7 February 2017.
4. I first reported these figures in this article: 'Meth's new frontier: the marshlands of Bangladesh', Public Radio International, 26 April 2017.
5. Author interview with Jeremy Douglas, Regional Representative of the United Nations Office on Drugs and Crime for Southeast Asia and the Pacific, June 2017.
6. I compiled this video and published excerpts along with this report: 'Meth's new frontier: the marshlands of Bangladesh', Public Radio International, 26 April 2017.

7. Duterte: 'Hitler massacred three million Jews. Now, there are three million drug addicts … I'd be happy to slaughter them.' Reported in the article 'Duterte willing to unleash a Hitler on PHL criminals', *GMA News Online*, 30 September 2016.

8. 'Soaring prison population prompts Thailand to re-think "lost" drug war', Reuters, 17 July 2016.

9. 'Thailand is moving closer to decriminalizing meth', Public Radio International, 8 September 2016.

10. That deputy chief's name is Prawit Wongsuwon, a deputy premier and defense minister who helped to engineer Thailand's military coup in 2014.

11. 'Combating corruption: the Hong Kong experience', by Dr Hui Wing-chi with the Independent Commission Against Corruption in Hong Kong.

12. 'Forty years since its creation, how the ICAC cleaned up corruption in Hong Kong', *South China Morning Post*, 15 February 2014.

13. 'People and corruption: Asia Pacific', Transparency International, February 2017.

14. '"You are corrupt to the core," Duterte tells cops', ABS-CBN News, 20 January 2017.

15. 'President Obama: Human trafficking must be called by its true name – human slavery', The White House, Office of the Press Secretary, 15 September 2012.

16. This sordid history is well covered in: Alfred McCoy, *In the Shadows of the American Century: The Rise and Decline of US Empire*, Haymarket Books, September 2017. McCoy is a University of Wisconsin-Madison professor.

17. '7 things you may not know about US foreign assistance', Oxfam, 14 April 2017.

18. 'US Image Suffers as Publics Around World Question Trump's Leadership', Pew Research Center, 26 June 2017.

19. This public discussion took place on 22 November 2017, at the Foreign Correspondents' Club of Thailand. Other panelists included: Kobsak Chutikul, a veteran Thai diplomat, and Prapat Thepchatree, director of the Center for ASEAN Studies at Thammasat University.

Acknowledgements

My earliest impulse to write a book on organized crime in Southeast Asia came many years ago. I couldn't tell you exactly where this notion first occurred to me – probably on the road in some noodle shop or one-star hotel.

But it took about two years to sift through enough notebook scrawl, recorded interviews and old photos to divine a coherent thread from nearly ten years of reporting. Add to that fresh reporting to shore up facts and new sources.

Compiling this book has proven humbling. The process has helped me to appreciate how much I've relied on the cleverness, hard work and guidance of others. Behind every chapter is a mostly invisible supporting cast.

My deepest appreciation goes out to:

Pailin Wedel, my brilliant wife. Life as I know it is largely defined by you. My work would be vastly inferior without your late-night counsel and narrative craftwork. Thanks for keeping me honest and loving me enough to tell me when my ideas are promising and when they're terrible.

To Kelly Falconer, my agent, who championed this project and boldly took a chance on a first-time author. Your expertise has been invaluable during my maiden voyage into the world of publishing. Your endless boosterism keeps me buoyant.

To the Icon Books team and, most of all, Tom Webber, who both commissioned and edited this book. Your guidance has helped crystallize this book's vision and your narrative instincts have vastly enhanced my copy. Publishing this book through Icon is a source of immense pride for me.

To Ying Panyapon, Sona Jo, Puchara 'Am' Sanford, Rica Concepcion, Muktadir 'Romeo' Rashid and several Vietnamese producers who must remain anonymous. Writing this book would have been impossible without your wits and tenacity. It's an honor to work with such talented journalists.

Special thanks to my 'nyi lay' in Myanmar. I can't print your name but you know who you are. Brother, you're one of the most good-hearted people I've ever met. I'm so proud to know you. Thank you for your bravery.

To Phil Balboni, Charlie Sennott and Tom Mucha with *GlobalPost*, the Boston-based news agency that first hired me as a foreign correspondent. Much of the field reporting that appears in this book began under their aegis. Under *GlobalPost*, you gave me the time, budget and platform to aggressively chase stories in a part of the world often neglected by Western outlets. Special thanks to Lizzy Tomei, editor extraordinaire, who also oversaw parts of this investigative work.

To Andrew Sussman and the talented newsroom at PRI's *The World* – a team of journalists who've so generously taught me the art of audio storytelling. Thanks so much for allowing me to vanish for a few months so I could properly complete this book. I'm so gratified to appear on the best foreign news program on American radio.

To Mark Oltmanns and Jonah M. Kessel, two supremely talented videographers who joined me on several reporting trips to Myanmar, Thailand and Vietnam. Mark and Jonah were present for some of the scenes depicted in this book. Sorry, guys, for excising you to avoid cluttering the storyline – a sin for which I beg forgiveness.

Acknowledgements

To anyone who'd like to see some of this book's characters in action, please watch our documentaries. Check out *Asia's Meth Wars* (featuring material depicted in Chapters I and II), *Red Light Jihad* (Chapter V) and *Dog Thief Down* (Chapter VI). All were filmed by Oltmanns in 2014 and 2015.

Also, in 2013, Jonah and I produced a 30-minute doc titled *Myanmar Emerges* that touches on the narcotic crisis in northern Myanmar. (This work earned us the Robert F. Kennedy Journalism Award, which I received in person from the namesake's widow, Ethel Kennedy.)

To my father, Ronnie Winn, whom I revere. From you, I developed an eye for the absurd and a deep skepticism of authority.

To my relentlessly cheerful mother, Teresa Knight, whose love and support knows no bounds. To my stepmother, Kathie, whose social work showed me, as a child, the dignity in aiding society's least fortunate. To Jack, my gifted brother, who shares my love of prose. To Alison, my cousin, who tormented me with her wizardry.

To my grandfather, Milfred Winn, who died before I was born. He was the first in my family to see Asia – albeit as a soldier deployed to rebuild parts of the Philippines during the Second World War. How strange it might seem to him – a man once haunted by Japanese snipers – that his grandson would come to this part of the world and make a happy life.

To Margie Winn, my grandmother and moral guiding light, who helped to raise me and always corrected my country grammar. You are the reason I no longer confuse 'brought' with 'brung'. You are a picture of female strength, a woman who has endured plenty yet loathes self-pity. Thank you for never criticizing me for selfishly moving so far away and only asking that I 'always remember my bringing's up'.

To Yuangrat and Paul Wedel, as well as Jinda and the entire Pattanapong family. Through all of you, I have gained a second family and grounding here in Thailand. I would not have made it this far without your generosity and wisdom.

To my NC crew: Biggs, Donna, Gullett, Jarf, Tanca, Hardcore Keith, Tedd, Miles and Jim Starr. We made it.

Most of all, I am indebted to all the people in Southeast Asia who have opened up their homes and lives to me. I am doubly grateful to those who have recounted experiences that are painful. I truly hope that I've done right by you. I have always tried to let sources know the limits of my power – that I might make their experiences better known, at least in the English-speaking world, but probably cannot do much to stop whoever is making their lives difficult. That so many have indulged my questions is deeply heartening.

Index

Index

ABOUT THE AUTHOR

Patrick Winn is an award-winning investigative journalist who covers crime and black markets in Southeast Asia. He enters the worlds of guerrillas and vigilantes to mine stories that would otherwise go ignored.

Winn has received the Robert F. Kennedy Journalism Award (also known as the 'poor man's Pulitzer') and a National Press Club award. He's also a two-time winner of Amnesty International's Human Rights Press Awards among other prizes.

His writing and short documentaries have been featured on NBC News, the BBC, The Atlantic, NPR and many other outlets. He is a co-creator of the film *Hope Frozen*, which will screen at international documentary festivals in 2018.

Winn has served as a consultant for *Anthony Bourdain: Parts Unknown* on CNN. Working closely with the show's director, he selected people, locations and food featured on the debut episode in Myanmar. The episode won multiple Emmys.

Winn is currently Public Radio International's Asia correspondent. He appears on PRI's *The World*, a BBC co-production. The show is broadcast on more than 300 NPR stations across America to reach roughly 3 million listeners each week.

Winn was raised in Eden, a dwindling North Carolina factory town that once manufactured carpets and beer. He graduated from UNC – Chapel Hill in 2003 with a journalism degree. His early reportage explored economic decay in the American south and crime within the US military.

Since 2008, Winn has lived in Bangkok and reported almost exclusively on Southeast Asia. He reads and speaks Thai – and occasionally sings it, badly, in upcountry karaoke bars.